AFTER THE GRIZZLY

The publisher gratefully acknowledges the generous support of the Gordon and Betty Moore Fund in Environmental Studies of the University of California Press Foundation.

The publisher also gratefully acknowledges the generous support of the Humanities Endowment Fund of the University of California Press Foundation.

Peter S. Alagona   •   AFTER THE GRIZZLY

Endangered Species and the
Politics of Place in California

University of California Press

Berkeley   Los Angeles   London

University of California Press, one of the most
distinguished university presses in the United States,
enriches lives around the world by advancing
scholarship in the humanities, social sciences, and
natural sciences. Its activities are supported by the UC
Press Foundation and by philanthropic contributions
from individuals and institutions. For more information,
visit www.ucpress.edu.

University of California Press
Berkeley and Los Angeles, California

University of California Press, Ltd.
London, England

Library of Congress Cataloging-in-Publication Data

Alagona, Peter S.
    After the grizzly : endangered species and the politics
of place in California / Peter S. Alagona.
        pages   cm
    Includes bibliographical references and index.
    ISBN 978-0-520-27506-5 (cloth : alk. paper)
    1. Wildlife conservation—California.   2. Wildlife
conservation—United States.   3. Endangered
species—California.   4. Endangered species—
United States.   5. Grizzly bear—California.
I. Title.
QL82.A42   2013
591.68—dc23

                                        2012038183

Manufactured in the United States of America

22   21   20   19   18   17   16   15   14   13
10   9   8   7   6   5   4   3   2   1

In keeping with a commitment to support
environmentally responsible and sustainable printing
practices, UC Press has printed this book on Rolland
Enviro100, a 100% post-consumer fiber paper that is
FSC certified, deinked, processed chlorine-free, and
manufactured with renewable biogas energy. It is
acid-free and EcoLogo certified.

CONTENTS

ACKNOWLEDGMENTS

This book was a long time in coming. Depending on how you count, it took half a decade, a decade, or a decade and a half to complete. I don't like to do the math. All I know is that without the support and encouragement of my family, friends, colleagues, mentors, and students, I *never* would have finished this project.

During my career, I have had the good fortune to work with an outstanding collection of mentors. At Northwestern Peter Hayes inspired me, challenged me, and invited me to consider history as a career. At UC Santa Barbara Frank Davis encouraged my interest in ecology and conservation. At UCLA my doctoral committee members—Jessica Wang, Stephen Aron, Ted Porter, and Rick Vance—each brought distinct and indispensible perspectives. I am especially indebted to Jessica for her sage advice and commitment to my cause. At Harvard I had the formative experience of working with Sheila Jasanoff, and at Stanford I benefitted immeasurably from my time with Richard White, who read a full draft of the manuscript and provided vital feedback.

It is a delight to thank my many friends and colleagues who contributed to this project with their insight, advice, and encouragement: Gregory Simon, Lissa Wadewitz, Lawrence Culver, Emily Scott, Jay Turner, Mark Barrow, Etienne Benson, Jeremy Vetter, Robert Wilson, Jenny Price, Roxanne Willis, Stefan Sperling, Matt Booker, Jon Christensen, Fritz Davis, Phil Garone, Anita Guerrini, Andrew Mathews, Patrick McCray, Gabriela Soto Laveaga, Simone Pulver, Stephanie Pincetl, David Igler, Erica Fleischman, Chris Pyke, Britta Bierwagen, Noah

Goldstein, Heather Rosenberg, Holly Doremus, Stephen Bocking, Paul Sutter, Nathan Sayre, Stephanie Pincetl, Carla D'Antonio, Stève Barnardin, and Jacquelyn Langberg among others. I also thank John Majewski and Josh Schimel, who served as the chairs of the History Department and Environmental Studies Program during my first few years as a faculty member at UCSB, for their extraordinary confidence and support.

I received help with my research from a number of scientists, agency officials, archivists, librarians, and editors. I am particularly indebted to Jan Hamber, Susan Snyder, Brian Cypher, Pete Woodman, Kristin Berry, James Moore, Cameron Barrows, Travis Longcore, John Mattox, Lloyd Kiff, Peter Sorensen, and Peggy Wood—each of whom spent valuable time with me—as well as the staffs of the California Academy of Sciences, Oregon State University Archives, California State Archives, Natural History Museum of Los Angeles County, Santa Barbara Museum of Natural History, Yosemite and Joshua Tree national parks, California Department of Fish and Game, U.S. Fish and Wildlife Service, and the Museum of Vertebrate Zoology and Bancroft and Bioscience libraries at the University of California, Berkeley. I also thank Cathryn Carson and her colleagues from the Office for the History of Science and Technology at UC Berkeley for welcoming me as a visiting scholar for two years of research and writing. A special thanks goes out to the three reviewers who read and commented on my draft manuscript. Kate Marshall, from the University of California Press, did a wonderful job producing the book, as did the superb editors I worked with at various stages of the writing process: Jenny Wapner, Blake Edgar, Dore Brown, Juliana Froggatt, and Audra Wolfe.

During the course of this project, I received generous support from the UCLA Graduate Division, The John Randolph Haynes and Dora Haynes Foundation, the Harvard University Center for the Environment, the Bill Lane Center for the American West at Stanford University, and the UCSB College of Letters and Science.

It is a great joy to thank my unwavering, irrepressible parents, Judy and Peter, and my sister, Robyn, who inherited the best of them both. And then there is my own growing family: first Bodie, then Ziti, and now Saul—a little person with a big personality who changed my life in an instant almost a year ago and has done it again every day since. I dedicate this book to Jessica who saw it, and me, through from beginning to end. Like everything else in our lives together, this too was a team effort.

INTRODUCTION

One hot morning in the spring of 2004, I found myself in a distant corner of the Mojave Desert, standing in a field surrounded by saltbush and sage, feeling disoriented, overdressed, and a little embarrassed. A biologist named Peggy Wood had agreed to let me tag along with her while she tracked a small population of desert tortoises in a fenced area to which they had been moved to make way for the construction of an automobile test track. Peggy had handed me a radio telemetry receiver and an antenna and explained how to use the two devices to locate the tortoises she and her colleagues had fitted with beacons as part of the project's wildlife translocation and mitigation effort. I set off on foot to search for a signal, and within a few minutes, sure enough, the receiver's faint, intermittent chirps merged into a loud, continuous buzz. According to the receiver, I was standing practically on top of a fifteen-inch-long adult desert tortoise with a plastic and metal radio glued to its back. I had heard that desert tortoises were masters of disguise, but this was absurd. Here I was, just feet from the Mojave's most famous endangered species, and I couldn't find it. All I could see in front of me, when I turned away from the graders and bulldozers next door, was miles and miles of desert.

I did eventually find the tortoise, with Peggy's help—it was lying as still as a rock, and looking like one too, against the gravelly desert floor—a couple meters away, in the shadow of a creosote bush. I had nearly stepped on the poor critter.

On the way home that evening, after the temperature began to drop and my pride started to heal, I realized that even though I had missed the tortoise, I had stumbled

FIGURE 1.
Street sign in the Mojave National Preserve near Cima,
California. Courtesy of Christopher Woodcock.

upon an invaluable insight. Studying an endangered species is only partly about
surveying populations, tracking movements, and documenting behaviors. It is also
an exercise in comprehending the politics of land use and natural resource management, the laws that structure our relationships with nonhuman beings, and the
drivers of regional economic and environmental change. Perhaps most important,
it is as much about the places where endangered species live as it is about the species
themselves. Don't get me wrong: many people care deeply about wildlife and the
threats of species extinction and biodiversity loss. But endangered species are by
definition rare, and, like the inconspicuous desert tortoise, most remain unseen
except by highly trained experts. It was clear to me that the conservation efforts I
had witnessed earlier that day were part of a much larger scientific, legal, and
bureaucratic project, which was as much about protecting the Mojave—fencing off
at least some of those vast desert miles—as it was about conserving the tortoises
that lived there (see figure 1).[1]

These observations are not new. Since the 1970s, dozens of endangered species
conservation conflicts have captured national media attention. Many commentators
have noted that in such struggles, the species in question often serve as proxies for

much larger debates involving the politics of place, which I define as an ongoing cultural conversation about who should have access to and control over lands and natural resources. Seen in this way, endangered species debates are about not only the conservation of biological diversity but also the allocation of scarce public goods, the appropriate level of government intervention in a market economy, the distribution of legal authority among state and federal bureaucracies, the proper role of scientific expertise in democratic institutions, and divergent visions for the political and economic futures of communities and even entire regions. Endangered species have become surrogates for environmentalists who use them to pursue broader political agendas—such as preventing development, establishing nature reserves, or reducing carbon emissions—and scapegoats for those who oppose further regulation or stand to lose from changes in government policies. When it comes to endangered species, one person's totem is another's effigy.

It is one thing to identify a proxy debate but a more complex matter to explain that debate's antecedents, origins, development, and peculiar political framings. How did the United States develop a political system capable of producing and sustaining debates in which endangered species serve as proxies for broader cultural conflicts with such far-reaching social and economic consequences?

In the pages that follow, I argue that the endangered species debates that have rocked American environmental politics since the 1970s are the product of a more than century-long history in which scientists and conservationists came to view the fates of endangered species as inextricable from the ecological conditions and human activities in the places where those species lived. Endangered species advocates adopted the concept of habitat to describe these circumstances and relationships, and over time habitat conservation became a central tenet of wildlife management. The word *habitat* has many contexts and meanings. This book shows how habitat became the concept that connects endangered species to contested places and how this connection has allowed people to use those species as proxies for a host of broader social conflicts. It describes how a particular version of habitat conservation—the "protected natural area"—became the dominant paradigm for endangered species management in the United States. Finally, it suggests that although the protected areas paradigm probably helped prevent many extinctions in the twentieth century, this approach has encountered a range of problems and paradoxes in the twenty-first century, jeopardizing the survival of myriad threatened and endangered species.[2]

Readers who have studied endangered species issues will notice that this thesis differs from most other accounts, which identify the federal Endangered Species

Act (ESA) as the source of so many subsequent conservation conflicts. The ESA, which calls for the protection of all plant and animal species, as well as vertebrate subspecies and distinct populations, no matter the cost, passed Congress with nearly unanimous support in 1973. By the end of that decade, however, it had become perhaps the country's most controversial environmental law. Today the ESA remains not only one of the most formidable and comprehensive U.S. environmental statutes but also the most ambitious biodiversity conservation measure ever enacted by any country.[3]

The ESA plays a central role in this book, but I consider it part of a much longer story. Concern about extinctions dates back to at least the 1880s in the United States, and ambitious species and habitat conservation efforts began during the first half of the twentieth century, decades before the ESA's passage. The ESA is important here not because it was unique or unprecedented but because it continued two long-term trends: increasing the government protection of imperiled species, and elevating habitat to the status of a key concept in environmental science, law, management, and politics. Indeed, one of the reasons the ESA has become so powerful and controversial is that after its passage it evolved—through a series of legislative amendments, court decisions, and administrative rules—from a species protection law into a habitat protection law far stronger than almost anyone could have anticipated.[4]

There is another important reason why the ESA became such a powerful and controversial law. During the 1970s and 1980s, at the same time that environmental law was beginning to mature as a legal subfield, conservation biology was becoming established as an interdisciplinary scientific profession in academia, government, and nongovernmental organizations. In its early years, conservation biology focused mainly on developing theories and models to guide the selection and design of nature reserves for the conservation of habitat and biodiversity. Practitioners in these two fields still complain about the gulf that separates science from law, which they believe hampers effective policy and management. With a little historical perspective, however, it becomes clear that the two fields emerged and grew together, informing and shaping each other along the way. This reciprocal process, known as coproduction, creates what science studies scholars call hybrid concepts. Today it is impossible to provide a complete definition of either *habitat* or *endangered species* without referring to both science and the law and the relations between them.[5]

This book also takes a different perspective than most other endangered species research on the subject of federalism, which remains at the heart of many environmental debates. Historians often note that over the past two centuries, the United States government has extended its authority to new regions, peoples, and resources, in the process growing in size and increasing the range of its powers. Although this has occurred in many ways and in many areas, few topics seem to represent the theme of federal expansion better than wildlife. Before the twentieth century, the states retained nearly complete authority over the fish and game within their boundaries. Beginning in 1900, however, Congress passed a series of laws that increased federal involvement in wildlife management. To many observers, the ESA, which is essentially a receivership program that authorizes the federal government to step in and act on behalf of species that have suffered under state authority, represents the culmination of a process through which the U.S. government gradually expanded its influence over wildlife and natural resources, often at the expense of states' rights and local control.[6]

A closer look reveals a more complicated story. First, the federal government is anything but a monolithic entity with a coherent set of interests and objectives. Federal agencies have diverse institutional cultures, histories, missions, and alliances, making interagency cooperation challenging under the best of circumstances. Even in cases where one agency, or one group within an agency, appears to have the legal authority to advance its agenda, complex power relations often thwart action. The two federal ESA-implementing agencies, the U.S. Fish and Wildlife Service (FWS) and the National Oceanic and Atmospheric Administration (NOAA), have seen their legal responsibilities increase, but they remain underfunded, understaffed, and underresourced.[7]

Second, although the states have lost some of their autonomy, they still have administrative control over almost all of the nonendangered wildlife inside their boundaries. In recent years they have continued to develop their regulatory frameworks and administrative capacities. By 2012 only four states lacked some form of endangered species legislation, and the fifty states together issued 90 percent of all regulatory permits related to the environment. Not surprisingly, many state officials now believe that laws and cooperative agreements other than the ESA grant their wildlife agencies, not the federal government, the lead role in endangered species programs. The states will only continue to reassert their authority in the future, as pressure builds to remove more species from the federal list and return them to state jurisdiction.[8]

The federal government has played a pivotal role, however, in the area of habitat conservation. During the nineteenth and early twentieth centuries, state fish and game programs focused on artificial propagation and the regulation of take: establishing open seasons, bag limits, and other rules meant to limit hunting and fishing to sustainable levels. The states owned little land, and they had few precedents or incentives to allocate space for wildlife habitat. Beginning in the 1930s, a series of conservation initiatives, including several associated with federal New Deal recovery efforts, set out to protect and restore habitat in the national parks and new national wildlife refuges. Laws regulating take remained, and divergent visions for habitat conservation competed for dominance in various agencies. Yet overall, increased federal intervention fostered a new approach that moved beyond managing fish and game by regulating individual animals to managing land as habitat for wildlife conservation.[9]

The federal government did not invent the notion of habitat conservation. The idea of managing land to produce fish and game probably dates back millennia, but a more modern rationale emerged during the 1910s and 1920s among the founders of the discipline of ecology in the United States. Key figures, such as Victor Shelford, the first president of the Ecological Society of America, argued that the concept of habitat—understood as the biophysical relationships among species and between species and their environments—could provide an organizing framework for the entire field. For Shelford, habitat provided the keys to understanding ecology, and ecology opened the doors to understanding evolution. Habitat also provided spaces for rare or imperiled species and for the scientists who studied them.[10]

Ecology and conservation have changed in many ways since Shelford's time, but at least one aspect of his philosophy has survived. During the early twentieth century, ecologists argued that protected areas—including national parks, wildlife refuges, and other nature reserves—offered the most value for science and conservation when in their "original" condition. This meant that the most pristine areas, in terms of human influence, held the greatest value for habitat conservation. "Unprotected" sites would prove of little use as human activities increasingly altered them, and this meant that nature reserves would need vigilant protection against outside forces to maintain their value. These same themes would reemerge among the first generation of professional wildlife managers during the 1930s and among the founders of conservation biology in the 1980s. This approach lives on today, in modified form, as the protected areas paradigm.[11]

Creating nature reserves is not the only way to protect endangered species or even safeguard their habitats, but in the United States, and increasingly elsewhere, it has become the preferred approach. People who advocate for more protected areas have good reasons for doing so. Protected areas enable efficient management and provide diverse social and ecological benefits. Their administration can prove controversial, but it tends to incite less conflict than regulating the take of protected species on private property or multiple-use public lands. Protected areas render nature more legible for bureaucratic institutions by reducing unruly patterns, dynamic processes, and blurry boundaries to lines on a map that define the extent of conservation programs. Protected areas build on a strong legal rationale in that they can be owned outright, as either public or private property—a concept with high regard in American society. The protected areas approach also has a cultural resonance, in reinforcing the traditional American penchant for preserving relics of pristine nature in the form of national parks and wilderness areas. Finally, in an era when habitat loss constitutes the most important driving force behind most species declines, the creation of nature reserves offers a practical conservation approach that has probably already prevented numerous extinctions. And for that, we can all be thankful.[12]

Since the 1990s, however, the protected areas paradigm has come under criticism from scholars in the social sciences and humanities. Historians such as Alfred Runte and Richard West Sellars have critiqued the political and bureaucratic processes by which U.S. national parks were selected, established, and managed. The geographers Robert Wilson and Nathan Sayre have completed similarly provocative and enlightening studies of political conflict and administrative folly for wildlife refuges in the American West. A series of authors, led by William Cronon, have argued that the modern American idea of wilderness is based on a peculiar and problematic cultural history that fetishizes primeval nature over the places where most people live and obscures the diverse human values and activities that have helped produce all contemporary cultural landscapes. Numerous researchers in the interdisciplinary subfield of political ecology have adopted postcolonial and neoliberal development theories to show how, in economically poor but ecologically rich regions of the world, nature reserves have often served as a form of enclosure that privileges the environmental objectives of wealthy northern and western countries while making it more difficult for local people to access scarce natural resources. In response, conservationist biologists have defended their work and rethought their approaches. Nevertheless, scholarly debates about protected areas have often devolved into contests pitting ecological protection against social justice—a dichotomy that drastically oversimplifies the issues.[13]

This book builds on these insights and debates but focuses on a somewhat different problem. It locates the origins and logic of natural areas preservation not only in broad cultural ideas about nature but also in the specific and intertwined histories of American ecological science, environmental law, and natural resource management. The result is that this book focuses less on debates about ecological protection versus social justice than on the question of how the protected areas paradigm emerged and spread as a principal approach for biodiversity and endangered species conservation and whether, in the face of much political conflict, nature reserves established for these purposes are fulfilling their goals.

The results to date are mixed. Efforts to manage wild species inside legally bounded but ecologically porous nature reserves have always proved difficult. Endangered species managers increasingly rely on privately owned reserves that have more administrative flexibility than public lands do but whose permanence remains in question. Government agencies are suffering from unprecedented short-falls in funding and resources, which have exacerbated conflicts over their land management priorities and raised the question of whether reserve administration is, in fact, less contentious than the regulation of take on nonreserve lands. Recent research suggests that wildlife-habitat relationships are more complicated and less understood than previously believed; some species that seemed relatively tolerant of human activities now appear to be much less so, while others once thought to require remote wilderness areas have found refuge in the most unlikely of built environments.[14] Species declines that were once assumed to stem from a few limiting factors actually resulted from complex, multifarious, and synergistic forces. Global climate change threatens to transform all habitats, including those "protected" in nature reserves. And although habitat conservation has probably helped forestall many extinctions, it has not yet proved to be an effective tool for recovering endangered species to self-sustaining populations.

Many endangered species need more nature reserves, not fewer, if they are to persist in a world of rapid environmental change and mounting ecological problems. And despite major achievements in using nature reserves to maintain biodiversity in the United States, the protected areas paradigm does not offer a panacea for the problems facing endangered species and their keepers in the decades to come. But the time has also come to rethink the role of protected areas in a broader program of land, wildlife, and biodiversity conservation for the twenty-first century.

This book explores these issues through a history of endangered species and habitat conservation, with a focus on vertebrate wildlife, in and around California. Since 1967 the FWS and NOAA have listed around fifteen hundred types of plants and animals throughout the country as threatened or endangered. Every state now has listed species. Yet none offers a richer ecological context in which to study endangered species than California. This state has a greater diversity of plant and animal species than any other. It has the second-largest number of endangered species—more than three hundred as of 2012—after Hawaii (see map 1). It also has

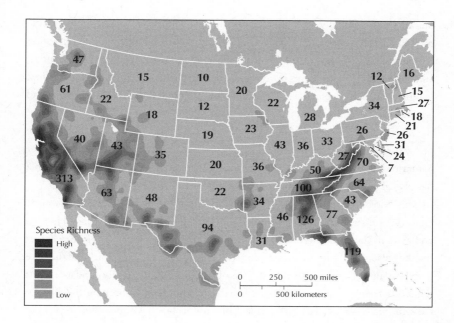

MAP I.

Species richness (combining both quantity and rarity) and
endangerment in the contiguous United States. The numbers
indicate species listed as threatened or endangered, per state.
Richness data courtesy of Oxford University Press.

by far the largest number of species at risk of becoming endangered in the future,
with at least 50 percent of its vertebrate fauna falling into this ominous category.
The California Department of Fish and Game (CDFG) estimates that seven vertebrate species or subspecies have gone extinct in the state since the gold rush.
Several factors have contributed to these patterns, but habitat loss, invasive species,
pollution, and a legacy of overhunting all rank near the top of the list.[15]

California's human history also makes it an ideal place for a study of this type.
The state experienced dramatic environmental changes during the nineteenth
century, was home to some of the first park and forest conservation movements,
and hosted several innovative early experiments in wildlife management. After
World War II, it developed a vast network of research universities, an influential
community of activists, and pioneering environmental policies that provided the
basis for similar measures by other states and the federal government. Wildlife
conservation initiatives began later in California than in the Northeast and Midwest,

but the state eventually built the country's largest wildlife management infrastructure. In the 1980s and 1990s, it became a hearth for the development of conservation biology, witnessed some of the country's most infamous endangered species battles, and hosted novel experiments in policy and management, including the nation's first habitat conservation plans (HCPs). California has spent far more on terrestrial and aquatic habitat conservation than any other state. In 1999 its legislators passed the Marine Life Protection Act, which launched a process for designating marine protected areas along the state's 840-mile coastline and made it the national leader in marine habitat conservation. In American endangered species history, California has played an outsize role at once unique, representative, and influential.

This book recounts a series of stories told from the perspectives of scientists, conservationists, bureaucrats, farmers, ranchers, developers, and others who live and work in California. These characters most often deal with issues close to home, but they also travel and correspond and collaborate with colleagues around the state and the country. The species they discuss often cross boundaries too, and as a result this book frequently wanders beyond the state's borders. By writing this history from the view—instead of at the scale—of California, I have attempted to give the state's experience a broader context while maintaining my conviction that endangered species debates are best told as historical narratives about the politics of place.

The first part of the book, chapters 1 through 4, is organized chronologically and thematically and spans from the late eighteenth to the late twentieth century. Chapter 1, from which the book takes its name, focuses on the epic tale of the rise and fall of the California grizzly, the state's official mascot and a ubiquitous symbol from a formative time when residents were debating what kind of place California should become. Chapter 2 moves on to the Progressive Era and the state's first wildlife conservation campaign, led by the zoologist Joseph Grinnell and his Berkeley circle of students and colleagues, who set out reform state fish and game laws and in the process laid the foundation for future endangered species and habitat conservation efforts in the state. Chapter 3 follows the Berkeley circle's shift, in the decades that followed, from grassroots campaigning in state-level politics to working for bureaucratic reform and habitat conservation on the growing federal lands. Chapter 4 picks up in the postwar era, when diverse social forces converged to enable the passage of the ESA, a law that would have profound and unexpected consequences as it evolved from a species protection measure into a broader mandate for habitat conservation.

Part 2, chapters 5 through 8, presents four case studies of endangered species in California, including the events that resulted in their declines and listings, and the conservation debates, failures, and occasional successes that followed. The four species hail from different taxonomic groups and represent regions of California with different economic geographies, political dynamics, and endangered species–related conflicts. Chapter 5 considers the California condor controversy, which exposed an awkward split between wildlife managers and wilderness preservationists but eventually led to a philosophical consensus among conservation biologists that combined scientific management with habitat preservation. Chapter 6 follows the story of the desert tortoise, a species whose decline helped launch a new era of land management in the Mojave Desert but which has continued to suffer despite having vast areas set aside on its behalf. Chapter 7 introduces the San Joaquin kit fox, the flagship species of an industrialized agricultural landscape, whose history illustrates our still limited understanding of wildlife-habitat relationships. Chapter 8 turns to the delta smelt, an indicator species for the California Bay-Delta that became embroiled in a water war and whose predicament casts doubt not only on the protected areas approach to endangered species recovery but also on the very idea of habitat conservation as Americans have traditionally understood it.

The emergence of habitat as a key concept in environmental science, law, management, and politics is one of the great, untold stories in American conservation history. It is also essential for understanding contemporary endangered species debates. This book concludes with an epilogue that reflects on the importance and accomplishments of the protected areas paradigm while highlighting the limitations of nature reserves as a conservation strategy. It ends with a call for a broader vision that moves beyond an approach that served conservationists well in the past but has little chance of recovering endangered species in the future.

Californians are surrounded by bears. Most of these creatures are not the coy, mischievous black bears that prowl Yosemite campgrounds after dark, raiding ice chests and eating bologna sandwiches out of "wildlife resistant" trash bins. No, these are massive, fearless, humpbacked, barrel-chested, dagger-clawed grizzly bears—and they are everywhere. They lurk behind picnic tables in city parks, patrol the entrances to government buildings, gnash their teeth next to bus stops, and splash in fountains alongside children. Sometimes they wear plastic pink leis and funny hats. During an hour's walk on the campus of the University of California, Berkeley, an intrepid naturalist can view at least twenty-seven resident grizzly bears in an area of just three square miles. Scientists have not attempted a current census, but the state's grizzlies must number in the hundreds of thousands. California truly is the land of the bears.[1]

Of course, none of these animals are *alive*. They are all only images and monuments. In the mid-nineteenth century, California was home to as many as ten thousand living, breathing grizzly bears—a greater population density than in present-day Alaska, and around a fifth of all the grizzlies in the United States at the time. Zoologists believe that the California population constituted a unique subspecies: the California grizzly, or "chaparral bear," a label that referred to its affinity for the region's scrubby foothills and brush-covered mountains. The chaparral bear's numbers seem to have peaked around the time of the gold rush, in 1849, then plummeted during the second half of the nineteenth century. The last captive

California grizzly died in 1911, and any remaining wild individuals probably perished before 1930.

By the time it went extinct, the California grizzly had become an indelible icon. It appeared on the state flag and seal. Artists had immortalized it in paintings and murals. The University of California had adopted it as a mascot. And hundreds of monuments commemorated its role in the state's Indian, Spanish, Mexican, and early American histories (see figure 2). Today the grizzly's image appears on pendants and billboards and is inscribed on T-shirts and logos, carved in stone, and cast in bronze. These representations are all that remain of the chaparral bear. Most people hardly notice them. Yet references to the California grizzly—a once-celebrated totem now vanquished, extinct, and largely forgotten—remain a ubiquitous presence in the lives of millions.

The California grizzly went extinct long before conservationists coined the term *endangered species*. Its story can serve only as a prelude to the debates that followed and that are the focus of subsequent chapters in this book. Yet the epic history of the grizzly bear in California, in addition to offering a grand tale of the American West, illustrates a crucial point for understanding more recent endangered species controversies. Although debates about wildlife extinction and conservation have changed much over the years, one thing remains the same: they have always been about the politics of place. In California there is no better species to illustrate this essential insight than the one most closely associated with the state's indigenous history, colonial encounters, frontier origins, early development, political symbolism, and contemporary cultural landscape.

MONARCH—AN URSINE ENCOUNTER

In the spring of 1889, the reporter Allan Kelly left the cosmopolitan comforts of his San Francisco home bound for the rugged mountains of Ventura County in a still-remote corner of Southern California. He worked for the *San Francisco Examiner*, and his boss, William Randolph Hearst, had sent him on an extraordinary assignment. Kelly's goal was to capture and return with a live California grizzly bear. Doing so would prove the animals still existed. It would also enable Kelly's ambitious employer to generate publicity for his newspapers by presenting the citizens of San Francisco with a marvelous gift.

Kelly was a quick-witted observer and eloquent author. He loved the mountains, penned self-effacing accounts of his outdoor misadventures, and wrote about people and animals with humor, precision, and respect. According to Kelly, Hearst

FIGURE 2.
California grizzly monuments: *(above)* the Bruin mascot on the UCLA campus in Westwood (courtesy of Jacquelyn Langberg); *(below)* a statue near the central coast town of Los Osos ("The Bears"), on the approximate site of the first European encounter with California grizzlies (photo by the author).

had selected him for the job because although the reporter had no experience as a trapper, he was "the only man on the paper who was supposed to know anything about bears."[2] Hearst sent Kelly on the expedition only after having tried and failed to purchase a captive grizzly, for which he would have fabricated a harrowing tale of pursuit and capture. As Kelly would discover on the publication of his own heavily edited grizzly story, Hearst made a habit of encouraging his employees not to allow the facts to constrain their imagination.

Kelly set out for the little farming town of Santa Paula, where he would begin his adventure, in May. He spent a month in the area learning to build bear traps from stout oak beams, to ignore the locals' eccentric advice, and to distinguish real paw prints from the fake ones left by his untrustworthy advisers. By June he was ready to proceed, and he moved to a camp at seventy-five hundred feet on the forested slopes of Mount Piños some forty miles to the north. Three grizzlies visited Kelly and his assistants during their time on the mountain, but none of the bears took the crew's bait or wandered into the traps. In July Kelly's editor at the *Examiner* decided that the adventure had gone on long enough and ordered his reporter back to San Francisco. Kelly pleaded for more time, but the editor responded by revoking his funding and suspending his salary. With no assistants and no support, the unemployed journalist was on his own.

Having failed on Mount Piños, Kelly decided to move his camp, his burro, and his few remaining possessions east to the Tehachapi Mountains near Antelope Valley, where he hoped to find a bear that the locals called Old Pinto. To Kelly's surprise, tracking Old Pinto proved relatively easy. The bear strutted about the area as if he owned it, leaving tracks in the soil and scratches on the trees wherever he went. But capturing Old Pinto, who was wary enough to avoid the temptations of honey-and-mutton-baited traps, was another matter. Kelly was impressed with the bear's intelligence and instincts. He found himself surprised by the serenity of the forest and the reticence of the animals that lived there, and he grew ambivalent about what he increasingly viewed as his nefarious objective. "Many of my prejudices and all my storybook notions about the behavior of the carnivorae [*sic*] were discredited by experience," he wrote, "and I was forced to recognize the plain truth that the only mischievous animal, the only creature meditating and planning evil on that mountain . . . was a man with a gun."[3]

Word of Kelly's search soon spread, and mountain men for fifty miles in every direction set out their own traps in the hope of catching a suddenly valuable bear. In October Kelly got word that a syndicate of shepherds and trappers had captured a grizzly on Gleason Mountain, in what was then called the Sierra Madre and is now known as the San Gabriel Mountains, north of Los Angeles. Sure enough, when Kelly arrived at the site he found a massive grizzly in a stout cage. The group's watchman, a vaquero named Mateo, unaware of the visitor's identity, told Kelly that he planned to sell the animal to a big-city newspaperman for an exorbitant price. He was, however, open to other offers. The two men haggled a bit before Kelly purchased the bear for a bargain price. Kelly later wrote that it was "the only evidence of business capacity to be found in my entire career."[4] But now he was alone in the mountains, nearly broke after a five-month mostly self-funded expedition, the owner of an ill-tempered half-ton grizzly bear that he somehow needed to get to San Francisco, four hundred miles away, to deliver to an unscrupulous publisher who had recently fired him and who might not even still want the beast.

Fortunately for Kelly, Hearst was thrilled. Yes, he still wanted the grizzly; yes, he wanted to name it Monarch, after one of his newspapers; and yes, he wanted Kelly to return to San Francisco with the animal at once. Now came the hard part. Monarch was not exactly a docile creature. For his first week in captivity, the bear "raged like a lunatic." He "bit and tore at the logs, hurled his great bulk against the sides and tried to enlarge every chink that admitted light" into his box cage. Eventually the beast tired, allowing Kelly and his hired team to fit the bear with chains for the trip ahead. That process required several days, and it cost Monarch his canine teeth, which he splintered while trying to rip off his shackles. After the chains came the temporary gag, a thick rope lashed through the bear's mouth and strapped around his ears to form a bridle, which was attached to a collar made of heavy Norwegian iron. Once Monarch was fully restrained, his captors removed the gag and finished readying him for the long journey north.[5]

The trip took about two weeks. The first section, from the camp to the nearest wagon road, was the most difficult. Each evening Kelly's team would chain Monarch to a tree, and each morning they would load him up for the day's trip. This required roping the bear, binding him to "a rough skeleton sled," or "go-devil," then dragging the whole contraption, bear and all, down the mountain. It was not easy to find a team of horses that would submit to the task, and each morning Monarch fought back with "dogged persistency." He was an enormous and powerful animal, but in the end he was no match for four men on horses with chains and lassos. When they reached the road, the crew built a bigger cage, and Monarch spent the rest of the trip riding on wagons and trains. The bear had but one "tantrum" along the way, when a group of onlookers in the ramshackle depot of Mojave poked and prodded him with sharp sticks to try to make him stand. He had almost burst out of his cage when Kelly arrived to chase the gawkers away and pacify the bear with a sliced watermelon. After that, Monarch settled into the calm routine of a defeated but dignified captive.[6]

The journey left a lifelong impression on both man and animal. By the time they reached San Francisco, according to Kelly, Monarch would "allow me to handle his chain and would take food from my hand. . . . Close acquaintance with the grizzly inspired me with genuine respect for his character and admiration for his indomitable courage." But the trip was tough on Monarch. According to the *Examiner*, the grueling voyage had left the great bear "travel-worn and thin. . . . His broken teeth trouble him some and it will be some time before he will feel as well as he did before he was caught." The paper assured its readers, however, that Monarch was "brightening up, and when the abrasions of his skin, made by ropes and chains, are healed up and his hair grows again on the bare spots he will be more presentable."[7]

On November 10, around twenty thousand people gathered at Woodward's Garden—a long-shuttered zoo, museum, and theme park that was then in San Francisco's Mission District—to attend a reception celebrating Monarch's debut as the only California grizzly in captivity. It was a merry outing for most of the attendees. But for Kelly the day's festivities offered little cause for cheer. Looking back, he recalled that after Monarch's capture, the bear had "exhausted every means at his command to break out, and when convinced that he was beaten, he spent one whole day in grievous lamentation and then ceased his futile efforts. Monarch is a brave old fellow and he ought to be free in his native mountains. If he still regrets that he was captured I sympathize with him for I'm more than half sorry myself."[8]

Kelly never said exactly why he was sorry. But he knew that California's wildlife was declining rapidly and that zoos were miserable places for most animals. His experience with Monarch had challenged him and changed him, and it seems safe to say that he had decided that wild creatures, particularly large and intelligent animals such as grizzlies, belonged in wild places. This was not a common belief at the time, but Kelly would be far from the last Californian to reach that conclusion.

THE RISE AND FALL OF THE CHAPARRAL BEAR

Before the arrival of European explorers, settlers, and missionaries in the late eighteenth century, grizzlies roamed throughout most of what is now California. They lived on the seashores, in the valleys, in the foothills, and in the mountains all the way up to the alpine zone. They favored grasslands, wetlands, woodlands, and brushlands—especially chaparral—but they ranged widely throughout the region's diverse landscapes, from the Sierra Nevada and the Cascades to the Coast, Transverse, and Peninsular Ranges, into the Sacramento and San Joaquin Valleys, and along coastal bluffs and prairies including the San Francisco Peninsula and the Los Angeles Basin (see map 2). The only part of California that grizzlies probably did not frequent was the eastern deserts. They did, however, wander all the way out to the desert fringe, especially during the sporadic years when the piñon trees produced their sumptuous crops of buttery pine nuts.[9]

Unlike their relatives farther north, California grizzlies lived in a region with year-round resource availability. They remained active day and night, consumed a wide variety of foods, and had no need to hibernate. Grizzlies scavenged the carcasses of beached marine mammals, grazed on perennial grasses and seeds, gathered berries, and foraged for fruits and nuts. They rooted around like pigs in search of roots and bulbs, and after the introduction of European hogs, the bears ate them too. At times and places of abundant food—such as along rivers during steelhead spawning seasons or in oak woodlands during acorn mast years—grizzlies congregated in large numbers. Such a varied and plentiful diet produced some enormous animals. Male California grizzlies could grow to more than fifteen hundred pounds. This equals the maximum size of the largest grizzlies alive today, Alaska's Kodiak bears, which achieve their exceptional girth by the rather different strategy of specializing on salmon and hibernating for much of the year.[10]

No one knows how many grizzlies lived in California before European contact. The great naturalist Joseph Grinnell, who served as the first director of the Museum of Vertebrate Zoology at UC Berkeley and spearheaded California's first grassroots wildlife conservation campaign in the 1910s, calculated a pre-1830 population of 2,595 adult grizzlies. He based this number on historical records, assumptions about resource availability, and the size of grizzly ranges in other regions. He also noted that under favorable conditions, grizzlies were capable of rapid population growth.[11] Yet Grinnell's numbers are only estimates. All we can say for sure is that grizzlies were probably always common in California, and much more so than their smaller cousins, the black bears, whose populations grizzlies appear to have limited through territorial aggression and competitive exclusion. Black bears are common throughout much of California today, but they probably only became so after the grizzlies' eradication.

Despite their robust size and large population, grizzlies were never the dominant land animal in California. For the first million years of the species's existence, the grizzly was just one member of a spectacular group of Pleistocene megafauna that included such formidable beasts as the saber-toothed tiger, the dire wolf, the giant

MAP 2 (OPPOSITE)
Key sites in the history of the California grizzly.

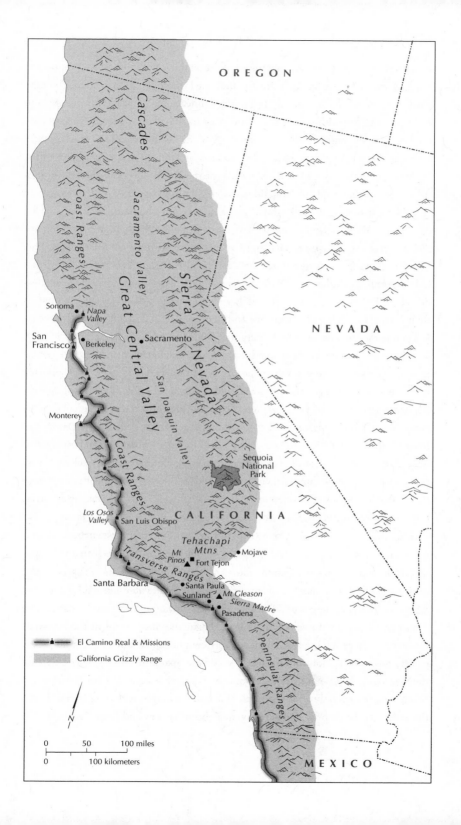

OREGON

Cascades

Coast Ranges

Sacramento Valley

Sierra Nevada

NEVADA

Sonoma
Napa Valley
San Francisco
Berkeley
Sacramento

Great Central Valley

Monterey

Coast Ranges

San Joaquin Valley

Sequoia National Park

Los Osos Valley
San Luis Obispo

CALIFORNIA

Tehachapi Mtns
Mt Pinos
Fort Tejon
Mojave

Transverse Ranges
Santa Barbara
Santa Paula
Sunland
Mt Gleason
Sierra Madre
Pasadena

Peninsular Ranges

━■━ El Camino Real & Missions

California Grizzly Range

N

0   50   100 miles

0   100 kilometers

MEXICO

ground sloth, and the woolly mammoth. Around thirteen thousand years ago, near the end of the last ice age and shortly after the arrival of the first human hunter-gatherers, many of these species began to decline. Some persisted for millennia in isolated areas, but within a few thousand years most had disappeared. Species with the largest body masses were the first to go, and they went extinct at a much greater rate than did the smaller ones. Grizzlies ranked well down the size hierarchy of the Pleistocene megafauna, but they were one of the largest terrestrial animal species to survive the subsequent extinctions. By ten thousand years ago, they were the second-most-dominant land animals in California, after humans.[12]

As late as the 1980s, many scholars of this period thought that California Indians did not have the capacity to challenge or control the grizzlies in their midst. This belief derived from scattered accounts by Spanish chroniclers who claimed that killing problem grizzlies proved their countrymen's benevolence toward the helpless natives. The Indians' supposed inability to control grizzlies was an example of their failure to civilize their country and thus contributed to a larger narrative of indigenous savagery and vulnerability that helped to justify colonization.[13]

Recent scholarship on pre-Columbian environmental manipulation by indigenous people has revealed the self-serving absurdity of the Spaniards' claims.[14] California before the Spanish was not a primeval wilderness; it was one of the most densely populated regions on the continent outside present-day Mexico, with human inhabitants who altered its environments through hunting, fishing, gathering, burning, and horticulture. Grizzly bears and people coexisted in uneasy proximity and often killed one another. But this was no balance of power. People almost certainly excluded bears from key resource sites, hunted them for food and ceremonial uses, and may even have culled their populations for community safety or to prevent raids on valuable resources. Grizzlies were formidable neighbors, but then as now, people ruled the land.

The Spanish did, however, bring superior firepower to their first encounters with California's bears. In September of 1769, a motley band of soldiers from the Gaspar de Portolá expedition landed on the shores of what is now San Luis Obispo County, near Morro Bay, and marched inland in search of freshwater and wild game. Not far from the coast, they found "troops of bears" foraging in a marshy basin. The famished soldiers mounted their horses and began the chase. None of these animals had ever heard or felt gunfire, and they were caught exposed in open country. One grizzly took seven shots and maimed two of the Spaniards' mules before chasing the men away. A 375-pound female, small by California standards but enormous to Spanish eyes, died only after receiving nine bullet wounds, including a final shot to the head. The bruin provided a hearty meal, both "savory and good," and gave the soldiers a taste for bear meat that, just a few years later, would prove their salvation. The site became known as La Cañada de los Osos: The Valley of the Bears.[15]

The Spaniards settled in the north at Monterey, and then at San Carlos and San Antonio, but their missions were miserable, squalid places. They had meager supplies, and the landscape that surrounded them seemed to offer few resources. The missions in the south, at San Gabriel and San Diego, were even worse off, and Junípero Serra, the leader of the Spanish mission system in Alta California, sent provisions to the southern outposts overland by mule. Within three years of their arrival in California, the residents of the northern missions also began to fear starvation.

Enter Don Pedro Fages Beleta, the Spanish navy captain who served as the maritime chief of the Portolá expedition. After Portolá's departure, in 1770, Fages became Alta California's second Spanish military governor, and he concocted a daring plan to resolve the increasingly desperate situation. He and his small band of soldiers marched 140 miles, from Monterey back to Morro Bay, to find food. They reached La Cañada de los Osos in 1772 and remained in the area for three months, during which time they killed some thirty grizzlies and sent about nine thousand pounds of jerked bear meat back to the northern missions. Fages became an instant hero, and for his accomplishments he earned the nickname El Oso.[16]

Why did Fages need to travel 140 miles to find food? There are several possible answers. First, the Spaniards were picky and prejudiced eaters. They were accustomed to consuming large quantities of red meat, but they preferred the beef of proper Spanish cattle. They knew little about hunting, fishing, or trapping, other than shooting bears, and because they believed they were the ones doing the teaching, they rejected the advice of the area's indigenous inhabitants. But there is something else to this story. Fages needed to travel 140 miles to find food because in 1772, wild game in Alta California appears to have been relatively scarce.[17]

Before European settlement, a population of some three hundred fifty thousand American Indians used the region's fish and wildlife resources and altered its ecosystems in myriad ways. Consider two well-known examples: Fisheries biologists have estimated that indigenous people in the Central Valley alone caught up to 8.5 million pounds of salmon annually. The largest Euro-American commercial harvests taken in the nineteenth and twentieth centuries ranged from four to ten million pounds. Indians also managed landscapes to maintain terrestrial game, such as deer, using fire to clear brush and promote forage, and they undoubtedly took large numbers of these animals too. Some of these practices had already diminished by the late eighteenth century, but indigenous environmental manipulation and resource harvests continued at significant levels for several decades. The consequences of these activities for fish and wildlife must have been profound and complex, but it seems clear that indigenous hunting and gathering limited the abundance of wild game in Alta California into the second half of the eighteenth century.[18]

This situation changed swiftly and dramatically during the mission era. Between 1769 and 1834, the number of Indians living along the coast between San Diego and Sonoma dropped by an apocalyptic 75 percent. Disease and migration contributed to further declines through the end of the Mexican rancho era in 1848. By 1855 there were only about fifty thousand Indians left in California. For the few who survived, ecological changes, including the proliferation of exotic plants and animals, made it more difficult to pursue traditional subsistence life-styles based on the harvest of native species.[19]

Aside from its human consequences, the demographic collapse of California's Indians had enormous consequences for the region's ecology. Hunting, gathering, fishing, burning, and horticulture all dwindled. European livestock proliferated on the range, denuded the vegetation, and formed huge feral herds. Some native wild-life species were forced to compete with introduced European species for resources. But for many others, particularly those that did not compete with or suffer from the presence of feral livestock, the mission era represented a period of diminished human pressure, abundant resources, and population growth.[20]

This process began almost immediately, and it soon reached epic proportions. As early as 1786, the French navigator Jean François de La Pérouse wrote that no country was "more abundant in fish and game of every description." Tales of California's bountiful elk, antelope, deer, salmon, ducks, geese, and of course bears became commonplace in travelers' and settlers' accounts. In 1826 Frederick William Beechey, of the British Royal Navy, found the San Francisco Bay region "abounding in game of all kinds, so plentiful, indeed, as so to lessen the desire of pursuit." In 1841 the American settler John Bidwell described the Great Central Valley as containing "thousands of elk, antelope, deer, wild horses, . . . incalculable thousands of wild geese, ducks, brants, cranes, pelicans, etc.," as well as "a great abundance of salmon in every stream." A complete list of such accounts could continue for many pages. California's boosters almost certainly exaggerated these reports in their attempts to attract new residents. Yet descriptions of plentiful wildlife were so common, among so many diverse and independent observers, that it would be folly to reject their essential veracity. By the 1830s, the same region in which El Oso had needed to travel 140 miles to find wild game had become a paradise for fish and wildlife—including grizzlies.[21]

No group of species profited more from this transition than the large carnivores, which benefited from a reduction in hunting but even more from an increase in resource availability. Eagles preyed on newly introduced agricultural livestock, including goats and piglets. Wolves stalked vast flocks of feral sheep. Coyotes and bobcats devoured house cats and Norway rats. Condors and vultures gathered around gruesome *calaveras*, or "places of skulls," where they and other scavengers picked at the discarded remains of animals slaughtered for the hide and tallow industries. And thousands of grizzlies became fat on the carcasses of Spanish live-stock. Grizzlies are opportunistic eaters. They can survive on largely herbivorous diets, but they will consume extravagant quantities of meat when the chance arises. Livestock provided an unprecedented caloric resource, and by 1848 the population of bears in Alta California had probably reached its historic peak. On the eve of statehood, the region contained about seventy-five hundred naturalized Spanish settlers, or Californios, one hundred thousand Indians, sixty-five hundred miscel-laneous immigrants, and some ten thousand grizzly bears—a staggering ratio of more than one grizzly for every twelve people.[22]

The historical record from California during this period abounds with stories about bears. In Southern California, grizzlies were "more plentiful than pigs," a situation that made ranching in the mountains above Santa Barbara and Los Angeles "utterly impossible." In central California, grizzlies loitered around the towns of San Luis Obispo and even Monterey, where El Oso had failed to find any just a few decades earlier. In Northern California, George C. Yount, one of the region's first Anglo-American pioneers, recalled that near his Napa homestead, grizzlies "were everywhere upon the plains, in the valleys, and on the mountains . . . so that I have often killed as many as five or six in one day, and it was not unusual to see fifty or sixty within twenty-four hours." In 1827 a grizzly bear astonished the crew of a boat sailing near Angel Island, in San Francisco Bay, when it surfaced nearby and began swimming toward them. The sailors dispatched the animal with "four balls . . . at close range" before it had an opportunity to board their vessel. As late as 1850, a grizzly wandered into the settlement at Mission Dolores on the outskirts of San Francisco.[23]

The Californios hunted and killed grizzlies. Yet unlike the Puritan farmers who had arrived in New England with a pious hatred of all things wild, the Catholic ranchers who settled in Alta California a century and a half later had no particular enmity toward the native animals. By the 1830s the region had an overabundance of livestock, and the ranchers, who never made much of an effort to maximize their profits, felt little urgency to control the predators or build their herds. Grizzlies became subjects of sport and leisure, and they assumed a central place in the grand festivals that defined the time (and still do in the popular imagination). Bear lassoing was one popular, if hazardous, diversion (see figure 3). Grizzlies also participated

FIGURE 3.

Roping the Bear at Santa Margarita Rancho of Juan Foster,
by James Walker (1818–89), c. 1870 (oil on canvas). Courtesy
of the California Historical Society; gift of Mr. and Mrs. Reginald
F. Walker Coll., CHS2009.165.

in the bear-and-bull fights that occurred in towns throughout the region. These fights continued a European tradition thousands of years old, but they reached their most elaborate development in Alta California. The bears almost always won these bloody contests, but the fights often turned into harrowing spectacles whose result was never a foregone conclusion.[24]

By 1840, Anglo-American pioneers were beginning to arrive in Alta California in larger numbers. Most had little appreciation for Californio culture and even less regard for wild animals. These newcomers killed grizzlies for a multitude of reasons—or sometimes for no reason at all—and they pursued their project with relentless enthusiasm. Grizzly killing soon became a rite of passage and a sign of manly virtue among a certain class of self-styled and self-promoting mountain men who sought fame and fortune in the Great West. They made guest appearances, toured with traveling shows, and published popular accounts, often ghostwritten, of their daring exploits. Hunters would even sell captured cubs as pets or performers. In Sacramento in 1858, one could purchase an untamed California grizzly cub for $15.50 and a trained bruin for $20.50, which was probably worth the modest markup. Men such as George Nidever, Colin Preston, and Seth Kiman all claimed to have killed

FIGURE 4.
Adams, the Hunter, and His Bears, by Edward Vischer, 1873.
Courtesy of the Bancroft Library, University of California,
Berkeley.

dozens or even hundreds of bears, and each became briefly famous. But none
achieved the mythical status of one John Capen Adams.[25]

"Grizzly" Adams arrived in California from Massachusetts in 1849, and from 1852
to 1856 he hunted and trapped bears in the Sierra Nevada and the Rocky Mountains.
Adams killed dozens of grizzlies. But he domesticated and cared for many others,
including a feisty, fifteen-hundred-pound behemoth named Old Sampson, and his
more sedate longtime companion, Ben Franklin, whom he walked on a leash and
fitted with a packsaddle. Adams became famous for parading his menagerie through
downtown San Francisco, and in 1856 he founded the Pacific Museum on the corner
of Clay and Kearney Streets in the heart of that city. The establishment was more
of a circus than a museum, and Adams was more of a clown than a curator. In the
building's cramped quarters, he staged bizarre evening shows that included bears as
well as elk, deer, lions, tigers, snakes, roadrunners, monkeys, and "numberless small
animals," all choreographed to a "fine brass band" (see figure 4).[26]

As Monarch's capture demonstrated, grizzlies did not succumb to death or the indignities of captivity without a spirited fight, and California soon contained scores of men who had proved their masculine virtue at the expense of death or disfiguring injuries. "If you kill a bear," *Harper's New Monthly Magazine* declared in 1861, "it is a triumph worthy [of] enjoying; if you get killed yourself, some of the newspapers will give you a friendly notice; if you get crippled for life, you carry about you a patent of courage which may be useful in case you go into politics. . . . Besides, it has its effect upon the ladies. A 'chawed up' man is very much admired all over the world." Adams died in 1860, at the age of forty-eight, from medical complications following a series of massive, bear-inflicted head wounds, several of which he received from the animals in his care.[27]

California's macho bear hunters were not the only people attempting to define the state's grizzlies. Another perspective, popular among Victorian moralists, portrayed grizzlies as benign creatures, righteous citizens, and even good parents. As early as 1850, U.S. Naval Chaplain Walter Colton wrote that the grizzly's child-rearing skills shone "like a good deed in a naughty world." Joaquin Miller, one of the most colorful characters in the late-nineteenth-century American West, had little in common with Chaplain Colton. He reportedly contracted scurvy while working as a cook at a mining camp and spent time in jail for stealing a horse before being elected a judge in Grant County, Oregon. But he agreed with Colton's assessment of the grizzly's character. In 1900 he published a book called *True Bear Stories,* much of which was undoubtedly false, in which he described the grizzly as "a good-natured lover of his family."[28]

The heyday for California's chaparral bears lasted little more than half a century—halted not only by hunting, capture, and commodification but also by the transformation of the state's rural landscapes into spaces of capitalist agricultural production where bears simply were not welcome. In the decades following the gold rush of 1849, the state's new Anglo-American elite succeeded in dispossessing the Californios of their lands and began converting the state's valley grasslands and wetlands into orchards and wheat fields. Ranching continued in the foothills and mountains, but the great drought of 1863–64 devastated California's overstocked rangelands and killed at least half of the state's cattle. Sheep weathered the drought better than cows but were more vulnerable to attack by large carnivores, and the woolgrowers, with their newfound political clout, took the lead in predator elimination.

No one knows how many domestic animals the grizzlies killed, but many clearly became habituated to livestock, and this earned them a place on the agricultural blacklist, along with numerous other species. Cattlemen awarded bounties for the scalps of special offenders, and hunters could profit several times from a single kill. After a hunter collected his reward, he would dismember the animal and sell off its oil, meat, hide, internal organs, and claws. This created a strong incentive for grizzly hunting. According to the naturalist Henry W. Henshaw, few species had "suffered more from persistent and relentless warfare waged by man than this formidable bear. . . . The number of bears is each year diminished, till in many sections where formerly they were very abundant they have entirely disappeared."[29]

Despite these landscape transformations and eradication campaigns, grizzlies remained common in some areas for decades. Sightings continued through the 1860s in the San Francisco Bay Area, from Carmel to Santa Cruz, Palo Alto, San Jose, and Livermore, where Grizzly Adams had lived in his wilderness cabin. In the 1870s, grizzlies were still abundant near Yosemite Valley and in the vast belt of chaparral-covered mountains that stretched across Southern California from Point Conception in Santa Barbara County to Fort Tejon in Kern County and the Peninsular Ranges east of San Diego. As late as the 1880s, grizzlies frequented the Arroyo Seco outside Pasadena, now home to the Rose Bowl, where they indulged in the unhealthy habit of raiding apiaries owned by beekeepers armed with poison and guns.[30]

The number of recorded encounters between humans and grizzly bears declined during the final decades of the nineteenth century. Grizzlies were shot in Santa Cruz County near Ben Lomond in 1886, in Ventura County near Mount Piños in 1898, and in Orange County at the head of Trabuco Canyon in 1908. A man named Cornelius B. Johnson killed Southern California's last known grizzly near the town of Sunland, in the San Fernando Valley north of Burbank, in October 1916. Johnson used some stale beef from a local butcher shop as bait for a Newhouse No. 5 bear trap, which he set out near some vineyards and weighed down with a fifty-pound drag log. He discovered the animal, a full day after it had become ensnared, half a mile into the foothills and nearly five hundred feet higher in elevation. The 254-pound bear had dragged the trap and log up the canyon until the whole tangled mess of bear and iron and wood got stuck in the brush. By the time Johnson found the exhausted sow, she was waiting to die.[31]

No one knows how long the last California grizzlies survived in the wild. In 1924, reports appeared of a massive, speckled, cinnamon-colored bear prowling the western slopes of the Sierra Nevada near Horse Corral Meadow in Sequoia National Park. Witnesses said it had a hump on its shoulders, which is one of the features that most easily distinguishes grizzlies from black bears. A local rancher named Jesse Agnew claimed to have killed another grizzly in the same area just a couple years earlier. Agnew's story received the support of C. Hart Merriam, the chief of the U.S. Biological Survey, who examined a tooth from the bear and proclaimed it a grizzly. The last reported sighting came in 1925, from a cattleman named Hengst, near the headwaters of Cliff Creek deep in the park, but no specimens, photographs, or other physical evidence ever emerged. And then the sightings stopped. It had taken just seventy-five years of statehood for Californians to exterminate their most spectacular land animal.[32]

A SYMBOL OF STATEHOOD AND BEYOND

The California grizzly may have gone extinct, but it did not disappear. In 1890 the historian and naturalist Charles Howard Shinn envisioned a future when the bear, having "impressed himself irrevocably upon the imagination," would achieve immortality. Farms and cities would replace wilderness, and the grizzly would fade away from the countryside. In its passing, however, the species would take its place alongside the American pioneer and other cherished anachronisms in a new chapter of national folklore—a "noble myth" of westward expansion, comparable in its grandeur to the epics of medieval England and ancient Greece. It was impossible to say exactly what this heroic legend would contain, because it would remain incomplete until the final California grizzly had vanished from its last mountain redoubt. For Shinn, the grizzly's extinction was not only inevitable but also essential for the patriotic reunification and rebirth of a country still reeling from half a century of internecine violence and frenetic change that included the Civil War, Manifest Destiny, and the Gilded Age.[33]

Shinn was not the only observer who believed that wild animal extinctions were necessary and inevitable in American progress. During the previous two decades, a wide variety of commentators, capitalists, and politicians had made similar statements about other species in other parts of the American West. They argued that the settlement of the region required a great transformation of nature and society—one that would see unruly wild beasts and uncivilized native peoples give way to domestic animals and an industrious white society. The California grizzly was just one creature among the many that had no place in this new American future.[34]

Shinn had good reason to believe that the grizzly would become a permanent feature of California's foundation mythology. His article coincided with the U.S. Census Bureau's announcement, in 1890, that the country no longer had a western frontier, which it defined as a single contiguous line beyond which the population density decreased to less than two people per square mile. The West was now, at least in official terms, settled. The western frontier had occupied a prominent place on the mental maps of white Americans since the seventeenth century, and its closure created an uncommon opportunity for collective reflection and mythmaking. This process was already well under way in California, where the grizzly bear had emerged as an icon of both the fading frontier and the new society that was replacing it.

In the Bear Flag Revolt, of June 1846, a band of Anglo-American interlopers, acting at the behest of U.S. Army Major John C. Frémont, marched into the town square of Sonoma, fifty miles north of San Francisco, and replaced the Mexican flag there with a makeshift banner featuring a star, a grizzly bear, and the words *CALIFORNIA REPUBLIC*. The bear symbolized power and defiance for a ragtag group of insurgents whose intention was to seize control of land that the Mexicans had wrestled from the Spanish, and the Spanish had usurped from the Indians. The California Republic was short-lived. It ended less than a month later, when army forces occupied Monterey and the Bear Flag rebels sided with the United States in the Mexican-American War. California joined the Union in 1848 and achieved statehood in 1850. A redesigned version of the insurgents' original Sonoma banner became its official flag in 1911 (see figure 5).

The Great Seal of the State of California, adopted at California's constitutional convention on the eve of statehood in 1849, also features a grizzly. This bear shares its space with grapevines, representing agriculture; a miner, embodying resource extraction; sailboats, signifying trade; and the Roman goddess Minerva, symbolizing wisdom, poetry, craft, and commerce. Native Americans, Franciscan missionaries, and Californios are nowhere to be found.

Shinn was right to identify the grizzly as an enduring symbol of early California. But he was wrong to think that most people would look back on the bear's destruction as a necessary step in American progress, and he underestimated its versatility as a cultural icon. By the time the California grizzly went extinct, people had seen it as a man-eater, a cattle killer, a test of masculine virtue, an exemplar of domesticity, and a source of meat for their starving communities. They had pressed it into service as a totem, a trophy, a varmint, a delicacy, a matador, and a jester (as in Grizzly Adams's grotesque basement circus). They had mobilized it as a symbol of revolt and statehood, of the fading frontier and the residual wilderness, of reckless consumption and the promise of conservation. People had even used grizzlies to hunt other grizzlies. The grizzly provided Californians with such a powerful symbol not only because it played a unique role during a formative historical period but also because it typified a much larger transformation that reordered the state's

FIGURE 5.
The California state flag.

ecosystems and rearranged its animal populations. We now turn to that larger context of wildlife exploitation and ecological change.

THE BELEAGUERED MENAGERIE

Not all wild animal species responded in the same way to the social, economic, and ecological changes that transformed California during the nineteenth century. Some, such as the grizzly, probably experienced brief periods of superabundance, in response to diminished human hunting and increased resource availability, only to become rare during the final decades of the century. Species that thrived in fields and farmlands probably increased their numbers. But many others declined in population due to habitat loss, increased competition, and predation from larger, more aggressive species. The net result of all of this change was that by 1900, many of the state's most valuable and charismatic fish and game species reached their lowest levels ever recorded, before or since. We must understand the grizzly's story within this broader context.

Marine species were among the earliest to suffer from exploitation. Beginning around 1780, the sea otter supported the first major wildlife industry in Alta California. By 1800, ships were arriving there from around the world, and sea otter pelts, which had become North America's most valuable natural resource by weight, were appearing in markets as far away as Shanghai and London. This was California's first "gold" rush. By 1840 the fur trade had nearly led to the sea otter's extinction. A sea otter harvest would briefly reemerge around 1890, and this second phase of hunting again almost annihilated the species, as well as several other marine mammals. The North Pacific Fur Seal Convention of 1911, the world's first wildlife conservation treaty, banned further exploitation, but by this time fewer than two thousand sea otters remained in the near-shore waters throughout western North America. Despite their long-predicted extinction and to the amazement of many naturalists, sea otters reappeared along the California coast in the 1930s. In 2010 there were more than twenty-six hundred sea otters in California waters. The resurgence of this species ranks among the most dramatic reversals in the annals of American wildlife conservation, but the otters' return remains controversial among fishers forced to compete with these voracious carnivores for valuable crabs, snails, clams, mussels, urchins, and abalone.[35]

A vigorous trade in freshwater aquatic species began almost as soon as sea otter populations started to decline. In 1827 Jedediah Smith led a hunting expedition to the San Joaquin River that bagged fifteen hundred pounds of skins. By the 1830s, French, British, and Anglo-American trappers were making regular visits to California's interior valleys in search of aquatic fur-bearing mammals, including beaver, river otter, mink, and muskrat. With its abundant wildlife and proximity to the port town of Yerba Buena, now San Francisco, the Sacramento–San Joaquin Delta soon became the hub of Alta California's inland fur trade. In 1840 the author Thomas Farnham noted that "beaver were very numerous . . . on the hundreds of small rush-covered islands" in the delta. "There is probably no spot of equal extent in the whole continent of America," he concluded, "which contains so many of the much-sought animals." By the time of Farnham's writing, the beaver market had already begun to crash in Europe, but large-scale trapping in California continued for several years.[36]

It did not take long for the fur trade to expand to terrestrial species. Bobcats, wolves, fishers, martens, wolverines, foxes, raccoons, skunks, badgers, and bears all provided luxurious winter furs, while deer, antelope, and elk supplied fat for tallow and hides for tanning. In 1833 John Work, an officer with the Hudson's Bay Company, recorded that his party had killed "395 elk, 148 deer, 17 bears & 8 antelopes" during a month in the Central Valley. According to Work, this was "certainly a great many more than was required, but when the [hunters] have ammunition and see animals they must needs fire upon them be wanted or not."[37]

One of the species that suffered the most from this onslaught was the tule elk, a diminutive subspecies of wapiti found only in California. Tule elk probably declined due to competition and diseases from domestic livestock and predation from wolves and grizzlies, but they also benefited during the early nineteenth century from a reduction in Indian hunting. By 1845 Charles Wilkes, of the United States Exploring Expedition, estimated that California was exporting three thousand elk and deer skins per year for the hide and tallow industries, at between fifty cents and a dollar each. The State of California banned all tule elk hunting in 1873, but by then many believed that the species had already gone extinct. The following year, a farmhand working for the Miller and Lux agricultural empire discovered a small band of elk hiding in the marshes near Buena Vista Lake in the San Joaquin Valley. The firm's proprietor, Henry Miller, gave orders to protect the animals, and in 1904 he donated a portion of his herd to the U.S. Biological Survey for keeping at Sequoia National Park. Ten years later, Miller gave more of the elk to the California Academy of Sciences, which began to distribute them to parks around the state. All tule elk now derive from that single bottlenecked population.[38]

As the numbers of hide- and fur-bearing mammals declined, hunters shifted their focus to birds. Between 1850 and 1856, collectors from the Farallon Egg Company harvested three to four million murre and guillemot eggs from the Farallon Islands, west of the Golden Gate. By 1900, merchants were selling at least two hundred fifty thousand ducks, many shot in Central Valley wetlands, in San Francisco markets each year, and more than five hundred thousand waterfowl, upland game animals, and shorebirds were passing through the combined markets of San Francisco and Los Angeles annually. Wealthy urban sportsmen and rural subsistence hunters also took considerable harvests.[39]

By 1900 the populations of most valuable fish and game species had reached historic lows. The wood duck, the Columbian sharp-tailed grouse, and the band-tailed pigeon had all declined. Rails and other shorebirds no longer frequented their ancestral haunts. Antelopes had vacated most of their range. Beavers and river otters lingered in only a few remote backwaters. The last herd of northern elephant seals retreated to Guadalupe Island off the coast of Mexico. Wolves withdrew into the Rocky Mountains, and jaguars vanished into the Sonoran Desert. Even the common mule deer became scarce.[40]

California was not alone in the loss of its native fauna. More than two hundred animal species have gone extinct in and around North America since the beginning of the colonial period.[41] The victims have included a disproportionate number of coastal and island-dwelling birds, such as the great auk, the Labrador duck, and the magnificent chickcharnie—a three-foot-tall flightless barn owl, elfin in appearance and endemic to the Bahamian island of Andros. Species such as the heath hen provided easy targets for mariners, lost their habitats to land-use change, succumbed to exotic predators, and became the targets of sportsmen, commercial hunters, and scientific collectors who canvased the countryside gathering specimens of dwindling species. The passenger pigeon became the subject of great seasonal hunts in the Northeast and the Midwest, until the birds abruptly disappeared. Thousands of Carolina parakeets died to become hats, as did millions of egrets, herons, terns, gulls, and hummingbirds. Island mammals, large carnivores, freshwater fish, and mollusks also fared poorly. Little information exists for most taxa, but it seems likely that no class of North American vertebrate escaped the nineteenth century with all its constituent species.

Historians have described California's nineteenth-century economic history as a chronicle of natural resource exploitation that progressed, with plenty of overlap, from animal to mineral to vegetable. The animal part—California's wild-game hunting frenzy—happened fast, happened late compared to other areas of the continent, and took place on a massive scale. But in the end, it differed little from the overall pattern. Newcomers of all races and classes consumed and wasted wild animals until few remained. Most seem to have believed either that California's fish and game were unlimited or that it was appropriate to exhaust a region's wildlife resources during the early stages of its capitalist economic development. As early as 1885, the historian Theodore H. Hittell wrote that the "days of fur hunting, which was once a great business in California, are gone; and it can not be long until wild fur-bearing animals will be curiosities in the country." San Francisco remained the market center of the Pacific game trade until around 1915, but by then the hunters and trappers had long since moved on to fresher fields in more-remote regions.[42]

The California fur trade followed a pattern of exploitation and decline that has become familiar to all students of natural resource economics. But this was no simple tragedy of the commons, in which rational individuals, acting independently and in their own self-interest, inevitably exhaust a common property resource. The wild animals that people captured and consumed in nineteenth-century California, from the grizzly to the sea otter to the tule elk, represented much more than just commodities. They served as instruments of cultural domination, of religious persecution, of economic imperialism, of power, and of violence. Those who controlled animals controlled the region's most valuable natural resources, and, in an economy based on resource extraction, they controlled other people too.

The history of the conservation movement that emerged in the late nineteenth century is in part a chronicle of efforts to restore decimated populations of fish and game. It is also, however, a tale of social conflict. Squabbles among various groups about access to and control over fish and game, as well as who should accept culpability for wildlife declines, sparked a series of debates throughout the country, including California's first major wildlife conservation battle, which began in 1912. By that time, it was probably already too late for California's grizzlies, but the stories of the chaparral bear and other lost wildlife species would serve as rallying cries and cautionary tales for generations of conservationists.

RESPONSES TO THE DECLINE

Californians responded to wildlife declines in several ways. They launched research expeditions, founded scientific societies, built academic institutions, started government conservation programs, and enacted dozens of laws that regulated the harvest of fish and game. These were typical responses for the late nineteenth century. Similar efforts were occurring throughout the country, and California's conservationists worked alongside their progressive colleagues in the Northeast, the Northwest, and the Midwest.

California may not have been unique in its loss of wildlife or in the efforts of some people to protect its fish and game, but it did offer a compelling perspective from which to view the momentous social and ecological changes that occurred throughout the United States during the second half of the nineteenth century. The state represented the culmination of Manifest Destiny in North America, and it would serve as the seat of American imperial power in the Pacific Basin. Between 1848 and 1880, San Francisco grew from a seaside village into the eighth-largest city in the United States, with a population of 234,000. The San Francisco Bay Area, meanwhile, contained more people than all other major western cities combined.[43]

The new Californians struggled to understand the deluges, fires, mudslides, and droughts that shaped the landscapes of the Pacific Coast. Economic development required natural resources, which California possessed in abundance. But it also required a modicum of stability, which nature failed to provide. There was a point in the mid-nineteenth century when Californians had a choice. They could work with the elements or stand and fight. They could, for example, relocate their state capital from a floodplain to higher ground or decide to stay put and build levees. They opted for the latter. Stephen Powers captured this mentality in 1869 when we wrote that "nature is eccentric and obstinate here and must be broken with steam and with steel."[44] So Californians raised capital in distant financial centers, imported cheap labor from Europe and Asia, and devised new technologies to reorganize their landscapes. They unearthed minerals, raised cattle, planted orchards, sowed wheat, cultivated grapevines, and built cities. They also denuded their rangelands, drained their marshes, channelized their rivers, felled their forests, and washed their mountains out to the sea.

As early as the 1870s, the scientists and conservationists who witnessed these changes in California began to develop a distinctive viewpoint, approach, and set of institutions that would shape the future of fish and game conservation there and elevate them to national and international leadership positions. The state's abundance and diversity of wild species, combined with its increasing wealth, growing civic institutions, and geography that placed large urban centers in close proximity to wild areas, contributed to the rise of California as a center for natural history research and conservation activism.[45]

Despite the havoc wreaked on its environment, California gained a reputation as a naturalists' haven. By the middle of the nineteenth century, San Francisco had become a required stop for all serious students of natural history. Those who came there found that the state still possessed wild tracts of land close to the city where naturalists could explore unsurveyed areas and discover new species unknown to science. The proximity of urban areas to wildlands enabled a legion of naturalists, even those with scant resources, to map California's physical and biological diversity and document the changes that were transforming its landscapes. The knowledge that development might eradicate many unique species only increased the naturalists' enthusiasm. First came the contract collectors, who gathered botanical specimens for museums in Europe and the Northeast. Then came the self-educated amateur naturalists, such as John Muir, who achieved notoriety in the state's small scientific community. Next came the government surveyors, who sought to document the state's resources for economic development. These included the members of the famed Whitney Survey, which traveled "up and down California" during the 1860s, as well as the Death Valley Expedition, which surveyed the state's eastern deserts in 1891. Finally, there were the professional academics—the museum researchers and the professors.[46]

Naturalists played central roles in the establishment of all of California's major scientific institutions. Californians founded the first scientific institution on the West Coast, the California Academy of Sciences, in 1853, with botanists and zoologists as its primary participants. During the early twentieth century, Barton

W. Evermann, a fisheries biologist, became one of the academy's longest-serving and most influential directors. The University of California, a publicly funded land-grant institution, began accepting students in 1868, and that same year Joseph LeConte offered its first course in zoology. Stanford University opened its doors in 1891 under the direction of its first president, the famous ichthyologist David Starr Jordan.[47]

It was not unusual for naturalists, who were much more prominent at the time than they are today, to play leading roles in scientific institutions. Yet their work revealed important aspects of California's scientific community that distinguished it from those of New York, Boston, and London. The state's new universities and museums lacked the libraries, specimen collections, and laboratory facilities of more-established and better-endowed institutions a continent—or continents—away. The California Academy of Sciences launched some foreign expeditions, but most of the state's researchers still lacked the philanthropic funding necessary to support far-flung adventures. They did, however, have a vast, sparsely populated, and easily accessible countryside all around them and available for research. California attracted scientists who stressed observation over experimentation and looked first to the landscape and only later to the laboratory for their subjects of study. Unlike their eastern counterparts, whose elaborate imperial expeditions have become both legendary and infamous, California naturalists tended to focus their research on the region where they lived.[48]

This regional focus had implications not only for the content of scientific knowledge but also for the role of science and scientists in California politics. Elected officials expected state-funded universities to conduct research that contributed to California's two major industries, mining and agriculture. Many scientists chose instead to study California's wild landscapes and diverse flora and fauna. As they traveled around the state, they witnessed the conversion of its landscapes and the eradication of its native species. Their experiences watching the decline of fish and game led them to argue against both the myth of resource inexhaustibility and the wisdom of unfettered exploitation, which played such central roles in the state's economic development. They soon found themselves in the uncomfortable position of asking for financial support from the state while denouncing the practices of its most important industries. By 1890 many of California's leading scientists were among its most active conservationists.[49]

Conservation meant different things to different people in different contexts. For fish and game, it could refer to the introduction or propagation of species for the purpose of augmenting wild populations, or to the enactment and enforcement of regulations establishing harvest seasons and bag limits. It could also refer to federal, state, or nongovernmental efforts. The federal government started the Bureau of Biological Survey in 1885 to facilitate research and conservation, but most public programs occurred at the state level because the federal government appeared to have little constitutional or statutory jurisdiction over wild animals within state boundaries. California began enacting fish and game conservation measures almost as soon as it joined the Union. In 1852 the state legislature passed its first such measure, a law that prohibited elk, deer, antelope, quail, mallard, and wood duck hunting for six months each year. Several codes attempting to restore depleted populations of valuable species followed. In 1870 California established the country's first wildlife refuge, at Lake Merritt in the city of Oakland. But this was an isolated event: the state had little authority or resources to purchase or set aside lands or waters for conservation, and the movement to establish wildlife refuges would not gain widespread support until the 1930s.[50]

The California legislature's most important move on behalf of fish and game during the first few decades of statehood was its establishment of a conservation commission. In 1870 it created the Commissioners of Fisheries, which it tasked with replenishing and building stocks of commercial and sporting fish, mainly through importation and propagation. Eight years later the state expanded the organization and renamed it the Board of Fish and Game Commissioners. This made California one of the first two states, along with New Hampshire, to establish an administrative agency for fish and game conservation. Others soon followed, and by 1910 most states had similar agencies.[51]

During its first two decades, the California commission enjoyed widespread popularity. It pursued uncontroversial programs, such as introducing popular fish species from other regions, constructing hatcheries to rebuild diminished salmon runs, and educating the public about the value of wild species. The commission had an early success in 1879, when it imported striped bass from New Jersey and planted them in the Carquinez Strait. Within five years the species was appearing in San Francisco markets, and today it is one of the delta's most important sport fish. By 1900 the commission had become a model for similar organizations around the country, and it could boast a "well-earned reputation for scientific achievement" and "great returns" despite only a "small annual expenditure."[52]

The commission's early programs may have been popular, but they helped create the context for a series of conflicts. Opinions differed about what had caused the decline of valuable species. Some observers recognized that the causes were numerous and diverse: hunting, development, pollution, the introduction of exotic species, and other factors had transformed the state's land and waterscapes and reduced the populations of many important fish and game species. Other commentators grasped for simpler and uglier answers. California had attracted immigrants from around the world who sought work in resource-based industries and provided convenient scapegoats for disgruntled whites who were only a generation or two from their own immigrant roots. Chinese and other East Asians often took the blame for over-fishing, while Italians and other southern Europeans received criticism for overhunting. Several decades passed before scholars began to understand that the commission deserved less credit than it claimed and the immigrant fishers and hunters received more blame than they deserved.[53]

After 1900 the state legislature began to enact a long list of fishing and hunting codes. By the end of the decade it had established much of the basic legal and bureaucratic infrastructure for fish and game conservation that remains in effect in California today. As the commission's duties—along with its budget and staff—increased, it extended its regulatory work into new arenas and bolstered its law enforcement capacities. It would soon become clear that the commission's job was not only to propagate and conserve wild animals but also to mediate debates about who should have access to and control over those species. This was a complex task, and the commission in California, like those in other states, often failed to promote the most equitable and sustainable solutions.[54]

MONARCH, REDUX

Monarch the bear lived in captivity for twenty-two years, most of which he spent in the zoo at Golden Gate Park. Toward the end of his life he no longer attracted crowds, though he did receive visits from naturalists, who sketched him, photographed him, fed him apples, or just stared in wonderment at this living symbol of the breathtaking changes that had taken place in California during the course of a single ursine lifetime. In May of 1911, zookeepers put the elderly, arthritic, nearly toothless beast to sleep. At the time of his death, Monarch was a corpulent 1,127 pounds. No one knows how many California grizzlies outlived him in the wild, but he was surely among the last of his kind (see figure 6).[55]

One of the naturalists who visited Monarch in San Francisco was the charismatic artist, author, educator, conservationist, and founding chair of the Boy Scouts of America, Ernest Thompson Seton. Years later, Seton offered a concise account of

FIGURE 6.
Glass case grizzly: Monarch on display at the California
Academy of Sciences in 2011, one hundred years after his demise.
© Brant Ward/Corbis.

the grizzly's decline in the American West. Grizzlies, he wrote, had been "left at the mercy of men with no mercy."[56] Few statements could more eloquently disguise the complexity of the truth. Many hunters and ranchers did fail to show the grizzly compassion, even as its numbers dwindled. Yet the grizzly's history in California is far too complex to reduce to a facile morality tale. The California grizzly, like so many other species, got caught up in a great economic, political, cultural, and ecological transformation. For a time these changes benefited the grizzly; only later did they lead to the bear's demise.

The extinction of the California grizzly took place long before the term *endangered species* entered the English lexicon. Even *wildlife* only became common, in its current compound form, in the 1910s. Yet the grizzly's story offers a crucial insight for anyone who wants to understand the subsequent history of wildlife and endangered species in the United States. This epic saga is only partly about an animal. It is also about a place, and about how the people who lived there understood, envisioned, portrayed, and promoted its political, economic, and ecological future. We could say the same of the stories of myriad other endangered species.

It is a paradoxical fate to be simultaneously adopted and eradicated, but such is the predicament of an extinct mascot. Most Californians are probably unaware of the grizzly's history in their state. Those who do know seem to view it with a sense of irony and regret similar to what Allan Kelly expressed after Monarch's debut at Woodward's Garden in 1889. Few Californians would likely want to see grizzlies patrolling the crowded trails of Muir Woods, Yosemite Valley, or Griffith Park in Los Angeles. But the extermination of this remarkable animal is not something to take pride in anymore either. Now when Californians speak of their departed grizzlies, they talk not about courage or progress or inevitability but about folly and destruction and the necessity for restraint. In the words of the author Susan Snyder, the grizzly's disappearance "evokes the absence of what else is now gone from California," including its lost landscapes and biological diversity.[57] The story of the California grizzly has become an allegory of ecological decline.

It is easy to embrace a story of ecological decline when you do not have to contend with thousand-pound omnivores in your daily life. When you do, things become more complicated. In other regions of the United States, controversies still surround living grizzlies, and outside Alaska their populations have continued to fare poorly.

It was not until 1973—almost fifty years after the chaparral bear's extinction— that the U.S. Fish and Wildlife Service began monitoring the country's remaining grizzlies, all of which lived in Idaho, Montana, or Wyoming. Two years later, the FWS listed the grizzlies in the lower forty-eight states as threatened, under the federal Endangered Species Act. By that time their total number had declined, from around fifty thousand individuals in the early nineteenth century to about one thousand in just six scattered populations. In 1982 the FWS completed its first Grizzly Bear Recovery Plan, and three years later a consortium of government agencies formed the Interagency Grizzly Bear Committee. A small group of grizzlies eventually returned to Washington State, and in 2007 the service announced that the Yellowstone population, which had increased from a low of 136 to more than five hundred bears, no longer qualified as endangered. Today, however, the grizzly's total non-Alaskan U.S. population is still less than fifteen hundred and remains limited to the North Cascades and Northern Rockies.[58]

More than a century after Monarch's death, Californians are still surrounded by bears. The state's living, breathing grizzlies are of course long gone, expelled decades ago from the fringes of an expanding society. Today's grizzlies are symbolic beasts of our own making. But we also have dozens of metaphorical grizzlies that are not bears at all. They may be condors, tortoises, foxes, smelts, or any other imperiled species that has become a symbol of the contested relationships between people and nonhuman nature in the places where they live. The rest of this book explores the wildlife and endangered species conservation debates that began in California around the time of the grizzly's extinction and grew to encompass all of these creatures and many, many more. As we will continue to see, these debates remain as much about the politics of place as about wild animals.

Monarch's arrival in San Francisco in 1889 captivated the city, but his death in 1911 went almost unnoticed. If his story had ended there, this would have been an anticlimactic conclusion to the life of a California icon, but the great bear's journey was far from complete. During the preceding decades, popular enthusiasm for recreational hunting and natural history museums had fostered advances in the art and science of taxidermy, and by the time of Monarch's death, expert technicians were capable of preserving animal remains almost in perpetuity. A local purveyor named Vernon Shephard accepted the job. He used part of the bear's skull to mount its hide but discarded the rest of its massive skeleton. The specimen first went on display at the de Young Museum in San Francisco and later moved down the street to the California Academy of Sciences, where curators placed it on a pedestal adorned with an image of the California flag. It appeared that Monarch would have two final resting places: his skin would occupy a station of honor at one of the state's oldest cultural institutions while his bones rotted at the bottom of a ditch in some weedy corner of Golden Gate Park.[1]

News of Monarch's unceremonious burial soon reached Joseph Grinnell, a young zoologist who in 1908 became the founding director of the Museum of Vertebrate Zoology (MVZ) at the University of California, in Berkeley. Grinnell set out to establish the West Coast's premier institution for research in zoology and evolutionary biology. His work used comparative morphology to illuminate patterns of evolution in the state's diverse fauna and thus required a large collection of biological specimens. By the time he accepted his position, however, the populations of many of California's most charismatic and sought-after wild animal species—from marine mammals to terrestrial fur bearers, large carnivores, ungulates, raptors, shorebirds, and waterfowl—had reached historic lows, and opportunities to acquire additional specimens were diminishing with each passing year.[2] Specimens of any vertebrate species could contribute to Grinnell's research, but none was more important for the museum than the state's mascot, the California grizzly. So six months after Monarch's death, Grinnell sent his assistant, Joseph Dixon, to San Francisco with a map and a shovel. Dixon located Monarch's grave, exhumed the skeleton, and brought it back to Berkeley, where he disinfected it and prepared it for storage.

Soon after Monarch's death, Grinnell and his "Berkeley circle" of students and colleagues decided that museum conservation, of the kind they had undertaken for Monarch's remains, was not enough—they needed to do more to save California's dwindling fauna. Grinnell was by no means the state's first wildlife conservationist, but he proposed an ambitious plan to launch a new political movement that would inform "the public of the great depletion of the supply of game in the state" and generate support for a comprehensive program of research, education, regulation, and enforcement. By 1914 the campaign had expanded from its initial focus on game animals to include all of California's native fauna.[3]

The Berkeley circle's campaign sparked the first major political debate about the conservation of terrestrial wildlife in California. Grinnell carefully guarded his reputation as a nonpartisan scientific expert, and he remained mostly in the background during the controversies that ensued, but from his office at the museum he dispatched a small army of emissaries, including several students who took classes and worked as research assistants at the university. Between 1912 and 1914 they raised money, founded activist groups, developed public relations campaigns, and lobbied politicians in Sacramento. Their campaign had several legislative goals, but the most important was an effort to pass a state law that would ban the commercial sale of wild-caught game.[4]

Grinnell and his allies focused on the sale of wild-caught game for two main reasons. The first and most obvious was that at the time, many conservationists believed that market hunting was the main cause of wildlife declines. A second but equally important reason was that state-level hunting and fishing regulations were already well established and widely accepted, whereas other options, such as habitat protection, had little if any legal or political precedent.

Despite longstanding legal precedents for state-level hunting and fishing codes, the Berkeley circle's campaign sparked a vigorous political debate that soon grew to encompass a variety of much broader issues. A debate about wildlife soon became a debate about the public good versus private interests, government regulation in a market economy, the role of bureaucratic versus democratic decision making, and the importance of race, class, gender, and citizenship in shaping access to and control over lands and natural resources. This debate began later in California than in other states with Progressive political majorities in the Northeast, the Midwest, and the Pacific Northwest. It also took a different course and came to a different conclusion, at least for a time. Yet by 1915, conservationists across the country were looking to California and the work of the Berkeley circle as a model for what had gone right and what had gone wrong in the Progressive Era wildlife movement. The insights they gained would shape subsequent conservation efforts into the New Deal era of the 1930s and beyond.

What is perhaps most remarkable about the Berkeley circle's work during the Progressive Era is how much it anticipated future developments in conservation science and environmental ethics. This is not to say that the group's members were somehow ahead of their time—they were very much creatures of it. Yet their story challenges, or at least complicates, the widespread belief that many features of contemporary conservation, including concern for nongame and uncharismatic endangered species, did not emerge until the second half of the twentieth century. By 1915 the Berkeley circle's members had developed an intellectual foundation for what, over the next two decades, with the addition of a strong focus on habitat management, would develop into a comprehensive vision for wildlife science and conservation backed by almost every major ethical rationale that supports the work of conservation biologists today.[5]

The Progressive Era wildlife debates in California are important to the story of American endangered species conservation for another reason. Scientists and legal scholars who write about the Endangered Species Act often cite its widespread popularity at the time of its passage, in 1973, as evidence that conflicts about species conservation emerged only later, in response to the act's unintended consequences. It would be unwise to underestimate the ESA's capacity to provoke controversy, but this version of the story tends to truncate the history of endangered species debates. Controversies that have surrounded the ESA since the late 1970s are part of a much longer legacy of disputes about species loss and conservation that began more than a century ago, have waxed and waned, and continue in modified forms today. To understand the origins of these struggles, there is nowhere better to start than with the life and work of the Berkeley circle's leader, Joseph Grinnell.

THE HOUSE GRINNELL BUILT

Joseph Grinnell was born in 1877 on the Kiowa, Comanche, and Wichita Indian Agency near Fort Sill in Indian Territory. His Quaker family traced its ancestry New England's earliest French Huguenot colonists, and his father worked as a physician on the reservation. They soon moved to the Pine Ridge Agency, in Dakota Territory, where Joseph spent his early childhood with the Oglala Sioux. During their time at Pine Ridge, Joseph and his father earned the friendship of a local patriarch, Chief Red Cloud. In 1885 the Grinnells moved to California and settled in Pasadena, then a small town surrounded by remote mountains and wild animals. Joseph spent the rest of his childhood and young adulthood hunting, fishing, and studying natural history near his home. One summer, he even found grizzly tracks in the lower Arroyo Seco. In 1898 he left for his first expedition, a voyage to Alaska, where he collected some fourteen hundred birds and eggs. He returned to California the following year and began his graduate work in zoology under the direction of Charles H. Gilbert and David Starr Jordan at Stanford University. In 1901 he became the youngest fellow in the history of the American Ornithologists' Union (see figure 7).[6]

Grinnell was still pursuing his doctorate and teaching part time at the Throop Polytechnic Institute, the future California Institute of Technology, in Pasadena, when he met Annie Alexander. Alexander was a remarkable woman. Born in 1867 in Honolulu, she was an heir to the Hawaiian Commercial and Sugar Company fortune. Her father, Samuel, introduced her to natural history at a young age, and in 1904 he took her on a trip to hunt big game in Africa. The two were setting up for a photograph on a ledge overlooking Victoria Falls when construction workers, building the now-famous bridge on the cliffs above, dislodged a boulder. The rock ricocheted off the canyon wall and struck Samuel. Doctors amputated his leg that night, but he died of his injuries the following morning. It was a disastrous end to what had begun as an exuberant expedition.

Undeterred, Alexander decided that her father would have wanted her to pursue her passions, and upon her return from Africa she enrolled in natural history courses at the University of California. She soon became one of the most accomplished female hunters and collectors of her time. Over the next four decades Alexander and her longtime partner, Louise Kellogg, took dozens of expeditions throughout the North American West. They collected tens of thousands of plant, animal, and fossil specimens, and they explored remote corners of the continent at a time when few women participated in scientific research or traveled alone. In 1947, at the ages of

FIGURE 7.
Joseph Grinnell at work in the field. Courtesy of the Bancroft
Library, University of California, Berkeley.

eighty and sixty-eight, Alexander and Kellogg set off with the botanist Annetta
Carter for a three-month plant-collecting expedition in Mexico's Baja Peninsula. The
trip would be Alexander's last. Yet when asked if she or her companions had ever
been frightened, as elderly women traveling without an escort in a foreign country,
Alexander replied, "*Somos tres mujeres sin miedo*": we are three women without fear.[7]

In 1906 Alexander contacted Grinnell to ask for advice in preparation for her first
collecting trip to Alaska. The Berkeley paleontologist Jon C. Merriam and the first
chief of the federal government's Bureau of Biological Survey, C. Hart Merriam (no
relation), had both recommended Grinnell to Alexander as an expert on Alaskan fauna.
Grinnell impressed Alexander, and she soon approached the young scientist with a
proposition. She wanted to use her inheritance in a way that would honor her father's
memory, and she had decided to donate a portion of her money to the University of
California for the establishment of a zoology museum. She hoped that Grinnell would
accept a position as its first director, an unusual opportunity for a young man who was
still pursuing his doctorate. Grinnell agreed, and Alexander spent the next year nego-
tiating with the university for space, resources, and administrative autonomy. It was
the beginning of a collaboration that would last for more than three decades.[8]

When the Museum of Vertebrate Zoology opened, in 1908, it joined the larger movement to establish natural history museums throughout the United States. Many of these museums began as "cabinets of curiosities"—the personal collections of specimens and artifacts that wealthy patrons donated for public education and entertainment. The contributors and board members of these institutions were among the country's richest and most powerful people. They represented a political elite that included politicians, leaders of industry, and prominent activists behind a variety of Progressive Era causes, from child welfare to occupational safety, public education, women's suffrage, and conservation. Some also participated in anti-immigration groups, and many supported efforts to "improve society" through eugenics.[9]

During the late nineteenth and early twentieth centuries, institutions such as the Smithsonian's National Museum of Natural History, the American Museum of Natural History, and the Harvard Museum of Comparative Zoology grew in scope and influence. They mounted ambitious expeditions to remote lands, assembled catalogues of specimens from around the world, constructed ornate Victorian buildings to house their collections, and produced elaborate public displays to represent the diversity of life. These were scientific institutions in the sense that they hosted research and promoted public education. But like zoos, they also promoted themselves as sites for leisure and entertainment. To attract patrons, they often emphasized the exotic: African mammals arranged in dramatic dioramas, reconstructed skeletons of immense blue whales, life-size models of snarling tyrannosaurs, and the obligatory aquatic scenes of quizzical duck-billed platypuses.[10]

The MVZ would develop a different approach. It would forego international expeditions and the collection of exotic specimens, and it would delegate the task of staging public exhibitions to other institutions, such as the California Academy of Sciences. Grinnell wanted to establish the West Coast's first major center for biological research, and like the generation of California naturalists who came before him, he focused his work on the region where he lived. Under Grinnell, the MVZ accrued a small staff of skilled researchers and collectors dedicated to the study of native fauna in and around California. The state became not only a study site but also an organizing framework and common bond for the museum's researchers, students, patrons, and network of local informants.[11]

Grinnell welcomed specimens from other areas of the North American West, especially those adjacent to California, but as early as 1907 he wrote to Alexander to protest her planned acquisition of specimens from more-distant regions. Alexander had proposed to purchase a large collection from the Galápagos Islands, which to many observers would have seemed like a coup for a small, upstart museum. Yet Grinnell argued that the Galápagos had been "worked over again and again, *better* than any area of similar extent in California." Unlike these islands, which had been popular with naturalists since Charles Darwin's time, California was "in the newest part of the new world" and still offered a fresh field for research. The state, Grinnell concluded a few years later, "is practically inexhaustible, is naturally of easiest access and should be of greatest interest to this institution."[12]

Grinnell viewed the physical collections of the MVZ not only as an important contribution to future generations of natural historians but also as the foundation of a comprehensive methodology that would foster his ambitious research program. Throughout his life, he focused on three interrelated areas of theoretical inquiry: the classification of biophysical environments, the spatial distribution of vertebrate species, and the ways that organism-environment interactions shaped animal evolution. These interests inspired one of the most innovative and energetic careers in the history of biology. Between 1893 and 1939, Grinnell published 554 books and articles. He extended C. Hart Merriam's life zone concept, developed the idea of the niche, and provided a basis for the competitive exclusion principle. He also popularized the use of trinomial taxonomic classification, the division of distinct species into less-distinct subspecies defined by their morphological differences and geographic ranges. Grinnell viewed these fine distinctions, identifiable only through close observation and laborious mapping, as essential for understanding the evolutionary processes that led to the emergence of new species.[13]

Some of Grinnell's most significant contributions involved his biogeographical research, which refined, revised, and extended Darwin's theories about speciation, including the role of physical geography in the processes of adaptation and radiation. As early as 1904, Grinnell's work on the chestnut-backed chickadee signaled his intent to develop the role of geography in evolutionary theory. A decade later he published two landmark works about the Colorado River, the first of which explored it as a pathway of species dispersal and the second of which considered it as a barrier. His nuanced thinking about the complexity of physical space and its importance in evolution provided a basis for countless future studies. Grinnell's many protégés built on his work and amplified its influence even further. In 1941, for example, his former student Alden Miller published a classic study on speciation in the avian genus *Junco*, which Ernst Mayr later cited as a crucial contribution to the modern synthesis in evolutionary biology.[14]

Several influences shaped Grinnell's work on spatial processes. At Stanford he studied among a group of naturalists who were developing theories of speciation based on geographical distribution. He arrived in Berkeley at a time when researchers in North America and Britain were beginning to think more rigorously about wildlife-habitat relationships, and the influences of a number of those individuals appear throughout his work.[15] By the 1930s and 1940s, members of this loosely knit community included such key figures in the history of ecology as Charles Elton, Paul Errington, Herbert Stoddard, Aldo Leopold, and David Lack.

Grinnell's most important influences, however, were the places where he conducted his research. In California's mountains and rivers, he found evidence for the importance of migratory corridors and impediments to animal movement. In its valleys, he saw isolated centers of evolution that contained large numbers of endemic species. And in its fires and floods, he witnessed the unpredictable forces of landscape change that altered the availability of resources and rearranged animal populations. California was Grinnell's mentor as well as his laboratory. Decades of fieldwork there taught him that one could not understand ecology and evolution without history and geography.

Building the kind of collection necessary to conduct this research required Grinnell to become an effective administrator. He maintained Alexander's crucial support, secured funds for expeditions, established survey priorities, sought the advice of distant colleagues, and served as a mentor, counselor, disciplinarian, cheerleader, and occasional therapist to his assistants in the field. He could be pedantic and demanding, but he earned the universal admiration of his students and colleagues. He also became a scrupulous curator who spent much of his time on technical details. Which caliber gun should fieldworkers use to collect songbirds? Should museum staff skin bats or preserve them in formaldehyde? How much cornstarch would protect a badger skull from damage during shipment? Which brand of India ink was best for labeling specimens? What color paint should coat the walls of the MVZ? These questions may seem trivial, but Grinnell regarded every detail of museum administration as essential to his vision of a comprehensive research methodology.[16]

His primary goal was to develop a collection of biological specimens that would represent California's diverse native fauna and enable researchers to answer basic biological questions about the evolutionary relationships between organisms and their environments. Yet by the time he began his work, hunting and habitat loss had already decimated many of the species he aimed to study. "Many species of vertebrate animals are disappearing; some are gone already," he wrote. "All that the investigator of the future will have . . . will be the remains of these species preserved more or less faithfully, along with the data accompanying them, in the museums of the country."[17] Museum work was not only part of a research methodology but also a form of conservation. The two were inextricably linked.

Collecting specimens in California required Grinnell and his assistants to stay one step ahead of the forces of land use and environmental change. They scrambled to survey aquatic environments before the dredgers, dikers, dynamiters, and dam builders arrived. They raced to collect in undeveloped valleys just days before farmers cleared the vegetation and leveled the soil. They spent weeks searching remote mountains for once-common game birds and fur-bearing mammals that had been driven to the far corners of their ranges. And they mapped the spread of exotic species, such as the European starling and the English sparrow, that had colonized the landscape and were expanding their ranges.[18]

Grinnell and Alexander discussed these problems as early as 1907, and they based the MVZ's early surveying priorities on the assumption that many native species would soon disappear. Before the museum even opened, Grinnell suggested to Alexander that its first official expedition should visit the Imperial Valley, in the flat, hot, low-elevation desert of southeastern California. The Imperial Valley had several endemic species, and Grinnell worried that some were about to go extinct. Water diversion from the Colorado River had enabled farmers to develop the valley for intensive agriculture. In 1905 one of the new irrigation canals ruptured, and for the next two years the Colorado River poured into the desiccated bed of an ancient lake. This deluge created California's largest body of water, the Salton Sea, and produced a new landscape populated by new plants and new animals. Grinnell later wrote that he found "nothing attractive about collecting in a settled-up, level country," such as the Imperial Valley. But he knew that "it *ought* to be done, and the longer we wait, the fewer 'waste lots' there will be" in which to find remaining populations of native species.[19]

Finding specimens of rare or recently eradicated species required careful detective work. It also required the museum's staff to cultivate a network of supporters and informants. Fieldworkers conducted oral histories, inquired about taxidermied trophies kept in private homes, and relied on locals for advice about when and where to search. In 1916, for example, Joseph Dixon issued a plea on behalf of the museum for information from "anyone who knows of the whereabouts of any parts of wolves killed in California, or who is conversant with *facts* relating to the past or present occurrence of the species within the state." The MVZ finally acquired a California wolf specimen in 1922. Such efforts involved a sizable commitment of the museum's limited resources, costly searches often failed to produce results, and the fieldworker might not even live to see the payoff. The value of these specimens "might not be realized," Grinnell wrote, "until the lapse of many years, possibly a century, assuming that our material is safely preserved." Yet he believed such work was crucial so that "the student of the future will have access to the original record of faunal conditions in California and the west."[20]

Preserving this record played a central role in Grinnell's vision for the MVZ. But why would he—a man who had grown up with Indians, knew about California's long human history, and studied the role of landscape change in vertebrate evolution—invoke a concept so apparently static and ahistorical as "original conditions"? Grinnell was not ignorant about history. He understood that no single date in the past represented the original state of nature in California and that the early twentieth century was an arbitrary moment at which to create an archive of the state's fauna. But he was also typical of naturalists of his time in the way he interpreted environmental history. He believed that, with the exception of their use of fire, Indians had lived lightly on the land; it was the Europeans, particularly those who came after 1849, who made the most significant impacts. These ideas informed generations of thinking in American ecology and environmentalism even as scholars in other fields realized that they had drastically underestimated the importance of indigenous societies in shaping North American landscapes and ecosystems.

Despite these shortcomings, Grinnell's approach had a remarkably contemporary objective. He knew that development would continue to transform California's fauna, and he based his plan for the museum on the premise that future researchers would want to understand those transformations. He viewed the MVZ's collections as baseline data for measuring change over time. This view has proved prescient. As part of the MVZ's centenary celebration, in 2008, researchers began resurveying sites that Grinnell and his assistants had visited a hundred years earlier. Their goal was to use the museum's data to track changes in the state's ecosystems. The team's first study, published in the journal *Science*, documented a five-hundred-meter average upward shift in the elevation ranges of fourteen small mammal species in and around Yosemite National Park.[21] Over the course of a century, climate and environmental change had rearranged the Sierra Nevada's biogeography and reshuffled its ecological communities. Grinnell studied change over time, and in his evolutionary research he explored the deep past. But when it came to baseline data, his interest was primarily in the history of the future—one that California's human and nonhuman residents are experiencing today.

The MVZ flourished under Grinnell's leadership. It developed special strengths in birds and mammals, and its geographic focus allowed it to achieve an unparalleled degree of detail in its collections. During its first five years, the museum catalogued nearly fifty thousand specimens. By 1937 C. Hart Merriam could praise it for having produced "a vastly more complete" record of fur-bearing mammals in California than existed for any other part of the world. Grinnell departed in 1939, but the museum's collections developed further under the direction of his successors. By 1955 it had accumulated the third-largest collection of mammals in the country, even though most of its specimens came from a single state, and it had begun building large collections in new taxonomic areas, such as herpetology. By the 1980s, the MVZ's collections, along with those of the state's other major natural history museums, had established California's status as a hot spot of global biological diversity.[22]

CONSERVATION ETHICS

Historians have often suggested that ethical arguments for wildlife conservation in the United States developed in a clear pattern. During the nineteenth century, people considered fish and game valuable only to the extent that they served human economic, recreational, or aesthetic interests. Pests that detracted from these interests were to be controlled or eradicated. During the first half of the twentieth century, scientists and conservationists gradually regarded increasing numbers of species as beneficial and called for more protection. After World War II, the range of their concern grew even further, to include all native species and ecosystems. The process by which human societies extend moral standing to animals and other things is called ethical extensionism and is often associated with the work of the famed philosopher-conservationist Aldo Leopold.[23]

Though attractive, the story of ethical extensionism suffers from several problems, not least of which is its teleological portrayal of American environmental history as an inevitable march toward increasingly enlightened ideas. The actual story is much messier, fraught with political contestation, social conflict, and the complexities and contingencies that define the past. Ethical disputes about wild nature did reach a wider audience over time, but almost all of the major arguments for wildlife and endangered species conservation that exist today emerged within the first two decades of the twentieth century. What followed was not a slow expansion or adoption of new ideas but rather a series of struggles that redistributed political power and elevated old ideas to new positions in science, politics, and the law.[24]

No group was more active in forging these ideas during the Progressive Era than the Berkeley circle. As with its scientific work, the group's contributions to conservation ethics resulted from the productive, although at times tense, partnerships between Grinnell and his protégés at the MVZ. Harold C. Bryant was one of Grinnell's first students, and he specialized in natural history education. Grinnell and Bryant borrowed arguments for conservation that other scientists, government officials, wilderness preservationists, and animal welfare advocates had developed in previous decades. They expanded these from fish and game to encompass the more general category of wildlife. To appeal to diverse constituencies, they adapted and sharpened their arguments and used different approaches with different audiences to achieve the greatest political results. By 1916 Grinnell and Bryant had articulated and employed almost all of the major ethical arguments for wildlife conservation that exist today.

Like many Progressive Era naturalists and educators, Grinnell asserted that natural history study promoted healthful recreation and an informed citizenry. He joined with activists who called for more nature study in the public schools and more educational programs from state and federal agencies. One of the best ways to achieve these objectives was to install his students in influential positions. In 1914 Grinnell helped Bryant find two part-time jobs, one as the first director of education for the California Fish and Game Commission and another as a member of Yosemite National Park's first cohort of interpretive naturalists, who gave campfire talks. These were new positions, but they came with considerable opportunities and support. Bryant soon emerged as the most prominent natural history educator not only in California but also, after 1916, in the new National Park Service. His career in the service continued until 1954, when he retired as the superintendent of Grand Canyon National Park, one of the organization's most prestigious positions. NPS historians today remember Bryant as the founder of the service's interpretive programs.[25]

To understand Grinnell and Bryant's approach to ethics, it is necessary to understand their approach to politics. When they spoke and wrote about conservation, they often stressed the pragmatic utilitarian justification that had already gained widespread general support among conservationists and that they thought would persuade the largest number of people: wild animals should be conserved to promote the country's economic well-being. This argument had two components. The first involved the animals' monetary value. Hunters, trappers, traders, and merchants— including those who sold supplies to recreational sportsmen and tourists—lost future profits when they squandered resources in the short term that could have remained viable for the foreseeable future. Grinnell and Bryant argued for stronger regulation of animal harvests, as well as the creation of game farms that could produce waterfowl and fur-bearing mammals as crops while allowing wild populations to recover from overhunting.[26] Both thus supported the regulated use of wildlife as an important aspect of utilitarian conservation.

The second component of the economic argument was the protection of "beneficial species" for pest control. The question of whether certain species were beneficial or injurious had particular salience during a time before modern chemical pesticides when many scientists believed that reckless agricultural development had disturbed the balance of nature. At the time, the federal government's first fish and game agency, the Bureau of Biological Survey, was sponsoring research on the economic value of various species. Foster E. L. Beal, an economic ornithologist from the bureau, visited California three times between 1901 and 1906 and conducted studies on the agricultural relations of seventy bird species. He concluded that only four of these—the house finch, the scrub jay, Stellar's jay, and the red-breasted sapsucker—were of "doubtful utility." All of the state's other common bird species benefited agriculture. "A reasonable way of viewing the relation of birds to the farmer," Beal wrote, "is to consider birds as servants, employed to destroy weeds and insects. In return for this service they should be protected."[27]

Grinnell and Bryant took Beal's argument and ran with it. They soon began to see economic benefits in almost every normal function of almost every native species. According to Grinnell, more than 90 percent of California's bird species qualified as "community assets." Bats were "desirable citizens" for consuming insects, gophers tilled and fertilized the soil, and beavers created habitats for juvenile fish by plumbing rivers.[28] As early as 1912, members of the Berkeley circle used the beneficial species argument to lobby for state protection of carnivorous mammals, which most people still considered pests. According to Grinnell and Bryant, predators helped to control undesirable rodent species and improve populations of game animals, such as deer, by culling the weakest members. By the 1920s, the Berkeley circle had emerged as a leading force in the nationwide effort to curtail predator control programs.

Grinnell and Bryant insisted that their arguments were utilitarian, not sentimental, but they viewed economic rationales at least in part as means to an end and sought to expand these arguments to incorporate noneconomic concerns. By 1913 Bryant was including not only fish and game but also nongame vertebrate species and even insects in his list of beneficial creatures. "Doubtless if our knowledge were not so limited," he wrote, "we would be able to see a use for every living thing. As it is, we brand life as useful, neutral, or injurious because of its effect on ourselves or our environment." According to him, this parsing of species had appreciable, damaging consequences: "Anything known to be useful is always assured protection, anything considered of no use is assured of speedy destruction. Hence, viewed from a utilitarian standpoint,

SACRED
TO THE MEMORY OF
VANISHED GAME
IN NORTH AMERICA
PASSENGER PIGEON
LABRADOR DUCK
TRUMPETER SWAN
ESKIMO CURLEW
SEA OTTER
ELEPHANT SEAL
IN CALIFORNIA
WOOD DUCK
SHARP-TAILED GROUSE
ANTELOPE
DWARF ELK
ROOSEVELT ELK
BEAVER
COMPLETELY OR NEARLY
EXTERMINATED
BY CIVILIZED MAN
1840-1913

FIGURE 8.

The "Monument to Game Conservation" appeared on the cover
of the first issue of *Western Wild Life Call*, in 1913, to draw
attention to extinct and endangered species.

there is a certain value in classifying life as injurious or beneficial." When addressing
friendly audiences, he often returned to the example of birds, which had a large constituency of advocates and a long tradition of aesthetic appreciation: "Somehow at
this day and age the convincing value of a bird lies in its usefulness. . . . This point of
view is exaggerated and the other real value,—the esthetic,—is left in the background;
but we must meet the demands of the times." Bryant understood the political value
of a utilitarian argument, but his real convictions lay elsewhere.[29]

If all wild animals had aesthetic value or even pure intrinsic value, then human-
induced extinctions posed a special problem that transcended mere economics
(see figure 8). Indeed, extinction was one area in which Grinnell and Bryant wrote
about conservation issues as explicitly ethical challenges. "It is now generally
recognized as ethically wrong," Grinnell wrote in 1914, "to jeopardize the existence

of any animal species." Bryant tied together economic and ethical arguments about extinction the following year when he wrote, "An extinct form of life can never be restored. In this ethical viewpoint we perhaps find the strongest argument of all. But add to this the economic viewpoint and we have an argument in favor of wild life conservation that defies every assailant."[30]

Grinnell's commitment to the aesthetic and intrinsic values of wild animals did not prevent him from killing them in large numbers. He was a prodigious collector who bagged thousands of animals during his lifetime and facilitated the slaughter of tens of thousands more. He offered his motives, his credentials, and the uses to which he put the remains as justification for this carnage. According to him, animals that were killed for food or profit only benefited a few people for a few days, but animals preserved in a museum would benefit society for centuries. He encouraged amateur naturalists to avoid collecting eggs and to watch birds with opera glasses instead of killing them. But he chastised professional naturalists who shot pictures when they should have been shooting guns and argued with animal welfare advocates who called hunting inhumane or questioned the need for further scientific collecting of rare species. In 1915 he published a manifesto on the subject, "Conserve the Collector," which argued that future biological research would depend on scientists having open access to vertebrate specimens, even in protected parks and reserves.[31]

Grinnell also lectured Bryant on the subject. As part of his job at the California Division of Fish and Game, Bryant handled requests for permits to collect specimens of protected species. He balked when his friend and fellow Grinnell protégé, Loye Miller, requested a permit to collect a white-tailed kite. Miller was a respected young researcher who would go on to found the Department of Life Sciences at UCLA. When Grinnell heard about the delay, he intervened on Miller's behalf. "I do not believe that the species is anywhere near the point of extermination," he wrote in a letter to Bryant. "There cannot be less than 100 of the birds alive in the State. . . . Specimens of the species should be preserved for science; and they can be without, I believe, jeopardizing the existence of the species."[32]

If the population of a charismatic raptor such as the white-tailed kite dropped to one hundred individuals in California today, scientists would consider it on the brink of a regional extinction and would call for a major mobilization of conservation resources. Yet Grinnell seemed almost blasé about the bird's small population. The white-tailed kite has since rebounded in California, and today it is fairly common, but that outcome was by no means assured in 1915. Grinnell was correct in arguing that sport, market, and subsistence hunting, predator control, and habitat destruction were more important than scientific collecting in driving the decline of such species. Yet he must have known that with so few individuals the loss of even one could alter a population's demographic trajectory and that small populations were especially at risk from scientific collecting. Grinnell was overconfident about the white-tailed kite's status, but his mistake did not result from indifference to the species's plight. Instead it stemmed from his stubborn support for science and his attribution of blame. "This wastage is not to be debited to the collector," he insisted, "but to the average and very ignorant and numerous hunter."[33]

By 1916 Grinnell and Bryant had articulated a multifaceted argument for the conservation of California's native fauna. It combined economics with ethics, utilitarianism with aesthetics, and instrumentalism with a concept of intrinsic value. They argued that wildlife was important for science, education, recreation, tourism, agriculture, natural resources, and even something akin to our contemporary notion of ecological services—the idea that wild species and healthy ecosystems perform essential functions for society that would be costly and difficult to replace by artificial means. Grinnell and Bryant were not alone in developing these ideas; they were part of a large network of conservationists throughout the United States and beyond. Yet these conservationists were not all of the same mind regarding the vital issues of the day. Three key groups shaped wildlife conservation during the Progressive Era, and each had a distinctive view on the contentious topic of hunting regulation.

HUNTING AND THE POLITICS OF CONSERVATION

Debates about fish and game regulation involved a variety of economic, political, and ethical issues, as well as basic conceptions of social status and identity. Groups on all sides claimed to have the support of moderate political majorities that advocated the most equitable and democratic solutions. But to gain such support, they portrayed social and economic differences as antagonistic dichotomies: rich versus poor, citizen versus alien, white versus nonwhite, rural versus urban, masculine versus feminine, ethical versus unethical, honorable versus dishonorable, public versus private, occupied with leisure versus consumed by work. The struggle over hunting regulation and its enforcement in California, as in other parts of the country, thus grew to encompass issues far beyond the conservation of wildlife and became a surrogate for much larger conversations about the social and moral order.

The three main groups of conservationists that debated these issues in California were the same as those that participated in fish and game controversies in other parts of the country. Among the advocates for additional regulations were the professional and amateur naturalists, such as the members of the Berkeley circle, who advocated for measures to conserve wildlife as a public good. Then there were the humanitarians—Protestant clergy, women's club members, and temperance unions—who worried that cruelty toward animals, including unnecessary hunting, damaged the moral fiber of society. And finally there were the sportsmen, a group mostly made up of wealthy, white, urban men who wanted to secure a privileged place for recreational hunting and fishing as a way to maintain what they considered the rough, masculine virtues of the fading frontier and to combat the feminizing aspects of Victorian culture. They also tended to view working-class men, immigrants, and anyone who relied on fish and game to make ends meet as illegitimate users of these resources.[34]

In practice these three groups overlapped, but rhetorically they often worked to maintain their boundaries. Sportsmen indulged in bird watching with female companions and sought to mobilize women's groups for conservation campaigns, but they disregarded, and even belittled, sentimental arguments for animal welfare. Women's groups played outsize roles in many conservation efforts, including the establishment of some of the country's first environmental organizations, but they railed against the corrosive moral influence of bloodsports and were often excluded from the grounds of private sporting clubs. Individual women who crossed gendered boundaries or controlled significant financial resources, such as Annie Alexander, who did both, wielded considerable political influence, but they were few in number.

As for the naturalists, many amateurs were women, but most professionals were men who were also accomplished hunters. Naturalists often required sportsmen's support to fund their projects and organizations. But a large fraction were middle-class academics and professionals who avoided identifying with sportsmen's groups, which seemed to constitute a kind of New World aristocracy. In public, for example, Joseph Grinnell distanced himself from the sportsmen's clubs, but in private he worked with them and courted their support. He or his assistants submitted anonymous dispatches, under the pseudonym Golden Gate, to the country's preeminent sporting magazine, *Forest and Stream*, updating its subscribers on the California conservation campaign. Grinnell worked to retain the sportsmen's financial support, including a $4,500 donation in 1914 on behalf of the Berkeley circle's conservation efforts. And throughout his career he remained a member of the Boone and Crocket Club, a famous cabal of prominent sportsmen that included the former U.S. Forest Service chief Gifford Pinchot, Aldo Leopold, and the club's founder, Theodore Roosevelt.[35]

It is impossible to say exactly how different groups of hunters and different forms of hunting contributed to the game declines of the late nineteenth and early twentieth centuries. Market hunting must have made a significant impact. In 1895 and 1896, markets in Los Angeles and San Francisco alone sold 501,171 game birds, and this was only a fraction of the statewide total.[36] In a biological sense, however, market hunting was no different than subsistence or recreational hunting conducted lawfully under the same seasons and bag limits. The class, gender, nationality, ethnicity, citizenship, rationale, fashion, style, and intention of the shooter mattered less than the number of animals taken, where, and when. What is clear is that hunting of all types—for sport, sale, science, and subsistence—rearranged wildlife populations, decimating some and creating new opportunities for others.

Hunting was, of course, not the only problem facing fish and game in the early twentieth century. Astute conservationists realized that complex factors—such as pollution, disease, exotic species, and habitat loss—all contributed to the decline of native fauna. No one knew this better than Grinnell, who had spent his early career watching the transformation of California's wildlife habitats. At the time, however, conservationists had few policy or management tools available to address larger issues related to land use and environmental change. So most wildlife conservation efforts focused on hunting: who should be allowed to do it and for what purpose, how it should be conducted, and where and when it should be done. By the 1910s, many conservationists had come to believe that the only way to restore depleted wildlife populations was to turn hunting into a purely recreational endeavor by banning the sale of wild-caught game.[37]

STATE REGULATION

During the Progressive Era, the states retained almost all of the legal authority over the fish and game within their boundaries, with the exception of a few areas such as Indian reservations. This authority derived from a series of court rulings in the nineteenth century that named the states as the lawful successors of the British crown and the colonies under common law. In the case of *Martin v. Waddell* (1842), the U.S. Supreme Court ruled that after the American Revolution, the states became sovereigns with a general police power and the jurisdiction to maintain navigable waters, soils, and other natural resources in public trust for the common use of their citizens. The public trust doctrine remains a cornerstone of state wildlife and natural resources law.

Half a century later, in 1896's *Geer v. Connecticut,* the court went even further when it ruled that the states *owned* the fish and game within their boundaries. This decision drew criticism for its flawed conception of property, and in 1979 the court overturned *Geer* when it ruled that Congress had the authority to govern wildlife on federal lands within state boundaries under the supremacy clause of the U.S. Constitution. Yet *Geer* was only one of many court decisions that empowered the states to take the lead in most areas of fish and game conservation—a role they continue to play today.[38]

By 1910, most states, including California, had extensive catalogues of fish and game codes. Yet these regulations remained limited to the harvest and sale of wild animals acquired through hunting, gathering, trapping, or fishing and did not include other measures such as habitat protection. There was little legal precedent for habitat protection, and few politicians believed state governments should own or manage nonessential properties. Instead of acquiring land or restricting its use, states sought to strengthen the rights of private landowners through measures such as increasing the scope and power of trespass and nuisance laws.[39]

Conservationists advocated for new regulations on take and sale, but they encountered two main problems: cooperation and enforcement. The first was the lack of cooperation among the various agencies involved—within a state, among the states, and between the states and the federal government. Many conservationists regarded this as the single most important problem for fish and game. As early as the 1870s, government officials began to call for uniformity of closed seasons and bag limits so that hunters in one state could not monopolize the fish and game that the citizens of a neighboring state were attempting to protect. One vocal advocate for state cooperation was the activist, photographer, and Oregon state game warden William Finley. In 1913 he complained that sportsmen in Oregon had grown "tired of keeping seasons closed on certain birds for the sole purpose of allowing the California hunters to kill without regard to the breeding season." The band-tailed pigeon, he wrote, was disappearing for exactly this reason "and may become extinct before many years."[40]

The federal government's first two national wildlife laws both aimed to increase cooperation. The Lacey Act of 1900 made it a federal crime to engage in interstate commerce with wild animals that had been taken in violation of state laws. It also allowed the federal government to regulate the import of exotic species into the United States and authorized federal programs to restore native species in areas where they had declined. The purpose of the act, which came just four years after the Supreme Court's *Geer* decision, was to strengthen the states by buttressing their laws with federal enforcement. Yet as the first national wildlife law, it created a context for further federal involvement in wildlife conservation. The Lacey Act not only increased cooperation among the states and the federal government, but also set an important precedent for the application of the U.S. Constitution's commerce clause as a rationale for federal environmental policies.

Intrastate cooperation also posed a challenge. Counties and municipalities passed ordinances that contradicted state laws and conflicted with those of neighboring jurisdictions. Different state agencies pursued their own agendas and even struggled to coordinate their internal programs. The California Division of Fish and Game had the responsibility of administering conservation laws in a state twice the size of New England. It attempted to do so by forging partnerships with other agencies, organizing the state into districts, and soliciting support among its diverse and divided constituents. "We recognize," the Board of Fish and Game Commissioners wrote in 1913, "that we are administering a public trust, that to us has been assigned the duty of protecting and conserving the fish and game interests of the State for the benefit of all the people, and that to be successful we must have their active coöperation."[41]

The board's call for cooperation was both a plea and a threat. The Fish and Game Commission had adopted the motto "conservation through education," but each year it dedicated more of its resources to law enforcement. Enforcement of fish and game codes was weak or nonexistent in most states until the twentieth century. Between 1902 and 1915, however, California established one of the country's most aggressive fish and game law enforcement programs. It dispatched wardens to every corner of the state, deputized more than three hundred U.S. Forest Service rangers, and prosecuted about ten thousand cases of fish and game code violations. Fines collected from the convictions went back into the Fish and Game Commission's coffers. Along with fees from hunting and fishing licenses—which favored and legitimized those who had the money to purchase them—these funds enabled the commission to hire 120 employees, based at offices in Sacramento, San Francisco, Fresno, and Los Angeles.[42]

Despite these efforts, law enforcement remained a major challenge. Game wardens could not detect more than a small fraction of the violations. According to Ernest Schaeffle, the commission's executive officer, conservationists were "compelled to realize that laws are being violated every day and that the fish and game supply is suffering correspondingly." Hunters ignored new laws, landowners refused to allow officials to work on their property, and sympathetic judges declined to hear game cases. "He has read history to very little purpose," wrote one such California judge, who was unaware that game codes were a "fruitful source of oppression of the masses of the people. . . . It was better to exterminate the game at once than to preserve it for the special benefit of a favored few."[43]

People violated the new fish and game codes for many reasons. In some cases, these laws reversed older statutes that many people thought still made sense. For example, proposals for new regulations to ban the sale of wild-caught game reversed previous laws in many states that had required hunters to bring their excess catch to market. The rationale behind the earlier laws was that demand, not supply, should dictate the size of the commercial harvest. In other cases, people violated the new codes, such as closed seasons, to feed their families or because they were following cultural traditions from their homelands. Sometimes people were simply not aware of the new codes, but they also broke the law to protest regulations that appeared to single them out for discrimination.[44]

Racism and xenophobia were rife in California, as in other parts of the country, and on full display in fish and game debates. Wealthy white sportsmen championed legislation that prevented nonwhite immigrants from owning property and firearms. The California Fish and Game Commission studied instances of lawbreaking and concluded that most fish and game code violators were aliens and other immigrants from southern Europe. Schaeffle blamed poaching on the "irrepressible mountaineer or the unschooled immigrant."[45] Conservationism, like other Progressive Era political movements, included elements of what today seem like both liberal reform and reactionary conservatism—often represented in the same policies and embodied in the same individuals.

By 1912 many California conservationists had decided it was impossible to prevent fish and game code violations by patrolling the state's vast mountains, deserts, forests, and waterways. So they adopted a strategy that had worked in other states: they turned their attention from the vast rural places where wild animals were hunted to the dense urban spaces where animals were sold. The nonsale of game campaign shifted the focus of law enforcement from market hunters to game dealers, restaurateurs, and hoteliers who sold wild animals for profit in cities such as Los Angeles, Oakland, and San Francisco. Concentrating on the site of sale rearranged the spatial organization of police power and made law enforcement more feasible. It also stirred opposition among some wealthy and powerful businessmen who banded together with hunters and game dealers and resolved to fight against this new form of government incursion into the free market.

THE FLINT-CARY DEBATE

In the summer of 1912, less than a year after Monarch's death, Joseph Grinnell recruited another one of his students, Walter P. Taylor, to lead the Berkeley circle's legislative campaign. Taylor worked to mobilize scientific societies, reform state agencies, lobby politicians, disseminate the results of scientific research, coordinate outreach programs, and establish new wildlife refuges. Under Grinnell's direction, he also founded a new activist organization, the California Associated Societies for the Conservation of Wild Life, staffed by volunteers from the Berkeley circle. The Associated Societies advocated a platform of conservation laws, but by the end of its first year it was focusing on getting a law enacted that would ban the sale of wild-caught game. The following winter, Taylor published the first issue of the group's newsletter, the *Western Wild Life Call*, which became the voice of the campaign. "It is a fixed principle that every wild species of mammal, bird, or reptile that is pursued for money-making purposes eventually is *wiped out of existence*," he wrote. "Even the whales of the sea are no exception."[46]

By the time Taylor began this campaign, thirty-one states had passed laws prohibiting the commercial sale of ducks and other wild-caught game.[47] Legislation had stalled elsewhere due to opposition from hunters and businesses that depended on the trade. It also met with resistance from people who believed that such laws were unconstitutional or saw wild-caught game as an essential source of income or food for the poor. Yet by 1912, California was the largest and most progressive state that had not yet banned the sale of these animals. In the absence of national legislation, which seemed out of the question, a nonsale law in California represented the biggest prize for wildlife conservationists in the United States.

The Associated Societies campaign for a California nonsale of game law lasted about a year. In April of 1913, Taylor took a leave from the MVZ and moved to Sacramento, where he stayed for two months to lobby for a collection of fish and game bills. The work was exhausting and frustrating but also exhilarating, and Taylor seemed to thrive on the politics. He wrote letters to Grinnell almost daily, and his boss in Berkeley encouraged him to work "energetically and judiciously until all the legislation pertaining to our field is 'finished business.'"[48] The result was an impressive, if temporary, success. In May of 1914, a little more than a year after the campaign began, the state legislature passed the Flint-Cary Act, which banned the sale of most wild-caught game, and California's Republican governor, Hiram W. Johnson, signed it into law.

But the battle was far from over. Johnson had swept into office in 1910 with the promise that he would reform the state's government, control monopolies such as the Southern Pacific Railroad, and hand political power back to the citizenry. The following year, his progressive majority amended the state constitution to include three new mechanisms of direct democracy: the initiative, the referendum, and the recall. Opponents of the Flint-Cary Act seized this opportunity. A coalition of market hunters, game dealers, restaurateurs, and hoteliers formed the People's Fish and Game Protective Association and began to mobilize support. The Protective Association was not antiprogressive or even anticonservation. The group proposed new fish and game laws that its members believed would improve wild stocks without damaging their businesses or constraining the free market. Its members did, however, believe that the Flint-Cary Act singled them out unfairly and would fail to restore wildlife populations. The association began collecting signatures, and by the spring of 1914, it became clear that a referendum to overturn Flint-Cary would appear on the November ballot.

Now on the defensive, Grinnell directed Taylor to shift his efforts from lobbying in Sacramento to spearheading California's first grassroots wildlife conservation campaign. The Associated Societies produced twenty thousand copies of the *Western Wild Life Call*, ninety-five thousand informational pamphlets, sixty thousand letters, one hundred public lectures, and three press releases for each of the state's 825 newspapers. Advertisements appeared on streetcars in San Francisco, Sacramento, and the Napa Valley. A separate but coordinated effort took place in Southern California. Taylor estimated that the campaign's literature had reached at least a million Californians, or about a third of the state's population. The Associated Societies also received support from prominent national activists. By September it had a council of officers and advisers that reads like an honor roll of Progressive Era reformers, including American Federation of Labor president Samuel Gompers, National Consumers' League president Frederick Nathan, American Museum of Natural History president Henry Fairfield Osborn, and National American Woman Suffrage Association president Anna Howard Shaw—not to mention William T. Hornaday, Theodore Roosevelt, and John Muir. (This would be Muir's last campaign endorsement before his death that Christmas Eve.)[49]

With such a formidable roster of backers and the support of state lawmakers who had voted for the Flint-Cary Act, the nonsale of game seemed like a tough cause to defeat. In the words of one noted Progressive Era historian, market hunters and game dealers posed "no match for the politically powerful and wealthy people who supported conservationism."[50] But the situation in California was more complicated than that. Both sides of the Flint-Cary debate spanned the socioeconomic spectrum and drew supporters from urban and rural settings around the state. Each side accused the other of speaking on behalf of society's most privileged people and charged that its opponents were dominating resources at the expense of the majority. Both sides claimed the mantle of Progressivism and argued that they spoke for the true conservationists. Both wielded considerable political power and labeled the other as undemocratic. The opponents were well matched, and the outcome was impossible to predict.

The campaign started out relatively tame. The *Western Wild Life Call* listed nineteen reasons to uphold the Flint-Cary Act, most of which focused on its general benefits to society. Proponents of the act argued that fish and game codes prevented private control and established equal ownership of public goods. Unlike the commercialization of game, which benefited a minority of the population, Taylor argued, regulations benefited everyone, without exception or prejudice. By maintaining a strong nonsale of game law, California would remain in the ranks of progressive states and become a leader not only in conservation but also in national politics.[51]

The People's Fish and Game Protective Association portrayed the situation differently. Its members argued that onerous regulations already delayed the delivery of lawfully killed game, so meat spoiled before it reached the market. Nonsale of game laws deprived the populace of cheap food, granted "special privilege to so-called sportsmen," and allowed rich hunters to monopolize public goods. Under the guise of conservation, such laws represented an exercise of power by the rich over the poor. According to the Protective Association, a more equitable game law would cancel these special privileges. It would repeal hunting and fishing license fees, levy a special tax on private preserves, and transfer law enforcement powers from the state Fish and Game Commission to the county boards of supervisors.[52]

After a few months of this back and forth, things started to get ugly. The *Western Wild Life Call* argued that the Protective Association's referendum petition contained thousands of false signatures. Most of these, Taylor claimed, had come from San Francisco or Oakland, where wealthy French restaurants charged exorbitant prices for the privilege of overfeeding on fancy meat; poor San Franciscans and Oaklanders had been deceived into signing a petition that would benefit only the gluttonous and corpulent few. The newsletter asserted that those behind the referendum had committed fraud, forgery, and perjury and had attempted to incite class conflict. It even claimed that the Protective Association was a front for Chinese mobsters who, when they were not lobbying against wildlife conservation, "engaged in the sale and traffic of women and the protection of murderers."[53]

In a survey of California's newspapers conducted just days before the election, Taylor found that fourteen publications, with a combined circulation of 214,442, opposed the Flint-Cary Act, while 170 publications, with a combined circulation of 617,416, favored it. On November 1, however, the *San Francisco Examiner,* the same

Hearst newspaper that had sponsored Allan Kelly's expedition to capture a California grizzly twenty-five years earlier, published a front-page lead story titled "180—and More—Reasons for Voting for Sale of Game to People." This article accused Fish and Game Commission president Frank Newbert of breaking his own laws by exceeding the bag limit for mallards. It was a short article, but it was printed on the front page and included a large photograph that showed Newbert and six of his hunting partners standing behind a row of 180 dead ducks strung on a line. For years conservationists had published photographs they said illustrated the wastefulness of "game hogs" who hunted for profit. The *Examiner* showed that this allegation could go both ways.

The following day, Californians overturned the Flint-Cary Act by popular vote. Voters in Southern California supported the act by a margin of two to one, but the larger population in Northern California overwhelmingly rejected it. Opposition was particularly strong in the urban centers of San Francisco and Oakland. Some urban elites supported the Flint-Cary Act, but a significant fraction opposed it. The Protective Association also convinced many working-class urban and rural residents that the act would allow the rich to restrict access to the state's resources. This was a humbling defeat for the Berkeley circle conservationists in a battle they had initially won and certainly not expected to lose. A week after the election, Grinnell had to write to Harry Swarth, his former student and now the editor of the *Condor*, to retract an article Grinnell had submitted before the election claiming a premature victory.[54]

The state and federal governments eventually managed to curtail the sale of wild-caught game. Not long after the Flint-Cary debate, the California legislature passed a law that fixed the number of game birds any person could posses in a single day to the normal recreational bag limit, which made the sale of wild-caught game unprofitable without actually outlawing it. Resistance emerged once again, but in 1918 Congress passed the Migratory Bird Treaty Act, which outlawed the sale of most avian species nationwide. This act met with well-organized opposition, including not only individuals and organizations involved in the wildlife trade but also state governments that viewed it as a violation of their property rights as defined in *Geer vs. Connecticut*. Two years later, however, this conflict led to another landmark legal case, *Missouri v. Holland*, in which the Supreme Court ruled that the supremacy clause of the U.S. Constitution enabled the federal government to enact treaties that superseded the rights of the individual states. The treaty power thus joined the commerce clause as a legal justification for federal involvement in wildlife conservation.

The nonsale of game debate left an important legacy for wildlife conservation in California. Before 1915, East Coast conservationists viewed their colleagues there as little more than an eccentric, provincial West Coast subculture. During the Flint-Cary debate, however, California moved from the periphery to the center of national wildlife politics. The nation's most famous wildlife conservationist, William T. Hornaday, even singled out the work of the Berkeley circle as a national model. He pointed to the University of California as the first educational institution to actively engage in wildlife conservation, and he called the California Associated Societies for the Conservation of Wild Life the finest organization of its kind in the country. No other state, Hornaday noted, had such a combination of forces working for wildlife conservation.[55]

Despite this praise, the controversies of the early 1910s took a toll on the California Fish and Game Commission, which had opened itself to criticism by assuming a prominent role in political advocacy. It had developed an impressive bureaucratic infrastructure for coordination and enforcement, but it lacked both widespread public support and the confidence of the state legislature, which refused to grant it plenary powers to enact its own regulations. Unlike wildlife agencies in many other states, the California Fish and Game Commission would not achieve this level of autonomy until the 1940s. In the years that followed the Flint-Cary debate, the chastened commission turned its efforts away from divisive political campaigns and refocused its work on education, propagation, and law enforcement. Commission officials, including some Berkeley circle alumni, talked less about conservation ethics and the threat of extinction and more about their efforts to supply fish and game for the hunting and fishing license holders who funded the commission's work.[56]

By 1915, Grinnell's first cohort of student assistants began to disperse. Joseph Dixon and Harold Bryant remained with the National Park Service. Harry Swarth accepted a curatorial position in Los Angeles and continued to act as the editor of the *Condor*. Tracy Storer served in World War I and later founded the Department of Zoology at the University of California, Davis. Loye Miller left for UCLA. And Walter P. Taylor accepted a position with the Bureau of Biological Survey in Arizona.

The second cohort of Berkeley circle students would adopt a different approach to conservation. They never embarked on a legislative campaign, instead focusing on the equally challenging but lower-profile work of bureaucratic reform. During the 1920s they worked for the reduction of predator elimination programs. They also began to think less about state hunting codes and more about federal land management. By 1930 a trio of former Grinnell students working at Yosemite had established the National Park Service's first science-based wildlife conservation program. These shifts in the Berkeley circle's focus—from legislative to bureaucratic politics, from state to federal programs, and from hunting regulations to habitat management—would shape wildlife conservation in California and the American West through the New Deal era and beyond.

CHAPTER THREE · The Official Landscape

In September of 1916, less than two years after the Flint-Cary referendum, Joseph Grinnell and his student Tracy Storer published an essay titled "Animal Life as an Asset of the National Parks" in the journal *Science*. Their paper served as a manifesto for the next generation of Berkeley circle conservationists. According to Grinnell and Storer, the national parks offered more than just sublime scenery, healthful recreation, and a chance to view big game. They were also some of the last sanctuaries where visitors could observe wild animals and ecological processes relatively free from human influence. They provided opportunities to preserve "natural conditions" for research and education. And they could serve as nurseries for wildlife populations that had become depleted through excessive hunting in adjacent "unprotected areas." This would be possible only if the National Park Service—which Congress had created less than a month earlier—avoided overdevelopment and unnecessary artificial manipulation and launched a new program of scientific management.[1]

By suggesting that the national parks should be viewed as wildlife refuges, Grinnell and Storer helped initiate a new phase in American conservation history. The 1920s and 1930s were a time of great advancement in wildlife ecology and conservation, and Berkeley circle members played essential roles in this movement. During this period, they abandoned Progressive Era–style legislative campaigns and worked for change by reforming government bureaucracies from the inside out. They shifted their focus from the state to the federal level and from hunting regulations to habitat protection. They also continued to argue that scientific evidence should guide the management of wildlife in national parks and other nature reserves. In the process, they outlined almost all of the key scientific concepts that would inspire the field of conservation biology decades later, and they described most of the management problems that would shape endangered species debates in the postwar era.[2]

By 1955 A. Starker Leopold, the eldest son of Aldo Leopold and a lifelong Berkeley circle member, could describe the "complicated legal machinery" of hunting and fishing codes, which had formed the "backbone" of fish and game conservation during the Progressive Era, as flawed and insufficient. In the years since, scientists and managers throughout the country had come to appreciate the role of "habitat as the transcendent force that, more than any other, determines the level of wild populations." According to Leopold, the idea of habitat conservation had been slow to catch on, but change was under way. It was "now an accepted truism," he concluded, "that maintenance of suitable habitat is the key to sustaining animal populations, and that [game] protection, though it is important, is not itself a substitute for habitat."[3]

The story of wildlife conservation in California and the rest of the United States from the end of the Progressive Era, around 1916, to the beginning of the environmental era in 1964 is, in large part, about the emergence of habitat as a key concept in science and management. Agreement on the centrality of this concept did not, however, lead to a consensus about who should manage habitats, by what means, and for which species. Divergent ideas about the meaning and purpose of habitat conservation fractured scientific societies, split the profession of wildlife management, and led to a division of labor and philosophy among government bureaucracies.

Habitat conservation is a complex endeavor, and disagreements about its techniques and objectives continue to this day. Yet Leopold's larger point remains: after World War II, habitat conservation became an overarching framework for wildlife management in the United States. After the passage of the federal Endangered Species Act in 1973, however, this framework was increasingly turned on its head. Whereas scientists and managers had initially conceived of habitat conservation as an approach to managing wildlife, environmental activists would come to see wildlife conservation as a way to protect habitat. Setting aside habitat—in the form of parks, wilderness areas, nature reserves, and myriad other land management designations—eventually became an end in itself.

"NATURAL AREAS" IN AMERICAN ECOLOGY

Some of the earliest habitat conservation initiatives in the United States began among ecologists who wanted to preserve natural areas for scientific research. During the first three decades of the twentieth century, the field of ecology in the United States was searching for a mission and a clientele that would demonstrate its social relevance and promote its growth and development. The first ecologists set out to address the unintended consequences of westward expansion, population growth, resource extraction, and agricultural development. Several of the discipline's leaders worked in the Midwest and the Great Plains, where these changes had been particularly dramatic. They believed that the landscape transformations of the nineteenth century had thrown dynamic but orderly communities of plants and animals into disarray. Understanding how North America's pre-Columbian landscapes functioned thus became a key aspect of their work to reestablish an equilibrium in the balance of nature.[4]

But the ecologists had two problems. First, they needed a set of objectives and a repertoire of methodologies that would distinguish their discipline. These would have to combine the broad, integrative perspective of field-based natural history observation with the scientific rigor and control of laboratory-based experimentation. It was not immediately clear what this new approach would look like, and ecology's pioneering figures struggled to define their discipline's best practices. Second, the ecologists were being outcompeted by specialists in the related resource management fields. New disciplines such as forestry, agricultural entomology, fisheries biology, and range management were already building their professional reputations, specializing in particular economic sectors, developing methods to investigate pressing problems, and winning the allegiance of patrons in government and industry.[5]

Two of ecology's founders in the United States, Charles C. Adams and Victor E. Shelford, offered a solution to these problems (see figure 9). They argued that ecologists should move beyond the customary zoological approach of collecting and analyzing biological specimens to a new focus, the study of "natural areas." They also believed that their fledgling professional organization, the Ecological Society of America—founded in 1915, just a year before the National Park Service—should advocate for the establishment of nature reserves to facilitate this research. According to Adams, it was not enough to preserve skins and bones in dusty museums. It was ecologists' scientific duty to protect at least some areas where researchers could study "unified assemblages" of animals interacting under normal conditions in their primeval habitats and original associations. "The animal remains themselves are only a very incomplete record," Adams wrote in 1913. "Their activities and environments are an essential part of the animals and should also

FIGURE 9.
Victor Shelford. Courtesy of the University of Illinois Archives.

be preserved." Shelford echoed this sentiment when he noted that "from a philosophical and practical standpoint, the unified assemblage of organisms is commonly more valuable than the isolated rare species."[6]

The natural areas that Adams and Shelford wanted to create would serve several functions. They would provide classrooms for teaching, storehouses of native plants and animals, opportunities for scientific research, benchmarks for measuring changes in the surrounding landscapes, and demonstration sites for projects in wildlife management and ecological restoration. "We must *know* nature," Shelford wrote, as a "whole, if we wish to treat the simplest everyday problem of our relations to animals intelligently and justly." Natural areas would also enable ecologists to acquire a professional identity distinct from those of practitioners in other fields who worked in spaces dominated by farming, ranching, logging, or other resource industries. "A branch of biological science which obtains its inspiration in the natural order in original habitats," Shelford concluded, "must depend upon the preservation of natural areas for the solution of many problems."[7]

If ecologists were going to build a new discipline based on the study of natural areas, they had to move fast. "Ecology," Adams wrote, "has developed only at a late stage in civilization, after much of the environment has undergone great changes, so that in order to study the original conditions, which are of such great historic and genetic significance, he must make long journeys, or invade swamps or sterile uplands which man has not yet been able to reduce to the average conditions best suited to his needs." Wild places were being destroyed, degraded, simplified, and transformed before scientists had a chance to study them—a lesson Grinnell had learned all too well in California. "One can but wonder," Adams continued, "if the naturalists of the future will commend our foresight in studying with such great diligence certain aspects of biology which might be very well delayed, while ephemeral and vanishing records are allowed to be obliterated without the least concern." These records included not only species but also habitats and ecological relationships.[8]

Adams and Shelford had status in their young discipline, and they used their influence to promote an agenda of natural areas preservation. Both men had received their doctorates from the University of Chicago, and they were among the country's first animal ecologists. In 1915 Shelford became the first president of the Ecological Society of America, and two years later he appointed himself head of a new Committee on the Preservation of Natural Conditions that oversaw the society's most ambitious initiative. The committee sent out queries, conducted field surveys, and assembled a massive amount of geographical information. By 1921 it had identified about six hundred sites worthy of protection. Shelford's committee published its study five years later as a 761-page tome, *Naturalist's Guide to the Americas*.[9]

The *Naturalist's Guide* was more than just an inventory. Its main objective was to locate natural areas and make them more accessible for scientific research, but it also offered a professional agenda for the discipline of ecology that included a broad critique of the traditional biological sciences. According to Shelford, research specialization in particular objects and organisms was impeding crucial integrative studies on "the entire life of natural areas." Ecologists rejected not only narrow specialization but also "fads" and "crude ideas," such as "the survival of the fittest." These notions had given biologists in most other fields a myopic view of nature better suited to sterile laboratories than to the landscapes where organisms actually lived. When he described those landscapes, Shelford used *environment* and *habitat* as synonyms. He argued that there could be "no adequate knowledge of fitness to environment without knowledge of environment" and insisted that "knowledge of habitats can be organized into science." By studying species in their natural habitats, Shelford and his colleagues hoped to transform scientists' understanding of evolutionary biology.[10]

Over the next decade, Shelford continued to update the *Naturalist's Guide* with additional assessments, reports, articles, and recommendations. These included a new framework for prioritizing and designing nature reserves. "First-class" sanctuaries would be "areas of natural vegetation containing as nearly as possible all the animal species known to have occurred in the areas within historical times." Second- and third-class sanctuaries would encompass more modified landscapes, such as sites with altered vegetation and extinct or introduced species. All sanctuaries should have core natural areas that would remain unavailable for human uses other than scientific research. Core areas would be surrounded by buffer zones, which would provide additional habitat for the wide-ranging species that needed the most protection, particularly large carnivores.[11]

This focus on natural areas helped set ecology on a different path in the United States than in other parts of the world. In Britain, where the field had also taken root, ecologists were not nearly so interested in the types of places that American scientists and conservationists called wilderness. British ecologists, such as Arthur Tansley, regarded traditional land uses as components of the cultural landscape that were essential for the maintenance of many indigenous ecological communities. American ecologists came to view human land uses as disturbances—cattle grazing is a classic example. Yet for Tansley it was the removal of such activities that counted as the disturbance. Only when British ecologists traveled outside Europe to other regions of their empire did they adopt a more American-style approach, which embraced the idea of wilderness, dismissed customary indigenous practices, and provided a convenient scientistic justification for their seizure of lands and natural resources.[12]

During the 1910s and 1920s, Shelford's work gained support in the Ecological Society of America, which adopted his sanctuary protection plan and became one of the first national organizations to work for habitat protection. Yet by the 1930s, support began to wane. Most ecologists still backed efforts to establish nature reserves, but the society's membership, which had grown to 653 people by 1930, was shifting toward the view that a national scientific organization should remain apolitical. As early as 1933, members debated whether scientific societies should endorse land preservation efforts or leave this task to the country's growing collection of activist conservation organizations. The society's constitution prohibited lobbying on "nonscientific" issues, so part of the question was whether preservation work was sufficiently scientific. This was just the first of several struggles in the society over the proper relationship between science and activism.[13]

In 1937 Shelford threatened to leave the organization he had helped to found more than two decades earlier if it did not amend its constitution to permit his conservation projects. Seven years later he wrote a letter to *Science* complaining that the Ecological Society of America had made little progress in its preservation work. "With wartime and post-war pressure to destroy nature mounting," he reflected, "it is well for those interested in its preservation for scientific purposes to look over the machinery by which some of it may possibly be saved." Later that year he circulated a survey to the society's members, and 85 percent of the respondents supported his committee's efforts. The society's governing board opposed the program, however, and in 1945 it blocked a petition to amend the constitution. The following year the board voted to abolish Shelford's preservation committee.[14]

Shelford did not follow through on his threat to leave the society, but he did partner with sympathetic colleagues to establish a new organization to continue the work of the preservation committee. In 1946 he and more than a dozen other senior ecologists, including four past Ecological Society of America presidents, founded the Ecologists Union. It advocated for the protection of primitive areas in the national forests, passed resolutions against the transfer of federal lands to state and private control, and shifted its focus from Washington, DC, to regions with important natural areas. Once the union established its independence, the Ecological Society of America's board endorsed its work as a scientifically grounded conservation organization. In 1950 the union changed its name to the Nature Conservancy (TNC). TNC would become one of the world's largest conservation organizations, and from the beginning it has dedicated its efforts to protecting biodiversity and endangered species through habitat protection.[15]

The Ecological Society of America's shift away from natural areas preservation had another effect: it helped to facilitate the emergence of wildlife management as a profession. Wildlife management coalesced in the 1920s and 1930s, combining features of forestry, ecology, natural history, and fish and game conservation and often focusing on the vast new public lands created by the New Deal. The first generation of wildlife managers believed that public officials should administer natural resources for the common good, but they held diverse opinions on what this meant in practice. Academic scientists, government officials, recreational hunters, conservation activists, and landowners and users, including farmers and ranchers, thus waged a series of struggles over the meaning and purpose of wildlife management that shaped the young profession and created a context for future conflicts about endangered species and habitat conservation. The most important of these battles was over predator control.

PREDATOR CONTROL

In the early twentieth century, most people viewed predators as varmints. This included animal welfare activists concerned about the plight of prey species, hunters worried about the loss of game, and ranchers anxious about the security of their livestock. It also included many scientists and government officials. In 1925 Edward A. Goldman, a prominent scientist from the Smithsonian Institution and the Bureau of Biological Survey, expressed a common sentiment when he wrote that "large predatory mammals, destructive to livestock and to game, no longer have a place in our advancing civilization." Other prominent authors, such as Ernest Thompson Seton, expressed regret that large carnivores, such as the wolf and the grizzly, were disappearing from the North American landscape, but even Seton agreed that such extinctions were the inevitable price of progress.[16]

Beginning in the 1880s, the Bureau of Biological Survey, under the direction of C. Hart Merriam, published a series of reports on the economic effects of predators. Its early work took a relatively positive position compared to that of its later work, which focused on the damage that predators caused. Merriam, Albert K. Fisher, and other bureau officials emphasized the services predators provided, such as culling sick animals, consuming carrion, and devouring rodent pests. They even took positions on public policy. As early as 1886, Merriam publicly criticized a law passed the previous year in Pennsylvania, dubbed the Scalp Act, that issued a bounty of fifty cents on hawks, owls, weasels, and minks. Using a simple cost-benefit analysis, he calculated that in its first year the program had operated at a loss of more than $3.8 million. The same could be said, he believed, of similar programs in states throughout the country.[17]

Merriam's moderate view was an exception to the rule. Predator control remained a ubiquitous practice throughout the United States into the 1920s. Federal agencies, state fish and game departments, university extension programs, county animal control boards, livestock organizations, and private landowners all pursued their own programs. Control efforts in California grew along with its farming and ranching industries. Between 1919 and 1947, the state employed two full-time mountain-lion hunters, Jay Bruce and C. W. Ledshaw. In his autobiography, *Cougar Killer*, Bruce claimed to have bagged 669 of the animals. According to a study published in 1931 by Jean Linsdale, another of Joseph Grinnell's students, poisoning programs aimed at predators and rodent pests were under way on more than a third of California's land, at a cost of $812,478. Grinnell calculated that these programs were killing more than fifty million animals per year, including members of many "non-target" species, some which were in danger of extinction.[18]

Early in his career, Grinnell seemed conflicted about how to deal with predators. He supported the control of rattlesnakes and mountain lions, advocated the sustainable harvest of fur-bearing mammals, proposed experiments in game farming, and accepted that scientific management would require some limited local culling of problem species. But he thought it was wrong to poison animals or subject them to unnecessary suffering, and programs that sought to eradicate rather than control predators horrified him. Over time, he became convinced that most control programs were wasteful, destructive, and unsupported by scientific evidence, and he called for an end to indiscriminate shooting, trapping, and poisoning. By 1930 Grinnell had emerged as the country's foremost opponent of predator control policies and practices.[19]

During the 1920s, several of Grinnell's protégés worked on questions of predator ecology and behavior. Lee Dice wrote about "the scientific value of predatory mammals," and E. Raymond Hall argued that an infestation of house mice in Kern County, California, had resulted from the removal of their predators. Joseph Dixon examined the stomach contents of more than one thousand fur-bearing mammals to determine their diets and found that the majority of wild carnivores consumed little valuable game or livestock. Local patterns undoubtedly varied, but "in many instances where extermination is advocated, we are getting 'the cart before the horse.'" Dixon concluded that most "so-called predatory" species were, "in the aggregate, beneficial and not harmful to human welfare."[20]

The Bureau of Biological Survey had shifted its position, however, since the time of Merriam and Fisher, becoming allied with cattlemen, woolgrowers, and farmers—groups that supported continued aggressive predator control. Woolgrowers, whose animals were the most vulnerable to predation, were particularly adamant about reducing populations of coyotes and bobcats, the species that most often killed sheep. They viewed predator control as a matter of economic necessity and often took matters into their own hands, shooting predators and leaving poisoned carcasses on public and private lands.[21] The bureau's efforts also received support from recreational hunters, who saw game species proliferate as predator populations declined. For most sportsmen, predator control remained an essential aspect of game conservation.

Grinnell proceeded cautiously in his critiques of these programs, to protect his reputation and his institutional position at Berkeley. Frequently he used his students and colleagues as surrogates to take public positions on issues he supported. After the Flint-Cary defeat (see chapter 2), he grew even more wary about legislative politics. He did, however, speak his mind to government bureaucrats. Early on, Grinnell complained that officials at agencies such as the Bureau of Biological Survey had ignored his "frequent solicitous enquiries" about their policies. As his career continued, he used his professional stature and network of allies to cajole, convince, and coerce government officials on issues such as predator control. Eventually, however, his ambivalence and cautious political maneuvering gave way to frustration, and by the early 1930s he was condemning the bureau's programs. "It is a curious perversion," Grinnell wrote in 1931, "when 'conservation' is appealed to to justify *destruction*."[22]

Grinnell had more success in shaping opinions outside the Bureau of Biological Survey. By the mid-1920s, the California Fish and Game Commission had announced its opposition to most predator control programs and was criticizing the bureau, arms manufacturers, sportsmen, and other groups that supported such programs. "Where would we end," read a 1925 article in the commission's journal, *California Fish and Game*, "if we started in consistently killing everything that eats something else?"[23]

At the time, Harold Bryant was serving as the commission's director of education, publicity, and research, and he used his position to disseminate the Berkeley circle viewpoint. Grinnell also found allies in other agencies, including the National Park Service. During the mid-1920s, Walter Fry—a Grinnell associate who served as a federal judge, a naturalist, a ranger, and Sequoia National Park's first civilian superintendent—wrote a series of articles in defense of carnivorous animals. He referred to such creatures as "man's best friends" for their part in maintaining the "balance of nature," including eating pests. He spoke out against control programs that lacked scientific evidence, and he defended some of the state's most reviled predators: ring-tailed cats, badgers, skunks, raccoons, snakes, hawks, and coyotes. Even the wolverine, with its "bad morals"—by which he apparently meant its aggressive behavior and taste for meat—deserved protection for its role in culling sick deer and other game during outbreaks of contagious diseases.[24]

Berkeley circle members also worked to change the minds of their fellow biologists, including no less than Aldo Leopold. In 1922, more than a decade after

Leopold's famous epiphany about the ecological value of predators, which supposedly came to him after he shot an "old she wolf" and her pups on the piney slopes of White Mountain in northern Arizona, he submitted an article to the *Condor*, Grinnell's journal of western ornithology. In this essay, he discussed his recent discovery that roadrunners preyed on quail, a popular game species. "I have never before killed a road-runner," Leopold wrote, "but they are now on my 'blacklist' and will stay there until somebody proves that this was an exception to their usual habits." Harry Swarth, the managing editor of the *Condor*, begged to differ: "It seems to me that the road-runner is just as desirable a bird to have around as the quail! I suppose, though, that you look at the matter from the 'game protective' standpoint." After reconsidering the matter, Leopold agreed that he had been "a bit hasty" and assured Swarth that he was "heartily in sympathy" with his Berkeley colleagues. Leopold asked the editor to remove the passage before his manuscript went to print.[25]

Not all scientists and government officials were so humble and open-minded. In 1924, Dixon teamed up with Charles C. Adams and Edmund Heller to build support in the American Society of Mammalogists for a resolution against government-sponsored predator eradication programs. The debate that followed revealed how controversial the issue had become. The society's members quarreled about predator-prey relationships and the ecological factors that regulated animal populations. Both sides argued for policies to conserve precious resources but disagreed about what those resources were and how they should be managed. Neither side had adequate data to support its arguments, and both appealed to aesthetic notions about the balance of nature. Bureau of Biological Survey officials who were members of the society, including Goldman and Vernon Bailey, defended their predator control work as an economic necessity. W. L. McAtee and A. Brazier Howell, both of whom were friends and allies of Grinnell, responded by challenging the bureau's claims about predator-related agricultural damage and about the harm that predator control programs inflicted on nontarget species. The bureau's then-chief, Paul Redington, claimed that his agency's policies would merely "hasten the inevitable" extinction of large carnivores, which was out of its control, and its future chief Ira Gabrielson quit the American Society of Mammalogists in protest.[26]

In 1931 the society issued two reports on this topic. One represented the Berkeley circle view that most control programs were harmful and unwarranted; the other represented the Bureau of Biological Survey's argument that although no species should be driven to extinction, aggressive predator control constituted an effective use of public funds and an economic necessity. The Ecological Society of America issued its own report, which endorsed the notion of limited predator control but criticized the bureau's approach and called on it to abandon its proposed ten-year predator management plan. Not surprisingly, this report also highlighted the need for more research.[27]

If the Bureau of Biological Survey was not yet ready for change, then maybe the National Park Service would be more receptive. During the service's early years, park superintendents often contracted with the bureau to control the predators on their lands and allowed rangers to earn extra money by moonlighting as trappers. In 1916 Grinnell and Storer called for an end to hunting, trapping, and predator control in the parks, except for scientific purposes: "As a rule predaceous animals should be left unmolested and allowed to retain their primitive relation to the rest of the fauna, even though this may entail a considerable annual levy on the animals forming their prey." This was a radical idea. Most western parks were surrounded by forests and rangelands stocked with hunters and ranchers who supported predator control. Yosemite even made a spectacle of the policy, hosting fireside lectures by Jay Bruce, California's famous mountain-lion hunter. The Park Service's first two directors, Stephen T. Mather and Horace Albright, both favored predator control to protect tourist-friendly species such as deer and elk.[28]

Despite these inauspicious signs, the National Park Service proved more amenable than other federal agencies to reform in this area. Grinnell lobbied the service's leadership and had Berkeley circle members placed in important positions. Over the course of a decade, he convinced a succession of directors and superintendents to change their predator policies from eradication to control and eventually to conservation. In 1925, Superintendent W. B. Lewis banned all trapping for nonscientific purposes in Yosemite National Park, where Grinnell and his students conducted much of their research. In 1931, Albright adopted a policy of giving "total protection to all animal life," including predators. The following year, Yosemite officials announced that rangers would kill only individual predatory animals that were jeopardizing public safety or the existence of other native species.[29]

The predator control debate of the 1920s and early 1930s was a formative episode in American conservation history. It helped elevate the realm of wildlife conservation debates from local advocacy groups and state legislatures to national professional organizations and federal agencies. Philosophical divisions about the role and value of predators developed within academic zoology and game management, and government agencies began to diverge in their policies and practices. The participants in this debate used science, especially ecology, more than ever before to support their arguments. The debate expanded the range of protected species to include a much wider variety of fur-bearing mammals and birds of prey, at least in the national parks. By the 1930s, radical new activist groups, such as the Emergency Conservation Committee, were forcing more established organizations, including the National Audubon Society, to denounce the very predator elimination programs they had once supported.[30]

The predator control debate had another effect that few have recognized. When the Berkeley circle and its allies criticized predator control programs, they questioned the ability of officials to manage wildlife through the direct removal or addition of individuals to a population. Direct manipulation of wildlife populations continues today. Yet the predator control debate of the 1920s and 1930s was the beginning of a long-term shift toward the view that the most effective approach to wildlife management is not culling or controlling certain species—it is the conservation, restoration, and improvement of those species' habitats.[31]

This debate also taught Grinnell's group a crucial lesson. Agencies such as the Bureau of Biological Survey—which had labored to cultivate relationships with hunters, cattlemen, woolgrowers, and private landowners—would remain loyal to and advocate a conservation philosophy that supported the goals of their clientele. The National Park Service—which was still searching for its identity, philosophy, and constituency—had proved far more receptive to the ideas of natural areas preservation and the conservation of all native species. Therefore, in the 1930s Grinnell and his students turned to the national parks as spaces to develop their vision for wildlife management based on a comprehensive new approach to habitat conservation.[32]

WILDLIFE MANAGEMENT IN THE NATIONAL PARKS

Wildlife conservation provided a rationale for the establishment of several early national parks, including Yellowstone and Denali, but most were created to protect spectacular scenery or promote tourism. During the Park Service's early years, architects and engineers, not ecologists, were the agency's most influential professionals. Their projects obviously affected wildlife, but they had little knowledge about park fauna and no coherent plans for conservation. Superintendents outlawed poaching and grazing—much to the chagrin of local residents—but they also fed elk, herded bison into corrals, kept deer in cages, poisoned coyotes, permitted trapping by rangers, and constructed bleachers for viewing bears feeding at garbage dumps. For the first fifteen years of its existence, the Park Service had no coordinated science or resource management programs, and its wildlife conservation efforts were, at best, ad hoc.[33]

In this way, the Park Service was similar to the federal government's other major land management agency, the U.S. Forest Service. Both agencies set aside small tracts as research natural areas for studies of native flora and fauna, but neither established a coherent scientific research, education, or management program. For wildlife projects and services, both contracted with the state departments of fish and game or the Bureau of Biological Survey. This created potential competition between the state and federal wildlife agencies, but many states still had greater administrative capacity than the federal government in this area, and officials usually took pains to emphasize their cooperative efforts. State fish and game departments benefited from cooperative arrangements with the Park Service and the Forest Service that enabled them to maintain their traditional authority even on areas otherwise administered by the federal government. Yet state projects on federal lands usually involved limited and discrete game protection and predator control projects. They were neither coordinated nor comprehensive management programs.[34]

No individual played a more important role in changing these policies in the national parks than Joseph Grinnell, who conducted the first systematic surveys of the fauna in Yosemite and other California parks. He came to believe that the national parks offered the best remaining opportunities to protect large areas where the whole "biotic mosaic" would survive "uninjured—to the benefit of all its constituent species and populations." Around 1915 Grinnell began a regular correspondence with Park Service officials, and by the end of his career he had become what the historian Alfred Runte has called "the conscience of the National Park Service." Through his persistence, he persuaded Yosemite officials to support public education, outlaw trapping, curtail predator control efforts, and develop restoration programs for species, such as beavers, that had disappeared elsewhere. "You must forgive me for thus expressing concern about things to do with administrative policies in Yosemite Park," Grinnell wrote to Superintendent Charles G. Thomson in 1929, "but the fact is that I feel a sort of proprietary interest in the welfare . . . of the wild animal life in Yosemite."[35]

Some of Grinnell's most important contributions came indirectly, through the work of his former students. In 1929 three of his protégés—George Wright, Joseph Dixon, and Ben Thompson—began a survey of faunal conditions in the national parks (see figure 10). Two years later they moved into offices in the Park Service's Branch of Research and Education, run by Ansel Hall, on the campus of the University of California, Berkeley. In 1932 the agency's director, Horace Albright, recognized Wright and his colleagues as the Wildlife Division of the National Park

FIGURE 10.
George Wright interviewing Maria Lebrado, popularly known as
"the last Yosemite Indian," in 1929. Photograph taken by Joseph
S. Dixon. Courtesy of the National Park Service.

Service. The Park Service's first venture into ecological science began on a shoestring budget with money Wright donated from his family's fortune. But he was no
dilettante. While still in his twenties, he led the Wildlife Division in developing a
new approach to conservation, based on habitat protection, restoration, and
management in nature reserves.[36]

   This approach involved four steps. First, Wildlife Division members described
the pre-European ecological history of a park, with a focus on the area's indigenous
fauna. They regarded this as the "original status," or baseline, necessary to measure
subsequent changes and develop conservation and restoration objectives. Next they
searched for information on the "history of fauna under man's influence" in the
park since European contact. Then they conducted an extensive biological survey
to determine the current status of the park's fauna. Finally they developed a management plan designed to meet a set of conservation goals. The notion that a management plan should seek to achieve a set of clearly defined objectives was itself

groundbreaking. In 1932 the Wildlife Division published the first comprehensive description of this approach, *Fauna of the National Parks of the United States*, or simply *Fauna 1*.[37]

Wright, Dixon, and Thompson intended *Fauna 1* to be the first in a series of publications on wildlife in the national parks. The field of wildlife management was just beginning to coalesce, and given the sorry state of wildlife in the parks, they had an almost endless amount of work. Of all their studies, however, *Fauna 1* and its successor, *Fauna 2* (*Fauna of the National Parks of the United States: Wildlife Management in the National Parks*), had the greatest impact. These publications built on Grinnell's writings on science and conservation, as well as the work of many others, including Victor Shelford, Charles Adams, and Aldo Leopold. Yet they also included a set of insights and approaches so original that historians who have studied these documents regard them as a rare, even unprecedented, "cognitive leap" in conservation thinking.[38]

Consider a few of these insights. The Wildlife Division members described how landscape fragmentation could lead to local extinctions and worried that geographically isolated populations might disappear, even from protected areas. They noted that the national parks did not constitute whole ecological units and therefore recommended the expansion of park boundaries to match patterns in the landscape. They documented external influences on the parks, and based on Shelford's recommendations, they called for the establishment of core research reserves surrounded by buffer areas. They proposed that the Park Service should select new units based on biological criteria, such as species representation, and that managers should maintain and monitor parks as ecological baselines. They cautioned against the introduction of exotic species and worried about the genetic consequences of moving individual members of native species from one place to another. They knew that animal populations exhibited dynamic fluctuations, but they worried that when populations dropped below a certain level they could die out due to random factors. Wright suggested that for some populations, this threshold level may be around five hundred breeding pairs, the same number conservation biologists independently identified five decades later. Finally, the Wildlife Division argued that contrary to the principles of game management, no species should take precedence over another. Instead, the goal of wildlife management should be to restore the entire suite of native species in a park or nature reserve.[39]

The Wildlife Division's insights and approaches were all responses to two related problems in animal populations: artificial scarcity on the one hand and overabundance on the other. Some native species, such as antelope and bighorn sheep, had continued to decline despite the efforts of state fish and game commissions to regulate hunting, while others had proliferated, had become pests, and were even damaging the very habitats on which they depended. According to Wright, Dixon, and Thompson, both of these problems were consequences of an inescapable conundrum—"the sharing of a common habitat by man and animal." Habitat management, with the goal of preserving native species and restoring natural conditions, thus became the focus of their work.[40] ·

Unlike many of their contemporaries, such as Leopold, the Wildlife Division's members did not express much interest in the protection of wilderness for its own sake. Yet wilderness and wildlife became so intertwined in their work that it was often difficult to tell the two apart. In their foreword to *Fauna 1*, they wrote that they were developing a park management program to promote the conservation of "wilderness life." Were they talking about wildlife or wilderness? Like Grinnell, they argued that areas with the least human interference presented the best conditions for wildlife, but they also advocated intensive management in the form of "biological engineering." The division's members never distinguished wilderness preservation from wildlife conservation, and they never resolved the tension between hands-on and hands-off management strategies. These issues reemerged decades later in the California condor conservation debate, discussed in chapter 5, with yet another Grinnell protégé playing the role of a leading protagonist.[41]

The Wildlife Division met with considerable success during its short tenure. In 1931 Albright acknowledged the national parks' role as "the last stand" for many native species. Three years later, his successor, Arno B. Cammerer, adopted the twenty management recommendations contained in *Fauna 1* as official Park Service policy, and the book soon became a "working bible" for Park Service wildlife programs. The division moved its offices from Berkeley to Park Service headquarters in Washington, DC, and by 1935 it had grown to twenty-seven biologists. Its members soon found themselves spending less time on research and writing than on reviewing proposals for new projects. They spoke out against many park development schemes, and they soon emerged as a "minority opposition group" within the Park Service.[42]

During the 1930s, Park Service administrators found their staffs divided between two equally idealistic factions: the developers, who wanted to increase public access, and the resource managers, who wanted more conservation. So, like good bureaucrats, they attempted to do both. The service obtained funds from Congress and labor from the Civilian Conservation Corps for a wide range of infrastructure projects, including remote trails, scenic highways, and grand hotels. It also enacted progressive new wildlife policies. By 1933 it had established twenty-eight research natural areas in ten national parks and acquired several new units—including Joshua Tree National Monument in California and Everglades National Park in Florida— based at least in part on ecological justifications. The Wildlife Division remained unsatisfied with many of these policies. Yet over the course of just five years, from 1932 through 1936, the Park Service went from having no coordinated science or resource management effort to possessing the most innovative wildlife conservation program of any government agency.[43]

In 1935 Grinnell wrote to Wright to congratulate him on his accomplishments and express his pride in his former students. He praised Wright's dedication to "high ideals," including "the aesthetic and educational, as well as the more 'practical'" aspects of wildlife management. "I would far rather trust men of such convictions and background," Grinnell wrote, than those "trained under game-hunting auspices or under 'control' organizations." "The supreme 'hope' for pure, uncontaminated wildlife conservation," he concluded, "is the National Park Service, under its Wildlife Division."[44]

It was not to last. In 1936 Wright died, at the age of thirty-one, in an automobile accident near Big Bend National Park in Texas. Thompson, Daniel Beard, Victor Calahane, Adolph Murie, and others continued the work of the division, but by 1938 it had dwindled to just ten biologists. The following year, the Franklin D. Roosevelt administration launched a reorganization scheme for the Department of the Interior that renamed the Bureau of Biological Survey the U.S. Fish and Wildlife Service (FWS). As part of this effort, Cammerer agreed to transfer the Wildlife Division from the NPS to the FWS. With the division gone, the Park Service dropped the words *Research and* from the title of its Branch of Research and Education.[45]

The Fish and Wildlife Service's first chief, Ira Gabrielson, had always viewed the Wildlife Division's work with skepticism bordering on hostility for its subversive departure from game-oriented conservation objectives. Most conservation programs had their budgets slashed during World War II, so Gabrielson took the opportunity to allow the Wildlife Division to wither from a lack of funding. The Park Service rehired eight biologists who had been forced to leave the division, but repeated bureaucratic reorganizations had demoralized the remaining participants. After the war, the Park Service developed its Mission 66 initiative, which called for enormous infrastructure investments to increase access for millions of newly affluent, newly mobile Americans by the time of the agency's fiftieth anniversary, in 1966. Many NPS veterans view this as a golden age for the service, but for wildlife advocates it was a "period of eclipse." The service scrapped most of the reforms it had adopted in the 1920s and 1930s and reduced its support for research. References to the Wildlife Division's work disappeared from most Park Service documents and faded from its institutional memory. Some officials believed that the division had gone too far, while others remained reluctant to acknowledge the ecological value of the parks for fear that conservation would interfere with other agency priorities. As late as 1972, the Park Service's aging patriarch, Horace Albright, insisted that the national parks were not created to "preserve an 'ecosystem.'"[46]

WILDLIFE REFUGES

The New Deal spawned several other wildlife conservation initiatives, including the establishment of a vast system of national wildlife refuges under the authority of the Bureau of Biological Survey. Before 1930 many wildlife refuges were privately owned or administered. Sportsmen's clubs maintained hunting clubs, which they somewhat disingenuously called preserves, for the exclusive enjoyment of their members. State Audubon societies acquired lands in the Southeast and Gulf Coast regions to protect key bird breeding rookeries, and the National Audubon Society followed with its own acquisitions. Audubon groups also provided staff support for the few existing public refuges, including armed security guards charged with enforcing game codes. This practice often met with resentment in the divided local communities where the refuges were located, and the conflicts sometimes ended in violence.[47]

State governments had established a handful of small refuges in the late nineteenth and early twentieth centuries, but none were big enough to provide much habitat protection. As early as 1869, the federal government designated its first refuge, in Alaska's Pribilof Islands, to restore populations of fur seals and other marine mammals and to control the area's game market in the territory it had purchased from Russia two years earlier. It did not establish another refuge until 1903, when Theodore Roosevelt signed an executive order creating the country's first federal bird refuge, at Pelican Island, Florida. During his time in office, Roosevelt established fifty bird reservations, four wildlife refuges, eighteen national monuments, and one hundred forest reserves—in every case but that of the forest reserves using the Antiquities Act to designate new sites without congressional authority. These were pathbreaking contributions, but most of the sites Roosevelt established for birds and other wildlife were too small, isolated, or otherwise impaired, and it soon became apparent that they would prove inadequate for fostering the recoveries of depressed game populations.[48]

The federal government's role in habitat conservation remained limited during the Progressive Era due to several factors that hindered the creation of refuges on a larger scale. As we have seen, the courts had ruled that the states "owned" the wildlife within their boundaries, and legislators had no desire to infringe on states' rights or acquire lands that might pose a burden for future taxpayers. Many conservationists argued that instead of creating new refuges, the federal government should provide more aid to the state fish and game commissions for law enforcement. Even without these arguments, federal acquisitions probably would have remained limited for one crucial reason: few private landowners wanted to sell their property to the government. That is, until the stock market crash of 1929.[49]

A year before the crash, Aldo Leopold, who had been working for the U.S. Forest Service, left his job to conduct a national study on the status of wild game, funded by the Sporting Arms and Ammunition Manufacturers' Institute, which was concerned that the decline of waterfowl and other popular game could hurt the hunting industry. The following year, when he presented his findings to the sixteenth annual American Game Conference, he emphasized that collapses in waterfowl populations—down, by some estimates, from one hundred million to twenty million in the contiguous United States—were only partly due to overhunting. According to Leopold, hunting regulations were "already well developed as far as legislation can do it," but "control of other factors is not developed at all." These included "food, cover, predators, disease, and parasites." "*The one and only thing we can do to raise a crop of game,*" he concluded, in italics, "*is to make the environment more favorable.*" And by that, he meant habitat management. The conference's host, the American Game Protective Association, responded by requesting that Leopold form a committee to author a new national game policy. The committee's report, issued in 1930, stressed, above all, the need for habitat conservation.[50]

The timing was fortuitous. Conservationists were beginning to recognize that the economic disaster of 1929 had created an unprecedented opportunity. Now there were willing sellers everywhere, and the U.S. government had a chance to acquire inexpensive land while reducing agricultural production—widely thought to be a cause of the agricultural crisis that had resulted in a 70 percent decline in farm income by 1934. Withdrawing "submarginal" farmlands from production had become a priority for the Franklin Roosevelt administration's New Deal recovery effort, and Leopold and his colleagues recognized that such lands could serve as habitat conservation areas.[51]

In 1933, Leopold joined the cartoonist Jay "Ding" Darling and the publisher Thomas Beck on the President's Committee on Wild Life Restoration. The Roosevelt administration had launched the Beck, or "Duck," Committee, as part of the New Deal conservation initiative, but its recommendations went well beyond what Roosevelt had envisioned. The Duck Committee recommended that the federal government appropriate fifty to seventy million dollars for the purchase of submarginal farmlands as wildlife refuges for the conservation of all species, not just valuable or popular game. That summer Leopold accepted a position as the new chair of game management at the University of Wisconsin, and Darling became the director of the Bureau of Biological Survey. The Duck Committee—which now included a prominent bureaucrat, a prominent academic, and a prominent publisher—was well positioned to influence policy.[52]

Congress had already taken a few small steps to facilitate habitat conservation. In 1924, legislators had allotted funds for the creation of a new refuge on the upper Mississippi River. In 1929 Congress passed the Migratory Bird Conservation Act, or Norbeck-Anderson Act, which authorized federal expenditures to protect migratory bird habitats in the form of "inviolate" sanctuaries. Within a year, Bureau of Biological Survey officials conducted studies for land acquisition in twenty-four states and approved the acquisition of two sites, while executive orders designated two new refuges on federal lands. Despite these achievements, the bureau's program was hurtling toward a barrier. Congress had allocated only one million dollars per year for ten years for the program, and most legislators still believed that this minor expenditure would be sufficient to "care for the more pressing and essential needs of the birds" and other wildlife.[53]

Officials at the bureau realized that their work would receive more support in Congress if they could find a way to fund the refuges outside the federal budget. For a model, they looked to the state fish and game commissions, which for decades had generated funding through the sale of hunting and fishing licenses. In 1934 the bureau endorsed the Duck Stamp Act, which created a fee for licenses to hunt on federal wildlife refuges. Congress followed this act with a series of similar laws—including the Pittman-Robertson Act of 1937, which taxed sporting goods and ammunition, and the Dingell-Johnson Act of 1950, which did the same for fishing tackle. These laws created a reliable revenue stream for the refuges and cultivated a constituency of sportsmen who would support the bureau's efforts to improve hunting and fishing conditions.

Bureau officials also helped convince Congress to enact legislation that would facilitate the growth and development of federal wildlife refuges and give the agency a broader mandate. In 1934 Congress passed the Fish and Wildlife Coordination Act, which authorized the federal government to take a variety of actions to increase the supply of game—such as research, restoration, and consultation with other agencies. The act's primary purpose was to mitigate the negative effects on wildlife that resulted from modifications to rivers, streams, lakes, and other bodies of water. It was the first law that gave the federal government the general authority to undertake a wide range of wildlife management activities, including habitat conservation.[54]

As the bureau's chief, Darling played a prominent, and highly successful, role in efforts to establish new wildlife refuges. In 1934 the Roosevelt administration allocated twenty-five million dollars in emergency funds for land purchases, and within a year the bureau acquired 840,000 acres, divided into thirty-two units. The bureau also conducted a national study of potential new refuges, and in California alone it identified nineteen sites covering 198,000 acres. Many of these parcels, such as those around Klamath Lake in Northern California, included drained wetlands that had once attracted multitudes of birds. But not all were formerly prolific habitats. As pressure to expand the agricultural bailout increased, the term *submarginal lands* likewise expanded, to include almost any distressed, degraded, or abandoned farm. Between 1929 and 1945, the federal government acquired 4.7 million acres of new wildlife refuges in this way—almost 50 percent of the land it has ever purchased for conservation throughout the course of American history.[55]

Roosevelt and his administration achieved a tremendous amount on behalf of various conservation causes. Many important advances came early in his presidency, but his second term was no less productive than his first. In 1936 Roosevelt convened the North American Wildlife Conference to set an agenda for future programs. The attendees included representatives from industry, universities, and the government who spoke on a wide variety of issues. One was the former Grinnell student and current Park Service biologist Ben Thompson, who led the "Problem of Vanishing Species" session. During his second term, almost 40 percent of FDR's executive orders dealt with conservation issues, broadly conceived—an all-time high for any U.S. presidential administration.[56]

Unlike his cousin Theodore, however, FDR was not a wildlife enthusiast. He claimed to care little about "the welfare, health, and happiness" of birds, and he often argued that the federal government should spend its money on more worthy problems, such as public health and urban poverty. He tolerated wildlife programs because he viewed them as a means to an end. And he was not alone. His liberal allies questioned the allocation of scarce resources for wildlife, and his conservative critics worried about overspending and creeping federal authority. Even Darling expressed concern that an overly ambitious conservation agenda, such as the one that Leopold increasingly supported, could result in too much federal control. "You are getting us out into water over our depth by your new philosophy of wildlife environment," Darling warned in a letter to Leopold. "The end of that road leads to socialization of property which I could only tolerate willingly if I could be shown that it would work."[57]

For all his accomplishments, Darling served just two years under Roosevelt as the director of the Bureau of Biological Survey. Ira Gabrielson assumed his position in 1935 before becoming the first director of the reorganized U.S. Fish and Wildlife Service, in 1940. Gabrielson was, in many ways, a traditional "hook and bullet" conservationist. He saw recreation as the highest use of fish and game and continued the agency's predator control efforts. Under his leadership, however, the service expanded its programs to nearly every area of wildlife conservation, including some once considered solely under state or National Park Service jurisdiction, such as the conservation of imperiled species.

In 1932 the bureau acquired the Red Rock Lakes National Wildlife Refuge in Montana, which provided seasonal habitat for a remnant population of trumpeter swans. It also collaborated with the National Audubon Society on several initiatives to protect rare and declining species. Gabrielson's staff worked for the passage of the Bald Eagle Protection Act of 1940 and authored popular publications that drew attention to the issue. Yet efforts to protect charismatic bird species were exceptions to the rule. As late as 1961, the service's year-end report contained no references to any endangered species conservation efforts.[58]

Gabrielson's agency also developed an approach to habitat management that sharply diverged from that of the National Park Service's Wildlife Division. Unlike the Park Service, which saw its mission as administering the nation's most important natural areas and cultural sites, the Fish and Wildlife Service recognized that most of its refuges were degraded areas that would require intensive management to become productive once again. The service created and maintained these artificial habitats, or "duck factories," with labor supplied by the Civilian Conservation Corps and other government agencies. By the 1950s it was erecting dams, rerouting waterways, and cultivating crops, all to produce abundant waterfowl. It also deployed army surplus equipment from the Second World War—including helicopters, floodlights, and grenades—to contain its waterfowl in refuges that were often still surrounded by farms.[59]

By 1946, when Gabrielson left the service to become the president of the Wildlife Management Institute, he could point to numerous accomplishments. Over the next three decades he championed many more wildlife conservation efforts, and he was a founding member of the International Union for the Conservation of Nature. In 2000, *National Wildlife* magazine memorialized him as the person who "brought order to America's wildlife management efforts."[60] Yet his legacy remains mixed. The Fish and Wildlife Service that emerged in the 1950s and 1960s was, in large part, his creation. For a short time during those two postwar decades, it developed a clear sense of mission, identity, and connection with its patrons. It promoted itself a production-oriented agency that managed land to supply wild game for the use and enjoyment of sportsmen. But Gabrielson also disregarded the Berkeley circle's insights, dismantled the National Park Service's Wildlife Division, adopted an unsustainable engineering approach for habitat management on many wildlife refuges, and endorsed aggressive predator control programs based on scant scientific evidence. He was a skilled bureaucrat and effective advocate for conservation—but unlike Leopold or Wright or Grinnell, he was no visionary. The same could be said of the agency he helped build.

THE BERKELEY CIRCLE'S LEGACY

On May 29, 1939, Joseph Grinnell died of a heart attack at his home in Berkeley. He was only sixty-two years old. The following day, Robert Sproul, the president of the University of California, eulogized Grinnell as the person who had done more than any other "to promote public knowledge of wild life in the west, and to arouse public interest in its enjoyment and conservation."[61]

Grinnell's ideas lived on, through the students he trained, the research he published, and the institution he built. Yet he had always maintained a relatively low public profile, and several factors helped diminish his notoriety as a conservationist even after his death. Controversies in the Ecological Society of America and the American Society of Mammalogists muted the influence of Berkeley circle members and allies who called for more protection of natural areas and diverse species. The Fish and Wildlife Service's embrace of a production-oriented philosophy, including aggressive predator control and habitat manipulation, shaped the profession of wildlife management into the 1970s. The California Fish and Game Commission's shift away from its Progressive Era activist roots also probably contributed. But no single factor played a more important role in reducing Grinnell's posthumous recognition, particularly during the immediate postwar era, than the Interior Department's decision to relocate and later dissolve the National Park Service's Wildlife Division.

This was not, however, the end of the story, or of Grinnell's influence. In 1938 Aldo Leopold's oldest son, A. Starker Leopold, transferred from his father's alma mater, the Yale University School of Forestry, to the University of California to pursue his doctorate under Alden Miller, another former Grinnell student. Leopold received his PhD in 1944 and went on to serve as the Museum of Vertebrate Zoology's assistant curator of mammals, chief conservationist, and then acting director from 1965 to 1967. He spent most of his career at Berkeley, eventually taking Grinnell's place as California's most influential wildlife conservationist. He was his father's son: an avid sportsman, eloquent author, passionate conservationist, and savvy political actor who cultivated an expansive network of friends and colleagues. In 1963, Secretary of the Interior Stuart Udall appointed Leopold chairman of an advisory board to assess the status of wildlife conservation in the national parks. The board titled its report *Wildlife Management in the National Parks,* though today most people refer to the document simply as the Leopold Report.[62]

The Leopold Report contained almost no original information or insights. There was little specific to say. The Park Service knew less about the wildlife in its parks in the 1960s than it had during the 1930s, so Leopold and his colleagues possessed little data from which to draw new conclusions. They did know, however, that the parks were still facing the same old problems—too many of some animals but too few of others, and too much environmental manipulation based on too little evidence—that the Wildlife Division's members had identified a generation earlier. They also knew that the service had made little progress in defining the goals, policies, and methods of its wildlife management activities. The report sought to raise awareness about ecological problems in the national parks—including the continuing issue of predator control as a management strategy in many units and the effects of overdevelopment associated with the Mission 66 program—and the need for better-coordinated programs based on scientific research.[63]

The Leopold Report revived and repackaged the Berkeley circle's insights from the 1910s, 1920s, and 1930s. It returned to the themes of Grinnell and Tracy Storer's 1916 manifesto, "Animal Life as an Asset of the National Parks," and echoed ideas about natural areas, ecological baselines, imperiled species, and habitat conservation from the Wildlife Division's *Fauna of the National Parks* series. In some cases, the Leopold Report reproduced the Wildlife Division's prose almost verbatim. Its most famous passage argues that "the biotic associations within each park [should] be maintained, or where necessary recreated, as nearly as possible in the condition that prevailed when the area was first visited by the white man." Many readers today rightly bristle at the report's ethnocentric viewpoint that national parks should represent the state of nature first encountered by "the white man." Yet for Leopold, as for Grinnell, the preservation of pre-European "biotic associations" was more an attempt to preserve history than to erase it. "A national park," the report concluded, "should represent a vignette of primitive America."[64]

What differentiated the Leopold Report from *Fauna of the National Parks* was not its content or even its implementation but its reception. By the time the advisory board completed its work, officials, critics, and patrons of the Park Service, including a new generation of activists and watchdogs, had become much more receptive to these kinds of conclusions. Six months after the report's publication, the National Academy of Sciences completed an assessment that came to similar conclusions and added weight to the advisory board's findings. The National Park Service responded by adopting the Leopold Report as official policy—just as it did with *Fauna 1* three decades earlier.[65]

The Leopold Report was a foundational document in the postwar conservation movement, but its most important contribution was only partly related to national park management. It is best remembered today for having reinforced the link between wildlife and wilderness—between native species and natural areas—which American ecologists and conservationists had begun developing and promoting decades earlier. The report helped provide a scientific rationale for land preservation during the debate over the Wilderness Act, which Congress passed in 1964, and it revived the idea of national parks as sanctuaries for imperiled species. Over the next two decades, habitat protection efforts in the new fields of conservation biology and environmental law linked wildlife and wilderness even further.

In 1967 Leopold accepted a position as the Park Service's chief scientist, and under his influence it seemed that the agency might undergo a qualitative change. A year later, however, he resigned and returned home in frustration. In 1969 the service once again reorganized and demoted its science program, including its wildlife research and management branch. Eleven years later, a Park Service report to Congress noted that "very few park units possess the baseline natural and cultural resources information needed to permit identification of incremental changes. . . . The priority assigned to the development of a sound resources information base has been very low compared to the priority assigned to meeting construction and maintenance needs." The sentiment behind this observation was now at least seventy years old. As late as 1986, the Park Service official Rich Baker issued a call for assistance in identifying natural areas in California's national parks.[66]

In the years since, the Park Service has remained ambivalent about the role of science in policy and management, and its employees have continued to debate many of the same ideas that Grinnell and Storer first introduced in their "Animal Life" manifesto, now almost a century ago. Some reform efforts have come from dedicated employees inside the Park Service, but much of the progress that has occurred there has resulted from outside pressure. It was not until the 1970s and 1980s, when the courts began to force state and federal agencies to comply with new environmental laws such as the Endangered Species Act, that policy and management, particularly in the key area of habitat conservation, began to change in more substantial ways. This is the subject of chapter 4.

CHAPTER FOUR · The Laws of Nature

On December 28, 1973, President Richard Nixon addressed a festive crowd of Republicans and Democrats who had gathered during Congress's holiday recess to witness his signing of the federal Endangered Species Act. "Nothing is more priceless and worthy of preservation," Nixon declared, "than the rich array of animal life with which our country has been blessed." His administration had worked with states and nongovernmental organizations to attract bipartisan support for a law that would "provide the kind of management tools needed to act early enough to save vanishing species." According to the Michigan representative John Dingell, "scarcely a voice [had] been heard in dissent" of the bill in the House of Representatives. In July it passed the House by the whopping margin of 390 to 12, and in September it sailed through the Senate by a unanimous voice vote of ninety-two to zero.[1]

The environment was not the only area of government reform during the dynamic phase in American legal and institutional history bookended by the John Kennedy and Gerald Ford administrations, but it probably saw the most sweeping change. Between 1964 and 1980, Congress passed twenty-two major pieces of environmental legislation. These laws introduced regulatory schemes, as in the Clean Air Act and the Clean Water Act; resource management programs, as in the Wild and Scenic Rivers Act and the Marine Mammal Protection Act; funding mechanisms, such as the Land and Water Conservation Fund; and administrative procedural mandates, as in the National Environmental Policy Act. Congressional action also resulted in the establishment of new federal agencies, including the Council on Environmental Quality, the National Marine Fisheries Service, the Federal Energy Regulatory Commission, and the Environmental Protection Agency.[2]

The Endangered Species Act was part of this broad transformation. Yet of all the changes that occurred during the golden age of environmental legislation, the ESA stands out in at least three important ways. Unlike most environmental laws, it took an explicitly ethical approach to wild nature. The conference committee's report on the bill called for "a certain humility" among humans who had become the "custodians" of the planet's species and ecosystems. "Like it or not," the authors concluded, "we are our brothers' keepers, and we are also keepers of the rest of the house." The ESA was also unusual in that it prohibited the consideration of economic factors in conservation programs; all imperiled species were to be preserved, no matter the cost. Finally, the ESA offers perhaps the best example from this period of bold legislation leading to unintended consequences. Few of those who wrote, lobbied for, voted for, or signed the ESA understood its implications—and almost everyone involved underestimated its future impact. Within five years, the ESA would go from a relatively minor and universally popular law to one of the country's most powerful and controversial environmental statutes. It was also, according to the U.S. Supreme Court in *Tennessee Valley Authority v. Hill*, "the most comprehensive legislation for the preservation of endangered species ever enacted by any nation."[3]

Why did the ESA become so unexpectedly powerful and controversial? Scholars have usually offered two answers to this question. First, although legislators pledged to protect all plant and animal species, they failed to grasp the number of species, including some with little economic value or charisma, that would eventually qualify for protection. Second, the ESA's authors imbued the act with clear and bold language but did not foresee that such unequivocal language would require courts to interpret its provisions broadly, in some cases with considerable social costs.

This chapter offers a third explanation, which builds on and complements the previous two. The ESA became so powerful and controversial, in part, because few of its early supporters or framers recognized that it would evolve into a law that protected not only listed species but also the habitats—including lands, waters, and resources—on which those species depended. Habitat protection played a role in the ESA from its conception, but in the decades after the act's passage, its habitat and ecosystem protection provisions expanded dramatically through legislative amendments, administrative rules, and court decisions. Conservationists still complain that the ESA's regulations and enforcement are too weak to achieve the level of habitat protection necessary for preserving biological diversity—and they are probably right. Yet the changes that have occurred in this area since the ESA's passage have been both sweeping and consequential. The ESA has had dramatic effects on land and wildlife conservation in the United States. But this story also shows that, rather than constituting a sharp departure from the past, the act continued a decades-long trend of elevating habitat into a key concept in American environmental science, law, and politics.

This chapter focuses on the political history of the ESA and its role in the growth of habitat conservation programs in the United States since the dawn of the environmental era. Although the pages that follow often refer to events that are national in scope, many of the important episodes occurred in California. In some cases the state has served as an innovator or outlier, and in others it exemplifies broader trends. In all cases, it is central to the larger, national narrative.

THE ORIGINS AND PROVISIONS OF
THE ENDANGERED SPECIES ACT

While the first Earth Day, in 1970, served as the symbolic start of the modern environmental movement, the cluster of social movements commonly recognized today as environmentalism had started to develop more than a decade earlier. The World War II and immediate postwar era represented a period of retreat for New Deal–era conservation efforts, such as those of the former Wildlife Division of the National Park Service. By the late 1950s, however, the community of scientists and activists concerned with land and wildlife conservation was beginning to grow again. This created an essential context for the popular concern and legislative activism of the following two decades.[4]

A series of publications during this period raised awareness about the status of wildlife and called for stronger conservation efforts. In 1942 the Fish and Wildlife Service published *Fading Trails: The Story of Endangered American Wildlife*, which described the declines of several large game and charismatic species. Peter Matthiessen's *Wildlife in America*, published in 1959, drew attention to the plight of a much larger range of nongame species—particularly those in danger of extinction through habitat loss or predator elimination programs. In 1962 Rachel Carson's classic book, *Silent Spring,* exposed the unintended effects of industrial chemicals on wildlife. A year later the Leopold Report revived and repackaged the Berkeley circle's ideas about wildlife for a new generation of scientists and managers. In 1965

A. Starker Leopold's former student Ray Dasmann published *The Destruction of California,* a widely read book that described the ecological consequences of the state's postwar demographic and economic explosions.[5]

Increasing awareness and concern led to unprecedented growth in environmental science and conservation organizations. Between 1968 and 1986, the total number of conservation organizations in the United States rose 109 percent, from 185 to 387. Some of these groups specialized in particular issues, places, or species, while others focused on research, education, policy making, litigation, or land acquisition. Individual organizations also grew. The Ecological Society of America, for example, quadrupled its membership between 1945 and 1960. By 1990 the Nature Conservancy, which had begun as a preservation committee within this society, was the world's largest nongovernmental organization dedicated to biodiversity and habitat conservation.[6]

By the mid-1960s, diverse groups were calling for legislation to address a variety of environmental problems. At the time, wildlife was already the most regulated natural resource in the United States. The expansion of federal laws and lands during the New Deal era gave federal agencies a greater role in wildlife management. Yet the states remained the constitutional sovereigns, with a long history of court decisions ensuring their legal authority over, public trust responsibility for, and even ownership of the fish and game within their boundaries. At the beginning of the environmental era, therefore, the fundamental question for legislators pondering additional national wildlife regulations was how to improve conservation in a complex federalist system.[7]

Unlike the states, Congress does not have a general police power. It does, however, have enumerated powers under which it can enact legislation that supersedes state laws. By the 1970s, courts would agree that the Constitution provided Congress three powers under which it could pass fish and wildlife laws: it had the right to protect the federal government's property, it had the authority to enact international treaties, and it had the jurisdiction to regulate commerce among the several states. Of the clauses that guaranteed these three powers, the commerce clause was the most general in its wording and therefore had the potential for the broadest application. In the 1930s, under pressure from the Franklin Roosevelt administration, the courts embraced an expansive interpretation of this clause. Over the next sixty years, the Supreme Court deferred to Congressional authority in every case, without exception, where the outcome could conceivably affect interstate commerce. During the golden age of environmental legislation, the commerce clause was the closest thing the federal government had to a general police power, and it provided a constitutional justification for dozens of new laws, including the ESA.[8]

Although the federal government had a legal rationale for getting involved in wildlife conservation, disagreement remained about how far it should extend its authority. Congress responded by adopting three approaches that would form the foundation for federal wildlife law. It bolstered state laws by authorizing federal enforcement in cases that involved interstate trade, provided funding and logistical support for state conservation efforts, and facilitated the acquisition and management of public lands where state and federal agencies could engage in cooperative conservation programs. With each new law, both the states and the federal government increased their authority and capacity for wildlife management.[9]

In 1964, federal legislators and bureaucrats undertook three measures that created a context for future endangered species and habitat conservation. Congress passed the Wilderness Act, which promised to protect large tracts of public land for "primitive" recreation and wildlife habitat. It established the Land and Water Conservation Fund, which enabled the acquisition of new areas for recreation, conservation, and "the preservation of species of fish or wildlife that are threatened with extinction." And the Fish and Wildlife Service created the Committee on Rare and Endangered Species. The committee compiled a list of imperiled species, recommended an expansion of FWS programs to save species such as the whooping crane, and identified pollution, overhunting, and habitat loss as the main causes of species declines. The following year, Congress debated the first proposed federal law to protect endangered species.[10]

In 1966 and 1969, Congress passed the first two in a series of three increasingly ambitious endangered species acts. The Endangered Species Preservation Act (ESPA) of 1966 was the first federal law that focused on endangered species as a single, broad category. Previous laws had dealt with fish and wildlife more generally, without any special regard for species in danger of extinction, or had focused more narrowly on a particular group of imperiled species, such as eagles or marine mammals. The 1966 act required the FWS to develop a list of endangered species and promoted habitat conservation as a recovery strategy. It consolidated FWS refuges into a single National Wildlife Refuge System, outlawed the "take" of endangered species on refuges, and directed the service to manage its refuges for the benefit of listed species. It also required the FWS to consult with other federal agencies about projects that might affect endangered species and encouraged interagency cooperation wherever practicable.[11]

The Endangered Species Conservation Act of 1969 broadened the scope to include international affairs and commerce in protected species. It generated more opposition than the 1966 act, because it had obvious economic implications for the fur, tanning, and exotic pet industries, which objected to its trade restrictions. It enabled the addition of non-U.S. species to the endangered species list and authorized the inclusion of other species beyond just birds, fish, and mammals. Finally, it directed the secretary of the interior to organize a conference that would facilitate the conservation of endangered species around the world through further trade regulations. The conference took place in February of 1973 and later that year led to a landmark agreement known as the Convention on the International Trade in Endangered Species of Wild Fauna and Flora, which by 2012 had 175 signatory countries.[12]

Unlike with the 1969 act, there was little debate about the Endangered Species Act of 1973. The Nixon administration helped shepherd it through Congress, and the bill that emerged from the conference committee faced no significant opposition. A few legislators wanted assurances that it would respect states' rights, and some tinkering took place with the language in its definition of *take*. But none of the other issues so prevalent in today's endangered species controversies emerged during the floor debate. A series of legislators rose to speak for what they believed was a safe and popular cause—the protection of iconic species such as the bald eagle and the blue whale—but none seemed to recognize the bill's broader implications for land use or natural resource management. Scientists and scientific societies supported the ESA, but they too failed to comprehend its importance. The *New York Times* endorsed the bill during its preparation but barely noted its passage. Legal scholars seemed equally unimpressed. According to the then undersecretary of the interior, Curtis Bohlen, "there were probably not more than four of us who understood its ramifications" at the time.[13]

The 1973 ESA largely replaced the previous two acts. It contained a sweeping mandate, unconditional language, and regulatory requirements that could pertain to diverse economic activities. Indeed, the ESA is an unusual piece of legislation in that it is so clearly written, straightforward, general, and concrete. As legal scholars have often noted in the years since its passage, much of the ESA's power stems from its plain and unambiguous language, which offers little latitude for flexibility in administrative discretion or judicial review.[14]

The ESA has more than a dozen key provisions. Like other laws passed during the golden age of environmental legislation, it gives citizens and organizations standing to sue for enforcement. It authorizes the federal government to purchase habitat for listed species, calls for international cooperation, allocates funds, and establishes penalties and enforcement mechanisms. It defines *endangered species* as any member of the plant or animal kingdom that is "in danger of extinction throughout all or a significant portion of its range" and *threatened species* as those that are likely to become endangered "in the foreseeable future." These may seem like simple definitions—and compared to terms defined in many other environmental statutes, they are—but their meanings remain far from settled. As recently as 2009, for example, the FWS was still struggling to operationalize phrases such as "foreseeable future" and "a significant portion of its range." The ESA also outlines the processes for listing species as threatened or endangered and delisting species that have recovered to sustainable levels. These processes position the ESA as a temporary receivership program for species that have suffered under state authority and thus require the protection of the federal government.[15]

The ESA also directs the two federal agencies charged with enforcing its provisions—the FWS for terrestrial and aquatic species, and the National Oceanic and Atmospheric Administration (NOAA) for marine and anadromous species—to cooperate with the states "to the maximum extent practicable." This federalist clause was a crucial factor in gaining support for the ESA's passage because it recognized that endangered species conservation was not solely a federal affair. Indeed, some of the first endangered species programs in the United States began at the state level.[16]

In 1970 California became the first state to adopt endangered species legislation. The California Endangered Species Act (CESA)—one of a series of laws passed in the state for the conservation of flora and fauna and their habitats—prohibited the importation, possession, sale, or taking of any listed vertebrate species. Unlike the Progressive Era fish and game codes, these more modern endangered species laws set restrictions on a much wider variety of actions that might limit endangered populations. Several other states followed California in developing endangered species programs. Those that emerged as leaders—such as Massachusetts, New York, Connecticut, Oregon, Washington, and Hawaii—had strong fish and game departments, often with charismatic leaders and constituencies dedicated to non-game conservation. The threat of federal incursion also created an incentive for the states to adopt preemptive programs. By the time President Nixon signed the federal ESA, eighteen states had endangered species laws. In 1976 the Department of the Interior signed a cooperative agreement with eleven of them, and by 1999 at least forty-five states had some form of endangered species legislation.[17]

In addition to their interaction with the states, the ESA also describes the roles of the FWS and NOAA with respect to other federal agencies. Unlike previous statutes, it includes a binding clause that requires the FWS and NOAA to consult with other federal agencies regarding any project or activity that might jeopardize a listed species or adversely modify its habitat. In practice, informal consultations have become the norm. If the proposed project has the potential to pose a significant threat to a listed species, then the appropriate ESA agency must produce a "biological opinion" that describes the risks, issue a decision as to whether the activity constitutes a taking, and define the actions necessary to alter the project or mitigate its impacts.

Perhaps the most important part of the ESA is the section on take, which makes it illegal to "harass, harm, pursue, hunt, shoot, wound, kill, trap, capture, collect, or attempt to engage in any such conduct" toward a listed species in the United States or its territorial waters. Of all the activities listed in the definition of *take*, "harm" was the least well defined and, as such, had the potential for the broadest interpretation. More than twenty years passed before the Supreme Court ruled on what Congress meant by this word. The decision, discussed later in this chapter, was one of the most important in American conservation history.[18]

The ESA's key provisions give the FWS and NOAA broad authority, but these agencies have often taken a cautious and reluctant approach in their execution of the act. They have challenged state authority on certain issues, but they have never had the ambition or the resources to dominate or displace the more popular state fish and game departments. Even within the federal government, the two ESA agencies have conducted their work among a loose collection of diverse and divided institutions, many of which have aligned with state or local governments in key debates and resisted conservation programs that might hinder their missions. To understand this dynamic, we now turn to the years after the ESA's passage, when the golden age of environmental legislation gave way to a longer period of political conflict and administrative reform. During the 1980s and 1990s, controversies over the ESA's implementation emboldened efforts to roll back its authority, increase its flexibility, and expand its loopholes and exemptions.[19]

CONFLICT AND REFORM

Shortly after the ESA's passage, a few observers noticed that it could have considerable implications. In 1974 the ESA had its first significant test in federal court. In *United States v. Cappaert*, Judge Roger D. Foley issued a permanent injunction that enjoined the defendants from pumping groundwater near Death Valley National Monument, to preserve springs for an endangered desert pupfish. This was the first case in which the protection of an endangered species restricted the activities of individuals on private land. It was also the first time a federal court considered the

ESA as a tool not only to protect individual members of a listed species but also to prevent the adverse modification of that species' habitat. Little of value was at stake, however, in this remote area, and Foley's decision did not provoke much debate.[20]

For the first major endangered species debate of the environmental era, we must turn to the Tellico Dam snail darter controversy, which took place in the late 1970s. It pitted environmentalists and other opponents of the Tellico Dam project, on the Little Tennessee River, against the dam's supporters and its sponsor, the Tennessee Valley Authority. Congress passed a law that allowed the project to continue as planned, but only after the Supreme Court ruled that the act imposed a constitutionally valid prohibition on federal agencies' engaging in activities that jeopardized listed species. The episode ended in a political defeat for the dam's opponents, but it demonstrated that the ESA could serve as a legal tool for challenging powerful interests in government and industry. The snail darter controversy had other broad implications. It fueled a backlash among business groups and property rights activists who believed that environmental regulations had gone too far. Congress passed a few more environmental laws over the next several years, but the snail darter case helped bring an end to the golden age of environmental legislation. Finally, this case also began a new phase in the history of the ESA. In the years that followed, environmentalists sought to push the act further without risking its repeal, courts interpreted it broadly in ways that expanded its scope, and Congress tried to increase its flexibility and limit its economic impacts.[21]

In 1978 Congress amended the ESA for the first time. It added a provision that created a cabinet-level committee, which came to be known as the God Squad, that could exempt federal agencies from having to comply with the ESA under certain circumstances. Congress also increased the act's procedural requirements, making it more difficult to list new species. The following year, in a dramatic response, the FWS withdrew pending proposals to list 1,876 new species because it could not reach its decisions under the new rules within the two-year statutory time limit.[22]

Three years later Congress amended the ESA again, this time to increase its flexibility even further while reducing bureaucratic discretion. The 1982 amendments sought to make the act's language even clearer and more specific in several areas. They also included a new clause that allowed exemptions, or "incidental take permits," for proposed projects with habitat conservation plans. HCPs are mitigation schemes that aim to protect listed species, usually by conserving habitat through the creation of nature reserves, while enabling development to continue in other portions of the protected species' range. The HCP idea had existed for some time, but it came to legislators' attention as the result of a conflict near San Francisco.

Developers, planners, environmentalists, and biologists had become locked in a battle over the future of San Bruno Mountain, a popular open space that was also home to three listed butterfly subspecies. The developers proposed an HCP as a way to preserve the butterflies' habitats while proceeding with commercial and residential projects on other portions of the site.[23] The ESA's new HCP provision did not seem like a big change at the time, but it had enormous implications in the coming decades as HCPs gained in popularity.

Congress amended the ESA two more times, in 1988 and 2004, but these later amendments have proved less important. All four sets of amendments represented political compromises between legislators seeking to weaken the act and others aiming to strengthen it. The possibility of repeal, while remote, was never unthinkable, but the more likely threat was always an amendment that claimed to streamline the act while actually reducing its scope and effectiveness. By 1980, environmental organizations had realized that they would need to fight not only for the protection of endangered species but also, in the face of often hostile administrations, for the future of the ESA itself.[24]

A crucial moment came after the landslide midterm election of 1994, when Republicans gained control of the House of Representatives for the first time in four decades. The following year, several members of the new majority launched a legislative campaign against the ESA and other environmental laws. Conservative stalwarts such as Don Young of Alaska and upstarts such as Richard Pombo of California took the initiative. But their leaders, including Majority Whip Tom Delay of Texas and Speaker Newt Gingrich of Georgia, soon realized that this effort was reducing the party's popular support. According to Gingrich, the polling data were "overwhelming. Most Americans agree with the goals of the environmental movement." He quieted his colleagues, but he did not stop subsequent attempts to alter the ESA. Between 1995 and 2002 alone, members of Congress introduced at least fifty bills to reauthorize or amend the act, none of which passed.[25]

Despite this Congressional gridlock, the ESA has continued to evolve outside the legislative process, through rule making by government agencies, court decisions, and efforts by states to reassert their traditional authority and build new administrative capacities. Indeed, the ESA's history shows how federal laws can remain dynamic even without legislative intervention. Congress passed little environmental legislation in the 1990s. Yet even in the absence of congressional action in this arena, the Bill Clinton era administration fostered a vibrant period of reform now known as the era of regulatory reinvention. For endangered species, this meant a shift away from prohibitive, bureaucratic, eleventh hour, single species management toward a new model of flexible, collaborative, and proactive management focused on the conservation of ecosystems and habitats.[26]

Around this time, the ESA began to show signs of evolving into something the country had never seen before: a general conservation law. This was a function for which Congress had never intended it, and when the act fell short, it received criticism from across the political spectrum. Environmentalists considered it their most powerful tool for pursuing a wide variety of conservation objectives, and they fought repeated attempts to dilute or repeal it. But they also argued that the ESA agencies were doing a poor job of administering the statute, and environmental organizations launched hundreds of lawsuits to force more aggressive implementation. Scientists expressed concern as well. They worried that the ESA focused too much on single species instead of ecosystems and habitats, and complained that its rigidity precluded the kind of adaptive management necessary to incorporate new knowledge, manage dynamic ecosystems, and respond to changing conditions.[27]

The ESA also attracted criticism from the political right, but for different reasons and toward different ends. Conservative economists lamented its failure to consider the costs and benefits of endangered species protection in ways that would facilitate rational decision making and lead to more-efficient economic outcomes. Property rights groups argued that the act should not penalize individual landowners with endangered species on their lands, because doing so shifts the costs of conservation to individuals while the benefits accrue to society at large. Instead of rewarding people for protecting species and conserving habitats, they contended, the ESA antagonizes those whose cooperation is necessary to recover listed species. This turns endangered species into liabilities and creates a perverse incentive for landowners to eliminate species and destroy their habitats before those species receive protection. Industry groups and developers have issued many of the same criticisms, and they have long argued that the ESA is too absolutist and inflexible to accommodate economic development.[28]

These critiques seemed irreconcilable to many observers when Clinton took office in 1993. His interior secretary, Bruce Babbitt, a former Arizona governor, was familiar with battles over public lands and natural resources but arrived on the national scene during a time of escalating conflict. Federal agencies such as the U.S. Forest Service were under siege, jobs versus environment arguments were dividing communities, ESA-related lawsuits were beginning to drive natural resource management policy, and endangered species debates that once seemed contained had begun to proliferate and reverberate around the country. Babbitt soon realized, however, that two key groups in these debates, the scientists and the developers, saw many of the same problems in the ESA, only from different perspectives. Both wanted more proactive planning and less last-minute conflict, more assurances about future conservation efforts, less of an emphasis on single species and more of a focus on ecosystems and habitats, and more of a say in the decision-making process. These common concerns created opportunities not only for compromise on a case-by-case basis but also for a new approach to the conservation process.[29]

Babbitt embraced the idea that the ESA could, in fact, serve as a general conservation law for lands and natural resources, and he called it a "transcendent, overwhelming" mandate encompassing "all types of land use and development issues." He spent much of his time as secretary promoting the ESA's potential to serve as the framework for a national program of ecosystem management, based on collaborative planning and cooperative federalism. It was an approach he believed could improve conservation, reduce conflict, and protect "ecosystems while working with families and communities." Habitat conservation was central to this vision.[30]

THE POLITICS OF HABITAT

Secretary of the Interior Bruce Babbitt wanted to make the Endangered Species Act an "endangered ecosystems act." But how? By the time he took office, dozens of ESA-related cases were winding their way through the federal courts, the key participants in the national ESA debate seemed wedded to their positions, and the ESA itself had become a potent culture war symbol, which made compromise even less likely. It was unclear how much authority Babbitt had to order changes in his department's administration of the act, and even if the courts granted him broad discretion, the mechanisms for implementing such changes were not apparent. In the years that followed, however, three key issues emerged that clarified and strengthened the role of habitat conservation under the ESA.[31]

The first key development involved habitat conservation plans. The 1982 ESA amendments sought to make the act more flexible by allowing HCPs as a mitigation strategy, but in the years after the San Bruno Mountain agreement, which produced the country's first HCP, also in 1982, only a few planning processes began. Developers knew HCPs presented an option, but they had little incentive to engage in expensive and time-consuming processes that came with no regulatory assurance. Environmental groups grasped the potential benefits of proactive planning, but many believed that HCPs would ultimately weaken the ESA. Scientists remained divided on the issue, with some speaking out in opposition to HCP compromises and others seeing HCPs as a vehicle for scientifically based conservation planning on an unprecedented scale.

During most of the San Bruno debate, which began in 1980, the Fish and Wild-life Service remained reluctant to endorse HCPs as a new exemption process that could enable an end run around the ESA. By 1982, however, the FWS spokesperson Megan Durham could say that "everyone feels that this is really the wave of the future; that the FWS and the environmental groups and the developers will be working together on these conservation plans to conserve species—perhaps sometimes instead of listing them as endangered." In 1986 the service approved its second HCP, this time for the Coachella Valley fringe-toed lizard in the sand dunes near Palm Springs, California. By the early 1990s, HCP planning processes were under way in Nevada, Texas, and Washington. In the first decade, however, only fourteen plans received FWS approval. These early efforts tended to focus on small areas and single species, and they began only after lawsuits forced the parties to work together. HCPs received little support from the Ronald Reagan and George H. W. Bush administrations, and in the absence of leadership or motivation, the program languished.[32]

It took action at the state level, in California, to jump-start the national adoption of HCPs. Endangered species conflicts were mounting around the country, but no state had more at-risk species or more to lose from restrictions on real estate development, resource extraction, or agriculture than California. The California Department of Fish and Game (CDFG) warned that 71 percent of its state-listed species were decreasing in number, and biologists estimated that more than nine hundred of the state's native species were in "serious decline." Protecting each individually seemed out of the question. In 1991 a consortium of state and federal agencies in California signed the Memorandum of Understanding on Biological Diversity, which created an executive council and several bioregional councils to facilitate cooperative work on regional conservation planning.[33] That process was still beginning when a new conflict emerged that threatened to dwarf the previous controversies.

Between 1950 and 1990, the human population of Southern California increased from five and a half to seventeen million. Much of the development that accompanied this boom occurred on the semiarid shrublands of the region's coastal plains, interior valleys, and foothills. These areas of southern coastal sage scrub—a type of soft, silvery, low-lying chaparral—formed scattered pockets of vegetation within a coastal strip that extended less than a hundred miles inland from the Pacific Ocean. Coastal sage scrub habitat seemed to hold little monetary value for anything other than development, but it did host a diverse native biota that included endemic species such as the California gnatcatcher.[34]

California gnatcatchers, small insectivorous birds related to wrens, were still common in Southern California in the 1940s, but by 1990 only a few thousand remained, and they had disappeared from large areas of their former range. Biologists estimated that less than 20 percent of the region's coastal sage scrub was in habitable condition for gnatcatchers, but this still included up to 444,000 acres in Los Angeles, Orange, Riverside, and San Diego Counties. Coastal sage scrub covered some of the region's most valuable real estate, and about 80 percent of it was privately owned. With these statistics in mind, the Building Industry Association of Southern California braced for more conflict and offered a gloomy prediction. According to Lee Jones, a Building Industry Association consultant, a gnatcatcher listing would "inevitably lead to more confrontation, to hopelessly deadlocked habitat conservation programs, and to significant economic hardship. Litigation would be inevitable. Efforts to weaken the Endangered Species Act itself, which are already under way since the recent listing of the Northern spotted owl, would only gain momentum."[35]

In 1991 the state legislature amended the California Endangered Species Act to include a Natural Community Conservation Planning (NCCP) program. The state NCCP program would be similar to the federal HCP program in that most of its resources would go toward the establishment of reserves through land purchases, transfers, and easements, and an approved plan would receive an incidental take permit. The California program would be different, however, in offering more flexibility and in shifting the focus from single species to regional multiple species conservation.[36]

Republican governor Pete Wilson announced the NCCP program, on Earth Day 1991, as part of a new initiative he called Resourceful California. By that time, the CDFG had already begun working on a plan for coastal sage scrub in Southern California, but it was off to a shaky start, as several legislative attempts failed to provide adequate incentives for participation. In 1993 the FWS listed the gnatcatcher as threatened, but Babbitt supported the state planning process by promising to coordinate federal efforts under the NCCP umbrella, agreeing to issue a federal incidental take permit for a completed state NCCP, and threatening full enforcement of the federal ESA in the absence of a state plan.[37]

Over the next year, the state and federal governments accomplished together what neither could achieve alone: the completion of a landmark coastal sage scrub conservation plan. In 1993 Babbitt praised the NCCP process as "an example of what must be done across the country if we are to avoid the environmental and economic train wrecks we've see in the last decade." The following year, the FWS provided additional encouragement for participation in NCCPs and HCPs when it proposed its "no surprises" rule, which said that the service would not hold HCP signatories accountable for unforeseen problems that might occur after it issued an incidental take permit. This policy provided a strong incentive for participation by local governments and private firms that wanted regulatory assurance before they signed on to conservation plans or invested in new projects.[38]

By 1994, NCCP and HCP efforts were under way throughout Southern California. The Orange County plan, spearheaded by the Irvine Company in 1992, served as a model for open space preservation by private development firms. In 1995 the metropolitan Bakersfield plan became the country's largest HCP, covering seventeen species in a 408-square-mile planning region. By 2001 the San Diego Multiple Species HCP included eighty-five species, and even larger plans were under development in Nevada, Texas, and Arizona. HCPs also began to expand from one-time mitigation efforts covering a single project, species, or permittee into stakeholder-based, multispecies, collaborative processes administered by regional government consortia. These groups often linked HCPs to county general plans, which helped ensure their enactment and execution and worked to increase public participation in ways exemplifying the collaborative approach to conflict resolution that shaped so much of American environmental policy during the 1990s and 2000s.[39]

By 2010, NCCPs and HCPs covered or were proposed for much of Southern California—including most of San Diego County, almost half of Riverside County, and portions of Orange, Imperial, and Los Angeles Counties (see map 3). Together, these plans encompassed nearly one and a half million acres of conservation areas. Nationwide the number of HCPs increased from 14 in 1992 to 709 in 2010. FWS Region 8, which includes California and Nevada, accounted for 145. Most of the remaining 564 were in the Northwest, the Southwest, and the Southeast. The Great Lakes and the Northeast had a total of just seventeen HCPs, but planning efforts were only beginning in those areas. In less than two decades, the HCP program had grown from an obscure loophole in the ESA into a central feature of its implementation.[40]

The second key development that increased the ESA's role in habitat conservation involved the legal question of whether and to what extent the act protected not only listed species but also their habitats. This led to a related question, which was whether habitat protection would extend beyond federal lands and into private property. At stake again was the much broader issue of whether the ESA would

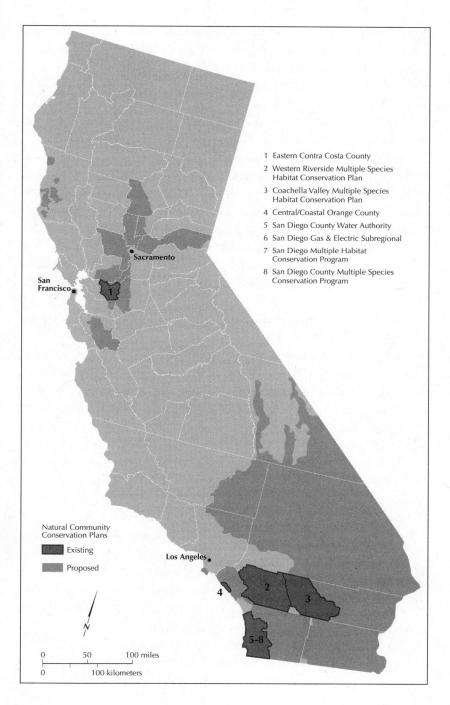

1 Eastern Contra Costa County
2 Western Riverside Multiple Species Habitat Conservation Plan
3 Coachella Valley Multiple Species Habitat Conservation Plan
4 Central/Coastal Orange County
5 San Diego County Water Authority
6 San Diego Gas & Electric Subregional
7 San Diego Multiple Habitat Conservation Program
8 San Diego County Multiple Species Conservation Program

Sacramento

San Francisco

Natural Community Conservation Plans

Existing

Proposed

Los Angeles

4

2

3

5-8

N

0   50   100 miles

0   100 kilometers

MAP 3.
Areas covered by or proposed for Natural Community
Conservation Plans in California by 2010.

serve merely as a species protection law or evolve into a habitat conservation and ecosystem management law. The answers to these questions relied, in part, on the meaning of the word *harm* in the ESA's definition of *take*. Did Congress intend for it to include only direct bodily damage or also indirect damage caused by habitat loss?[41]

The legislative history of the act offered some clues. The 1966 Endangered Species Preservation Act protected both listed species and their habitats, but only on certain federal lands, such as wildlife refuges. In the debate that preceded the passage of the 1973 ESA, however, legislators held a broader discussion about habitat loss. Democratic representative Frank Annunzio, of Illinois, expressed a common sentiment when he declared that "nearly a thousand species are endangered today because of man's interference with natural habitats, because of his greed, and because he fouls the air and the waters." The conference committee report reached a similar conclusion, stating that the purpose of the ESA was "to provide a means whereby the ecosystems upon which endangered species and threatened species depend may be conserved." Environmental activists, scientists, and lawyers and have cited this language as evidence that Congress intended to protect endangered species habitat regardless of where it was.[42]

The ESA's critics interpreted its language differently. Section 5 of the act authorized the secretaries of the interior and agriculture to purchase land for habitat protection. To some, this suggested that Congress had intended to protect habitat only through the acquisition of more federal land, not through the regulation of private land. The ESA's detractors also focused on the word *harm*, which was the vaguest of the prohibited activities in the act's definition of *take* and one of the only key terms in the ESA not derived from previous legislation. *Harm*, they argued, included the direct injury or death of an individual organism but did not extend to indirect damage caused by habitat loss.[43]

In 1981 the U.S. Court of Appeals for the Ninth Circuit, in San Francisco, upheld a district court injunction in *Palila v. Hawaii Department of Land and Natural Resources* that required the state to eradicate feral goats and sheep from forests surrounding the Mauna Kea volcano on the big island of Hawaii. The state administered the area in part for sport hunting of feral livestock, but the animals were gobbling up what remained of the native vegetation, denuding the soil, and imperiling an endangered species of finch-billed honeycreeper called the palila. The courts agreed that Hawaii's failure to protect the palila's habitat constituted harm as defined in the ESA. In 1988 the Court of Appeals for the Fifth Circuit, in New Orleans, reached a similar conclusion in a case that involved logging in the habitat of the red-cockaded woodpecker.[44] A legal precedent was starting to emerge, but the courts had not yet heard a case that addressed the issue specifically with respect to private lands.

In 1994 a new case, *Babbitt v. Sweet Home Chapter of Communities for a Great Oregon*, reached the U.S. Court of Appeals in the District of Columbia. In a split decision, the court ruled that the ESA's prohibition on take did not extend to habitat on private lands. This created a conflict between the Washington, DC, and San Francisco courts, so the case continued to the U.S. Supreme Court for a resolution. The justices found that Congress had failed to provide a clear definition of *harm;* the court thus turned to the question of whether the FWS had acted appropriately when interpreting vague language. Most of the justices found little evidence, in either the ESA's text or its legislative history, that Congress had intended to limit endangered species protection to death or injury by direct force. The six-to-three majority also noted that because "a word is known by the company it keeps," the meaning of *harm* must build on but not replicate other prohibited activities. *Harm* had a unique definition, they reasoned, which must include habitat modification.[45]

In the words of one legal scholar, *Sweet Home* brought an end to the "open season" on wildlife habitat that land developers and resource extraction firms had enjoyed for decades. Others were less sanguine. In a spirited dissent, Justice Antonin Scalia argued for a narrow interpretation of *harm* that required direct force, evidence of injury or death, and intent to break the law. More broadly, he lamented the threat *Sweet Home* posed to property rights and economic prosperity. "The Court's holding that the hunting and killing prohibition incidentally preserves habitat on private lands," he wrote, "imposes unfairness to point of financial ruin— not just upon the rich, but upon the simplest farmer who finds his land conscripted to national zoological use."[46] ESA opponents continue to echo Scalia's words, but ever since the *Sweet Home* decision, the act's definition of *harm* has included habitat degradation and destruction.

The third key issue that emerged in the 1980s and 1990s involved the designation of "critical habitat." The ESA requires that activities "authorized, funded, or carried out" by the federal government not "result in the destruction or modification of habitat . . . which is determined by the Secretary . . . to be critical." But what is critical habitat? Instead of defining it in 1973, Congress deferred to the ESA agencies, expecting them to determine the habitat necessary for any species. Two years later the FWS published its official definition of *critical habitat,* which it said included the air, land, water, or any "constituent elements thereof, the loss of which would appreciably decrease the likelihood of the survival and recovery of a listed species."[47]

During the ESA's early years, the FWS embraced critical habitat as a useful tool. FWS officials reminded observers that a critical habitat designation did not create new reserves or impose new regulations on private property. Its chief purpose was to alert federal agencies that an ESA consultation might be required for any project scheduled to take place inside the area it specified. In most cases, the service noted, such consultations would not significantly alter or delay the proposed projects. Yet from the outset, designating critical habitat proved to be a major logistical challenge. Estimating a species' population turned out to be much easier than mapping its distribution, and it soon became clear that scientists lacked adequate biogeographic data for most listed species, including even basic information about wildlife-habitat relationships.[48]

In its 1978 ESA amendments, Congress affirmed the importance of critical habitat while emphasizing the need for more flexibility to accommodate economic development. Legislators required that a species' critical habitat be designated at the time of its listing, amended the definition of *critical habitat* to include only those areas "essential for the conservation of the species," and precluded the ESA agencies from designating a species' entire range as critical habitat. Congress also allowed the interior secretary to avoid making a critical habitat designation if doing so seemed "not prudent" and expanded the criteria for critical habitat beyond scientific data, to include economic impacts. Congress did not call for a full cost-benefit analysis for every species, but the requirement to consider economic issues helped make the critical habitat designation process a unique—that is, a uniquely complicated and contentious—aspect of the ESA.[49]

ESA opponents continued to insist that critical habitat infringed on property rights and hindered economic growth. So the Reagan administration, which sympathized with this view, attempted to reduce the effects of critical habitat even further. It redefined *critical habitat* as the area necessary for a species' survival, not its recovery, authorized the FWS to refuse to issue a designation when it deemed critical habitat "not determinable," and required the service to consider current economic impacts and the opportunity costs of forgoing future economic activities in its decisions. ESA proponents responded that critical habitat designations were even more important than species listings and that species with critical habitat tended to fare better over time than those without it. They believed they had the law on their side, and they began mobilizing for the legal battles ahead.[50]

The FWS attempted to manage the increasingly volatile situation by reducing the number and scope of its critical habitat designations. By 1978 it had designated critical habitat for just twenty-nine of more than two hundred threatened and endangered species. In 1979 it began withdrawing controversial critical habitat proposals, and in 1986 only four of forty-five newly listed species received designations. By 1992 only 16 percent of all listed species had critical habitat, and by 2002 that number had declined to just 9 percent. To justify their decisions, officials argued that designations for most species were either not prudent or not determinable.[51]

In addition to reducing the number of new designations, the FWS also launched a broader political effort to diminish the role of critical habitat in its endangered species programs. It tried to convince skeptical scientists and environmentalists that designating critical habitat was divisive and unproductive and diverted scarce resources from more important tasks. It even attempted to define critical habitat out of existence with administrative rules. For example, the ESA prohibited federal agencies from approving or engaging in activities that "jeopardized" individual members of a listed species or resulted in the "adverse modification" of a listed species' critical habitat. The adverse modification standard was one of the act's clearest mandates for habitat conservation. Yet in 1986 the FWS announced that it considered jeopardy and adverse modification the same thing. Its critics pointed out that in cases where species had disappeared from portions of their historic range, the adverse modification standard was the only thing preventing further destruction of habitat essential for their recovery.[52]

In the 1990s and 2000s a series of lawsuits examined the scientific, legal, and bureaucratic complexities of critical habitat. A court decided the most dramatic and important of these, *Conservation Council for Hawaii v. Babbitt*, in 1998. By that time the FWS had listed seven hundred species of plants in the United States as threatened or endangered but designated critical habitat for only twenty-four. More than a third of the listed plants, 264 species, lived in Hawaii, but only three of these had critical habitat. The FWS announced that it intended not to designate critical habitat for 245 of the Hawaiian species because such designations would not confer any additional benefits and could even have detrimental consequences, such as encouraging vandalism or collecting. The U.S. District Court for Hawaii disagreed. It ruled that the ESA required critical habitat designations except in rare cases and warned that the FWS could no longer ignore this essential feature of the law.[53]

This decision led to a barrage of lawsuits that tested the limits of critical habitat. Some industry associations argued that the critical habitat process could serve as a constraint on regulation because it was the only part of the ESA that required the FWS to consider the economic impacts of its policies. But most conservative groups, such as the Pacific Legal Foundation, challenged the critical habitat process in court, forcing the service to retract some of its more expansive designations. In far more cases, however, environmental groups, such as the Center for Biological Diversity, won judgments that compelled the service to expand critical habitat areas. The courts also invalidated many of the administrative restrictions on critical habitat issued during the Reagan era. Within a few years of the *Conservation Council* verdict, critical habitat had emerged as perhaps the most controversial and litigious feature of the ESA.[54]

For federal government agencies, responsibility and power are not the same thing. Despite the broad new responsibilities it gained through the ESA, the FWS defended itself poorly in court, and each loss diminished its autonomy and discretion. It lacked the resources to fulfill most of the court orders to which it was subject, its backlog of unresolved designations grew, and its failure to comply with judgments led to threats that its employees would be held in contempt of court. In 1999 the service published a letter in the *Federal Register* describing the gravity of the problem and pleading for help. "We have been inundated with citizen lawsuits," it read. "The consequence . . . is that we are utilizing much of our very limited listing program resources in litigation support defending active lawsuits and Notices of Intent (NOIs) to sue relative to critical habitat, and complying with the growing number of adverse court orders." Almost all of the 504 comments submitted in response to this letter advocated stronger regulations and more critical habitat—hardly the reaction FWS officials had hoped to receive. Four years later the Interior Department's assistant secretary for fish and wildlife and parks testified that the critical habitat program was "'broken' and in 'chaos.'" As of this writing, the FWS still had no solution, Congress had offered no guidance, and federal judges were increasingly assuming control over the critical habitat process.[55]

The FWS's aversion to critical habitat stemmed from several sources. The most obvious was the simple political reality of how controversial and litigious it had become. But the FWS worsened the problem by failing to comply with the ESA. Courts responded by forcing the service to designate large areas of critical habitat, often with inadequate data. This exposed the FWS to further lawsuits for making arbitrary and capricious decisions in violation of the Administrative Procedure Act and the National Environmental Policy Act. The service continued to argue that critical habitat was unnecessary and redundant, but most judges ruled that it was a distinct and indispensible aspect of the ESA. These rulings forced the FWS to designate even more critical habitat with insufficient data, leading to even more criticism of its decision-making process (see map 4). It was a vicious cycle.

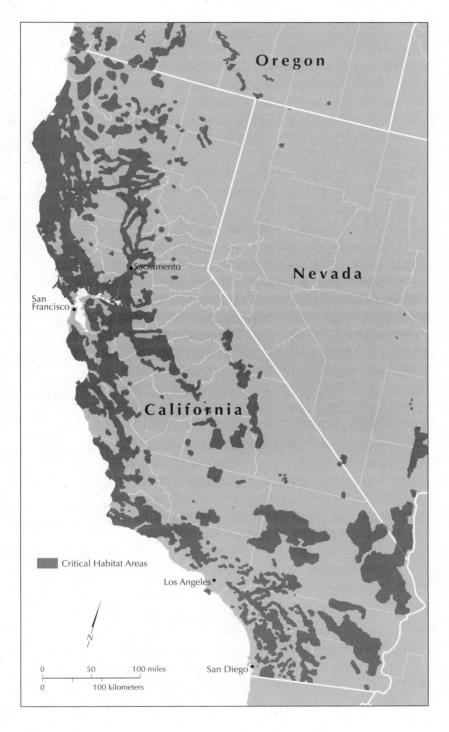

MAP 4.
Geographic areas designated as endangered species critical
habitat in and around California.

There is another equally important reason why the FWS continues to exhibit such distaste for critical habitat. Since the time of Ding Darling and Ira Gabrielson in the 1930s, federal wildlife officials have developed a strong preference for managing wildlife in refuges instead of regulating human activities that affect wildlife on multiple-use public lands or private property. Part of the service's inclination toward refuges over regulations results from its deference to the customary authority of state fish and game departments on nonrefuge lands. Over time, FWS officials have also learned that although refuge administration can be contentious, it is often less divisive than habitat regulation on lands that would otherwise be outside the service's jurisdiction. A final reason that FWS officials tend to prefer refuges over regulations is that beginning in the 1930s, but especially since the 1970s, an overwhelming body of science has convinced them that nature reserves offer the best hope for most endangered species.[56]

SCIENCE AND THE ENDANGERED SPECIES ACT

Conservation biology's roots extend back to the 1930s, but it only began to assume its contemporary form decades later. By the 1980s, conservation biology had become an international movement, with communities of scientists and managers in Australia, Europe, India, North America, and elsewhere adopting approaches that suited their national or regional context. In the United States, the generation of conservation biologists who came of age in the quarter century after the passage of the ESA had studied ecology but were dissatisfied with its lack of political engagement, knew the outdoors more as naturalists or backpackers than as hunters or fishers, and found themselves increasingly drawn to technological tools, such as computer modeling, in addition to conventional fieldwork. Unlike the generations of wildlife managers who came before them, many of whom had grown up in small towns, in rural areas, or on the still-wild fringes of expanding metropolitan areas, most of these new conservation biologists were middle-class kids from cities and suburbs who had grown up experiencing wildlife on occasional visits to parks and reserves.

The most important feature that distinguished the conservation biology of the 1970s and 1980s from what had come before was its emphasis on spatial analysis. From the outset, conservation biology was a spatial science. The modern era of conservation biology began in 1967, with the publication of Robert H. MacArthur and Edward O. Wilson's classic book *The Theory of Island Biogeography*. MacArthur and Wilson drew from multiple sources to develop a general theory of faunal colonizations and extinctions on islands. Islands were important because they had been the sites of most of the vertebrate extinctions documented in the historical and archeological record and provided natural laboratories for studying basic ecological and evolutionary processes in comparatively simple and bounded systems. The theory's mathematical elegance attracted many supporters. Perhaps even more important, it offered testable hypotheses. A small army of researchers went on to assess MacArthur and Wilson's theory through observational research, and it inspired some of the most famous experiments in the history of ecology.[57]

By the mid-1970s, conservation-minded scientists had adopted MacArthur and Wilson's model of islands as a metaphor for nature reserves. Some authors, including Wilson's protégé Daniel Simberloff, almost immediately noted conceptual problems with the comparison. Yet other field researchers, such as William Newmark, found empirical evidence that processes of local extinction similar to what MacArthur and Wilson described for islands were occurring in national parks and other so-called protected areas. Other authors, including the now-famous physiologist and biogeographer Jared Diamond, encouraged the use of island metaphors for advancing conservation theory. In a 1980 paper, Diamond and his coauthor, Michael Gilpin, wrote that the "fundamental assumption" of the new conservation theory was that "nature reserves act as habitat islands in an inhospitable sea of environment that has been modified by man."[58]

The comparison of islands to landlocked nature reserves was a tenuous leap. Yet it provided the framework for a series of theoretical advancements that helped foster the field of conservation biology as a spatial science. During the 1990s, the metapopulation approach, which viewed species as groups of populations linked through dispersal and interbreeding, superseded the theory of island biogeography in the scientific literature. Proponents of the metapopulation approach embraced a more nuanced view of landscapes, not as islands of safety surrounded by hostile oceans of human development but as complex mosaics comprising habitat patches, linkages, and barriers. These landscapes changed over time, and different species experienced them in different ways. Conservation biologists soon began using the metapopulation approach to determine the optimal design for nature reserves and to build population viability models for endangered species. Their work required new technological tools—satellite imagery, global positioning devices, geographical information systems, numerical modeling software, and powerful desktop computers with Internet access—as well as young minds capable of mastering them.[59]

The research theme that united conservation biologists in the field's early years was the creation and design of nature reserves and reserve networks. As early as 1972, Ray Dasmann, of the University of California, Santa Cruz, argued for the creation of natural reserve networks to protect endangered species and biological diversity by including representative samples of natural habitats. Other authors soon began to theorize about the optimal size and configuration of nature reserve systems in an ideal world. They also explored how species were using parks, refuges, and the landscapes around and between these spaces. Ideas and terms not discussed at any length since the 1930s, such as the creation of "buffer zones" to shield "core" protected areas, became the subjects of entire research programs. Some academic conservation biologists became so engaged in spatial methods that they found themselves working in geography departments in research universities.[60]

Expertise in spatial analysis made it possible for conservation biologists to contribute to land use planning. They began by working with nongovernmental organizations, such as the Nature Conservancy, to identify high-priority sites for acquisition and to design regional reserve networks. The Nature Conservancy also worked with state departments of fish and game, in California and elsewhere, to develop natural diversity databases that would facilitate habitat conservation for rare, endemic, and endangered species. In 1997 three well-known conservation biologists—Reed F. Noss, Michael A. O'Connell, and Dennis D. Murphy—published *The Science of Conservation Planning*. It was one of dozens of publications on the topic that signaled the arrival of conservation biology as a force in land use planning. The authors described several mechanisms for participation in planning processes, but their central focus was habitat conservation planning for endangered species. HCPs had become one of the main pathways, in addition to the listing and recovery planning processes, by which conservation biologists could shape the administration of the ESA.[61]

Environmental scientists and legal scholars often lament what they perceive as a gulf between their fields. Science and law must work more closely together, they say, if we are to develop better policies and practices based on the latest knowledge. Yet environmental law and science already have a long history of influencing each other in profound and consequential ways. This dialogue can seem obscure in the minutiae of the moment, but over the course of decades it is unmistakable. The history of the ESA, and of endangered species conservation in the United States more generally, provides an excellent example of this process at work. Science has helped generate support for conservation legislation, provided principles for policy and management, contributed evidence for legal proceedings, and supplied expertise to administrative agencies. Law has created a framework for the application of theories and findings, generated demand for usable knowledge, catalyzed the formation of new disciplines and institutions, and provided forums for scientists' participation in decision-making processes.[62]

The Fish and Wildlife Service's preference for refuge management over habitat regulation on nonrefuge lands is one expression of the profound influence science has had on endangered species policy and management. But the science-law relationship goes much deeper than that. It has shaped the organization of landscapes where people live and work, in the process reflecting and redistributing political power and creating new geographies of land use and management. Go a bit further and you will find that something even more profound is under way. The very concepts of endangered species and habitat, which are at the heart of this book, are in large part hybrid products of this law-science relationship. It is no longer possible to define either term without referring to both science and the law and the relationship between them.[63]

ENDANGERED SPECIES OR ENDANGERED HABITATS?

There are several reasons why the Endangered Species Act became one of the country's most powerful and controversial environmental laws. Legislators failed to foresee how many species would qualify for protection, even though by the end of 1973 federal officials had already protected more than one hundred endangered species under previous laws and were predicting hundreds or even thousands of additional listings. Buoyed by a political consensus about the need for stronger environmental regulations, legislators and their staffs passed a bill with bold and unequivocal language to protect those myriad species. The ESA's language compelled the courts to order administrative action even as the politicians who had voted for the bill and the bureaucrats who were responsible for administering it began to doubt the wisdom of their prior convictions.

Ultimately, the ESA became so controversial because at the time of its passage so few people anticipated that it would become not only an endangered species act but also an endangered habitats act. The ESA continued the trend of elevating habitat into a key concept in environmental science, law, and politics, and in the years after its passage a series of legislative amendments, administrative rules, and court decisions furthered this process. The second part of this book comprises four case studies of threatened or endangered species from different landscapes in and around California, including the conflicts that have developed over both their protection and the conservation of the lands, waters, and resources on which they depend. Like the ESA itself, these debates have been as much about endangered habitats as about endangered species themselves.

CHAPTER FIVE

The California Condor

From Controversy to Consensus

> Like large dark
> lazy
> butterflies they sweep over
> the glades looking
> for death,
> to eat it,
> to make it vanish,
> to make of it the miracle:
> resurrection . . .
>
> MARY OLIVER, "Vultures"

On Easter Sunday 1987, a team of scientists and Fish and Wildlife Service officials finally caught up with AC-9. Adult condor number nine, otherwise known as Igor, had developed an uncanny ability to evade his would-be captors. The team had pursued the seven-year-old male for months and lured him with regular offerings of fresh meat. But Igor, who had been captured and released twice before, refused to take the bait. It was the biologist Peter Bloom's job to catch the wary bird safely. Between recurring nightmares about all of the things that could go wrong—failed equipment, an injured colleague, a broken wing—Bloom had developed an approach based on hundreds of hours of observation and experimentation. He used a trap consisting of a covered earthen pit, a line of remote-controlled, cannon-powered nets, and the ripe carcass of a stillborn calf. He had built his trap on the rolling hills of the Bitter Creek National Wildlife Refuge, northwest of Los Angeles, a range-land reserve that the federal government had purchased just a few years earlier to protect the few free-roaming members of Igor's species. As Bloom waited, a group of team members watched anxiously nearby.[1]

Meanwhile, Igor was enjoying a lazy Sunday morning. He slept late, then spent several hours lounging on some sandstone rocks. Bloom knew where AC-9 was and what he was doing because a second group of biologists was watching the bird with binoculars and tracking his movements using the radio telemetry device clamped to his wing. Igor eventually left his perch and coasted north toward his feeding grounds in the foothills overlooking the San Joaquin Valley. He spotted the carcass,

FIGURE 11.

The trapper Pete Bloom (left) and the FWS biologist
Greg Sanders holding AC-9, the last wild condor in North
America, during his capture in April of 1987. Courtesy of the
Santa Barbara Museum of Natural History.

swooped down, landed a few yards away, and peered around suspiciously before
hopping over to the bait.

For a brief moment there was a blur of dust and feathers and nylon, but it was
finished almost as soon as it began. Bloom pulled the trigger to launch his nets,
pounced on the tangled bird, and stuffed him into an extra-large dog kennel in the
back of a van on its way to the Oxnard Airport (see figure 11). Igor had been the last

wild condor in North America. Now he was headed to the San Diego Wild Animal Park to join twenty-six other condors in a captive breeding program that proponents hoped would save the species from extinction. The team had decided not to send Igor to the Los Angeles Zoo, which was its original plan, so it could avoid the protesters there who were demanding that at least a few condors be left in the wild.[2]

The dramatic events of that spring afternoon represented the culmination of a more than thirty-year battle over how best to protect the California condor. By the middle of the twentieth century, the condor had become both an object of scientific study and an icon of the American wilderness movement. For decades these dual identities had existed in harmony, since most observers agreed that the condor's survival depended on the preservation of its wilderness habitat. Yet as the species' population dwindled, a controversy developed over the extent to which scientists should intervene on its behalf. As the environmental historian William Cronon has observed, "vigilant and self-conscious management" of endangered species may come into direct conflict with an ideology of wilderness that opposes any human intervention in wild nature.[3] The story of efforts to recover the California condor illustrates how these two seemingly compatible pursuits— wildlife management and wilderness preservation—unexpectedly clashed in the years following the passage of the Endangered Species Act (see figure 12).

This chapter explores the prehistory, origins, development, and resolution of the California condor conservation controversy. Its goal, and that of the chapters that follow, is to better understand endangered species politics by tracing the role of habitat conservation—especially through the establishment of nature reserves and other protected areas—in wildlife science, law, and management. Soon after the ESA's passage, habitat conservation emerged as an organizing framework for endangered species policy. Yet divergent visions about the meaning and purpose of habitat conservation persisted, in the condor's case creating an ideological rift between different groups of conservationists. By the early 1990s, this controversy had run its course. The result was a new synthesis, even a consensus, that combined wildlife management and wilderness preservation under the banner of conservation biology. This synthesis has continued to shape endangered species science, law, and politics ever since, for better and for worse.

CAUSES OF THE CONDOR DECLINE

At the end of the Pleistocene epoch, around twelve thousand years ago, condors ranged widely throughout North America, from what is now British Columbia to

FIGURE 12.

A captive-bred California condor, with identifying wing tag.
Courtesy of Ian Tait / Natural Visions.

Mexico and from Florida to New York. Over the succeeding centuries, however, a series of ecological changes transformed the species' physical and biological environment. The glaciers receded, the climate warmed, and hunter-gatherers colonized much of the continent. During the next several thousand years, thirty-one of forty-four genera of large mammals went extinct in North America. Scholars continue to debate the role of humans in this mass extinction episode. Yet the net effect for condors is clear: as carrion scavengers, they lost much of their former food supply.[4]

Although these changes reduced the resources available to condors, the species seems to have remained present, though in lower numbers, throughout large areas of the American Southwest and Pacific Coast until the past several hundred years. Condors continued to thrive in areas with eroded, pockmarked cliffs suitable for nesting and roosting; open landscapes in which to forage for food; climatic conditions, such as thermal updrafts, that facilitated their gliding manner of flight; and populations of ungulates, marine mammals, or other sources of animal protein. California's Great Central Valley, which was surrounded on all sides by steep mountains and contained large populations of grazing animals, was ideal.[5]

Condors were probably also common around American Indian settlements, where they scavenged from the carcasses of leftover meat, and several indigenous groups took a particular interest in the species. The condor is one of the most common animals in California Indian oral traditions, and it appears in the legends of several linguistic and cultural groups. Archaeological excavations, rock art, and modern-day anthropological studies indicate that condors frequently played ritualistic roles. Some groups used the bird's feathers in their ceremonial garments, and condor remains appear in burial mounds from the Central Valley to the San Francisco Bay. It remains unclear whether the American Indian use of condors constituted a sustainable harvest, but the gathering of feathers may have been an important source of condor mortality and could have placed significant pressure on some local populations.[6]

In 1602, Father Antonio de la Ascensión became the first European to document condors in North America. From the bow of his ship, he recorded a remarkable sight: a congregation of condors feasting on the carcass of a beached whale. Condors scavenged marine mammals when both were more abundant along the West Coast, before human communities began to efficiently dispose of animal carcasses that washed up on their beaches. During the mission era, the Spanish knew condors as one of the many scavenger species that loitered around the outskirts of their communities and "contended with the coyote[s] for the offal and carcasses of cattle slaughtered for their hides and tallow."[7]

Anglo-American explorers recorded condors all along the West Coast of the United States. Meriwether Lewis and William Clark recognized that condors were probably the largest birds in North America, at least in terms of wingspan. Sergeant Patrick Gass, who accompanied them on their expedition, documented condors feeding around the mouth of the Columbia River. In 1827 the botanist David Douglas confirmed the presence of condors in Oregon Territory when he noted the birds feeding on dead horses at Fort Vancouver, near present-day Portland. These reports led one prominent biologist to speculate that in the past some condors may have migrated seasonally, moving north to feed on Columbia River salmon runs in the spring and summer and returning south to California in the winter. Nothing like this has occurred, however, since at least the beginning of the nineteenth century.[8]

The proliferation of livestock in California during the 1830s and 1840s provided a new food source for condors that roosted in the Coast Ranges and the Sierra Nevada. But the time of plenty was short-lived, as the gold rush gave rise to a host of new dangers. During the gold rush, some forty-niners were said to have outfitted themselves with condor quills, to be used as lightweight vials for carrying gold dust, although there is scant evidence to document this claim. Other condors perished from lead poisoning, the result of inadvertently ingesting bullets in the carcasses of animals that had been shot. Some also probably succumbed to strychnine poisoning after feasting on livestock that shepherds had purposefully tainted to kill the bears, cougars, and coyotes that stalked their sheep. The most frequent cause of mortality for condors in the late nineteenth century seems to have been the most obvious and immediate: death by gunshot. Attacks with blades or blunt instruments were also common.[9]

Condors suffered from collecting too. Oology enthusiasts gathered hundreds of condor eggs in the first century after California achieved statehood. More than thirty live condors were placed in zoos or kept as pets. One account from the 1850s describes the capture of a live condor by Alonzo Winship and Jesse Millikan, who spotted the bird while working at a mining facility in El Dorado County on the western slope of the Sierra Nevada. Apparently, Winship was so moved by the sight of "the great grand daddy of all birds" that he could think of nothing better to do than throw a shovel at the unsuspecting creature. It was an impressive toss. The shovel hit the bird squarely, breaking one of its wings and sending it hopping and hissing down the canyon. The two men managed to catch the injured bird and keep it in captivity for a year until it escaped. Other condors were killed for their skins in the name of science. A survey of the world's natural history museums conducted by the biologist Sanford Wilbur in the 1970s found 177 California condor specimens.[10]

By the late nineteenth century, the California condor had declined from a wide-ranging generalist able to exploit a variety of resources in diverse environments throughout North America to a narrowly distributed endemic species with a population of probably less than two hundred individuals, all in central California (see map 5). Many commentators believed that it was no longer a viable species. In 1890 James Cooper, the founder of the Cooper Ornithological Society, published an article on the California condor titled "A Doomed Bird." Eight years later, the annual report of the New York Zoological Society listed the species under the heading "Becoming Extinct." In 1906 the naturalist C. W. Beebe predicted that the condor's "doom is near; within a few years at most, the last individual will have perished." The following year, Graham Renshaw called the condor's shrinking range "a miserable remnant . . . a mere dot on the map." As late as the 1930s, H. H. Sheldon argued that scarce resources should not be wasted and wild areas should not be closed to recreation in a vain effort to save a species that "has outlived its time and is on the trail of the dodo."[11]

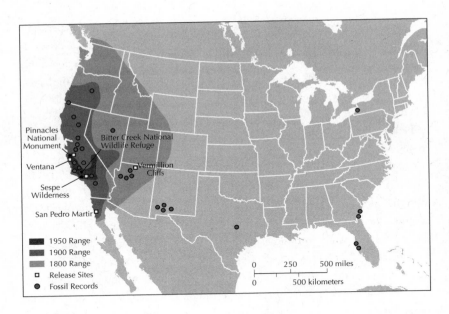

Pinnacles
National
Monument

Bitter Creek National
Wildlife Refuge

Ventana

Vermillion
Cliffs

Sespe
Wilderness

San Pedro Martir

- ■ 1950 Range
- ■ 1900 Range
- ■ 1800 Range
- □ Release Sites
- ● Fossil Records

0   250   500 miles
0   500 kilometers

MAP 5.
The range of the California condor over time.

CONDOR SYMBOLISM

Beginning in the early twentieth century, naturalists gave the California condor
an image makeover that transformed it from a lowly pest and opportunistic
scavenger into a venerated wildlife icon. First they changed its name. Native
Californians knew condors by a variety of names, such as *wee-itch* (Yaulamne) and
molloko (Chumash), that reflected the linguistic and cultural diversity of the
region's peoples. Anglo-American explorers, settlers, shepherds, and cattlemen
referred to the species simply as *buzzard* or *California vulture*. Naturalists coined
the name *California condor* in 1833, to highlight the recent scientific conclusion that
the species had more in common with its majestic Andean cousin than with other
New World vultures. Yet this new name did not appear in the common written
vernacular until around 1900, at about the same time that observers began to record
the species' decline. In the prevailing Victorian sensibility of the day, such a rare
and wonderful creature clearly deserved a title that conferred a sense of romantic
splendor. *California condor* worked nicely.[12]

By the mid-twentieth century, the condor's admirers had succeeded in creating
a new popular image of the species as a "living fossil"—a creature from another

time and a symbol of North America's primeval past. In 1953 the *Los Angeles Times* began a tradition of describing condors as flying anachronisms, "carryovers from the Pleistocene Age of 1,000,000 years ago, having come down virtually unchanged from that ancient era." Lloyd Kiff, who served as the Fish and Wildlife Service's Condor Recovery Team leader from 1986 to 1993, summed up this sentiment when he wrote that people found it "hard to be indifferent about condors. They seem like a creature out of another geologic age."[13]

The California condor is not, in fact, that ancient a species. Its nearest relative is the Andean condor, but it is also closely related to other vulture species in North and South America. New World vultures first appear in the fossil record in the Eocene, some fifty million years ago, but most of the current species date back less than ten million years, to a time during the Pliocene and the Pleistocene when their lineage radiated into its many modern forms. The fossil record of the genus *Gymnogyps*, of which the California condor is the only surviving member, is even shorter, dating back only about one hundred thousand years. This record is shorter than those of many related bird species and considerably shorter than that of anatomically modern *Homo sapiens*, which extends back about twice as long. Nor are the condor's roots much deeper than those of North America's other fauna, almost all of which are thought to survive in forms almost identical to those of their ice age ancestors. Condors may appear primitive, but they are no more ancient than blue jays, house sparrows, Norway rats, or human beings—all of which lived through the Pleistocene and once shared their environments with woolly mammoths, dire wolves, saber-toothed tigers, and giant ground sloths.[14]

Why did naturalists celebrate the condor's ancient origins when the evidence clearly demonstrated that the species was so unexceptional in that regard? For National Audubon Society president John Baker and others who referred to the condor as a link to a lost ice age, the bird's archaic-looking profile presented an opportunity to connect it in the public imagination with the ancient, unspoiled North American landscape. They hoped that doing so would help generate support for conservation efforts on behalf of the species, including the establishment of refuges to protect it. By 2002 the *Los Angeles Times* could report that "hundreds of biologists, volunteers and academics . . . have spent years trying to keep condors a living symbol of American's primordial past."[15]

The image has stuck, but it has not always benefited the species. According to Kiff, portraying the condor as an ancient species has misled people into believing that it is evolutionarily backward and ill suited for contemporary life. Even Loye Miller, a Joseph Grinnell protégé and the father of Alden Miller, Grinnell's successor at the Museum of Vertebrate Zoology, seemed to fall for this line of reasoning, arguing that the condor had passed its prime as a species. Yet as Kiff has repeatedly noted, condors are no less well adapted to their current habitats than the dozens of other vulture species around the world, many of which still have healthy populations.[16]

During the mid-twentieth century, writers and activists also transformed the California condor into a mascot for the wilderness preservation movement. According to the nature writer and literary scholar Charles Bergman, the condor represented "an ancient heritage of large spaces and unbroken stretches of time. . . . To modern people crowded by the millions into cities like Los Angeles, the condor came to symbolize both wilderness and prehistory." Of particular importance was the bird's relationship to the vast, mountainous region that encompassed the Los Padres National Forest backcountry, in Santa Barbara and Ventura Counties. This rugged, fire-prone land of canyons and cliffs and crumpled, chaparral-covered ridgelines was the largest nondesert wildland in Southern California. The U.S. Forest Service and the Bureau of Reclamation had proposed various development schemes for the area, which was just a few hours by car from Los Angeles. By the 1970s, however, the condor had become the flagship species for this region, and it had begun to command a sort of "mystic reverence" among people who wished to preserve its habitat in an undeveloped state. Ian McMillan, a rancher and naturalist who studied condors near his home for fifty years, wrote that the bird symbolized freedom, land, and sky.[17]

Some, like the famed conservationist and former Sierra Club executive director David Brower, took this logic even further. Brower met Carl Koford, a condor specialist and one of Grinnell's last students, in Berkeley in the 1940s, and he found a kindred spirit in the young biologist. The two men remained in contact for the next three decades. For Brower, the condor was more than just a fitting symbol of wilderness—its very value as a species depended on the wild country it symbolized. It did not matter that condors foraged on valley ranchlands that had been grazed since the nineteenth century. What mattered was that the condor, with its terrific size and prehistoric appearance, seemed to embody primeval wild nature, or at least Brower's idea of it. Condors were more than just surrogates. They were incarnations of the wild country Brower had sworn to defend, and "soaring manifestations of the place that built them and coded their genes." According to him, condors were "five per cent feathers, flesh, blood, and bone. All the rest is *place*." "Condors in zoos," Brower concluded, were "like feathered pigs."[18]

For people like McMillan, Koford, and Brower, condors and wilderness existed in a mutually dependent, symbiotic relationship. Condors embodied wild nature and justified the protection of wilderness areas as crucial endangered species habitat. In return, wilderness endowed the condor with its symbolic capital, which conservationists used to promote the bird's protection. This meant that *real* condors lived *only* in the wilderness, and intensive scientific management by definition robbed them of their true, wild essence. Some condor advocates even began to argue that the remaining wild condors would be better off left alone under any circumstances, even if the failure to intervene on their behalf would eventually lead to their extinction. Brower preferred for the species to meet "death with dignity" in its wilderness habitat rather than waste away behind bars at a zoo. If condors disappeared, at least the symbol would survive. And their martyrdom might make the symbol even more potent. By the 1970s, proponents of this hands-off approach to condor conservation were clashing with a new generation of scientists who argued that only intensive management, and later comprehensive captive breeding, could save the species from certain extinction.[19]

CONDOR SCIENCE

In 1906 the photographer and conservationist William Finley undertook the first study of condors in the wild. He wanted to observe and photograph the birds in their native habitats, make basic observations about their life history and behavior, and dispel some of the outlandish myths that had engendered ill will toward them. In Finley's view, the condor was a misunderstood species. It did not, as some had suggested, prey on live animals, and no condor had ever been seen "sailing away with a hind quarter of venison in its talons." Condors did not even have sharp talons like ordinary raptors; their claws were blunt and weak and not adapted to killing or carrying prey. "The habit of this vulture," Finley noted, "is to wait until after death." But if the condor was associated with death, then it was also in danger of annihilation. According to Finley, overhunting and predator control programs had harmed this already uncommon species. "The report that the California condor . . . will soon become extinct," he concluded, "is not without foundation."[20]

One of the things that impressed Finley most about the condor was its habitat. Setting out from the Los Angeles Basin—with his two young guides, Joseph Grinnell and Walter P. Taylor—he could not help but marvel at the transition he saw as he made his way into the mountains. "At eight o'clock in the morning, we were in the midst of pleasant homes and gardens, and two hours later we seemed to be almost in a different world." It was one of the "roughest, wildest" places imaginable. "Wild indeed," Finley wrote, "because this was the natural haunt of the California condor."[21]

Like so many other naturalists and conservationists of the time, Finley was gloomy about the condor's prospects. In 1937, however, his onetime companion Grinnell offered a different assessment of the bird's future. The condor's problem, Grinnell argued, was not its biology but rather that people lacked the will to act on its behalf. The species would disappear only if Californians failed to learn more about it and continued to fail to protect it. Grinnell was not the first to suggest that the condor be preserved. James Cooper called for legal measures to do just that in 1890, and in 1905 members of the Cooper Ornithological Society convinced California legislators to pass a law that prohibited condor hunting and egg collecting. A quarter century later, however, biologists still knew little about the species, and California's game wardens had rarely enforced the law, and then to no avail.[22] Something more needed to be done.

In 1937 John Baker approached Grinnell with a proposition. The Audubon Society was interested in creating a scholarship that would fund a study of the condor's biology and natural history, to be conducted by a doctoral student under Grinnell's direction. Grinnell discussed the idea with Alden Miller and others at the Museum of Vertebrate Zoology, and although they were delighted to receive such an offer, they worried that the society's influence might compromise the rigor or influence the conclusions of the project. Grinnell decided to accept the offer under certain conditions. The Audubon Society agreed, for example, not to release any information about the project to the press before the MVZ had vetted it.[23]

Grinnell's choice for the scholarship was a promising young student, Carl Koford, who seemed to have the combination of patience, intelligence, endurance, and stubbornness that Grinnell himself possessed. Koford began his fieldwork in 1939, and when Grinnell died later that year Miller took over as his adviser. Koford spent thousands of hours observing condors and documenting their behavior and biology. He used the traditional Grinnellian method of note-taking in the field, augmented with a historical and contextual analysis that he adapted from the work of George Wright's National Park Service Wildlife Division. At first, Koford often entered condor nests and handled wild birds, but later in his career he argued against what he had come to see as overly invasive management techniques, and unlike most of Grinnell's earlier students, he never took live specimens (see figure 13). These practices were due, in part, to the specific nature of his project, but they also represented a generational shift among the Berkeley circle's members and wildlife biologists nationwide. In 1941 Koford joined the military, and during World War II he flew reconnaissance missions and sorties in the Pacific theater. He resumed his studies in 1946 and completed his definitive work, *The California Condor*, six years later.[24]

FIGURE 13.
A boyish-looking Carl Koford holds a California condor while
conducting field research. Courtesy of the Santa Barbara Museum
of Natural History.

Koford's research began at a key moment in the history of California's national
forests—a coincidental fact that shaped his understanding of the condor's predicament. During the 1920s, a series of major fires charred national forest lands
in Southern California. Over the next decade the Forest Service launched a
campaign to battle wildland fires, in part by reducing "attack time," or how long
it took to reach the site of a new fire. Officials from Los Padres National Forest,
one of the country's most flammable landscapes, hoped to lower the service's
three-and-a-half-hour average response time by constructing new roads into
previously inaccessible areas. The Depression-era Civilian Conservation Corps
would provide the necessary labor. But this was also the heart of the condor's
breeding territory, and Koford believed that to reproduce successfully, condors
required a nesting habitat far from human disturbances. Road development posed
a direct threat. From the very beginning, therefore, he focused his research
and conservation efforts on the condor's breeding habitat in the Los Padres
backcountry.[25]

Koford's research revealed much about the condor's population. In his seminal monograph, he gave population estimates, recorded life history information, documented behavior, and mapped habitat use. He also noted that given the species' tenuous status and the fragile balance between fertility and survivorship, "the prevention of the death of a single condor . . . may mean that the population will show an increase rather than a decrease for that year. Persons in a position to influence the welfare of individual condors, and especially of their nests, should keep in mind that the precarious natural balance of the population can be easily upset in the direction leading to extinction of the species."[26]

Many factors contributed to condor deaths. Under the heading "Major Mortality and Welfare Factors," Koford listed shooting, collecting, poisoning, trapping, accidents, starvation, fire, roads and trails, oil development, and photographers. Counting photographers among the condor's enemies may seem odd, but years earlier Finley had almost killed a condor chick while attempting to capture its portrait, and Koford was concerned that photographers were harassing the birds and revealing the locations of nests. Under the heading "Minor Mortality and Welfare Factors," he included sickness and disease, eating foreign objects, storms, killing for quills, Indians, penning, the quintessentially Californian scourge of lassoing, and the scientists' ubiquitous complaint, false information. For wild condors, the world presented numerous pitfalls.[27]

On the positive side of the population equation, condors did seem to be breeding successfully. Like most other large, intelligent, long-lived species, condors have low fertility rates that even under the best circumstances can limit their population growth. Yet according to Koford's data, some 45 percent of condors observed at five sites between 1936 and 1946 had not yet reached maturity. In isolated populations without sources of immigration, a high proportion of immature individuals usually indicates one of two things: either the population is growing or excessive mortality is offsetting fertility. Since the total number of individuals appeared stable, Koford reasoned that high mortality, not just low fertility, must have been preventing population growth. Later condor biologists recognized this seemingly minor detail as a revelation.[28]

Koford believed that a combination of nest disturbance, forest mismanagement, development, and general harassment had caused the condor's decline. Human activities had endangered condors in the past, and future intervention, including the overly invasive research and conservation techniques used by some scientists, could only harm them further. Koford thought that nature knew best, and so the most effective management approach for condors, or any other wildlife species, would involve as little human interference as possible. Scientific studies would be essential for conservation, but their chief value would be in helping officials identify the habitat areas that should receive the most protection. More habitat, according to this logic, would result in lower mortality, leading to population growth. Shortly before his death in 1979, Koford argued eloquently against the "drastic artificial procedures" that the Audubon Society had recommended in one of its reports. "Must we further dilute the natural scene by manhandling the birds and injecting cage-raised stock into condor society?" No, he wrote, we must "keep condors forever free."[29]

During the 1970s and 1980s, zoos and other wildlife research facilities were experimenting with new approaches to improve the success and efficiency of captive breeding. Captive breeding is an ancient endeavor, but the emergence of conservation biology gave such efforts for endangered species new resources and urgency. Koford objected to this approach—and sought to prevent institutions such as the San Diego Zoo from receiving condor breeding permits from the California Department of Fish and Game—in part because he believed that condors had a culture. They learned from their parents, and robbing them of this experience would produce dysfunctional adults unable to survive in the wild. Koford also opposed captive breeding because he thought it endangered eggs and chicks, even though his field research, particularly early in his career, had involved similarly invasive techniques. Finally, Koford objected to captive breeding for aesthetic reasons. The "beauty of a California condor is in the magnificence of its soaring flight," he wrote. "A condor in a cage is uninspiring, pitiful, and ugly to one that has seen them soaring over the mountains."[30]

The condor controversy crystallized in the 1970s and early 1980s as more people began to call for a captive breeding program to supplement conservation in the wild. Yet the debate about hands-on versus hands-off management was not new to wildlife conservation in California. Grinnell had discussed the problem decades earlier, as did Wright and his colleagues in the Wildlife Division. In its *Twenty-Seventh Biennial Report*, published in 1923, the California Fish and Game Commission wrestled with this quandary as it applied to the pronghorn antelope. The question was whether to grant a local chamber of commerce permission to "'round up' and 'corral'" a remnant population of the species to protect its members and facilitate their propagation. After consulting with several conservation groups, the commission decided that "the animals should be left in a state of nature, with all possible done in their behalf. Whenever any so inherently wild a species as the 'Prong-horn' is reduced to slowly perish in the protracted misery of captivity, its status as 'wild-life' is admittedly at an end."[31]

Koford had speculated about the causes of condor deaths, but his research did not quantify these factors. As late as the 1960s, the exact causes of the condor's decline were still unknown. But the field of wildlife ecology was growing rapidly, and a new generation of scientists and managers—including Fred Sibley, Sandy Wilbur, Lloyd Kiff, and Noel Snyder—began to study the species in different ways. They expanded their work beyond the condor's nesting and roosting sites in the Los Padres backcountry, to the valleys and foothills where condors foraged below the national forest boundaries. What they saw seemed to contradict some of Koford's key ideas, and their research sparked a transformation in condor conservation.

The first thing they noticed was that central California's valleys and foothills seemed to have plenty of food resources available, in the form of dead cattle and deer, to support a much larger condor population than the one that currently existed. In a 1965 research report, Miller, Ian McMillan, and Eben McMillan observed that although land use developments and feedlots had destroyed some condor foraging territory, increased grazing on the remaining rangelands had already compensated for those losses. Wilbur made a similar observation, writing that despite land use developments that had eliminated some of the condor's foraging territory, there remained "vast acreages well stocked with livestock and deer." Condors were still circulating throughout the region, but they were failing to exploit significant caloric resources within their home range.[32]

Vacancies also remained in high-country roosting and nesting sites. Thousands of acres in Los Padres National Forest contained remote, structurally appropriate nesting habitat, and most of this area was under public management. In 1936 the U.S. Forest Service issued regulation T-9-1, which allowed it to close off certain areas for the protection of rare or vanishing species, important biological communities, or historical or archaeological sites. The service issued its first closure the following year when it established the twelve-hundred-acre Sisquoc Condor Sanctuary in Santa Barbara County. In the early 1940s, Baker attempted to convince Fish and Wildlife Service director Ira Gabrielson to endorse the creation of a condor refuge, but Gabrielson demurred. In 1947 the Forest Service moved forward on its own, establishing the Sespe Condor Sanctuary (see map 5), which it expanded from thirty-five thousand to fifty-three thousand acres four years later. In 1968, Congress established the San Rafael Wilderness, which was the first area it designated under the Wilderness Act of 1964. The San Rafael was also the first of several wilderness areas created in the Los Padres backcountry, in part for condor conservation. The Forest Service never built most of the roads it had planned for fire protection in the 1930s, and in 1967 wildlife and wilderness activists helped fight off a Bureau of

Reclamation plan to dam the Sespe River, which would have led to increased development. In 1978 Wilbur calculated that of the 36 percent of the condor's range in public ownership, almost all was mountainous terrain. Most of the rest was foothill and valley rangeland held in large parcels by private owners.[33]

If so many resources and so much habitat still existed, then why were there so few condors? For some, the answer was that there was still not enough protected land. Since the 1930s, land protection had become so central to wildlife management that it was now the chief tool for conserving endangered species not threatened by hunting or collecting. The logic that habitat preservation should take precedence over all other management approaches had become an article of faith among wilderness preservationists. Yet according to Kiff, the tendency to blame habitat loss for every wildlife problem was "an acquired reflex." In the case of the condor, it failed to capture the complexity of the situation. Kiff pointed out that condors disappeared from most of their Pleistocene range long before the habitat reductions of the twentieth century, and their population was below its "apparent carrying capacity" within the habitat areas that still existed. The word *apparent* was important here because it suggested that some factor, still unknown, was depressing the condor's population well below its potential. Kiff suspected that reproductive failure due to DDT toxicity was one explanation, but he knew that multiple factors were probably at work.[34]

The condor was one of the first species listed under the Endangered Species Preservation Act of 1966. Three years later, Wilbur replaced Sibley as the Condor Recovery Team leader, and he ushered the bird into the era of the Endangered Species Act. The condor was one of the first species to receive a critical habitat designation, and its recovery plan was one of the first such documents created for an endangered species. This plan provided a model for future ones in some important respects, but it was unusual because it included a contingency plan that the FWS could invoke if extinction seemed imminent. The scheme called for a captive breeding program that would include all members of the species.[35]

Everyone involved in condor conservation still agreed that habitat protection was an essential component of any effort to recover the species. Yet the research of the 1970s suggested that the condor's problems stemmed from the quality—not the quantity—of its habitat, and this led many scientists and officials to conclude that land preservation alone could not save the species. According to Snyder and his wife, Helen, prior to this time "a central operating assumption for condor conservation was that the species was threatened importantly by habitat loss and human disturbance of nesting areas and that the key to its conservation lay in habitat preservation and isolating the species as much as possible from direct contact with humanity." Yet the Snyders soon came to believe that "habitat loss and disturbance of nesting areas" were only "minor factors in the condor's decline."[36]

Between 1982 and 1986, poisoning emerged as the single most important source of condor mortality, causing a quarter (four of sixteen) of all deaths. No one knew to what extent lead poisoning, cyanide poisoning, and DDT toxicity had affected condors in the wild. Yet the fact that each of these four deaths appeared to have occurred independently suggested widespread danger. The more scientists knew about the effects of these toxins on condors, the less they believed in the hands-off approach and the worse things looked for the few remaining wild birds. If all condors, in all habitats, were now in danger of being poisoned to death, then no amount of wilderness could save them.[37]

Snyder replaced Wilbur as the Condor Recovery Team leader in 1980 and soon emerged as a strong voice for intensive research and captive breeding along the lines of Wilbur's contingency plan. Several other ornithologists, including Kiff, still believed that some condors should be left in the wild for biological reasons. In the winter of 1985, however, the species reached a turning point. In a single season, six adults (40 percent of the remaining wild flock) died, leaving just one breeding pair. At this point, the debate about the role of captive breeding in conservation abruptly turned to the question of whether any condors should remain in the wild. In January of 1986 the decisive moment arrived when, despite a dramatic emergency veterinary effort at the San Diego Wild Animal Park, a key breeding-age female succumbed to lead poisoning. Recovery team members had considered Santa Barbara Female, or SBF, a lynchpin in the future of the tattered flock, and without her the wild population no longer seemed viable. The species was now in immediate danger of extinction.[38]

Snyder turned to the contingency plan, which called for all wild condors to be enrolled in the captive breeding program. His proposal attracted widespread criticism. Celebrity biologists, including Paul Ehrlich and A. Starker Leopold, wrote editorials denouncing the plan. Some observers, who remembered the chick that had died years earlier during a routine examination, questioned the recovery team's ability to care for the animals in its custody. Other critics were unconvinced that condors could reproduce successfully in confinement. There were also many people who supported captive breeding but argued that at least a few birds should remain in the wild to preserve the species' social structure and act as custodians of its habitat. Members of the Chumash tribe protested, saying that if condors ceased to exist in the wild, their religion would suffer irreparable damage. Even the long-standing alliance between the National Audubon Society and the recovery team broke down. In 1977 the society had stepped forward as one of the first environmental organizations to endorse captive breeding. Just weeks before SBF's death, however, it filed a lawsuit in federal court to prevent the capture of additional birds. The FWS won the suit on appeal, in part because of evidence that SBF had died from lead poisoning.[39]

Despite this controversy, most condor biologists and agency officials supported the recovery team's recommendations. Brian J. Kahn, of the California Department of Fish and Game, was one. He believed that the physical survival of individual animals must take the highest priority. Kahn agreed with Snyder that officials should capture all the remaining wild birds because if left on their own, they would probably perish in the next few years anyway. The prospect was daunting, but no other choice remained for those who wanted to save the species. In the spring of 1986, the FWS issued its final decision to capture all of the remaining wild condors.[40]

One of the last protests against the recovery team's plan came from the literary scholar and environmental critic Charles Bergman, whose 1990 book, *Wild Echoes: Encounters with the Most Endangered Animals in North America,* offered an expansive critique of condor management. According to him, the condor episode marked a crossroads in endangered species history. "The methods we have used to save endangered species must fail," he wrote, "because the scientific approach to animals is part of the cultural mentality that created endangered species" in the first place.[41]

In the years that followed, Noel and Helen Snyder reflected on how perspectives such as Bergman's, Koford's, and Brower's had shaped the politics of condor conservation. According to the Snyders, "the concept of captive breeding condors was apparently so repugnant and divergent from [many environmentalists'] image of the condor as the essence of wilderness, that they proclaimed their preference for 'death with dignity' for the species, should captive breeding be its only salvation." Condors came to "glorify wilderness" even though they spent much of their time foraging on cattle ranches. But managing a symbol was about as easy as "trying to manage smoke rings. We had to prove the condor was a bird."[42]

Igor's capture changed the terms of the condor debate. Critics of the FWS's comprehensive captive breeding program no longer had anything tangible to fight for, because condors had gone extinct in the wild. So something surprising began to happen. Within a year, the various groups in the condor controversy, which had fought so doggedly before, began to come together around a set of common goals and interests. Everyone involved in the debates of the previous decades had hoped to keep a viable free-roaming population, even if they had disagreed on the best approach, and nobody wanted to see all condors permanently locked up in zoos. With the entire species now in captivity, all parties could agree on a single goal: returning condors to the wild. A new coalition suddenly stood on common ground. The condor's immediate welfare depended on state-of-the-art biology and intensive veterinary care—but its ultimate recovery would rely on the preservation of its habitat.

By 1988 most of the condor's advocates concurred that the hands-on versus hands-off debate, which had attracted so much attention and resulted in so much rancor, had proved fruitless. The condor's survival required both habitat preservation and intensive scientific management, and in the years to come, they formed the twin pillars of condor recovery efforts. These two approaches also emerged as central themes in the field of conservation biology in the United States.[43]

THE (BUMPY) ROAD TO RECOVERY

For five years, condors were extinct in the wild. But during its time in confinement, the species thrived. Condors first bred in captivity in 1988, and by 1992 the population had nearly doubled, from twenty-seven to fifty-two birds. In the years that followed, recovery team biologists continued to produce chicks using a battery of approaches in a highly controlled environment. These included intensive veterinary care, breeding techniques such as multiple clutching, and DNA fingerprinting, which allowed them to build a genetic map for the entire species and determine suitable mating pairs. The next, and more foreboding, phase of the project— reintroduction and reestablishment in the wild—required cooperation among government agencies and nongovernmental organizations, generous funding, and the establishment of a safe habitat for condors in the wild.[44]

Reintroduction posed several potential problems. Condors learn their survival skills through social interactions, and they require the tutelage of older, more experienced birds. Birds raised in captivity have a distinct disadvantage when it comes to acquiring the basic knowledge needed to live in the wild. The biologists involved in the breeding program hoped to solve this problem with a number of innovative solutions. In one approach, they "armed" themselves with hand puppets designed to look like adult condors, in an attempt to raise the chicks in disguise. No one knows whether this charade fooled the chicks or improved their chances of survival outside captivity—subsequent studies indicate at best mixed results—but concealment nonetheless seemed necessary because birds that associated humans with food would have been at great risk in the wild.[45]

To ensure that the chicks learned to stay away from people, their stealthy trainers also enlisted them in an aversion-therapy program—a sort of boot camp designed to instill fear in the hearts of young birds. Described by some as "tough love," the curriculum included exercises such as moving "a person into the [bird's] line of sight. Just as [it] sees the person, a group of biologists will rush the bird and turn it upside down." Mock power lines, carrying "mild" electric charges, hung in the birds' pens, and "dysfunctional parents" were eliminated from the rearing pool. According to Michael Wallace, the San Diego Zoo biologist who became the head of the Condor Recovery Team in the late 1990s, it was a "good day . . . when you have condors throwing up all over at the mere sight of a person." Through these extreme and sometimes painful measures, recovery team members hoped to break the condor's destructive "culture," eliminate individuals with detrimental "traditions," and train their pupils for new lives in a modern environment.[46]

In January of 1992, after five years of exile for their species, two California condors, along with two of their Andean counterparts, settled into the Sespe Condor Sanctuary in Los Padres National Forest. During the next decade, scientists released dozens more of the birds in Ventura County, Monterey County near Big Sur, and the Vermillion Cliffs region on the Utah-Arizona border. The culmination of these efforts came in May 2002, when Igor finally returned to the wild after a decade and a half in protective custody. Twenty-seven years and some thirty-five million dollars after its inception, the condor recovery program had achieved remarkable success: 68 condors survived in the wild, 16 more birds were almost ready for release, and 113 others waited in captivity, pampered and procreating.[47]

Breeding and releasing birds were only the first steps in the recovery program. The free-roaming condors needed to survive, reproduce, and establish self-sustaining populations. Yet more than a decade after the reintroduction program began, managers were still keeping the birds near established safe sites by enticing them with a steady supply of fresh livestock remains—what some have called "a carcass leash." Leaving them to forage on their own would have resulted in almost certain death. In one necropsy conducted at the San Diego Zoo in 2002, pathologists discovered "12 bottle caps, shards of glass, electrical fixtures, screws and washers inside [a] turkey sized chick." Since the reintroduction phase of the recovery program began, other condors have met gruesome fates, including being poisoned, colliding with power lines, drowning, and dying of bullet wounds.[48]

Reintroduction presented political challenges as well. In Southern California the condor enjoyed broad popular support. Even the *Los Angeles Times* made a rare exception to its normal standard for celebrities, saying that in the condor's case "ugly is okay." But the recovery team also hoped to establish a population in southern Utah and northern Arizona, where residents were considerably less enthusiastic. Some were downright hostile. People there had recent experience dealing with other endangered species, such as the Mexican spotted owl and the Mojave desert tortoise, and some believed that conservation programs for these species had stifled economic growth and limited public access to land and natural resources. One letter written to the FWS declared that "the condor is not a majestic bird but a common buzzard which lives on road kill. . . . If you think that we or any tourist would be excited to see these birds gnawing away on a dead animal's carcass along the road you are very mistaken." The service responded by signing a memorandum of understanding with other agencies in the region that allowed it to proceed while providing local governments and businesses with assurances against potential liabilities. In the fall of 1996, when officials released the first condors at the Vermillion Cliffs, seven hundred people showed up for the ceremony. The attendees included Interior Secretary Bruce Babbitt and Arizona Republican politicians Senator John McCain and Governor Fife Symington.[49]

Despite the condor's popularity, conflicts eventually emerged even in Southern California. Occasional proposals to expand fossil fuel exploration in Los Padres National Forest alarmed wildlife and wilderness advocates alike. Yet by the early 2000s, the most controversial land use issue within the condor's range was a plan to develop portions of the 270,000-acre Tejon Ranch—one of California's largest private landholdings—in the Tehachapi Mountains near the Grapevine portion of Interstate 5 north of Los Angeles. The Tejon Ranch Conservation and Land Use Agreement, reached between the Tejon Ranch Company and a coalition of environmental groups in May 2008 with the support of the Arnold Schwarzenegger gubernatorial administration, provided a framework for development and conservation on the site that may lead to some form of protection for up to 90 percent of the ranch. The California condor, not surprisingly, served as the flagship species for this habitat conservation effort.

Continued efforts to protect habitat notwithstanding, critics are right to point out that condors will require intensive and costly management into the foreseeable future. Some of these critics have argued that scarce resources would be better spent on different species or conservation efforts. Others have called the recovery program an avian welfare fund or, in Noel Snyder's words, a "stocking operation." Conservationists have saved the species from extinction, and its prospects for the future have improved now that a diverse coalition of environmental activists, scientists, officials, and the general public supports recovery efforts. It may not be long before the recovery team reaches its goal of 450 individuals in three populations, each with fifteen breeding pairs. But the program still has a long way to go and will require much more financial and institutional support before scientists can claim victory and curtail their intensive management. For now, the condor has the unfortunate distinction of being the best-known example of a class of plants and animals that biologists have begun to call "conservation dependent species."[50]

It is difficult to remain gloomy, though, when the recovery team has reported so many advances and successes. By 2010 there were 350 condors in existence, with at least 180 living outside captivity. Eggs had hatched in locations as diverse as Grand Canyon National Park in Arizona, Pinnacles National Monument in central California, and Sierra San Pedro de Mártir National Park in Baja California, Mexico, where the San Diego Zoo has established a collaborative recovery program with the Instituto Nacional de Ecología. In another encouraging sign, condors have begun doing things that are typical for their species but that none had done for at least a century. The wildlife biologist Joe Burnett even glimpsed two condors—birds that had been hatched in captivity and puppet-reared—devouring the carcass of a sea lion on the beach near Big Sur. It was a sight similar in almost every respect, except for the radio telemetry devices and bright white tags fastened to the birds' wings, to what Father Antonio de la Ascensión must have seen from the bow of his galleon in 1602.[51]

Moreover, despite all the evidence to the contrary, condors have several qualities that increase their chances for recovery. The species breeds well in captivity, and it tolerates constant surveillance and occasional human presence in its nests. Its survival does not stand in direct opposition to powerful economic interests, so it has been comparatively free from the economy-versus-environment debates that have shaped the stories of so many endangered species. Condors lack nasty habits such as preying on live cattle or stalking domestic pets. Leadless bullets have entered the market, and if put into widespread use they could dramatically reduce the danger of condor poisoning. Large portions of the bird's range are closed to development and managed for conservation. These factors give it a clear advantage compared to dozens of other endangered species that occupy specific ecological niches, have lost most of their former habitats, conflict with economic development, act as pests, or do not possess a broad political constituency. Indeed, the most important political problem in the condor's conservation history was not a conflict between its supporters and its detractors but a contest between different groups of environmentalists, all of which thought they knew what was best for the bird.[52]

MAKING SENSE OF THE CONDOR

How did the participants in the condor saga reconcile such profound and long-standing philosophical differences in such a short time? According to Noel Snyder, they didn't: The various camps held such different perspectives that their views about hands-on versus hands-off management remained irreconcilable. Intensive management, including captive breeding and vigilant protection in the wild, always represented the condor's only hope. Yet as Snyder has acknowledged, the hands-on versus hands-off dichotomy ultimately crumbled because even the most sophisticated and best-funded research and management programs could not ensure the species' survival. To succeed, the recovery program also required a secure wildland habitat for reintroduction, plus unified political support from the very scientists, activists, and officials who had once clashed over condor management.[53]

In addition to the emergency that faced condor managers and advocates in the late 1980s, two broader trends in American conservation history contributed to the resolution of this debate—and both are related to changing ideas and practices of habitat conservation. The first involved shifts in values and patterns of land protection. Until the late twentieth century, most national parks and wilderness areas were in cold, rugged, foreboding, inaccessible, and often fire-prone terrain. Efforts to establish mountain parks—such as Yellowstone, Yosemite, and Mount Rainer, three of the country's first national parks—drew from Romantic conceptions of the sublime, as well as capitalist imperatives to render otherwise useless areas profitable as tourist destinations. Mountain landscapes of rock, fire, and ice were often beautiful and popular playgrounds—and undoubtedly important for water conservation, as in the case of the Los Padres backcountry—but they were not very biologically diverse or productive compared to warmer, low-lying areas. The FWS had long managed valley wetlands as wildlife refuges, but it had dedicated most of these sites to the singular goal of waterfowl production.[54]

In the 1970s, conservationists in western North America began to focus on the intermediate spaces between the mountain parks and the wetland refuges. It turned out that in places such as California, these valleys, foothills, and coastal plains contained the most endangered species and the greatest biological diversity. Along with the trend toward valley and foothill dry land conservation, the FWS and the Nature Conservancy began to focus on the maintenance of biodiversity in working landscapes, such as rangelands used for livestock production. The realization that condors depended not only on mountain roosting and nesting sites but also on lower-elevation foraging areas led to the establishment of new rangeland refuges, such as the Bitter Creek National Wildlife Refuge, where Igor was captured in 1987. Habitat conservation patterns for the California condor thus followed larger historical trends.

The second broad factor that contributed to the resolution of the condor debate was the role of conservation biology in shaping the relationship between wilderness preservation and wildlife management. In 1991, Reed Noss, a future editor of the journal *Conservation Biology* and the president of the Society for Conservation Biology, wrote about the new alliance of wilderness and wildlife in his field. He argued that wilderness should serve as a foundation of conservation biology because wild areas offered scientific knowledge, ecological values, and a source of humility. They also had "intrinsic value." He developed this theme in the inaugural issue of the journal *Wild Earth*, founded by the longtime wilderness activist Dave Foreman, which sought to promote native biodiversity through wilderness preservation. According to Noss, science offered "an appropriate 'left-brain' complement to the ethical and spiritual reasons for wilderness preservation that attracted so many of us to this business in the first place." In the same issue, in an article titled "Wilderness: From Aesthetics to Biodiversity," the author Jim Eaton recalled that most "wilderness activists in the '60s were backpackers who wanted to protect [their] favorite tramping grounds." Now they worked as environmental professionals, government officials, and even scientists to protect endangered species and biological diversity.[55]

In 1997 the Ventana Wilderness Society, based in Salinas, California, joined the Peregrine Fund as one of the first nonprofit organizations to release and manage condors in the wild. Since its inception, the society had cited spiritual health and the intrinsic value of wild nature as the bases for its education, restoration, and research programs. Over the next several years, its collaborative efforts with government agencies to manage condors in the Big Sur area met with tremendous success. In 2005 the organization changed its name to the Ventana Wildlife Society to better reflect its goals and activities. Today the society's mission is to conserve native wildlife and habitats.

The Ventana Wildlife Society provides just one example of how the emergence of conservation biology as a discipline in the mid-1980s helped resolve the awkward conflict between wilderness preservation and wildlife management that arose after the passage of the Endangered Species Act. Conservation biology, which embraced science and ethics, offered a way to combine the symbolic capital of wild nature with academic respectability and technical expertise. The result was a new political consensus within the environmental movement. Habitat conservation would not be sufficient in every case, and it would have to allow for active management, but it would always form the foundation of endangered species recovery.

Noss and his colleagues had little new to say about the relationships between wilderness and wildlife or the importance of habitat. Most of their ideas dated back to the writings of A. Starker Leopold, George Wright, Aldo Leopold, Joseph Grinnell, and Charles Adams, to name just a few. Conservation biologists from other parts of the world tended to view wilderness as a uniquely North American interest. But in the United States the field came of age at a time when its synthetic approach offered a way for diverse groups in the environmental movement to reconcile their differences and build on one another's resources and successes.

One final question remains. What kind of story is the history of the California condor? Is it a tale of failure or success; is it unique or is it a model; who won and who lost? For science journalists, the condor's saga is often a story about how one group got it wrong. The Kofords and Browers of the world could not let go of their cherished beliefs about the importance of wilderness, even in the face of mounting evidence to the contrary, and modern science corrected their mistakes just in time to avert disaster. For government watchdogs, the condor's story serves as an example of wasted public resources—a textbook case of high costs leading to few benefits. For federal officials who are under pressure to demonstrate the effectiveness of the Endangered Species Act, the story is one of gradual success, cautious optimism, and scientific research leading to better land management. For the famous conservationist Jane Goodall, the condor's tale is nothing less than a "huge success story."[56]

Perhaps the most evocative version of the story has no words at all. It is the image that appears on the California quarter, which Governor Schwarzenegger selected from more than eight thousand submissions to a design competition for the commemorative coin in 2004. The winning image features a venerable John Muir, walking stick firmly in hand, standing on a granite slab with Yosemite National Park's Half Dome in the background and a California condor soaring overhead (see figure 14). According to Schwarzenegger, Muir was "a model to generations of Californians and conservationists around the world," without whom "Yosemite wouldn't be the cathedral that it is today." As for the condor, he said he hoped its "amazing comeback" would inspire future conservation efforts. Schwarzenegger's wife, Maria Shriver, called the coin simply "the people's quarter." A better way to read the image, though, would be to compare it to the California state flag, and its depiction of the long-extinct chaparral bear. If the flag seems ironic, given the grizzly's demise, then the quarter seems earnest in its hope for the future. Seen in this

FIGURE 14.
The California quarter.

way, the California quarter is not only a recovery narrative for the condor but also a redemption narrative for the grizzly and other lost species and landscapes.[57]

The story of the decline, near extinction, resurrection, reintroduction, and potential recovery of the California condor includes many problems and paradoxes. In this saga, wilderness conflicted with wildlife, conservationists quarreled with preservationists, environmentalists argued against acting to save an endangered species, scientists fought against the notion of scientific management, and an animal supposedly adapted to the world of the Pleistocene thrived in twentieth- and twenty-first-century zoos. The majority of condors roaming freely today were bred in captivity, receive top-notch veterinary care, eat food provided by their managers, and had to be trained to act like wild animals. Yet perhaps the most remarkable aspect of the condor's story is that even after its confinement, it has continued to serve as a powerful symbol.

In 2000, *Audubon* magazine reflected on its own role in the condor's saga after more than a decade of distancing itself from the recovery program. In a commentary titled "On Human Intervention," editor Lisa Gosselin wrote about wildlife conservation, wilderness preservation, captive breeding, and the hands-on-versus-hands-off management debate: "Only by interacting with nature can we come to appreciate it, understand it, and, we hope, preserve it. What we have learned from the condor may help us to alter our behavior enough to save these birds, or other animals. At the very least, it may prevent us from killing off another symbol of the wild."[58]

In 2002, fifteen years after his capture, FWS officials released AC-9 back into Los Padres. On the morning of his release, he seemed reluctant, clumsy, even confused. But he soon reacquainted himself with his surroundings and left his perch, and he has continued to survive even as numerous other condors have died in the same area, often of lead poisoning. As of this writing, Igor, at the age of thirty-two, remains the only free-flying bird born outside captivity before 1987. No matter how committed you are to a belief in the potential for effective scientific management of endangered species, it is difficult not to see Igor as a symbol of the wild.

CHAPTER SIX

· The Mojave Desert Tortoise

Ambassador for the Outback

In the summer of 1989, the U.S. Fish and Wildlife Service used its emergency authority to list the Mojave desert tortoise—a docile, long-lived reptile and common backyard pet throughout much of the American Southwest—as endangered in California, Nevada, Utah, and Arizona (see figure 15). Desert tortoises spend much of their lives hibernating in subterranean burrows, but after springtime rains they emerge to roam across millions of acres of federal lands that include national parks, monuments, recreational sites, and wilderness areas, as well as military bases, rangelands, and infrastructure projects from pipelines, power lines, and freeways to dams, wind farms, and nuclear waste disposal facilities. At the time of the tortoise's listing, its range also included state parks, desert resorts, Los Angeles bedroom communities, and the entire Las Vegas Valley (see map 6).

According to James E. Moore, a biologist with the Nature Conservancy based in Las Vegas, the tortoise situation in the Mojave "had all the right components for another spotted owl–type train wreck."[1] Just two months earlier, the FWS had listed the northern spotted owl as threatened throughout its range in the Pacific Northwest, sparking a political crisis over the management of that region's forest resources. Despite their dissimilar histories and geographies, Moore was right that these two species had much in common. Like the spotted owl, the desert tortoise still had a large population and range for a listed species. It lived mainly on public lands under the jurisdiction of government agencies that were facing novel political pressures

FIGURE 15.
A desert tortoise. Courtesy of Jessica Liberman.

and tumultuous institutional changes. It became a symbol of the landscape it inhabited and of a national debate that pitted economic growth against environmental protection. It provided a justification for broader efforts to transform land use and natural resource management in the region where it lived, including campaigns to establish or expand national parks, wilderness areas, and other nature reserves. And a vast area of habitat was ultimately allocated or managed for its protection. Yet like the spotted owl, the desert tortoise has continued to decline, and its situation today appears more dire than ever.

This chapter examines the environmental history of the Mojave desert tortoise to understand the changing role of nature reserves in endangered species recovery from the 1980s through the 2000s. By the time of the tortoise's listing, the awkward and unexpected conflict between wildlife management and wilderness preservation that had emerged in the years after the passage of the Endangered Species Act, and come to the fore in the California condor conservation controversy, was giving way to a new approach that combined habitat protection and intensive scientific management. Efforts to protect the desert tortoise built on this approach, fostered the further development of conservation biology, and helped create stronger links between environmental law and science. Yet the

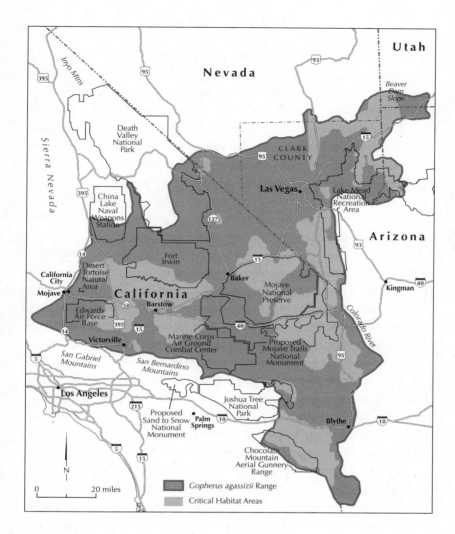

MAP 6.

Geographic range and critical habitat areas of the Mojave desert
tortoise (*Gopherus agassizii*).

tortoise's story has also come to exemplify the limits of a species recovery
approach that relies on habitat protection through the establishment of nature
reserves—even when backed by a large and ambitious community of scientists,
managers, and preservationists in a region with vast, undeveloped public lands
and "protected areas."

EVOLUTION AND EXPLOITATION

The story of the desert tortoise is, in many ways, the story of the Mojave itself. The Mojave may seem old, even timeless, to the casual visitor, but by geologic standards it is a young and dynamic landscape. When the first humans arrived there, at the end of the Pleistocene, they found an environment unlike the one of today. The Mojave was not yet a desert. The region experienced cooler temperatures year-round and probably received at least double its current precipitation. Pinyon-juniper woodlands and bunchgrass prairies thrived in many areas now dominated by thorny shrubs and annual plants. A full cast of Pleistocene megafauna roamed the plains. Perennial streams carried runoff from snow-covered mountains to dozens of enormous pluvial lakes fringed by wetlands and gallery forests. These waters have long since evaporated, and today only arroyos and playas remain.[2]

American Indians have hunted tortoises for food and for use as tools and in cultural rituals for as long as they have lived in the American Southwest. Archaeologists have found more than 150 midden sites containing tortoise remains, the oldest of which date back approximately ninety-five hundred years. Tortoises have been an important resource for native peoples, but the historical record offers no conclusions about how long-term human use affected their populations. Ethnographic research from the Sonoran Desert in Mexico, where local people still harvest desert tortoises, suggests that social structures and cultural mores may have prevented overharvest by regulating the species as a common property resource. Yet at least one archaeological study has found evidence of unsustainable exploitation. What we do know is that interactions between people and tortoises varied over time and space and that the two species shaped each other's destinies in the Southwest for several millennia before the arrival of European and Asian immigrants in the nineteenth century.[3]

The gold rush of 1849 transformed the Mojave Desert in three crucial ways. It became a transportation corridor for people trying to make their way to the Pacific Coast. The desert also attracted prospectors who staked their claims throughout the region. By the 1880s, the Mojave was producing gold, silver, and other minerals. Bustling towns emerged around some of the mines, but no bonanzas were ever found, and the settlements rarely lasted for more than a few years before the deposits declined, the residents fled, and the structures burned to the ground. Mining altered the desert ecosystem with its excavations, toxic chemicals, buildings, and fires, the scars of which are still visible at hundreds of abandoned sites. The third and probably most important impact, however, was the increase in access to remote areas, provided by horse, wagon, locomotive, and eventually automobile.[4]

Mining is an intensive activity that transforms local sites in dramatic fashion, but grazing is an extensive activity that can alter the ecology of an entire region. The effects of grazing vary depending on the location, season, intensity, and species of plants and animals involved. Even under the best conditions, grazing can alter the ecological structure and species composition of arid ecosystems. During dry periods, as in the decade from 1893 to 1904, sheep and cattle in the Mojave compacted the soil, eroded the riverbanks, and denuded the vegetation in their search for food and water. As early as 1898, H. L. Bentley could conclude that the rangelands of the American Southwest "have been ruined, and if not renewed will soon be past all hope of permanent improvement." Grazing peaked in the Mojave around 1920, before another cyclical drought of commonplace historical magnitude decimated herds and devastated the industry.[5]

Overgrazing left scars on the landscape, but it also created new niches for opportunistic species. Ranchers documented ecological changes, such as the shift from perennial grasses to tough woody shrubs, and were among the first to attempt rangeland rehabilitation programs. One common approach was to seed the range with exotic annual forage plants. Some of these proliferated on the desert floor. But so did a new cast of species that altered the soil chemistry, consumed more groundwater earlier in the season, and increased the fuel load in a system that had experienced little historic burning. As forage productivity declined, each cow or sheep required more land upon which to graze, and the whole endeavor became less profitable. The production of beef and wool for California's urban markets led to momentous, irreversible ecological changes, and the result was a diminished rangeland.[6]

The Mojave Desert's ecological transformation had profound effects on the distribution and abundance of its wildlife, including the desert tortoise. But desert tortoises are long-lived animals, and their populations appear to have responded slowly, at least at first, to changes in the environment. During the first half of the twentieth century, the collection of tortoises for the food and pet trades presented the greatest threat to the species in the wild.

The first European to taste the flesh of a desert tortoise was probably Friar Francisco Garcés, the Franciscan missionary who traversed the Mojave and Sonoran Deserts on five entradas between 1771 and 1781. For Garcés and those who followed him, "turtle soup" offered a welcome reprieve from "the desert men's menu of salt and meat." No cultural mores or government regulations limited tortoise consumption in the rough encampments that characterized the Mojave in the nineteenth century. But the total harvest probably remained small, due to a decline in Native American hunting, the small size of the region's human population, and the lack of an accessible market for tortoise meat.[7]

During the early twentieth century, the scattered harvest of tortoises for subsistence became a business. In 1922 the great desert naturalist Edmund Jaeger lamented that tortoises were being "piteously slaughtered . . . piled by the dozens in great crates and ruthlessly taken to the city markets, there to be butchered to satisfy the gormandizing epicures who can afford and will pay such fancy prices as this meat brings." The sight of them being boiled alive, he wrote, "must elicit the sympathy of anyone who has any sense of pity for God's sentient creatures."[8]

Jaeger's call for the protection of desert tortoises does not appear to have aroused much sympathy for the species' plight, but the burgeoning pet trade had an altogether different effect. In 1907 Raymond Ditmars, the curator of reptiles at the New York Zoological Park, wrote one of the first descriptions of a desert tortoise in captivity. According to him, tortoises "exhibited considerable intelligence, becoming exceedingly tame within a few days after their arrival from the deserts. They learn to take food from the hand and appear to possess actual affection." In addition to having a genial disposition, desert tortoises were abundant, were easily captured (at least during the spring), and required little care—all factors that made them excellent household pets. During the 1930s, their popularity grew even further, due to increased interest in and appreciation of the desert itself.[9]

With the help of new roads, trails, and campgrounds built by state and federal agencies during the New Deal era, large numbers of tourists encountered the Mojave for the first time in the 1930s. To the astonishment of many a leathery old-timer, they fell in love with the place. The Mojave's great distances and uncooperative weather ruled out travel by foot or horseback for most visitors, so desert sightseeing required automobiles and an extensive infrastructure of roads. The motorists who traveled these freshly graded byways discovered geological marvels, historical relics, and biological curiosities. They read books by Mary Austin and John C. Van Dyke, who had written about the stark beauty of the California desert decades earlier.[10] They started to experience the Mojave not as a godless wasteland but as a space of extraordinary natural beauty and as a gigantic playground. And in the springtime, when the conditions were right, they often crossed paths with desert tortoises.

The number of tortoises collected as pets soon surpassed the number collected for food. A tourist who encountered a desert tortoise often made the spontaneous decision to adopt an animal that could outlive its new owners. The hapless beast might soon find itself packed—alongside tents, lawn chairs, coolers, and canvas duffel bags—in the trunk of a dusty sedan headed west at sixty miles per hour on a warm Sunday evening. Like the food trade, the pet trade soon grew into a business. During the 1950s and 1960s, gas station operators along Route 66 alone probably sold hundreds of the animals. Desert tortoises appeared in pet stores and vivaria as distant as Chicago and London. As late as 1970, the California Department of Fish and Game fined a man five hundred dollars for shipping 105 desert tortoises to a Utah pet store and having 185 more in his possession at the time of his arrest. No one knows how much money changed hands in this pet trade or how many desert tortoises people collected over time. What we do know is this: in 1989 the FWS estimated that one hundred thousand desert tortoises existed in captivity—about the same number that remained in the wild. Today the desert tortoise is the only federally listed threatened or endangered species that is also a common household pet.[11]

TORTOISE SCIENCE AND LAND MANAGEMENT

In 1922, John Van Denburgh of the California Academy of Sciences noted that biologists knew almost nothing about the habits of the desert tortoise.[12] By the end of the twentieth century, however, the tortoise was one of the best-documented wildlife species in the American Southwest.

Early studies, often conducted by amateur naturalists and pet owners, concluded that female tortoises laid a clutch of six to eight eggs each year. Yet in the wild, most immature tortoises succumbed to predation, and as few as 2 or 3 percent survived to begin breeding, sometime after the age of fifteen. Those that did reach maturity became nearly impervious to native predators and under normal circumstances could live for several decades.[13]

These studies often began with statements about the species's ability to endure in such a harsh environment. Desert tortoises can survive for more than a year without drinking, and they tolerate annual temperature oscillations of more than one hundred degrees Fahrenheit. During times of scarcity they become torpid and wait patiently in their burrows for the return of water. Desert tortoises show remarkable fortitude, but the idea that they are evolutionarily and physiologically adapted to their current environment may be wishful thinking. Traits that appear to aid the species in its desert life—such as its affinity for salt, sluggish metabolic rate, and large impermeable eggs—first emerged in ancestors that inhabited moist tropical and subtropical climates not nearly as demanding as the contemporary Mojave. Ten thousand years ago, tortoises lived in more verdant landscapes. And unlike other desert herpetofauna, such as chuckwallas and leopard lizards, which seem to relish the summer sun, tortoises avoid the desert's extremes by hiding in burrows for up to 90 percent of their lives.[14]

In 1948, Angus Woodbury, of the University of Utah, and Ross Hardy, from Weber College, published the classic study of desert tortoises in the wild. Their paper provided key insights into the species' physiology, life history, and ecology, and it served as a basis for subsequent research into tortoise evolutionary biology, biogeography, and epidemiology. In addition to their biological research, Woodbury and Hardy provided a brief evaluation of the tortoise's general welfare. They described a species whose low rate of reproduction, lack of mobility, and ease of capture rendered it vulnerable to collection, highway traffic, poisonous plants, brush fires, trash burning, floods, and overgrazing. Woodbury and Hardy concluded that tortoises were already "in dire need of protection" and recommended new regulations to end hunting, prevent habitat loss, and reduce harm to tortoises wherever they occurred in the wild.[15]

By the time Woodbury and Hardy published their landmark essay, the California legislature had already made a gesture toward tortoise protection. In 1939, California became the first state to outlaw the sale or purchase of any desert tortoise. In 1961 the state strengthened its game code by adding the words *harm, take, shoot,* and *illegal possession* to its catalog of tortoise-related prohibitions. In 1970 the desert tortoise appeared on an initial list of thirteen reptiles and amphibians with full protection under the California Endangered Species Act. By 1973, Arizona, Nevada, and Utah had all established laws protecting tortoises in the wild and restricting their trade and transport.[16]

State game codes helped reduce tortoise collection, but they failed to provide sufficient protection for the same reasons that limited the effectiveness of conservation efforts for other imperiled species. First, state-level regulations lacked adequate enforcement and penalties. The state departments of fish and game, which received the majority of their budgets from the sale of hunting and fishing permits, used these funds for the management of species favored by sportsmen. Nevada did not even have a nongame wildlife program until the mid-1970s, when it hired just two biologists to manage all zero-bag-limit species, including birds, fish, mammals, amphibians, and reptiles. Pursuing tortoise collectors on millions of acres of remote desert rangelands did not seem like an effective or rewarding use of such limited resources, particularly when so many of the offenders were just uninformed tourists. When game wardens did find someone with a trunk full of tortoises, the punishment was usually insufficient to discourage future collecting.[17]

The second reason that state regulations failed to protect the tortoise was that habitat degradation was becoming an even more important problem for the species than collection. Major mining operations affected only about fifty square miles of the Mojave, but a network of roads serviced each of these operations, and thousands of smaller digs perforated the desert's surface. Grazing never completely rebounded from its crash in the early 1920s, yet in 1968 there were still twenty-five thousand cattle and one hundred thirty-eight thousand sheep on public lands in the California desert—all of which competed with tortoises for scarce forage. The U.S. military operated nine bases in the Mojave, which it used for training exercises and as bombing ranges. The Atomic Energy Commission (later the Department of Energy) conducted hundreds of nuclear tests at the Nevada Test Site. Highways and other linear corridors crisscrossed the desert, creating hazards and barriers to dispersal for terrestrial wildlife. By 1980, Bureau of Land Management (BLM) lands alone would contain thirty-five hundred miles of power transmission lines, twelve thousand miles of pipelines, fifteen thousand miles of maintained roads, and incalculable thousands of miles of off-road tracks.[18]

Off-roading started as hobby in the 1950s and then expanded during the 1960s with the introduction of light, inexpensive motorcycles imported from Japan. By 1968, Californians owned nearly two million off-road vehicles, including at least a million motorcycles and two hundred thousand dune buggies. Over the next five years, recreational use of California desert BLM lands tripled, with almost two-thirds of the increase attributed to off-road motorized recreation. Long-distance competitions, such as the infamous Barstow to Vegas race, attracted thousands of riders. What was once a hobby became a community, a culture, even a way of life for riders such as Bob Perkins, who came to know the desert as "a place of beauty and joy where you could have thrills that most people only dream about."[19]

One person's dream was another's nightmare. In 1974 the *Los Angeles Times* announced that a battle had begun over the future of the Mojave. "The bikers, seeing more fences, freeways and No Trespassing signs each time they ride the desert, are mindful of days when they could unload their machines and ride in any direction as long as their fuel would last." Meanwhile, the conservationists, "seeing marks lacing the desert and dust plumes on the horizon, hearing the annoying whine of engines, remember when only the wind moved the sand and the only sounds were of birds and of small animals scurrying." The two sides seemed irreconcilable, but they actually had much in common. Both wanted to "keep the wide open spaces open" and save the old Mojave they once knew, with all its freedoms and beauties, from encroachment and destruction.[20]

One of the most eloquent voices for desert conservation was Robert Stebbins, a herpetologist from the Museum of Vertebrate Zoology in Berkeley. What most people failed to understand, he argued, is that "nature isn't all that tough." Despite claims to the contrary, deserts were some of the most fragile environments on earth. Off-road vehicles were wreaking havoc on the land by churning its soil, flattening its vegetation, and disturbing its wildlife. Stebbins conceded that some form of multiple use should guide the management of the desert's public lands, but he also argued for a strong conservationist ethic that would connect wildlife conservation with wilderness recreation. "Let us set aside a few areas for off-road vehicles," he wrote, "but let us retain most of the desert in its pristine beauty. It is best savored by driving by road to remote areas, parking, and walking."[21]

Stebbins was advocating a radical change in the administration of the California desert, most of which was under the authority of the BLM. Congress had created the BLM in 1946 when it combined two agencies from the Department of the Interior, the General Land Office and the U.S. Grazing Service. The General Land Office had dispensed surplus government land to homesteaders, speculators, and businesses since 1812. The U.S. Grazing Service came later, after the passage of the Taylor Grazing Act in 1934. The ostensible goal of this act was to restore and maintain the vast nonforested, publicly owned western rangelands, but it also accomplished a political objective. By establishing a decentralized, production-oriented Grazing Service in the Department of the Interior, Congress halted the expansion of the Department of Agriculture's ambitious, bureaucratic, conservation-oriented, and more centralized U.S. Forest Service. The General Land Office and the Grazing Service had different histories, but they had something important in common. Both agencies were established to promote private economic development, minimize government interference, and maintain local control over public lands in the arid West.[22]

Upon its establishment, the BLM inherited one-third of the nation's public lands and one-eighth of its total land area. It also became the steward of about 75 percent of the desert tortoise's habitat. Like its predecessors, however, the BLM remained a weak and decentralized organization, allied with powerful interests from grazing, mining, and other resource extraction industries. Local BLM offices had the power, and indeed the obligation, to disburse permits for these activities to a wide variety of users. Yet the agency had no statutory authority to manage the land under its jurisdiction.

In 1970 the Public Land Law Review Commission, a federal committee charged with assessing the status of public land management in the United States, published *One Third of the Nation's Land*. This report attempted to balance the competing agendas of traditional conservation programs, extractive industries, environmental groups, and a range of recreational users. It concluded that like the Forest Service, the BLM should have the authority to manage its lands under a multiple use, sustained yield mandate. Exactly what *multiple use* or *sustained yield* might mean in the California desert remained open for debate.[23]

And debate there was. Mining corporations argued that under no circumstances should Congress alter the stipulations of the 1872 Mining Law or various other statutes that guaranteed their access to the desert. Ranchers maintained that grazing was an essential aspect of western culture and that local control had resulted in rangelands that were in better condition than at any other time in the previous century. Military leaders watched the process quietly but with the concern that in a new political environment, their operations—surrounded by a more intensively used desert landscape—might come under increased scrutiny. Energy firms, which at the time viewed the Mojave mainly as a transmission corridor between the oil and gas deposits of the intermountain West and the markets of coastal California, argued that their pipelines constituted essential infrastructure for the nation's economic prosperity. Off-road vehicle enthusiasts embraced a vision not only of limited government control but also of unimpeded mobility—and they pressed their case in the contentious debate over the BLM's ban on the Barstow to Vegas motorcycle race. Real estate agents and chambers of commerce argued that the BLM should sell more of its land to private interests for economic development. Preservationists saw the Mojave as one of the last remaining regions with large roadless areas suitable for wilderness designation. And tortoise advocates viewed it as an endangered habitat in need of scientific management and, of course, conservation.

In 1974 a group of state and federal government biologists formed the interagency Colorado River Wildlife Council. At their first meeting, held on a shoestring budget in a Las Vegas hotel room, the participants agreed that the desert tortoise should serve as the flagship species for wildlife conservation efforts throughout the region. The BLM and state departments of fish and game could not ensure the future of the tortoise and other desert wildlife species, but government employees could work for change inside their home agencies while going outside their professional roles to build new nongovernmental institutions and communities for research and conservation. In April of the following year, the members of this group founded the Desert Tortoise Council, which launched an interdisciplinary program that included research, education, advocacy, and annual conferences. By 1980 the Desert Tortoise Council had become the Mojave's most active and influential environmental science and conservation organization.[24]

Two other nongovernmental organizations emerged during this period to support tortoise research and conservation. The pet trade had decreased the number of tortoises living outside captivity in the Mojave. But the tortoise's status as a domestic companion lent it a large, enthusiastic, and diverse constituency, including many people who otherwise would not have become involved in wildlife conservation. In 1964, pet owners formed the California Turtle and Tortoise Club, which eventually partnered with the California Department of Fish and Game, the Desert Tortoise Council, animal shelters, and veterinary clinics throughout the region to find homes for hundreds of orphaned tortoises—some of which had been plucked from the desert decades earlier—and to study the effects of reintroducing captured individuals back into their desert habitat.[25]

The Desert Tortoise Preserve Committee, formed in 1974, had a more specific goal. It worked to establish a tortoise reserve on high-quality, densely populated habitat in the western Mojave near the town of California City, in Kern County. The preserve committee joined forces with the Nature Conservancy, and in 1980 the two groups succeeded in establishing the Desert Tortoise Natural Area. It was only about forty square miles, a minuscule fraction of the species' range, but it was an important site and a symbolic step for the conservation of tortoise habitat at a moment when the BLM was embarking on a much larger transition.[26]

In 1976, Congress passed the Federal Land Policy and Management Act. This law gave the BLM statutory authority to manage the lands under its jurisdiction for multiple uses—which included not only grazing, mining, and recreation but also the conservation of historical and archaeological sites, geologic features, water, wildlife, and endangered species. It demoted traditional extractive users and permit holders by forcing them to compete with upstart interest groups for access to the land. And it catalyzed the BLM's tumultuous transformation from a disempowered trustee of the federal estate into an active land management agency. The metamorphosis of the bureau was neither immediate, complete, nor uniform. It had a limited budget and few resources with which to implement the act, and the law remained flexible enough to accommodate diverse local interpretations. BLM officials in the inland West—including Nevada, Utah, and Arizona—generally sided with the rural communities in which they lived, and sought to maintain the preexisting policies their friends and neighbors had come to expect. In California, however, it was a different story.

The Federal Land Policy and Management Act contained a clause that directed BLM staff to develop a regional conservation plan for its California desert lands, which encompassed some twenty-five million acres in the state's southeastern quadrant. No other area in the country received such a specific directive. Congress chose the California desert as the site of a special conservation plan because the area had already experienced several nationally publicized land use conflicts and because powerful members of the state's delegation wanted to initiate a policy process that would include public input. After three years, eight million dollars, twelve hearings and workshops, and a fifty-one-day public comment period that elicited nine thousand written responses, the bureau completed its California Desert Conservation Area Plan, in 1980. James B. Rush, the bureau's California state director, struck a pragmatic, conciliatory, almost apologetic tone in his preface to the final draft. "Perhaps, as individuals, we may say, 'This is not exactly the plan I would like,' but together we can say, 'This is a plan we can agree on, it is fair, and it is possible,'" he wrote. After all, it was only the beginning. What really counts, Rush concluded, is "what happens on the ground."[27]

On the ground, the BLM had already begun to move forward several years before it completed the California Desert Conservation Area Plan. In 1974 the bureau hired a young scientist named Kristin Berry, who had recently received her doctorate under Stebbins's direction at the University of California, Berkeley, as the lead biologist for its new California Desert Program. Berry began her career as a herpetologist at a time when ornithologists and mammalogists still conducted almost all wildlife management. She was a woman in a profession still dominated by men. And she went to work in a region where wildlife managers, especially those interested in nongame species, had scant influence. Those who underestimated Berry, or the significance of her work, could be forgiven for doing so considering the circumstances.[28]

Berry's first job at the BLM was to develop the wildlife element of the California Desert Conservation Area Plan. She had not previously worked with the desert tortoise, but she soon understood that it could serve as a flagship species for the entire region. Berry attended the first meeting of the Colorado River Wildlife Council and helped found the Desert Tortoise Council. She soon launched a desert tortoise science and conservation program that led her to author dozens of publications, spearhead multiple research initiatives, participate in the founding of advocacy organizations, and develop new federal land management policies.

In 1984 Berry and her colleagues published an 848-page report titled *The Status of the Desert Tortoise (Gopherus agassizii) in the United States*. It assembled most of what scientists knew about the species and provided tortoise advocates with an agenda for research and activism. The report's most consequential claim involved historical changes in the distribution and abundance of tortoises in the Mojave. When Berry began her work, no one knew how many tortoises existed, where they lived, or how their populations had changed. Early naturalists had provided contradictory accounts, labeling the species "quite common," "tolerably common," "common at few places," and "formerly plentiful." Sampling problems were not limited to the historical record. Tortoises may seem big and slow, but, as the story at the beginning of this book illustrates, they are notoriously difficult to count. They spend nine-tenths of their lives underground, and when they venture outside their burrows they can look remarkably like stones parked on the desert floor.[29]

Despite these problems, the report offered a bold argument about the species' decline. Berry had grown up in the Mojave and could remember a time, just a couple decades earlier, when hundreds of tortoises would appear each spring near her family's home in Kern County. Her memories informed her science, and her interviews confirmed her observations. She concluded that tortoise numbers had plummeted, particularly in the western Mojave, where, prior to Euro-American colonization, population densities "may have ranged from 500 to over 1,000 tortoises/sq. mile in some areas." This estimate was double to quadruple the maximum density of 250 tortoises per square mile that biologists had recorded since they had begun conducting surveys a decade earlier. Some observers regarded Berry's data as anecdotal and her inferences as conjecture. Yet the report was an impressive step forward, and most biologists agreed with her conclusions. The *Status* report's findings soon became inscribed in hundreds of scientific papers, popular articles, and government documents. By the end of the decade, the BLM was reporting to Congress that "tortoise populations in the Mojave Desert have lost 60 percent of their range and 90 percent of their numbers in the last 100 years."[30]

The same year that Berry and her colleagues published their report, a coalition of three national environmental organizations—Defenders of Wildlife, Natural Resources Defense Council, and the Environmental Defense Fund—petitioned the FWS to list the desert tortoise as endangered throughout its range. None of these three organizations had participated in previous tortoise research or conservation efforts. But as in the case of the spotted owl, the opportunity to obtain endangered species protection for charismatic wildlife that happened to occupy a vast and largely unprotected region eventually attracted attention among national environmental organizations.[31]

The FWS had already acted once to protect the desert tortoise. In 1980 it granted threatened status to the Beaver Dam Slope population in southwestern Utah, where Woodbury and Hardy had conducted the first major study of the species decades earlier. The 1984 listing petition covered much of the American Southwest, and it represented a political and institutional commitment on an entirely different scale. After reviewing the petition, the service agreed that the desert tortoise warranted further protection, but it sidestepped the issue when it declined to take action because of a backlog of more urgent pending proposals. This was a common justification for delaying action.[32]

The lack of urgency soon turned into a crisis. Pet owners had reported "runny noses" in captive tortoises since the 1930s, but the disease that caused those symptoms remained a mystery. During the 1980s, veterinarians began to conduct research on influenza-like symptoms in several species of captive and wild tortoises. Upper respiratory tract disease (URTD), a chronic flu-like ailment caused by the endemic pathogen *Mycoplasma agassizii*, may have existed in wild tortoises for millennia, but it began to spread during the twentieth century through the pet trade. Former pets that had probably acquired the disease while in captivity readily transmitted it when their owners released them back into the desert. Even sick tortoises can survive for a long time in captivity, but URTD is chronic, unrelenting, and difficult to treat. Wild tortoises living with the disease display sunken eyes and wet or crusted nostrils; they appear listless, experience nutritional deficiencies, and suffer from massive organ damage before they languish and die.[33]

Researchers reported URTD among desert tortoises in Utah in the mid-1980s. Then, in 1988 and 1989, biologists almost simultaneously reported finding it at study sites in Arizona, Nevada, Utah, and California. The initial numbers varied as field-workers struggled to identify the symptoms. In the western Mojave, initial surveys concluded that anywhere from none to more than half of the tortoises showed symptoms. Berry compiled the data and reported an epidemic at the Desert Tortoise Natural Area. Elliot Jacobsen, a professor of veterinary medicine from the University of Florida, concluded that URTD had "the capability of wiping out an animal population. The oldest, longest living land vertebrate in North American is dying."[34]

In May of 1989, the same coalition of national environmental groups that had submitted the first comprehensive listing petition for the desert tortoise five years earlier submitted an updated version that included Berry's data on the spread of URTD. The specter of a pandemic generated support for the petition among most of the relevant state and federal agencies, including the BLM and the California Department of Fish and Game. In August the FWS used its emergency authority to list the tortoise as endangered wherever it occurred inside the United States. The following year the service ruled that tortoises in the Sonoran Desert did not require federal protection, which narrowed the scope of their listing to only the Mojave Desert. It also downgraded the Mojave populations from endangered to threatened—a less critical designation but one that carried the same legal protections, as defined in the federal Endangered Species Act.[35]

Conservation biologists frequently complain that by the time the government lists a species, it is often too late to avoid a demographic collapse. At the time of its listing, however, the desert tortoise still had several factors working in its favor.

The Mojave populations included about one hundred thousand individuals—approximately ten times more than any other listed land animal and some five hundred times more than the California condor at the time of its listing. About the same number of tortoises remained in captivity. The Sonoran Desert populations in Arizona and Mexico still seemed stable. In the Mojave, the tortoise's range included two national parks and several wilderness areas. Perhaps most important, the species had a large, diverse, and well-organized community of advocates. The desert tortoise remained widespread and common, but it had received the highest levels of state and federal protection. This meant that future tortoise conservation efforts would have an enormous impact on land use and natural resource management throughout the Mojave Desert.

THE DESERT REORGANIZED

In the two decades that followed the desert tortoise's listing, a series of complex, intertwined political processes transformed land and natural resource management in the Mojave Desert. New federal laws, management plans, conservation initiatives, interagency agreements, and scientific assessments—as well as more than a few lawsuits—redrew the region's bureaucratic boundaries and established a new administrative geography. Some of these processes began with the goal of restoring desert tortoise populations. But the species also became entangled in debates that seemed only vaguely related to its conservation, as various groups used it to promote their visions for the future of the landscape. Like the spotted owl, the desert tortoise became more than simply a subject of conservation. It became a vehicle, a catalyst, a symbol, a diversion, a partner, an enemy, and a potential source of political power for those who could mobilize it for their cause. By 1990 all attention had shifted to Clark County, Nevada, just over the California state line in the northeastern Mojave, home to the city of Las Vegas.

In less than a century, Las Vegas had grown from a dusty outpost and railroad depot into a major American city. Most of this growth occurred over the span of a single human, or tortoise, lifetime. Yet few people now remember the landscape that preceded the contemporary metropolis, so its special qualities warrant mentioning. In Spanish, Las Vegas means "The Meadows." Before the city appeared, the Las Vegas Valley's desert steppe landscape supported some of the finest rangelands in the Mojave. Snowmelt from the Spring Mountains, which reach nearly twelve thousand feet in elevation, created freshwater seeps and seasonal streams, and the steep terrain surrounding the valley provided habitat for a diverse suite of plants and animals. It was a wonderful place to settle down and raise some cows. It was also home to thousands of desert tortoises.

In 1960 Nevada was still the least-populous state in the nation, with fewer than three hundred thousand residents, but population growth had already become its primary engine of development, and civic leaders had a clear vision for their economic future. To attract new businesses, the state would remove impediments to growth: taxes would stay low, corporate regulations would remain limited, and local governments would annex federal land for privatization wherever possible. Inexpensive real estate would attract development, and planning would focus more on facilitating construction than mitigating its impacts. According to one of the state's greatest boosters, Governor Grant Sawyer, Nevada's newfound attractiveness came down to one word: "It is the intangible that is responsible for Nevada's charm—we call it climate." Sawyer did not have Las Vegas's 110°F summers, parched autumns, frigid winter nights, or gale-force springtime winds in mind when he spoke of Nevada's "climate." As the *Los Angeles Times* put it, in 1961, "Chances are . . . you'll be able to do whatever you want to do there for quite a while."[36]

By 1990 Clark County had a human population of nearly eight hundred thousand and one of the nation's fastest-growing metropolitan areas. (By 2007 the population had reached two million.) Las Vegas was a sprawling suburban metropolis, but it was not yet a dense urban region. Decades of frenetic development had created a mosaic of land uses and left a patchwork of undeveloped BLM parcels interspersed among commercial clusters, rambling suburbs, and eight-lane freeways. Desert tortoises still emerged from their burrows each spring to search for food, water, and mates. But as their habitat patches shrunk, they encountered a more fragmented and dangerous landscape. Some of these animals became backyard pets, but hundreds lost their lives on the highways, and many more were entombed in their burrows.[37]

The tortoise's listing caused a panic among real estate developers and contractors who feared that their operations might violate federal law, or worse, that the government would stop their projects before completion. The Summa Corporation, a former Howard Hughes subsidiary, had already invested sixty million dollars on infrastructure for a twenty-five-thousand-acre, two-hundred-fifty-thousand-person housing development when the tortoise's listing halted construction. In 1989 the Summa Corporation, the City of Las Vegas, and Clark County sued the Fish and Wildlife Service to revoke the species's threatened status, but their case faltered in court when a federal judge backed the emergency listing decision. The tortoise problem was not going away.[38]

The pro-growth consensus, which had dominated Nevada's political economy since World War II, never came into question. Growth had generated unprecedented prosperity, municipal governments depended on tax revenues from development, powerful corporations had made large real estate investments—and the people just kept coming. The city, the county, and the corporation devised a new plan. If they couldn't beat the tortoise, they would have to join it; it must become part of southern Nevada's growth machine. So they proposed a deal. They offered to create a $2.5 million endowment for tortoise research and conservation, establish a $550-per-acre mitigation fee for new development, and sponsor a collaborative process that would lead to the creation of a habitat conservation plan. Modeled after the HCP developed for the fringe-toed lizard in Southern California's Coachella Valley, the tortoise plan would provide Clark County with an incidental take permit under the Endangered Species Act and allow development to continue in the Las Vegas Valley in exchange for conservation programs elsewhere.[39]

The process got off to a rocky start. The area's few remaining cattlemen, who saw little to gain from bargaining for future access to lands they had always controlled, abandoned the meetings. Pet owners wondered whether their longtime companions now qualified as contraband. A plan to euthanize tortoises captured inside the Las Vegas Valley, to save money and prevent the transmission of URTD, met with protests from as far away as Europe and Asia. People even feared for their own safety. For two years the organizers of the public planning process had to hire security guards to frisk the attendees for weapons before they entered the collaborative process meetings, which were open to invited stakeholders and representatives from the public and private sectors, as well as members of the general public. According to Ann Schrieber, a miner who participated in the process, "people walked into the room hating each other's guts and ready to slit each other's throats."[40]

The process meetings continued for eight hundred hours over the course of nearly a decade. Clark County hired the attorney Paul Selzer, who had overseen the Coachella Valley fringe-toed lizard effort, as a facilitator. He established three ground rules for the meetings: there would be no debating the validity of the ESA, no one could criticize the FWS's tortoise listing decision, and everyone had to be willing to compromise. With these rules in place, strife eventually gave way to cooperation. In 1995 the participants completed the Clark County Desert Conservation Plan, which instituted development mitigation fees, established habitat reserves, and provided funds for tortoise research and rehabilitation programs, such as those at the Desert Tortoise Conservation Center, or "Tort Resort," outside Las Vegas.

In return, the FWS issued a thirty-year permit for the development of one hundred thirteen thousand acres of tortoise habitat in the Las Vegas Valley.[41]

This was just the beginning. The desert tortoise was only one of several dozen species in southern Nevada that were already endangered or could be listed in the future. In 2000 the planning process participants completed the much more ambitious Clark County Multiple Species Habitat Conservation Plan. This plan extended coverage from one species, the desert tortoise, to 232 species living in twelve ecological zones, from alpine meadows to salt desert scrub. It authorized the purchase and retirement of grazing permits held by willing sellers on more than two million acres of rangelands. And it used funds generated by the sale of BLM lands in the Las Vegas Valley to support dozens of conservation and infrastructure projects. Clark County already had a comprehensive plan covering areas such as transportation, housing, schools, recreation, public buildings, and economic development. The Multiple Species Habitat Conservation Plan linked these basic governmental priorities to a regional conservation strategy for one of the most biologically diverse areas in North America.[42]

The Clark County Desert Conservation Plan and Multiple Species Habitat Conservation Plan have become models for collaborative planning under the federal ESA. Both were among the first of their kind. By 2010 the FWS had approved some seven hundred HCPS. The desert tortoise alone appeared in twenty-four plans scattered throughout four states. Many of these plans covered small areas and specific projects, such as the construction of a racetrack, a prison, a church, a landfill, and a performing arts center. But the FWS also approved, or was overseeing the development of, regional multiple species HCPs covering much of the American Southwest. These included plans for the Sonoran Desert around Tucson, the lower Colorado River, the western Mojave Desert, the Imperial Valley, and the Coachella Valley.

In 1998 Congress passed the Southern Nevada Public Land Management Act, which authorized the BLM to sell its remaining lands inside the urban matrix of the Las Vegas Valley. During the first ten years of the program, the average price paid per acre increased from $3,876 to an astounding $573,262, and the Department of the Interior reaped a profit of $3.3 billion. It spent $2.6 billion of the proceeds on infrastructure projects, capital improvements, conservation efforts, and land acquisition. Almost $53 million went toward the implementation of the Clark County Multiple Species Habitat Conservation Plan, and another $1.1 billion went toward the construction of parks and trails and the purchase of nature reserves.[43] The Southern Nevada Public Land Management Act was one of the most lucrative public land sale programs in American history. But even more important for this story, it represented the culmination of a shift in which desert tortoise conservation went from an impediment to development to a component of southern Nevada's growth machine in the period before the great recession that began in 2007.

A NEW LAND MANAGEMENT REGIME

The desert tortoise's listing had consequences for the Mojave Desert extending far beyond Clark County. Between 1990 and 1994, three additional political processes created a new context for tortoise conservation and recovery efforts. Two were administrative efforts that resulted directly from the tortoise's listing; the third involved a legislative campaign in which politicians and activists mobilized the tortoise as a rationale for wilderness preservation. Together, these three processes signaled a new era for land and wildlife management in the Mojave.

First, in 1994 a team of eight biologists, all based outside the Fish and Wildlife Service, completed the Desert Tortoise Recovery Plan. Its goal, like that of all recovery plans, was to reestablish the species to a point at which the service could remove it from the federal endangered species list. Peter F. Brussard, of the University of Nevada, led the team, and the group included the familiar figure of Kristin Berry, who by then had moved to the National Biological Survey. The team's first task was to define *recovery*, and its members did so in terms of population biology and biogeography. The plan divided the Mojave into six Recovery Units, each comprising fourteen Desert Wildlife Management Areas. The tortoise population in each Recovery Unit would be evaluated separately, as distinct and with its own protected status. To qualify for delisting, each population would need management and monitoring plans, commitments from the relevant agencies, at least a thousand square miles of protected habitat, and "strong biological evidence" that its numbers had stabilized or increased over several generations. According to its authors, the plan would require "unprecedented interagency cooperation," and progress would be "measured in decades or centuries."[44]

The second consequence of the listing was that the FWS had to designate critical habitat for the tortoise. The service failed to do so until 1993, when a coalition of plaintiffs sued to prevent the transfer of BLM land in Ward Valley, near the town of Needles, to the State of California for use as a low-level radioactive waste facility. The suit argued that if the service had designated critical habitat, as it was obliged to do under the ESA, it would have included the Ward Valley site. This would have forced the BLM to consult with the FWS, as mandated by Section 7 of the ESA, and possibly to complete an environmental impact statement, as required under the California Environmental Quality Act and the National Environmental Policy Act.[45]

The service settled the suit and thereafter began a yearlong process to define the critical habitat of a species whose biogeography it understood poorly and that ranged over dozens of political jurisdictions in four states. Ultimately, the service settled on what it viewed as the only defensible solution: it copied the geographic boundaries of the six Recovery Units described in the Desert Tortoise Recovery Plan. The final critical habitat map, like the recovery plan, encompassed 6.4 million acres (ten thousand square miles)—an area roughly the size of Massachusetts. The critical habitat designation did not preclude any actions within the area. But it did mean that any federal project or any project that required a federal permit could invoke a Section 7 ESA consultation or a third-party lawsuit. An expensive and time-consuming environmental review and mitigation process would undoubtedly follow.[46]

By 2000, BLM field offices in the California desert had conducted more than 150 Section 7 consultations on various species with the FWS. Yet this did not stop the Southwest Center for Biological Diversity, the Sierra Club, and Public Employees for Environmental Responsibility from suing the BLM in San Francisco's Ninth Circuit Court for not doing enough. Their suit charged that the bureau's actions were jeopardizing twenty-four endangered species—including the Mojave desert tortoise, the Peninsular bighorn sheep, the desert pupfish, and Peirson's milk vetch—and that it needed to amend its California Desert Conservation Area Plan to better address endangered species problems. BLM officials had already outlined changes they intended to make to the plan, so they simply accelerated the process that was already under way. The bureau closed roads, covered landfills, erected fencing, prohibited off-road vehicles, and retired grazing allotments on at least eleven million acres.[47]

In the summer of 1994, at the same time that the FWS was approving the recovery plan and completing its critical habitat designation, a third, equally important Mojave Desert conservation debate was unfolding in Washington, DC. Almost twenty years earlier, Southern California environmental activists Joyce and Peter Burke had written the first proposal for a new national park in the eastern Mojave Desert, between Interstate Highways 40 and 15 and the Nevada state line. It was a remote and spectacular place that contained sand dunes, cinder cones, lava flows, limestone caverns, dry lakebeds, forests of relict fir trees, and some ninety mountain ranges—not to mention thousands of desert tortoises. Even the BLM admitted that the area contained cultural and natural values "so diverse and outstanding that the area readily qualifies for national park or national monument status." But the bureau's final California Desert Conservation Area Plan, published in 1980, stopped short of recommending park status. Instead it proposed that Congress create a "national scenic area," which would preserve a "sense of discovery" for visitors while maintaining BLM control and permitting multiple use management.[48]

In 1986, Senator Alan Cranston introduced the California Desert Protection Act, thereby beginning a legislative odyssey. Three years later, frustrated with its lack of progress and in need of additional evidence to support his case, he asked the General Accounting Office to review the status of wildlife in the California Desert Conservation Area. The GAO concluded that the BLM had failed to develop or implement nearly half of the California Desert Conservation Area Plan's wildlife- and habitat-related management tasks. In October of 1989, Cranston summoned the GAO representative James Duffus to the Senate to testify about the BLM's failings. According to Duffus, the BLM had completed only forty-seven of the eighty-five habitat-management and area-of-critical-environmental-concern plans required of it by law. In cases where the BLM had completed plans, implementation often lagged far behind.[49]

In 1992, Cranston retired and California's new senator, Dianne Feinstein, began to promote the bill with the help of the Bill Clinton administration. The legislation began to move forward, and the Democratic majority in Congress finally managed to pass the California Desert Protection Act in October of 1994, just one week before Republicans regained control of both chambers of Congress for the first time in forty years. In the next budgetary cycle, the new conservative majority appropriated the legal minimum, one dollar, for the act's implementation. Not until 1996 did the Democrats muster enough support to establish an operating budget for it.[50]

The California Desert Protection Act set in motion a regional remapping exercise. It transferred three million acres from the BLM to the National Park Service, including the new 1.4-million-acre Mojave National Preserve (previously the East Mojave Scenic Area). It enlarged the administrative boundaries of Joshua Tree and Death Valley and upgraded both from national monument to national park status. This made Death Valley the largest national park in the contiguous United States. The act also created seventy-one new wilderness areas encompassing a total of 3.75 million acres. Political compromises determined the names, boundaries, and rules for the new administrative units. Yet on its passage, the California Desert Protection Act became the second-largest conservation law, by land area affected, in American history. It was mainly about wilderness, not wildlife, but wildlife and endangered species, especially the flagship desert tortoise, provided a key rationale.

Over the next decade and a half, the act joined a raft of other less-ambitious legislative, judicial, administrative, and scientific processes that, together, transformed the Mojave from a space of weak government institutions and loose administrative control into the region with probably the greatest concentration of parks and wilderness areas in the United States outside Alaska.

The events of 1994 transformed the Mojave from a space of natural resource extraction to one dominated by conservation and recreation. Consider the case of mining. During the 1930s, National Park Service officials often viewed miners, with their rusty pickaxes and willful mules, as picturesque symbols of the frontier West whose presence might even complement new parks such as Death Valley. By the 1970s, however, Congress began to regulate mineral exploration and extraction on public lands through laws such as the Mining in the National Parks Act and the Wilderness Act, which allowed prospecting to continue but made it more difficult by banning motorized transportation to often remote mines. During the George W. Bush administration, mineral and fossil fuel extraction increased in many areas of the intermountain West—but not in the Mojave. By 2008 there were no active mines in the Mojave's three national parks, hundreds of inactive claims had failed to survive federal reviews, and most of the industry, at least for a time, had consolidated at a few important sites.[51]

Grazing has met a similar fate. In 1970, ranchers still controlled the use and management of rangelands throughout the Mojave Desert, even though the profitability of their industry had been declining for decades. The election of Ronald Reagan, a self-declared "sagebrush rebel," and the appointment of James Watt as his interior secretary gave ranchers renewed clout in a time of diminishing economic importance. But the reversal of fortune was short-lived. In 1992 the GAO concluded that "livestock grazing activity on BLM allotments in hot desert areas risks long-term environmental damage while not generating grazing fee revenues sufficient to provide for adequate management." According to the GAO, the BLM's entire program of grazing leases in the Mojave, Sonoran, and Chihuahuan Deserts—which included the operations of about a thousand ranchers—warranted reconsideration and potential termination. The following year, Interior Secretary Bruce Babbitt failed in his effort to reform grazing in these areas by altering fee structures. In 1994, however, millions of acres in the Mojave became critical habitat areas, recovery units, wilderness areas, and national parks. None of these designations absolutely precluded grazing, but all of them diminished its prospects.[52]

During the 1970s, the number of cattle and sheep grazing on the BLM's fifty-four California desert allotments declined by more than half. By 2005 only two large operations remained on BLM lands in the California portion of the Mojave Desert, and the purchase of lands and the retirement of grazing permits in Clark County had all but ended grazing in southern Nevada. Some ranchers gave up and left the business, while others moved their operations to less-regulated states, such as New Mexico. Abandoned ranches, like old mines and ghost towns, were relegated either to the status of historical artifacts, subject to preservation and interpretation, or more frequently erasure and demolition, by government agencies such as the National Park Service. Tom Wetterman, whose herd of two hundred to four hundred cows occupied three hundred fifty thousand acres near Barstow, California, finally decided it was time to leave when the U.S. Army offered to purchase his ranch as part of its Fort Irwin expansion. The Department of Defense had become interested in tortoise conservation because after the end of the Cold War, military bases were under increasing pressure to obey federal environmental laws such as the ESA. At the time of the sale of Wetterman's ranch, the army was considering using his former home as a field station for desert tortoise research.[53]

The Mojave Desert no longer generates much beef or wool, gold, silver, borax, or tungsten. But that does not mean that it has failed to produce things or that people no longer work there. From military might and suburban lifestyles to wide-open spaces for conservation and recreation, the Mojave still offers things that people want and will pay for. On rangelands where ranchers once raised cattle, biologists now raise tortoises, or at least they try. Even the handful of ranchers who remain in the region admit that their work is more an avocation than a viable industry. This explains why—unlike in the Northwest forest, home of the northern spotted owl, where endangered species controversies have involved labor and industry—conflicts in the Mojave have so often pitted different forms of conservation and recreation against one another. The debate over off-road vehicle access versus wilderness designation epitomizes these struggles, as does the newer conflict over the use of public land for renewable energy development in the form of solar fields and wind farms.[54]

The transformation of the Mojave was not a planned or orderly process. The changes that occurred were in part the result of contingent historical events, from housing bubbles to reptilian epidemics. The consequence was a hodgepodge of new laws, institutions, court cases, management plans, administrative designations, interagency agreements, and scientific assessments that represented a diverse set of political interests. These changes had no particular ultimate goal, but they did have a clear trajectory. Power shifted, industries moved, attitudes changed, and maps were redrawn.

AND WHAT OF THE TORTOISE?

Tortoise conservation clearly served as a catalyst for many changes, and much of the conservation work in the Mojave has been accomplished in the tortoise's name. It is impossible, however, to isolate or quantify the role that the desert tortoise and its advocates played in the larger transformation of the region. Between 1989 and 1998, the federal government spent at least ninety-two million dollars on tortoise recovery, making this endangered species conservation program the seventh most expensive in the country during that period. But this figure underestimates the total federal expenditures and does not include spending by state and local agencies or nongovernmental organizations. Depending on the accounting method used, the total costs of desert tortoise recovery efforts, including private land purchases that cited tortoise protection as a primary objective, may already have exceeded one billion dollars.[55]

But what of the tortoise itself? How has the species fared in this process? And how has habitat conservation in the Mojave shaped the species's prospects? Even though vast areas of this desert are now national parks, wilderness areas, or other kinds of nature reserves, it remains a dangerous place for desert tortoises.

Consider the issue of tortoise predation, which has increased markedly in recent years. Ravens are effective predators of juvenile tortoises. They were once rare in the Mojave, but they now congregate at dumps and roost on transmission towers, telephone poles, and billboards. Coyote populations decreased during most of the twentieth century, due to aggressive control programs carried out by state and federal agencies in partnership with shepherds and cattlemen. Today coyotes once again patrol the desert in boisterous packs, with year-round access to human-provided water and garbage. Feral dogs and cats have also joined the ranks of the subsidized hunters. Land managers have made attempts to decrease tortoise predation, but for many conservationists these efforts elicit disturbing memories of predator control programs from the nineteenth and twentieth centuries, when managers sought to make the desert safe for cows and sheep. Predator control thus remains unpopular among most conservationists and animal welfare advocates, even when its goal is to protect an endangered species.[56]

The example of predator control helps to explain why the bureaucratic reordering and remapping of the Mojave will not necessarily lead to the recovery of the desert tortoise or any other threatened or endangered wildlife species. It has proved difficult even to assess whether progress is being made. In 2002 a report by the GAO found that—despite the formation of technical advisory teams, land managers' groups, and scientific institutes—a lack of research coordination and a failure to conduct regular reviews had made it impossible even to assess the efficacy of management actions, much less to improve upon them. No one knows, for example, how the removal of grazing has affected tortoises or changed the ecology of the places where they live. The GAO's conclusions suggest the inherent difficulty in establishing an effective research and conservation program on the scale of the Mojave Desert.[57]

In 2004 the Desert Tortoise Recovery Team reconvened to attempt just such an assessment. Its findings were sobering. The team found evidence of "trends leading away from recovery goals in some parts of the species range." Key components of the recovery plan had not been implemented, and the original plan had not accounted for the full nature of the species's "synergistic, interacting, and cumulative threats." A decade earlier, the team had assumed the existence of six relatively discrete population units, but new research suggested a more complicated scenario, of various populations linked through dispersal and interbreeding. This meant that tortoises traveled over long, hazardous distances more often than previously believed. It also meant that the definition of recovery might need to be changed, since maintaining "a population that is demonstrably increasing or remaining stable may not be possible." A new approach might instead focus on the attainment of certain achievable management goals. It also might require admitting that tortoises needed "more intense actions," such as "head starting, genetics management, habitat management and facilitated dispersal, herd immunization, and other artificially facilitated ecosystem management processes."[58]

Desert tortoises are in much the same situation as other chelonian species, and reptiles more generally, around the world. Collection, disease, exotic species, and habitat loss continue to reduce their fertility and increase their mortality. If this process continues, the remaining adults will constitute a "living dead" population that may linger for years without sufficient recruitment before slowly fading away. This is not the only possible scenario for the future of the desert tortoise. It has plenty of space to roam and many dedicated people working on its behalf. With luck and hard work it may still recover. Only two things are certain. During the past several decades, the Mojave Desert has undergone a comprehensive administrative transformation that has changed every aspect of its land and natural resource management. Today the desert tortoise has plenty of "protected" habitat, including millions of acres in which to roam, but its future remains more tenuous than ever. As with the northern spotted owl—and, indeed, the California condor—it appears that habitat protection, although crucial, cannot alone save the desert tortoise.[59]

CHAPTER SEVEN · The San Joaquin Kit Fox

The Flagship Fox

In 1888, C. Hart Merriam published the first description of a new type of fox he had identified, based on a specimen from San Bernardino County in inland Southern California. "It is not a little surprising," Merriam wrote, "that so large a mammal as a fox, inhabiting so well explored a region as California, should have escaped notice till the present time." The animal was a kit fox, one of three varieties native to the state, and it had escaped notice for several reasons. Kit foxes often live in flat, arid landscapes that are relatively unenticing for most naturalists. They spend their days in subterranean burrows and forage by the dark of night. They are the smallest wild canids in North America, and their warm-weather pelts had little value in the fur trade. They possess a familiar canine cuteness, but they are neither icons of the wild nor popular household pets. As late as 1937, Joseph Grinnell, Joseph Dixon, and Jean Linsdale referred to the San Joaquin subspecies as "one of California's least known fur-bearers."[1]

Today the San Joaquin kit fox is famous, or to some, infamous. San Joaquin kit foxes live only in California's greater San Joaquin Valley ecoregion, an area that includes the San Joaquin Valley and about a dozen smaller neighboring valleys east of the Coast Ranges and west of the Pacific Crest. With abundant fossil fuels and a landscape uniquely suited to industrial agriculture, this is one of the world's greatest commodity-producing regions. It is also home to a large collection of rare, endemic, and endangered species. By the 1990s, the San Joaquin kit fox had become the flagship species for habitat and biodiversity conservation in the region.

The story of the San Joaquin kit fox differs from those of the California condor and the desert tortoise. The condor symbolized a conflict and later a consensus between ideas about wildlife and wilderness in the years following the passage of the ESA. The desert tortoise's story revealed some of the problems with that kind of consensus approach—even in a thinly populated region dominated by public lands, where the creation of vast new parks, reserves, and wilderness areas should have portended a more auspicious trend toward recovery. The kit fox lives in a privatized, industrial landscape devoid of grandeur, bereft of beauty, lacking in charm. The San Joaquin Valley ecoregion has no wilderness areas and few wildland parks. Its wildlife refuges are almost all wetland sites established for the conservation of waterfowl. And although it does have an increasing number of upland nature reserves, inhabited by terrestrial animals such as San Joaquin kit foxes, these are novel additions to an otherwise developed landscape.

This chapter explores the history of land and wildlife conservation for an endangered species that makes its home in a place no one could ever mistake for pristine. How have political debates about endangered species conservation and recovery efforts unfolded in privatized, industrialized landscapes such as the greater San Joaquin Valley? And what does the kit fox's story tell us about the possibilities and limitations of a protected areas paradigm for endangered species management in urban and agricultural environments? It is not surprising that habitat conservation efforts in such areas have confronted even greater challenges than in regions dominated by public lands, such as the Mojave Desert. What is surprising is how much creatures in urban and agricultural landscapes still have to teach us about the complexity of wildlife-habitat relationships and the potential for new approaches to endangered species conservation.

THE SAN JOAQUIN VALLEY

The San Joaquin Valley is a place made distinctive, indeed made possible, by its contradictions. It is an arid landscape with abundant water. Its sweltering summer sun is matched only by its dismal winter fog. It contains some of the continent's most contaminated and denuded lands, but its main commodity products, food and fuel, come straight from the ground. It is one of the world's most intensively farmed regions, and with five of the top ten agricultural counties in the United States, it serves as the country's "salad bowl." Agricultural abundance has not, however, translated into prosperity for most residents, who see corporate profits leave the valley in tankers, pipelines, and fruit trucks. This region of aqueducts, monocultures, derricks, refineries, and migrant worker camps is also a biodiversity hot spot. Its people are poor, but its ecology is rich.[2]

The San Joaquin Valley's agricultural productivity and biological diversity both stem, in part, from its physical geography. The valley floor rests on more than thirty thousand feet of accumulated sediment. The oldest and deepest of these layers dates to the late Jurassic period, around 145 million years ago, when saltwater covered the region. These marine sediments are the basis of the valley's petroleum industry. More-recent sedimentary layers came from the surrounding mountains—the Coast Ranges, the Tehachapi Mountains, and the Sierra Nevada—as they uplifted during the past five million years. Their peaks receive the full, wet brunt of winter storms that approach from the Pacific Ocean. This orographic effect creates a rain shadow on the leeward slopes, lush forests on the windward slopes, and streams that carry seasonal floods and mineral-rich sediments to the valley below. The result is the rare and extraordinary landscape of the San Joaquin Valley, with abundant sunshine, plentiful water, fertile soils, and a year-round growing season.[3]

The nearby peaks also created barriers to the dispersal of and interbreeding among plants and animals, and this geographic isolation encouraged the development of new forms. The Tipton kangaroo rat, the blunt-nosed leopard lizard, and the San Joaquin kit fox are all endemic to the valley and its immediate surroundings. And they are but a few examples. Taken together, the San Joaquin and Sacramento Valleys have twenty-eight endemic vertebrate species and subspecies. The San Joaquin Valley alone has more endemic vertebrate species and subspecies than any area of similar size in the continental United States.[4]

The San Joaquin Valley has always been a diverse and dynamic landscape, but today it is a different place, ecologically, than it was when its endemic species evolved. The current valley emerged through two and a half centuries of colonization, settlement, and commodity production. Spanish soldiers, Franciscan missionaries, French trappers, and American pioneers had all explored the valley by the early nineteenth century, but few chose to remain there. Physicians believed that its torrid climate and swampy lowland terrain produced miasmas, and they considered the place unsuitable for the temperate constitutions of civilized white settlers. For the first hundred years of European colonization in California, most of the valley's inhabitants were American Indians, domestic livestock, and wild animals.[5]

The gold rush initiated a new era in land tenure and use. Anglo-American cattlemen and their San Francisco financiers rigged the legal system in ways that allowed them to usurp lands under Mexican ownership. On these lands, they built enormous livestock operations to supply meat and wool to the state's new miners and merchants. The flood of 1861 and 1862 devastated the valley's cattle industry, and many of the animals that survived the deluge died in the two-year drought that followed. Chaos in the livestock industry helped enable agribusiness corporations to consolidate their control over the state's most fertile valleys. They used railroads, barbed wire, and laws that favored crops over cattle to expand their holdings. They won lawsuits against mining facilities that were fouling headwater streams in the Sierra Nevada, used riparian laws to ensure their access to mountain runoff, and invested enormous amounts of capital and labor in draining marshes and digging irrigation ditches. Wheat replaced livestock, and by the beginning of the twentieth century, row crops and orchards replaced wheat. The valley's modern agricultural geography had begun to take shape.[6]

Droughts returned in the 1920s, and farmers lobbied hard for state and federal water projects. They got the Central Valley Project in the 1930s and the State Water Project in the 1950s. These helped to make the San Joaquin Valley one of the world's most productive agricultural regions in the years following World War II. By 2007 the valley's eight counties were producing more than $18.3 billion per year in dairy, poultry, fruit, nuts, cotton, alfalfa, and other crops. Today the San Joaquin Valley is synonymous with modern industrial agriculture.[7]

The valley also houses some of the country's largest oil fields. The first wells appeared in the area before 1900, and within a decade thousands dotted the landscape. Trustbusters and conservationists fought to maintain public control by creating federally owned petroleum reserves. Yet by the 1920s, pro-development Western judges and legislators had forced the U.S. government to grant a multitude of leases on the public lands. Competition for these leases often led to corruption, as in the infamous Teapot Dome bribery scandal. And for good reason: the San Joaquin Valley contained some of the most valuable fossil fuel reserves in the United States. The Midway-Sunset oil field alone has produced almost three billion barrels since its discovery in the 1890s, making it the country's third-most-productive field. The Elk Hills Naval Petroleum Reserve was, for a time during the 1980s, the most productive oil field in the contiguous forty-eight states. In 1996 the federal government sold it to a private corporation for $3.65 billion, the most lucrative sale of public land in U.S. history up to that point. Elk Hills is also now known as one of the few remaining haunts of the San Joaquin kit fox.[8]

Urban areas cover less than 10 percent of the land in the San Joaquin Valley, but their growth has had disproportionate effects on the region's economy and ecology. Residential and commercial development, often in the form of sprawling suburbs and exurbs, has altered the real estate market and increased property taxes for farmers with land near the expanding urban centers. Many farmers have sold or subdivided their properties, and new developments have replaced former farmlands. Residential subdivisions have also replaced open spaces once covered by piedmont grasslands, oak woodlands, and vernal pools.

The San Joaquin Valley's conversion to a landscape of industrial agriculture, petroleum production, and suburban sprawl has come with environmental consequences. The loss of topsoil through erosion and salinization, a by-product of irrigation in arid climates, has diminished farm productivity and sterilized large tracts of once-fertile land. The valley's air quality ranks among the worst in the United States. Agricultural runoff has concentrated chemical pesticides, organic compounds, heavy metals, and trace minerals such as selenium in contaminated sumps. One such basin, the Kesterson National Wildlife Refuge, became so toxic to birds, fish, and livestock that in the late 1980s the Fish and Wildlife Service closed it and buried the wetland under a blanket of dirt.[9] Storage and distribution systems that move water around the valley can no longer supply all of the competing demands, and they remain vulnerable to catastrophic failure. And then there is the issue of habitat.

The San Joaquin Valley has lost a greater percentage of its pre-European land cover than any other region of similar size in California and possibly in the United States. By 1960, intensive agriculture and development covered at least half of the valley. Over the next decade, increased irrigation and population growth led to the conversion of another 34 percent of the undeveloped areas within the ranges of the San Joaquin kit fox and other endemic species. By 1980 less than 7 percent of the San Joaquin Valley floor remained in an undeveloped state. By the end of the housing bubble, in 2007, that number had declined to less than 5 percent.[10]

The region's endemic species evolved in a landscape of grasslands, scrublands, seasonal wetlands, riparian forests, and vernal pools. The wetlands are mostly gone, vernal pools are increasingly rare, and riparian forests remain only in a few small nature reserves. Grasslands and scrublands still exist, mainly in the ring of foothills that surrounds the valley floor, and they account for most of the "natural lands" described in the FWS's 1998 *Recovery Plan for Upland Species of the San Joaquin Valley*. This document does not define *natural lands*, but the intended meaning seems to be something like "open space" and includes privately owned rangelands used for livestock grazing. *Natural lands* truly is a relative term in the San Joaquin Valley.[11]

When California's first wildlife scientists and conservationists arrived in the San Joaquin Valley, around 1910, agribusiness firms had already drained large tracts of its once vast seasonal wetlands. By 1930 the state had lost 90 percent of its wetlands, most of which had been in the Sacramento and San Joaquin Valleys. Over the next four decades, conservation and restoration efforts thus focused on the wet, low-lying areas that provided hunting grounds and habitat for waterfowl traveling along the Pacific Flyway.[12]

Few of those who worked to conserve the San Joaquin Valley's wetlands worried about the plants and animals that lived in its arid grasslands and scrublands. Most of these areas were privately owned farms, cattle ranches, or oil fields that offered little public access. Who would have wanted to visit them, anyway? For most of the year, these were dusty, hot, foreboding places. The arid flatlands of the San Joaquin Valley lacked the recreational potential of the nearby wetland wildlife refuges; the scenery of Death Valley, which was becoming the archetypal standard for California desert beauty; and the charm of the giant sequoia groves in the neighboring Sierra Nevada. The San Joaquin Valley was no sublime wonder; it was an industrial landscape, and at least in the view of many conservationists, it was ugly.

KNOWING THE FOX

In their classic 1937 study *Fur-Bearing Mammals of California*, Joseph Grinnell, Joseph Dixon, and Jean Linsdale assembled the first detailed analysis of the natural history, taxonomy, and relationships to humans of California's kit foxes. Using morphological and geographic evidence, the authors concluded that the state had three kit fox "races," or subspecies. The desert kit fox lived in the Mojave and Colorado Deserts; the long-eared kit fox lived in the foothills and valleys of the eastern Los Angeles Basin; and the San Joaquin Kit fox lived in the greater San Joaquin Valley ecoregion. All three subspecies had a common evolutionary origin; were similar in size, appearance, and behavior; and lived on arid plains with hot summers and loose alluvial soils suitable for the creation of subterranean burrows. Kit foxes were denizens of the desert—inhabitants of the low, flat places that constituted some of California's most austere environments.[13]

By the time *Fur-Bearing Mammals of California* appeared in print, two of these three subspecies had already suffered significant declines. The long-eared kit fox probably went extinct by 1910. By 1930 the San Joaquin kit fox's population had also declined, and the authors believed that its range had contracted to less than half of the former area. One cause of this decline was the fur trade. In 1919 the trapper Arthur Oliver killed one hundred kit foxes in an area about twenty miles long and two miles wide near Fresno. The pelts sold for between $2.50 and $5.00 each, which was not much money for the effort. Because of such prices, trappers never pursued kit foxes in large numbers. According to Grinnell and his coauthors, however, "in certain parts of the San Joaquin Valley [kit fox pelts] have given men a good income from barren uncultivated land which otherwise yielded no return except a crop of jackrabbits."[14]

In addition to fur trapping, kit foxes died from ingesting poisoned bait. In 1925 Oliver reported finding five dead San Joaquin kit foxes in just one square mile, all killed by strychnine poisoning. Predator control programs did not target kit foxes, but foxes often reached baited carcasses first, and they also suffered from secondary poisoning after eating animals that had consumed the tainted meat. Individual kit foxes were collateral damage in a much larger predator control campaign, but predator control and fur trapping were not uniformly detrimental to kit fox populations. Such activities also reduced the populations of coyotes, bobcats, and red foxes—all of which either hunted kit foxes or competed with them for scarce resources.[15]

Grinnell and his coauthors believed that kit fox populations were regulated mainly, though not entirely, from the bottom up. In *Fur-Bearing Mammals of California*, they wrote that there was "no open warfare" between coyotes and kit foxes. In many areas, they argued, kangaroo rats constituted "the staff of life" for kit foxes. By this they meant that the availability of prey, not the prevalence of predators, was the most important factor controlling kit fox populations. Then as now, proponents of the bottom-up view argued that kit fox fertility and survivorship correlate strongly with the availability of prey, including insects and rodents, which in turn correlate with annual precipitation. These relationships are complicated, however, because although most insect populations tend to increase with precipitation, kangaroo rat populations may show an inverse relationship with it, actually increasing to a point during mild droughts. Another important implication of the bottom-up view is that kit foxes may not have benefited much from reductions in the number of coyotes and bobcats through predator control programs.[16]

Proponents of a top-down model, on the other hand, argue that predators can place considerable pressure on kit fox populations. Unlike most fox species, which use burrows only during the mating season, San Joaquin kit foxes use their burrows year-round, which suggests that they require constant access to safe sites. During the 1980s and 1990s, state and federal agencies curtailed predator control programs in California, and coyote populations rebounded. Recent studies have shown that in some areas, coyotes are responsible for more than 75 percent of kit fox deaths. But on closer inspection, the situation is more complicated. Red foxes, which may compete with and kill San Joaquin kit foxes, were introduced into the Sacramento

Valley from the Midwest during the 1870s, and since then they have expanded their range all the way to Southern California. If coyotes also compete with and kill red foxes, then the rebound of their population may indirectly benefit kit foxes.[17]

Grinnell and his coauthors embraced the bottom-up model for kit foxes in most areas, but they also understood the complexity of these predator-prey relationships and knew that a variety of factors determined the viability of San Joaquin kit fox populations. "Intensive trapping plus poison campaigns against 'predatory' animals plus some extraordinary seasonal food condition unfavorable to the foxes," they wrote, "might conceivably completely wipe out of the great interior valley of California the last survivors of the race *mutica*." The authors found this lamentable, so they invoked a familiar conservation rationale, arguing that the kit fox served as a helpful ally in the farmer's battle against insect and rodent pests. The San Joaquin kit fox "has very few habits injurious to man or his possessions," they wrote, and exhibits "positive values which far more than counterbalance its faults."[18]

Fur-Bearing Mammals of California was a landmark volume, but it offered more questions than answers and thus provided a potential basis for future studies. Yet San Joaquin kit foxes received almost no scientific attention during the 1940s, 1950s, or 1960s. Beginning in the 1970s, Lyndal Laughrin, Stephen Morrell, and later Brian Cypher and others picked up where Grinnell, Dixon, and Linsdale left off. Their research provided a much richer and more detailed account of kit fox behavior and ecology. It showed that kit foxes inhabit grasslands and scrublands in the San Joaquin and neighboring valleys, where they try to avoid predators and eat small mammals, birds, and insects, supplementing their diets with grasses and other vegetable matter. Mostly nocturnal, kit foxes rear their pups in earthen dens, which they often share with a menagerie of other subterranean dwellers—from rattlesnakes and ground squirrels to pocket gophers and burrowing owls. Kit foxes live in a matrix of connected groups, called a metapopulation, linked geographically through dispersal and genetically through interbreeding. Corridors connect each population's habitat patches, which may be more than a hundred miles apart, and contain a network of dens that can provide safe havens from predators. The numbers of predators, populations of prey, availability of dens, quantity and size of habitat patches, and pathways for dispersal all contribute to kit fox fertility, recruitment, survivorship, and mortality.[19]

Other physical habitat characteristics are also important. Kit foxes show a strong preference for flatlands and low-angle slopes with unconsolidated soil substrates suitable for the creation of underground dens. They can excavate a den in a single evening, but many of the best dens develop over a long period through excavation by numerous occupants. The destruction of one of these multigenerational dens can represent an important loss of habitat, hindering the ability of kit foxes to rear young in the area and disperse between patches. Kit foxes occasionally pass through agricultural fields at night, but they generally avoid exposed, shelterless areas. They often hunt along linear corridors, such as road shoulders and power lines, but these areas can prove hazardous because larger predators may attempt to exploit such bottlenecks as well. Roads are also dangerous, but studies suggest that less than 10 percent of kit fox deaths result from traffic collisions.[20]

One of the most important questions that emerged from the body of kit fox research was the extent to which the subspecies's range had contracted. The first known San Joaquin kit fox range map, published in 1920, included most of the southern and western San Joaquin Valley and several neighboring valleys. By 1937, Grinnell and his coauthors concluded that the fox's range had already shrunk. "Because the kit fox occupied territory in western California much of which has been taken over for man's uses," they wrote, "it has pretty much vanished from the country west of the desert divides." Their map identified a smaller area on the west side of the southern San Joaquin Valley and a smaller strip in the valley's center as the fox's current range. Maps published in state wildlife documents in 1950 and 1975, however, maintained the 1920 range. The map in the 1998 *Recovery Plan for Upland Species of the San Joaquin Valley* did not include a rangewide boundary line but instead represented a collection of kit fox distributional records as hollow dots (see map 7). The dots ranged from Contra Costa County near Sacramento in the north to Santa Barbara County in the south, and from Monterey County in the west to Tulare County in the foothills of the southern Sierra Nevada in the east. This map did not include dates for any of the distributional records.[21]

The researchers who drew the kit fox's historical range maps possessed inadequate data to make reliable conclusions about the subspecies's distribution and abundance. And as one might expect from a dynamic metapopulation, the kit fox's geography was constantly in motion. Grinnell and his coauthors believed that the range of the species had contracted, and kit foxes did in fact disappear in some areas. But in other areas they temporarily disappeared, only to reappear later. Range expansions in the south and west—where foxes colonized new portions of Monterey, Santa Barbara, and Ventura Counties—seem to have offset losses in the east. The southern part of the range may have always served as a stronghold for the subspecies, but during the 1950s, kit foxes also moved westward, probably due to shifts in land use—including more intensive grazing, seasonal burning, and coyote control—that led to increases in the number of rangeland rodents. These practices

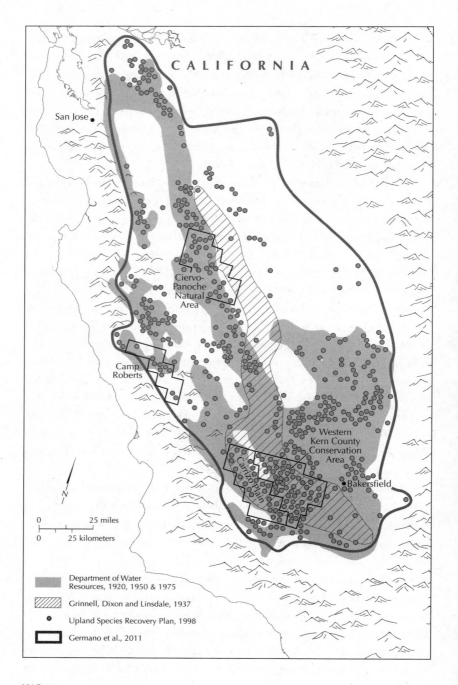

CALIFORNIA

San Jose

Ciervo-
Panoche
Natural
Area

Camp
Roberts

Western
Kern County
Conservation
Area

Carrizo Plain

Bakersfield

0   25 miles

0   25 kilometers

Department of Water
Resources, 1920, 1950 & 1975

Grinnell, Dixon and Linsdale, 1937

Upland Species Recovery Plan, 1998

Germano et al., 2011

MAP 7.

Kit fox range as represented by studies since 1920. This illustrates
the challenge of mapping the ranges of rare and endangered
species, as well as using ambiguous historical records and spatial
data for contemporary conservation efforts.

began to decline in the 1970s because of changes in livestock markets and environmental criticisms of postwar range management practices, and current geographic patterns may be continuing to shift as a result. By 1998, kit foxes still occurred in all fifteen of the counties where they had lived before the 1930s (and possibly an additional sixteenth), and range maps from the two periods looked remarkably similar. Researchers eventually concluded that although the kit fox's range might not have simply shrunk, in the manner that Grinnell, Dixon, and Linsdale had imagined, it had become increasingly fragmented by development, making travel between isolated habitat patches and populations more difficult for the foxes.[22]

These range maps said little about the number of individuals remaining in the wild. In 1970, Laughrin, of the University of California, Santa Barbara, and the California Department of Fish and Game, conducted the first postwar study of the San Joaquin kit fox's status. In a bleak assessment, he estimated a population of just one thousand to three thousand adults. Five years later Morrell revised the number upward, to at least 10,000 and possibly as many as 14,800 foxes. He arrived at his higher estimate by positing one breeding pair for every den he found along a series of transects that covered about 1 percent of the kit fox's range, and multiplying the total by one hundred. Today, however, biologists know that kit foxes use multiple dens, an insight that would have caused Morrell to lower his estimate. Despite the need for additional research, few investigations followed. When the FWS surveyed the literature in 1983, it found only twenty documents pertaining to kit foxes and just thirteen that dealt with the San Joaquin subspecies.[23]

The FWS's initial kit fox recovery plan, issued in 1983, made up for this lack of data with a combination of vague language, precise numbers, and bold assumptions. The result was a sort of mathematical alchemy. First, the document revised Morrell's 1975 estimate downward, obtaining a total of 6,961 adult foxes. Then it concluded that before 1930, the population of San Joaquin kit foxes "may have been between 8,667 and 12,134 assuming an occupied range of 22,447 square kilometers . . . and densities of 0.4 to 0.6 per square kilometer." These numbers meant "a possible population decline of 20 to 43 percent." When the FWS updated the recovery plan in 1998, it made no attempt to revise the population estimate of fifteen years earlier. To some extent, this was justifiable. More than thirty years after the San Joaquin kit fox had appeared on the first federal endangered species list and fifteen years after the publication of its first recovery plan, researchers had not yet completed a rangewide survey.[24]

Insufficient information about geographic ranges and population numbers almost always hinders endangered species recovery efforts, particularly in the early stages before researchers have the opportunity to gather data. Despite this lack of data, by 2005 researchers had concluded that the San Joaquin kit fox "was once ubiquitous throughout California's San Joaquin Valley and its surrounds" and that there remained only "a few thousand San Joaquin kit foxes, compared with tens of thousands that probably existed prior to European colonization of California." These conclusions may be correct, but little historical evidence existed to support them. Yet as is so often the case for endangered species, the emergence of a consensus about historical trends, rather than the strength of the evidence supporting it, was what really mattered in shaping subsequent management decisions.[25]

KIT FOX CONSERVATION

San Joaquin kit fox conservation efforts began in 1965, when the California Fish and Game Commission declared it a "protected fur-bearer." The kit fox became a member of the "Class of '67"—the group of seventy-eight vertebrate animal species that appeared on the federal government's first endangered species list—in March of that year. In 1971 the California Fish and Game Commission classified it as "rare" on the first list of protected species published under the new California Endangered Species Act. The state listing made it a crime to kill or possess a San Joaquin kit fox without a permit.[26]

Then nothing much happened. State and federal agencies allocated some funds for land purchases and facilitated mitigation efforts for public and private development projects in and around the San Joaquin Valley to aid the kit fox. But this was not a high-priority case. Most conservation resources in the valley continued to go to rivers and wetlands. Since the kit fox did not appear to be in imminent danger, the state and federal wildlife agencies focused their limited resources on listing more species and acting on behalf of those that seemed closer to extinction.

In 1983, sixteen years after listing the kit fox, the FWS published its *San Joaquin Kit Fox Recovery Plan*. This came at a time when the service had the authority to prohibit a wide variety of actions that could harm endangered species but little capacity to gather information, engage in collaborative projects, or pursue proactive conservation efforts. The plan's goal was to recover the kit fox so that it could be removed from the endangered species list. Yet its author had no idea "what population levels and degree of habitat protection are necessary to satisfy criteria for delisting" nor even enough information to make an educated guess.[27]

What did seem clear was that the available resources would limit opportunities for conservation. The 1983 plan envisioned a future in which agriculture and petroleum production continued to dictate virtually all land use in the San Joaquin Valley and few resources had become available to acquire land for endangered species conservation. It concluded that given inadequate funds and the high cost of real estate, "it would be unrealistic to propose that large blocks of land be acquired and preserved." The plan recommended a strategy that included the acquisition of just thirty-five thousand additional acres for kit fox conservation and recovery purposes.[28]

The 1983 plan became outdated almost as soon as the FWS adopted it. Over the next several years, environmental activists from around California started to take an interest in the San Joaquin Valley's rare species and to pressure the FWS to invest more resources in upland habitat conservation. The California Department of Fish and Game launched an ambitious effort to gain more state-level control over endangered species management through a variety of means, including the acquisition of state wildlife refuges in the San Joaquin Valley. Farmland retirement programs in areas with toxic drainage or degraded soils provided opportunities for additional land purchases. During the early 1990s, upland conservation projects in the valley ecoregion surpassed the recovery plan's habitat protection goals. By 1994, endangered species conservation and mitigation programs had resulted in forty-six major public land purchases and transfers within the kit fox's range in and around the San Joaquin Valley. These added up to 163,128 acres, or about 4.7 times the land area recommended for protection just over a decade earlier.[29]

In 1998 the FWS replaced its outdated kit fox document with a new recovery plan whose expanded scope included all threatened, endangered, candidate, and vulnerable species and subspecies living in the valley's upland environments. The *Recovery Plan for Upland Species of the San Joaquin Valley* covered thirty-four types of plants and animals, including twelve vertebrates and eleven federally threatened or endangered species or subspecies. According to the FWS, only one—the San Joaquin kit fox—had the "broad distribution and requirement for relatively large areas of habitat" that would allow it to "provide an umbrella of protection for many other species that require less habitat." The same animal that Joseph Grinnell, Joseph Dixon, and Jean Linsdale had once described as "one of California's least known fur-bearers" had become the representative of a multiple species recovery program in one of the country's most biodiverse regions and new mascot for conservation in the greater San Joaquin Valley.[30]

Even before the publication of the upland species recovery plan, the listing of so many plants and animals—and the threat of more listings—led to dozens of surveys, mitigation efforts, and conservation plans. In 1991 the California Energy

Commission conducted the first major study of biotic diversity in the valley ecoregion. Its Southern San Joaquin Ecosystem Protection Plan, published the following year, established a basis for future mitigation and conservation efforts. The City of Bakersfield used the energy commission's work in 1994 when it completed its multiple species habitat conservation plan. The Metropolitan Bakersfield Habitat Conservation Plan became one of the country's first multiple species plans, paralleling other early efforts in its approach and objectives, including the one under way for the desert tortoise and other species in Clark County, Nevada. The Bakersfield plan covered 408 square miles and included seven vertebrate and eleven plant species. Like the Clark County plan, it proposed opening up development in and around the city and then mitigating the effects of these projects by purchasing lands for conservation throughout the surrounding area.[31] By 2009 the kit fox appeared in twenty-one HCPs throughout the greater San Joaquin Valley ecoregion, and more were in preparation.

Conservation efforts had also begun in the region's few remaining open spaces and wildland areas. The most ambitious of these involved the Carrizo Plain— a broad, grassy rift valley that straddles the San Andreas Fault about thirty miles southwest of Bakersfield. In 1988 the Bureau of Land Management, the California Department of Fish and Game, and the Nature Conservancy collaborated to purchase eighty-two thousand acres of land that eight years later became the Carrizo Plain Natural Area. President Bill Clinton used the Antiquities Act to declare the Carrizo Plain a national monument in January of 2001, during the final days of his administration. In the years since, the monument has grown to two hundred fifty thousand acres. The plain had a long history of farming and ranching, but it was in a remote corner of the state. At an average of twenty-two hundred feet in elevation, it was perched well above the San Joaquin Valley and out of the reach of the state and federal water delivery systems that would have enabled large-scale agricultural development. In 2001 much of the Carrizo Plain either remained in a wildland state or had reverted to semiwild status after decades of mixed agricultural use.

Over the next several years the Carrizo Plain was the site of one of the West's most controversial range battles. The plot was familiar. Local ranchers and farmers—angered by environmental regulations of the 1970s, the Clinton administration's attempts to reform federal land grazing policy in the 1990s, and the establishment of the Carrizo Plain National Monument in 2001—pressured the Bureau of Land Management, which administered public lands in the area, to maintain its lenient grazing policies. In the words of the *Los Angeles Times*, the controversy that ensued over grazing regulations versus endangered species conservation devolved into "a morass of environmental politics."[32] Part of the conflict constituted a typical western range war, but part also related to the Carrizo Plain's unique condition and resources. Most observers considered it the closest contemporary analogue for what the San Joaquin Valley must have looked like in the late nineteenth century. The range remained productive for open cattle grazing, and the residents had largely avoided the development pressures that had shaped other rural landscapes throughout the state. The plain was also home to species, such as the tule elk and the pronghorn antelope, that had long since disappeared from nearby areas, and it contained the greatest concentration of federally listed endangered species in California.

The fight over the Carrizo Plain was particularly divisive, but it was only one of several conservation efforts that began in the greater San Joaquin Valley ecoregion in the 1990s and 2000s. Conservation and mitigation programs brought dozens of parcels into public ownership, conservation easements, mitigation banks, and land trusts. One such program has taken advantage of state and federal farmland retirement funds, which Congress intended to improve drainage, reduce contaminated runoff, and end irrigation on depleted, salt-encrusted soils. Conservation groups have joined with administrative agencies and local water districts to use the farmland retirement funds as a means of purchasing parcels that might facilitate endangered species recovery. In these cases, irrigation districts purchase lands and water rights from farmers, and wildlife agencies and partner organizations conduct programs to restore grasslands, replant woodlands, and install artificial kit fox dens. Programs such as these have protected most of the land that still has significant value for endangered species in the greater San Joaquin Valley ecoregion.[33]

A FOX ON THE FARM

Today the San Joaquin Valley ecoregion is well known as a national nexus for endangered species conservation efforts. Yet in the 1970s and 1980s, when urban conservationists, environmental organizations, and government agencies began to focus on the area, their interest came as a surprise to local farmers and ranchers. Agriculturalists in and around the valley had long-standing relationships with the FWS, which managed local wildlife refuges and migratory waterfowl. But the last time anyone had expressed concern about the valley's upland animals was in the late nineteenth century, and the species involved had been the iconic tule elk and pronghorn antelope. Now scientists and activists wanted to save species, from the Tipton kangaroo rat to the riparian brush rabbit, that few locals had ever seen or even heard of. As with ranchers on the Carrizo Plain, these new efforts were not an easy sell.

As a way of getting these farmers on board, many endangered species advocates worked hard to foster collaborative processes for conservation in and around the San Joaquin Valley. Beginning in the mid-1990s, however, a series of lawsuits forced the FWS to take a more aggressive approach to Endangered Species Act enforcement. The events that followed made the valley ecoregion the focus of a national debate about agriculture and endangered species.

In 1993 the Central Valley Project, which had delivered water to the valley's farmers for forty years, came up for reauthorization. Section 7 of the ESA requires all federal agencies to consult with the FWS on any project that may jeopardize a listed species. Because the Bureaus of Reclamation and Land Management administer the Central Valley Project, its reauthorization was subject to review through the ESA consultation process described in chapter 4. The FWS asked these agencies to conduct biological surveys of the project's irrigated areas as part of its permitting process. Without a permit, the two bureaus would need to shut off the taps or, at the very least, amend their preexisting water delivery agreements. Some farmers who hoped to sell their land to developers leaped at the offer of a free biological survey, and nearly 40 percent agreed to participate in the study. But many reacted with indignation at the prospect of facing government inspection or seeing their water cut off. According to Bob Krauter, of the Farm Bureau, the ESA was "changing agriculture in California. It really doesn't matter anymore how much snow falls in the Sierra. There's a regulatory drought." Scott Pearson, of the FWS, put it differently: people were upset because "water is money."[34]

Around this time, the FWS also began to use its regulatory authority to bring charges against individual farmers for violations of federal fish and wildlife laws. The service had never received much enforcement support from the Department of Justice, and by 1992 the federal government had prosecuted only four cases nationwide involving ESA violations. In 1994, however, the FWS pressed charges against three defendants in the San Joaquin Valley alone. On August 29, hundreds of farmers, many riding tractors, rallied in downtown Fresno to protest the arrest of a man who faced eighteen months in jail and three hundred thousand dollars in penalties for the alleged crime of killing endangered kangaroo rats while tilling his property. The man was a Taiwanese immigrant farmer and importer named Taung Ming-Lin, who claimed ignorance of the law but had received a registered letter from the service warning him not to proceed without an approved conservation plan.[35]

The San Joaquin Valley's farmers soon found their voice in Washington, DC. In 1991, Richard Pombo, a twenty-nine-year-old rancher from the city of Tracy, in

San Joaquin County east of San Francisco, captured a new seat in the House of Representatives created through congressional redistricting after the 1990 census. Pombo had served less than two years on the Tracy City Council when he won the election, and he rode into Washington wearing a white cowboy hat, boots, and a pencil-thin mustache.

Pombo was the sort of politician who fashioned his own mythology, and he did it so well that it is still difficult to distinguish fact from fiction. He ran for office as a Republican on a platform that combined rural western values, suburban Christian conservatism, opposition to environmental regulations, and a commitment to private property rights. In his 1996 book *This Land Is Our Land,* Pombo claimed that his antienvironmentalist views took shape during a dispute with the East Bay Regional Park District about a proposed public access trail along an old railroad right-of-way and cut through his ranch. But what really infuriated him, he told a Senate subcommittee in 1994, was the FWS's decision to designate his family's property as critical habitat for the San Joaquin kit fox. This reduced the property's value and gave the family "an unwanted, unneeded, un-silent partner—the federal government."[36]

Neither of these episodes actually happened. The East Bay Regional Park District did propose a new trail, but the project involved an old railroad segment some twenty miles from the Pombo family's property. Nor has the FWS issued a critical habitat designation for the San Joaquin kit fox. Pombo fabricated and embellished these events, but his message resonated with landowners throughout the country who had real complaints about the application of federal environmental laws. He became a star spokesperson for the national wise-use movement, which advocates for reduced environmental regulation and devolution of public land management to local control, by arguing that federal environmental laws infringed on the Constitution's Fifth Amendment guarantee against the taking of private property "for public use, without just compensation." And he gained a lot of supporters.[37]

In 2003, Pombo became the chair of the House Resources Committee and was soon the ESA's most zealous congressional adversary. Yet despite his enthusiasm, he failed to convert his agenda into law. During his first twelve years in the House, he passed only eight minor bills. Pombo introduced legislation to rewrite the ESA eleven times, but none of these attempts succeeded. After his party's electoral rebuke in 1996, House Republican leaders convinced him to tone down his rhetoric somewhat, but Pombo's views did not change. By the time he lost his seat in 2006, support for his agenda had waned and his proposals had little backing even from within his own party.

Pombo's policy proposals were ideological and self-serving, but his basic points—that landowners often bore the burden of conservation programs that benefited all members of society, and that stronger incentives would facilitate greater cooperation among landowners—had substantial merit. Indeed, organizations such as the Nature Conservancy have embraced similar ideas in their efforts to establish productive collaborations with farmers and ranchers that promote habitat conservation.

One such program, launched in 2002 by the Paramount Farming Company, sought to mitigate farming activities by constructing artificial dens that kit foxes could use to disperse across otherwise foreboding agricultural landscapes. This project resulted in California's second safe harbor agreement under the federal ESA, which rewards private landowners who enhance endangered species habitat on their land with permission to engage in authorized activities that may present risks to other endangered species. Safe harbor agreements offer one practical approach for promoting endangered species conservation on privately owned working lands and could lead to more flexible and effective efforts outside protected nature reserves. Yet in 2003, just weeks after the Paramount Farming Company received widespread praise in the media for its participation in the project, the company's chief executive gave a speech expressing frustration with the complexity and pace of the process and doubt about whether he would do it again. Other agribusiness firms, having met with similar problems, have scuttled safe harbor efforts.[38]

As early as 2002, FWS director Steve Williams recognized flaws in the safe harbor program and suggested solutions, but four years later the service had not implemented his recommendations. This has not stopped the program from growing. By June of 2005, more than 325 landowners had enrolled in twenty-three safe harbor agreements that sought to protect thirty-six listed species on more than 3.25 million acres. The fact that this program has continued to grow, despite administrative difficulties, offers yet another example of the need for more incentives and cooperation in endangered species conservation on private lands. This is especially the case in regions such as the San Joaquin Valley, where most land is still under private ownership and will remain so for the foreseeable future.[39]

In the San Joaquin Valley, as elsewhere in the American West, blame for a variety of agricultural problems, from erosion to lack of water, has often fallen on endangered species. Yet species conservation and recovery programs constitute only a small subset of the political, economic, ecological, and demographic changes that have led to such problems. From the 1940s to the 1970s, farmers in California enjoyed uncontested privileged status, and their industries benefited from favorable laws, generous subsidies, scant regulation, and massive public infrastructure investments.

In the years since, the political power of agribusinesses in California has slowly eroded. Farmers have faced challenges not only from environmentalists but also from air quality managers, fisheries advocates, water-hungry municipalities, and rising property taxes associated with rural population growth and real estate development. Seen in this way, endangered species debates, although important in their own right, represent just one aspect of a broader shift in political power, away from agribusiness and toward a more numerous and dispersed collection of interest groups. This is a complicated political and institutional landscape in which to attempt to recover a diverse cast of endangered species.

A FOX IN THE CITY

During the 1980s, Delbert Bowen worked as a sanitation engineer in the city of Bakersfield. Each morning he would arrive at work before dawn and begin the day by tending to the needs of an animal he had befriended that lived on the property where his office was located. This was no alley cat. It was an endangered San Joaquin kit fox, and every morning it would wait patiently for Bowen to arrive in the lot where he parked his pickup truck. The fox's favorite breakfast was a stale doughnut.[40]

Biologists knew that kit foxes lived in Bakersfield, but they considered the animals stragglers—the last remnants of a historic population that would ultimately succumb to habitat destruction, traffic fatalities, malnutrition, and disease. For decades, researchers focused on the foxes that lived in the region's rural rangelands, ignoring the city dwellers. In the late 1990s, they finally conducted the first systematic survey of Bakersfield's kit foxes and, much to their surprise, found that the city had a robust population of two hundred to three hundred individuals—the third largest in existence. Kit fox numbers appeared to be decreasing in other parts of the range, but the Bakersfield population was remaining steady or even increasing. This was due in part to the growth of the city itself, which created more urban habitat as it sprawled into the surrounding countryside.

Kit foxes live different life-styles on rangelands than in cities. On the Carrizo Plain, they live in earthen dens, keep watch for predators, and hunt for kangaroo rats and Jerusalem crickets. In Bakersfield they scamper around relatively safe from coyotes, den in storm drains under freeway embankments, and rear their pups on plush green fairways. In one case, a mating pair excavated a burrow under a median strip in the parking lot of an office complex that housed the local headquarters of a petroleum services corporation. Kit foxes enter a more dangerous landscape when they wander into the Kern River Parkway, an open space and wildlife conservation area that bisects the city and provides a corridor for coyotes and bobcats. Bakersfield is not the wilderness that many people imagine when they think of endangered species habitat. Yet it seems to work for San Joaquin kit foxes, which have access to abundant den sties and freshwater and live on a hearty diet that includes hot dogs, tamales, popcorn, cheeseburgers, and packets of ranch dressing—just look at the piles of garbage that mark the entrances to their burrows.[41]

This situation poses aesthetic, legal, scientific, and administrative problems with no easy solutions. One such problem involves the perceptions of local people. When researchers informed Bakersfield's residents that they had an endangered species living in their midst, many reacted with surprise. This was not because kit foxes lived in Bakersfield—they already knew that—but rather because it did not make sense that such a common and conspicuous critter could also be endangered. Some residents worried about risks such as attacks on pets or canine diseases, but most saw the foxes as harmless and endearing members of their community. They did not, however, consider the kit fox an endangered species that warranted federal protection.[42]

Another problem is the disparity between the expectations of environmental activists and the realities of wildlife ecology. Many environmentalists find it difficult to believe that kit foxes can survive in a place like Bakersfield, and they presume that this must be an unnatural and dysfunctional situation. Urban kit foxes may be cute, but they do not conform to romantic conceptions of natural beauty, and their habitat uses contradict the belief that threatened wildlife represents threatened wilderness (see figure 16). Yet beauty is not synonymous with ecology, and habitat is not the same as wilderness. The persistence of Bakersfield's kit foxes is not, as one nature writer put it, "more happenstance than anything else." Kit foxes are adaptable animals that have the capacity to exploit a wide variety of resources in diverse environments. Today the city as much as the country is kit fox habitat.[43]

This situation has created a set of contradictions and conundrums. In the transformed landscape of the San Joaquin Valley, it makes sense that nongovernmental organizations want to conduct habitat conservation and restoration projects in the few open areas available. It makes sense that planners want to use preexisting public lands and open space corridors as the foundations of a regional reserve network. It makes sense that environmental activists want to use the kit fox to establish open space preserves that would serve as de facto wilderness areas. It makes sense that scientists want to base an endangered species recovery program on the most sophisticated metapopulation viability analyses. And it makes sense that government

FIGURE 16.

A San Joaquin kit fox peeks out from between two buildings at a
high school in Bakersfield. Courtesy of Carrie Wingert and Brian
Cypher.

agencies want to create bounded refuges where they have the authority to manage
wildlife with the least economic impact and political conflict.

What does not make sense is that Bakersfield's kit foxes should be excluded from
conservation activities under the ESA. But this is exactly what has happened through
the adoption of the Metropolitan Bakersfield Habitat Conservation Plan. This plan
seeks to ensure that endangered species listings and recovery efforts will not hinder
the city's economic growth. Like the Clark County plan in southern Nevada, the
Bakersfield plan exempts new developments in the metropolitan area. It exports
conservation programs into the surrounding countryside by requiring developers
to mitigate the impacts of their urban projects through the acquisition of rural
habitat. When the FWS approved the Metro Bakersfield HCP, the city's kit foxes,
like the desert tortoises of Las Vegas, lost their protected status.

Many scientists, officials, and other conservationists argue that scarce resources
should be spent on more natural areas. With enough investment in restoration and
management, they say, kit foxes and other listed species in remote areas such as the
Carrizo Plain might someday reassume their traditional ecological roles and achieve
self-sustaining populations. This remains a worthy goal, and it is possible over the

long term, but getting to that point would require a significant departure from the current situation, in which intensively managed and monitored foxes live in landscapes that, while rural, are utterly different from what existed in those places hundreds or thousands of years ago.

The FWS excluded Bakersfield's kit foxes from the 1998 upland species recovery plan, and biologists have not generally included them in the population viability models that inform current conservation programs. Yet some of these same models have suggested that even in the region's largest habitat conservation area, the Carrizo Plain, the kit fox population may not persist in perpetuity without colonization from outside. Biologists have thus proposed that Bakersfield kit foxes could serve as a source population for reserves that need more individuals to augment their fragile populations. The implication is both counterintuitive and profound. To maintain San Joaquin kit foxes in nature reserves created in part to facilitate their recovery, wildlife managers may need to stock these reserves with individuals from an unprotected urban population.[44]

THE FOX OF THE FUTURE

Opportunities to conserve large areas of wildland habitat in the greater San Joaquin Valley are diminishing. This is partly due to development but also partly due to the success of land conservation efforts since the 1980s. Drainage improvement programs may supply some additional land, droughts and water wars may force farmers to fallow more of their fields, and the oil wells will all eventually run dry. But nongovernmental organizations and state and federal agencies have already purchased, transferred, or redesignated much of the land that could eventually serve as nature reserves for endangered species. So what does the future hold for the kit fox and other listed species in this unique region?

Despite millions of dollars spent on research, planning, and habitat acquisition, the San Joaquin kit fox has not made substantial progress toward recovery. Outside Bakersfield, most of its populations appear to be either stable or declining, and biologists continue to worry about the possibility of a catastrophic collapse due to diseases such as canine distemper. As with so many endangered species, conservation efforts have helped prevent the San Joaquin kit fox's extinction but shown little progress toward its recovery, and the future remains uncertain.[45]

Like many endangered species, kit foxes need more and better habitat. But scientists, managers, and environmental activists also need a better understanding of what constitutes habitat for species such as this and how different kinds of habitat areas—from wilderness to rangelands, farms, oil fields, and even cities—can contribute to the goal of recovering endangered species and integrating them into the broader cultural landscape. Narrowly distributed species with specific habitat requirements may need reserves specifically designed and managed for their recovery. The San Joaquin Valley certainly has several of those kinds of creatures. Kit foxes, however, do not fall into this category. Future conservation efforts in the valley, including the FWS's upcoming reauthorization process for the Metropolitan Bakersfield Habitat Conservation Plan, will offer opportunities to start thinking differently about wildlife-habitat relationships and integrating conservation into the places where people live and work. If that can happen in the San Joaquin Valley, it can happen anywhere.

CHAPTER EIGHT · The Delta Smelt

Water Politics by Another Name

In 2007 the national debate over endangered species and habitat conservation once again turned to California's Great Central Valley. This time it was not about iconic condors, amiable tortoises, or charismatic little foxes living on rangelands, oil fields, and vacant city lots. At risk was the single most important natural resource in the American West, and the culprit, according to most media reports, was a lackluster two-inch fish (see figure 17).

The delta smelt is endemic to the California Bay-Delta, the largest and most productive estuary on the West Coast of the United States. This is where the state's two great rivers, the Sacramento and the San Joaquin, converge in a maze of wetlands and waterways that covers some seven hundred square miles. Before 1849 the delta funneled runoff from the Sierra Nevada through the Carquinez Strait and into San Francisco Bay. Saltwater and freshwater converged to create a brackish mixing zone that fostered a diverse, dynamic, complex, and extraordinarily productive ecosystem.

Some water still flows all the way through the delta. But exactly how much freshwater reaches the ocean instead of being diverted upstream for urban or agricultural use has become the subject of an epic battle. And for good reason. Over the past 150 years, the delta has become the nexus of California's water control and distribution infrastructure: a vast network of levees, canals, aqueducts, pipes, and pumping stations operated by the state and federal governments, local irrigation districts, and hundreds of private users. As much as 70 percent of the runoff that enters the delta, much of which has already flowed through farms and cities, is diverted again for

FIGURE 17.
A delta smelt. Courtesy of the U.S. Fish and Wildlife Service.

further use, some of it as far south as Los Angeles. This intensively engineered and increasingly fragile system serves some twenty-five million people and five million acres of irrigated farmland.[1]

In December of 2007, federal district court judge Oliver Wanger issued an interim remedial order in the case of *Natural Resources Defense Council et al. v. Kempthorne et al.*, which temporarily closed the delta's pumping plants to protect the delta smelt, a federally listed threatened species. It was a dry year, and the pumping restrictions led to additional water reductions for downstream users, including farms in the San Joaquin Valley and cities in Southern California. Over the next two years, Wanger delivered a series of complex decisions that placed a tremendous amount of power over state water policy in the hands of a single unelected judge and temporarily reduced the total deliveries from California's two main water systems by 15 to 20 percent. Some farming areas with low-priority water contracts, such as the Westlands Water District in the arid western San Joaquin Valley, faced even greater losses.[2]

The crisis of 2007 continued into 2009, by which time the delta smelt, a once-obscure species known only to fisheries biologists, had become the subject of one of the country's most contentious and high-stakes endangered species debates. The *Economist* magazine declared that "with the stroke of a judicial pen," California had entered "an economic and political crisis." The *Wall Street Journal* called the water reductions a "man-made drought." And the *Orange County Register* informed its readers that they were paying a delta smelt tax to fund the federal government's "fish-before-people policy." Republican Representative George Radanovich, from the San Joaquin Valley city of Fresno, was more candid. He called the smelt "a worthless little worm that needs to go the way of the dinosaur."[3]

By the time most of these stories appeared, the pumping restrictions had already ended and various studies had concluded that about 75 percent of the 2009 water delivery reductions were due to a lack of precipitation, not endangered species regulations. But that is almost beside the point because, despite many claims to the contrary, the smelt's current condition is more a symptom than a cause of California's water problems. Since the nineteenth century, the delta has become so degraded and its maladies so complex and consequential that fixing it is now arguably the state's single greatest long-term political, economic, and environmental challenge. Simple explanations cannot explain this situation, and simple solutions will not solve it.[4]

The story of the delta smelt exemplifies a larger trend in which endangered species have assumed increasingly pivotal roles in the water politics of California and the American West. It reveals the challenges of environmental governance in a complicated federalist system where no single individual or organization possesses a majority of the political power. It provides an example of how, under the Endangered Species Act, even uncharismatic species now shape debates about land use and natural resource management. And it illustrates the difficulty of recovering endangered species in dynamic ecosystems that have been utterly transformed from the conditions in which those species evolved.[5]

The story of the delta smelt also illustrates the central argument of this book. The focus on habitat conservation in protected natural areas, which developed in American environmental science and law over many decades, has probably prevented the extinctions of numerous endangered species. Even under the most favorable circumstances, however, this approach can encounter serious problems, and it offers few insights into or solutions for thoroughly transformed environments such as the California Bay-Delta. No one is suggesting that habitat conservation, in the form of aquatic parks or wilderness areas, can repair the delta or save the smelt. Yet in the smelt debate, water has often taken the place of land, with calls for more water to sustain the fish echoing calls for more land to protect terrestrial species. The general mind-set of throwing more habitat at endangered species thus persists. California's business and government institutions have long operated on the assumption that if we had more water—enough for the fish and enough for the people—everything would be fine. But just adding more water, like just adding more habitat, can neither save the smelt nor fix the delta.

THE DYNAMIC DELTA

The California Bay-Delta is a seven-hundred-square-mile expanse of channels, sloughs, levees, and islands at the confluence of the Sacramento and San Joaquin Rivers, between the present-day cities of Antioch, Sacramento, Stockton, and Tracy (see map 8). Together, these two river systems drain 42 percent of California's land area and capture half of its annual runoff. Their combined watershed extends from the peaks of the High Sierra to the aquifers of the Tule Basin and from the leeward slopes of the Coast Ranges to the windward face of the Cascades.

During the last ice age, the delta was a freshwater marsh formed by runoff from the Sacramento and San Joaquin Rivers. It assumed its present geographic configuration only about five thousand years ago, as the sea level rose and saltwater intruded farther inland. Daily tides, seasonal weather patterns, annual stream flows, and frequent floods created a complex and dynamic landscape defined by shifting currents, water salinities, and vegetation patterns. Few places remained beyond the reach of the highest high tides, and at some point every inch of the delta was underwater.[6]

The region's dynamic ecology and relative isolation created the conditions for high productivity and biological diversity. The archaeological record from before European contact includes a unique and diverse assemblage of native species adapted to local conditions. Many of these species migrated or otherwise adjusted their life history strategies to take advantage of seasonal patterns in resource availability. The delta became a crucial node on the Pacific Flyway, attracting at least twenty-six species of migratory waterfowl and hosting a large fraction of the millions of ducks and geese that rested or overwintered in the Central Valley each year. Reports from the 1830s and 1840s describe a landscape with large populations of wild ungulates, fur-bearing mammals, and, of course, fish. About 80 percent of the fish species in the delta's watershed were endemic.[7]

Early Anglo-American travelers in the delta went there in search of wild game, but one of the first things they observed was the area's propensity for flooding. Many of these visitors had no intention of staying, but some did, and many more followed after

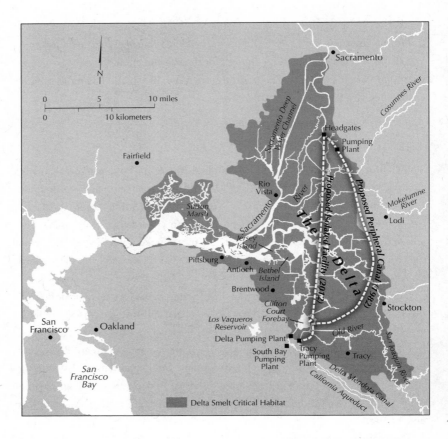

MAP 8.

The California Bay-Delta, with delta smelt critical habitat and other key features. The Isolated Facility, or conveyance system, is a reimagined and redesigned proposal to replace the never-implemented Peripheral Canal project.

1848. The city of Sacramento, which became California's state capital in 1854, was founded near the northeastern corner of the delta and flooded repeatedly in the 1840s and 1850s. In the winter of 1861 to 1862, four weeks of rain made commuting to work in this inland city a harrowing nautical adventure. In the years that followed, Californians began their epic struggle to contain the floodwaters, clear the channels, reclaim the wetlands, irrigate the farms, and reengineer the state's hydrologic systems.[8]

Everyone agreed about the need for flood control but disagreed about whether to embark on a coordinated public program or to allow private landowners and cooperatives to pursue their own solutions. The details of the epic struggle that followed are far too complicated to report here, but a few key points warrant mentioning. In 1850 Congress passed the Arkansas Act, which transferred all federally owned "swampland" to the states with the condition that they use the proceeds from future sales to fund agricultural reclamation projects. In 1868 the California State Legislature passed the landmark Green Act, which allowed developers to purchase swampland for just one dollar an acre, to be reimbursed after three years of cultivation. This act also enabled landowners to form "swampland districts," which later evolved into California's ubiquitous "irrigation districts," with the power to undertake local flood control projects.[9]

The Green Act, along with other state and federal policies, encouraged land speculation and the consolidation of delta landownership by a small San Francisco–based elite. It also helped start an infamous "levee war," in which each swampland district sought to fortify itself with ever-higher abutments while exposing its neighbors to even greater risk. The politicians, businesspeople, and financiers who orchestrated this process saw unlimited opportunity in the delta's agricultural potential, and levee building was just one step in a much larger project. The rivers needed to be dredged and confined to navigable channels; the swamps needed to be drained to reclaim dry land; the streams needed to be diverted to redistribute water; and the fields needed to be irrigated to produce crops. The profit motive would encourage investment, and economic growth would result, making everyone better off.[10]

By the 1870s, flood control and reclamation projects had created a new agricultural landscape in the delta and the surrounding region, with salt-tolerant crops, such as asparagus, growing on "islands" formerly exposed to regular seawater inundation. But problems soon emerged. Sediment and contaminated runoff from mining in the Sierra Nevada foothills polluted valley waterways beginning in the 1850s, a toxic legacy that remained for decades even after the landmark Sawyer decision of 1884, which brought an end to hydraulic mining. Floods worsened as hundreds of millions of cubic yards of mining debris washed down from the mountains and clogged the river channels. Poorly designed and constructed levees failed with startling frequency. Monopolies exercised nearly unlimited control over vast areas and the immigrant laborers who worked there. And a haphazard approach to governance slowed efforts to develop water distribution systems. By 1909 California still lagged behind even Colorado in irrigated acreage.[11]

Beginning in the late 1870s, ambitious politicians, landowners, and government officials attempted to adopt a more direct and coordinated approach to water management in California. In 1878 the politician and swampland speculator William H. Parks proposed the first coordinated plan for water management in the Sacramento River and Delta. That same year, the new state engineer, William H. Hall, began his famous study on the region's hydrology, which still serves as a benchmark for water resources in California. The ascent of Progressive Era republicanism during the 1880s and 1890s created new opportunities for state intervention, and frequent floods stirred public support for coordinated solutions. After the deluge of 1904, the *San Francisco Chronicle*'s editor, E. D. Adams, wrote that the levee wars of the previous decades could only continue "until all concerned are exhausted and can fight no more. . . . If the present flood season has proved to be the final knockout blow, it will be a blessing to the state." He called for the establishment of "a scientific commission in which confidence could be placed . . . to go ahead and protect everybody and all interests under some comprehensive plan."[12]

In 1921 the California legislature directed the state engineer to write a comprehensive water plan to promote flood control, storage, and distribution. The plan would also have to solve two long-term supply problems related to water quantity and quality. The first was the need for more irrigation water in the San Joaquin Valley, where farms had already overdrafted their groundwater and were experiencing land subsidence. The second was the demand for more freshwater, from factories in Contra Costa County, between San Francisco and Sacramento, which had become one of the largest industrial centers on the West Coast.[13]

In 1933, voters approved the proposed Central Valley Project (CVP) by the slim margin of 33,600 votes out of more than 900,000 cast. Voters in the Bay Area and the Central Valley supported the project by wide margins, while most Southern Californians opposed it. The whole scheme relied on bonds, but in the sour economic climate of the time the state failed to raise the necessary money. California officials turned to the Franklin Roosevelt administration, which adopted the plan as a Depression-era relief effort under the auspices of the Bureau of Reclamation. What began as a state project thus became a federal one. The bureau started construction in 1937, and the CVP soon became its biggest project. Over the succeeding decades, the CVP expanded to include a vast and complicated network of canals, pumping plants, aqueducts, dams, and reservoirs on the American, Sacramento, San Joaquin, Stanislaus, and Trinity Rivers (see map 9).[14]

MAP 9 (OPPOSITE).
Major California water projects, including the Central Valley
Project and the State Water Project.

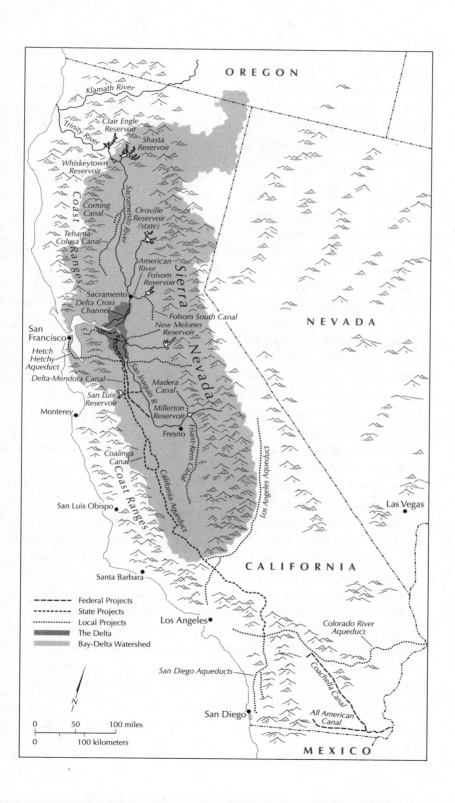

OREGON

Klamath River

Clair Engle
Reservoir

Trinity River

Shasta
Reservoir

Whiskeytown
Reservoir

Coast Ranges

Corning
Canal

Sacramento River

Oroville
Reservoir
(state)

Tehama-
Colusa Canal

American
River
Folsom
Reservoir

Sacramento

Delta Cross
Channel

Folsom South Canal

New Melones
Reservoir

Sierra Nevada

NEVADA

San
Francisco

Hetch
Hetchy
Aqueduct

Delta-Mendota Canal

San Luis
Reservoir

San Joaquin R.

Madera
Canal

Monterey

Millerton
Reservoir

Friant-Kern Canal

Coalinga
Canal

Fresno

Coast Ranges

California Aqueduct

San Luis Obispo

Los Angeles Aqueduct

Las Vegas

Santa Barbara

CALIFORNIA

Federal Projects
State Projects
Local Projects
The Delta
Bay-Delta Watershed

Los Angeles

Colorado River
Aqueduct

San Diego Aqueducts

Coachella Canal

N

San Diego

All American
Canal

0   50   100 miles

0   100 kilometers

MEXICO

By the 1950s, the CVP had enabled agribusiness corporations to reap tremendous profits. Yet the large growers realized that their success depended on continued cooperation from the federal government. Securing long-term public support and federal cooperation required yet another giant water project—one that would distribute benefits more widely and remain under state control. It would need to provide more water for Southern California's rapidly growing cities, as well as irrigation water to convert arid rangelands into industrial farms in the western San Joaquin Valley. Some of the country's largest corporate landholders—including Standard Oil, Shell Oil, the Southern Pacific Company, and the Times Mirror Company—owned property in this area, and they stood to reap a windfall from the delivery of state-subsidized water.[15]

As in previous water debates, sectional differences defined public opinion. This time, however, support flipped, with Southern Californians generally favoring the State Water Project (SWP) and Northern Californians mostly opposing it. The bond issue, structured with the support of the state's new pro-development governor, Edmund G. "Pat" Brown, amounted to $1.75 billion, the largest ever introduced by a state government. In 1960, Californians approved the measure by another thin margin: 174,000 out of 5.8 million votes. According to state water resource director William Warne, votes in favor of the project were votes for "growth and development." The SWP became the world's largest public water system, with thirty-four storage facilities, twenty pumping plants, five power plants, and some seven hundred miles of canals and pipelines.[16]

The delta's geographic site and situation made it an obvious choice to serve as the hub for the state's two major water diversion and redistribution systems, but its dynamic hydrology posed major technical impediments and political problems. Chief among these was the issue of saltwater, which sometimes flowed inland almost all the way to Sacramento. Local municipalities, industries, and agribusiness corporations all wanted to draw freshwater from the lower delta, but the Bureau of Reclamation argued that it was responsible for controlling salinity only farther upstream, at its pumping plants. Diverting freshwater upstream ensured supplies for distant farmers and cities to the south but not for industries and residents in the delta itself.[17]

Since the 1920s, several schemes, some outlandish and some rather fanciful, had emerged for dealing with the salinity problem and had received consideration from decision makers. These plans fell into two categories: saltwater barriers and upstream diversions. Barrier plans called for massive saltwater obstructions above the delta, in the delta, at the mouth of the delta, or even below the delta at the Golden Gate—which would have turned San Francisco Bay into a tepid freshwater pool.[18]

In 1963 an upstream diversion approach called the peripheral canal emerged as the leading contender. The peripheral canal would branch off from the main stem of the Sacramento River and circumvent the delta on its eastern side to connect with other SWP conveyance systems farther south. These included the Contra Costa Canal, which would bring freshwater back into the delta for agricultural, urban, and industrial use, the Delta-Mendota Canal, which would send water to farmers in the San Joaquin Valley, and the California Aqueduct, which would supply water to urban users in Southern California. Delta residents almost universally opposed the plan, because it diverted water and money to distant users and they feared that it might lead to the delta's infrastructure falling even further into decay. But they seemed to have little power compared to the forces allied against them. Southern California water managers, San Joaquin Valley farmers, the state Department of Fish and Game, and three consecutive governors, including Ronald Reagan, endorsed the plan. By the late 1960s, the peripheral canal's construction appeared all but assured.[19]

Yet the proposal soon ran into problems. In 1968 and 1978, the State Water Resources Control Board stirred controversy when it issued salinity standards for the delta that seemed designed mainly to protect the interests of Southern California municipalities and San Joaquin Valley farmers. A variety of interest groups soon began to challenge the board's authority and to cast doubt on the wisdom of the peripheral canal. Northern California politicians proclaimed it a Southern California "water grab," and environmentalists argued that it would cause the collapse of the delta's ecosystem. The Department of Fish and Game tried to convince environmentalists and local fishers that the canal would allow for better salinity regulation and improvements in habitat conditions. These groups agreed with the department's goals, but they opposed its means of achieving them. As support for the peripheral canal waned, doubt in the project came to reflect a broader decline in public trust of both big government and engineering-based solutions to complex environmental problems. In 1980 Governor Jerry Brown signed the peripheral canal bill into law, but two years later voters passed a referendum that repealed it by the not-so-thin margin of 63 to 37 percent. Cost played an important role in the referendum, which came during the recession of the early 1980s, but 48 percent of voters also said they believed the canal would damage the environment, and 28 percent expressed concern about the ecological health of the delta in particular. It was the first time since the 1920s that Californians had rejected a major water project.[20]

The peripheral canal's defeat at the polls in 1982 was a landmark event in California's environmental history. Additional shocks came in the succeeding years, when the state's water establishment faced challenges from cities, neighboring states, and even a ragtag group of University of California biology students who launched a campaign to reduce water diversions to the Los Angeles Aqueduct from Mono Lake in the eastern Sierra Nevada. In the 1986 Racanelli decision, a state appellate court ordered the board to develop new delta salinity standards that would protect not only big cities and San Joaquin Valley agriculture but also the interests of delta residents and the public trust values of fish and wildlife. The institutional and power structures that had emerged in the era of the great water projects were finally beginning to crack.[21]

Increased public scrutiny soon revealed a range of unsustainable policies and practices. Water managers were making rosy projections of future water supplies, which encouraged private investment and fueled even more demand; this led to further promises and provided a rationale for additional projects to develop more supply. It was a vicious cycle. By 2008 surface water contracts on the Sacramento and San Joaquin river systems totaled about 8.4 times the average streamflow. Only in extraordinarily wet years, when demand for long-distance deliveries declined anyway, did the CVP and the SWP have the capacity to meet their contractual obligations. Legally, water contracts are always conditional—the provider cannot supply water it does not have—but public agencies exacerbate the inherent uncertainty of water management when they enter into agreements based on misleading information and unrealistic promises.[22]

California's two great water projects fueled population growth, enabled the development of one of the world's largest economies, subsidized the construction of great cities, and created an unparalleled agricultural empire. But they also came with a host of unintended consequences. Today the Sacramento–San Joaquin Bay-Delta is not only the confluence of California's natural and engineered water systems; it is also the place where some of the state's most urgent and intractable economic, ecological, and political problems converge.[23]

THE DYSFUNCTIONAL DELTA

Since the 1840s, Californians have transformed the delta. It remains in the same location, but it is no longer the same place. People rerouted its waterways, reversed its flows, diverted its runoff, razed its forests, dredged its channels, and broke its tules. They erected more than one hundred dams in its watershed and reclaimed 95 percent of its wetlands. Most of all, they worked to standardize its dynamic hydrology and make it more predictable. The delta became an agricultural breadbasket, a recreational mecca, a geographical oddity, and one of the world's most intensively engineered landscapes. It also became a spigot for thousands of hoses, some literal and some figurative, that carried millions of gallons of water to quench a thirsty state.[24]

For most of the delta's Euro-American history, people considered saltwater the worst local pollutant because it contaminated precious freshwater. That view started to change in the 1960s, when SWP pumps began siphoning water from the delta for long-distance transport. These diversions changed the delta's flow patterns and salinity gradients, drew fish upstream, where some got sucked into massive pumps, and reduced the brackish mixing zone that served as important habitat for many species. Fisheries biologists soon realized that the freshwater-saltwater mixing zone had special biological significance in the delta's dynamic ecosystem. Most water managers and large purchasers no longer consider saltwater a pollutant, but many are still coming to terms with the idea that a variable, sometimes salty delta is both ecologically necessary and ultimately unavoidable.[25]

Other forms of pollution, however, are among the delta's most urgent problems. Pesticide-related fish and bird die-offs began in the 1950s, during the heyday of synthetic pesticides, and increased in the 1960s before declining in the 1970s and 1980s when new laws banned some of the most dangerous compounds. Runoffs from farms and cities carry a cocktail of pollutants into the delta, including dioxins, PCBs, pesticides, mercury, selenium, and pyrethroid pesticides, which began to replace organophosphates in the 1990s. Runoff treatment has improved some water quality issues in recent years, but fish consumption advisories have remained in effect because of concerns about toxicity.[26]

The delta also suffers from biological pollution. Scientists often remark that it is one of the planet's most "invaded" estuaries. Some of the area's exotic species were introduced intentionally, as was the case with American shad and striped bass in the 1870s, but many hitched rides on cattle or farm machinery or in the ballast water of ships visiting San Francisco Bay. Today the delta contains approximately two hundred nonnative species, which together constitute about 95 percent of its living biomass. The list of current residents includes a dazzling array of plants and animals from around the world: African clawed frog, Brazilian waterweed, Chinese mitten crab, New Zealand mud snail, South African sabellid worm, Mediterranean mussel, Asian clam, and the infamous shipworm—known to mariners and dock-workers as the termite of the sea. Although Americans have a history of nationalistic, even xenophobic, anxiety about immigrant species, there is nothing automatically wrong with a cosmopolitan biota. The problem is that some of these newcomers have altered and simplified the delta's ecosystem, making it less hospitable for native species and less conducive for human uses, from farming and fishing to shipping and swimming.[27]

The delta is becoming a riskier place too. Its levee system has aged and deteriorated at the same time that population growth in low-lying areas has placed more human life and property in flood zones. Peat burning and levee building have made the delta one of the world's most-subsided landscapes, with some areas more than fifteen feet below sea level. Of all major American cities, only New Orleans matches Sacramento in flood risk.[28]

Since the 1970s, California has appropriated more funding to shore up the delta's decaying levee infrastructure, but its resources have proved inadequate, and federal expenditures have lagged far behind. In one period during the late 1990s, the state contributed 174 percent of its estimated share to the delta's joint Levee System Integrity Program, while its ostensible partner, the federal government, contributed less than 1 percent of its share. The flooding that followed Hurricane Katrina in New Orleans, combined with the Upper Jones Tract levee failure, which occurred east of Stockton on a sunny day in June of 2004, brought more attention to the issue. Yet many scientists have concluded that massive levee failures are imminent and increasingly inevitable. Flooding has the potential to transform land use and settlement patterns in the delta, trigger a qualitative transformation in its ecosystem, and launch a new period in its history. For the scientists and managers who predict such scenarios, the current delta is little more than an "interim Delta." It is the settled, orderly delta of that fleeting period when Californians believed they could contain the "inland sea."[29]

Of all the problems facing the delta, the oldest is probably the fisheries crisis. Prior to European contact, the Sacramento River hosted the second-largest salmon runs on the West Coast of the United States, after the Columbia River. It is impossible to say exactly how many fish were involved, but at their peak, Chinook salmon, by far the most abundant anadromous fish in the delta watershed, probably numbered more than a million spawners per year. As early as 1879, however, David Starr Jordan was lamenting the decline of fisheries in the Sacramento River watershed, which he believed did not "contain one-twentieth the number of fish that it did twenty years ago." Fishers began focusing on other species, but their industry still suffered, and by the early 1880s the delta's short-lived canneries were beginning to shut down.[30]

In 1870 the California legislature established the Commission of Fisheries to restore and improve the state's fish stocks through conservation, importation, propagation, and law enforcement. The commission soon opened its first hatchery, in partnership with the California Acclimatization Society, and over the next ninety years it operated 169 fish hatcheries and egg-collecting facilities. In another early effort, the commission imported striped bass from New Jersey and planted them in the Carquinez Strait. By 1884, striped bass were appearing in San Francisco markets, and today the species is one of the delta's most important sport fish. The commission soon announced that it had saved the salmon in California, and its members began to congratulate themselves on their growing recognition as a model for other states.[31]

A variety of factors, including many unrelated to the commission's efforts, gave salmon populations a series of short-term boosts that maintained them at variable but reasonable levels for a century. Things seemed to be going moderately well, at least compared to many of California's other depleted fisheries, until 2007, when the total number of successful spawners plummeted to fewer than ninety thousand, down 88 percent from 2002. Over the next two years the number dropped to just 39,530, and the National Marine Fisheries Service (NMFS) responded by imposing an emergency ban on almost all salmon fishing off the coasts of California and southern Oregon.[32]

Halting fishing was probably the only option available to government officials during the salmon crash of 2007 to 2009, but it will not fix the fisheries crisis, because fishing alone did not cause the problem. California's sport and commercial fishing industries are tightly regulated, and they did not expand or change during the early 2000s in any way that could have precipitated such a dramatic decline. The problems now confronting salmon and other fish that live in or pass through the delta watershed are far more diverse and complex than fishing alone, and they are much more difficult to address than by simply regulating the catch. Indeed, the salmon decline was part of a much larger collapse in the populations of the region's fish, including the delta smelt.[33]

THE CHRONIC CRISIS

The delta fisheries crisis, which culminated in 2007 to 2009 and which the delta smelt came to symbolize, actually dates back to the early 1990s. From 1987 to 1992, California had below-average precipitation. This dry period differed from similar episodes not in its magnitude or intensity but in its scientific, legal, and political context. More than a decade earlier, biologists such as Peter Moyle, from the University of California, Davis, had begun to draw attention to the decline of California's native fish, particularly the noncommercial and nonrecreational species that the state had nearly forgotten. By 1990, freshwater fish had become one of the most imperiled groups of vertebrate species in the United States. Most of these species occurred in isolated watersheds west of the Rocky Mountains, and several were endemic to California. Many were still declining, and few had government conservation plans. Fishers and environmentalists were beginning to push for more endangered species listings, including for the delta smelt.[34]

The delta smelt is a slim fish about two to three inches in length, silver to partly translucent, with a steely blue streak on its side. Its habitat preferences, life history, biogeography, behavior, and physiology explain its vulnerability. It is pelagic and euryhaline, which means that it lives in open water and tolerates a wide variety of salinity conditions. It is endemic to the Sacramento–San Joaquin Bay-Delta, where it thrives under the same brackish conditions that water managers have been trying to eliminate, by separating saltwater from freshwater, for nearly a century. The delta smelt depends on a plankton-based food web that exotic species and other ecological changes have profoundly altered. Since most delta smelt live for no more than a year and have low fecundity, their population numbers are sensitive and prone to fluctuation. They have a weak stock-recruitment relationship, which means that spawning success does not necessarily lead to the survival of more young fish, and they handle stress poorly, often dying during transport. And because they are adapted to drifting with the currents in open water, they are, at least compared to most fish, relatively poor swimmers.[35]

There are no quantitative records of delta smelt abundance from before 1959, when the California Department of Fish and Game began conducting the townet surveys that now form the basis of our understanding of population trends. For the first two decades of the survey, the numbers varied by as much as an order of magnitude, with the peak catch occurring in 1978. Five years later, however, the numbers had plummeted, and they remained low for a decade. By the 1990s, biologists from universities, nongovernmental organizations, and government agencies began to view the smelt, with its extreme sensitivity to water quality and other ecological parameters, as an indicator of delta ecosystem health.[36]

On June 13, 1989, Moyle petitioned the California Fish and Game Commission to list the delta smelt as endangered. Over the next four years the commission rejected the petition twice, despite support for the listing from Department of Fish and Game staff who noted that the smelt had inadequate regulatory protection and no management plan. In 1990 Donald C. Erman, of the American Fisheries Society, submitted a separate petition to the FWS that requested federal protection for the smelt, and in March of 1993 the service listed the fish as threatened under the federal

ESA. A federal listing without a similar state listing would have limited California's ability to participate in consultations, planning, and management efforts. So the Fish and Game Commission relented, and in December of 1993 it listed the smelt as threatened under the California ESA.[37]

The delta smelt's listing coincided with the decline and listing of several other Bay-Delta fish species and anadromous fish runs. In 1989 the NMFS listed winter-run Chinook salmon in the Sacramento River as threatened. The run continued to decline, and in 1994, with about 1 percent of the former population remaining, NMFS upgraded its status to endangered. Other imperiled species and populations included the longfin smelt, the Sacramento splittail, the green sturgeon, Sacramento spring-run Chinook salmon, Sacramento late fall–run Chinook salmon, San Joaquin fall-run Chinook salmon, and the Sacramento perch. Even the State Water Resources Control Board admitted that despite efforts to safeguard these species, "the public trust resources of the Estuary are in a state of decline."[38]

In 1996 the FWS approved its Recovery Plan for the Sacramento–San Joaquin Delta Native Fishes. The plan, written by a team of fishery biologists from government and academia, described seven broad classes of recovery actions, including reducing the effects of exotic species, reevaluating commercial and recreational harvests, improving enforcement and regulation, and increasing research and public education. Its most important recommendation was to develop a broad strategy for habitat restoration and enhancement. In the case of the delta smelt, not only the size of its population but also the extent of its range would measure its recovery. To qualify for delisting, it would need a population and distribution equivalent to those recorded between 1967 and 1981. During that period, biologists had found delta smelt throughout the estuary, from Suisun Bay in the west, northeast on the Sacramento River, and southeast along the San Joaquin River to near Stockton. When the FWS published the smelt's critical habitat designation, in 1994, its map included the entire delta.[39]

By the time of the delta smelt's listing, and several years before the publication of the recovery plan, other federal agencies had attempted to quell the growing controversy over the delta and water resources. A combination of natural and political factors helped convince administrators to act. Between 1987 and 1992, the Sacramento and San Joaquin River watersheds received only about half of their average combined runoff. In the worst of these years, the SWP delivered only 10 percent of its urban demand. Reduced water quantity also exacerbated water quality problems by increasing the concentrations of pollutants. In 1988 the Environmental Protection Agency (EPA) responded by warning that if the State of California did not move to improve the delta's water quality standards, as mandated by the Racanelli decision, then it would intervene and impose the stricter federal standards.[40]

In 1992, Congress also sought to address these problems by passing the Central Valley Project Improvement Act. Several laws had refined or updated the CVP since its inception in the 1930s, but this new one clarified and redefined the project's purpose and obligations with respect to fisheries and wildlife. The act directed the Bureau of Reclamation to reconfigure its CVP operations to "protect, restore, and enhance fish and wildlife" and their habitats; dedicate up to eight hundred thousand acre-feet of water each year to increase streamflows and improve fish habitat; improve water conservation; and contribute to the State of California's efforts to protect the Bay-Delta. It also required the bureau to "make all reasonable efforts to at least double the natural production of six anadromous fish species" in the delta watershed, provide adequate water to state and federal wildlife refuges in the Central Valley, and investigate ways to further mitigate the CVP's impacts on fish and other wildlife. By 2002 the bureau had spent $342.2 million on research, restoration, infrastructure upgrades, and other projects designed to restore fisheries and prevent future water delivery reductions.[41]

The Central Valley Project Improvement Act, along with the state-level Delta Protection Act of 1992, brought more balance to delta resource management, but it did not solve the crisis. Environmental lawsuits mounted, and urban water managers and agribusiness groups howled that they were losing their water security. The State Water Resources Control Board produced new delta water quality standards to appease the EPA, but Governor Pete Wilson, a supporter of agribusiness, rejected them as too strict. Secretary of the Interior Bruce Babbitt responded by announcing that the EPA would issue overriding standards for delta water quality. Wilson had long argued that federal agencies had too much power over water in California, but he was left with few remaining options, so he called Babbitt to offer a truce. In June of 1994, the Wilson and Bill Clinton administrations reached a provisional agreement. Six months later, they signed the Bay-Delta Accord, which called for the collaborative management of the delta by ten state and federal agencies. This new attempt to fix the delta would be known as CALFED. According to Wilson, "peace [had] broken out."[42]

Politicians, bureaucrats, journalists, and academics all greeted CALFED with enthusiasm and high hopes. It represented a new approach to state-federal relations at a time when the older model of cooperative federalism—in which states set their own standards under federal limits and supervision—seemed to be failing, and it promised to address all of the delta's problems in a focused, coordinated, and scientific manner. It was also in the vanguard of the Clinton-era push toward collaborative environmental decision making that would move beyond traditional bureaucratic processes to incorporate more citizen participation. For its motto, CALFED adopted the feel-good phrase "getting better together."[43]

CALFED had a series of early accomplishments. It established a collaborative management structure led by a governing body called the Bay-Delta Authority, convinced its participating agencies to dedicate staff time and resources to the project, brought together diverse groups to discuss complex problems, created a citizen advisory council, and launched a research program. In 2000, CALFED published its final Environmental Impact Report and Statement and Record of Decision, which together presented a plan of action for the next thirty years. By 2004 the Bay-Delta Authority claimed to be pursuing more than three hundred target tasks and six hundred programmatic actions related to these two key documents. This was the biggest collaborative water management effort in the history of the American West, and it seemed to be going swimmingly.[44]

Two CALFED efforts held particular promise. The first was the Environmental Water Account, which enabled affiliated agencies to purchase water from willing sellers with excess supplies and then bank it for subsequent use when needed to promote endangered species conservation. This program constituted a first step toward establishing a more flexible water market with environmental interests as participants. A second area of progress involved habitat conservation. From 1995 to 2000, CALFED purchased or created conservation easements on 16,300 acres, while other California state and nongovernmental organizations acquired 4,600 acres. Acquisitions increased during the early 2000s as other groups, including the Nature Conservancy and the California Wildlife Conservation Board, became more involved. By 2005 there were more than three hundred habitat conservation or restoration projects under way in and around the Bay-Delta. They promised many benefits, halted some unpopular development schemes, and received widespread support. Many participants also hoped that conserving and restoring habitat would help prevent the need for future water delivery reductions.[45]

During the late 1990s, the delta's native fish appeared to recover somewhat. Surveys showed tentative population increases among delta smelt, threadfin shad, longfin smelt, and striped bass. As late as 1998, an ambitious study on the historical ecology of the Bay-Delta concluded that the pelagic habitats where these species lived were among the least degraded in the estuary.[46] After 2000, however, the populations of all four plunged. Native species declined more than introduced ones, though even introduced species, such as the striped bass, suffered. In 2003 the number of delta smelt declined to its lowest level ever recorded. By 2005 this multispecies collapse had become known as the "pelagic organism decline."

The once-abundant, now-endangered delta smelt soon emerged as an indicator species for the entire delta ecosystem. Scientists such as Moyle gave interviews in which they portrayed the delta smelt as a canary in the coal mine, and CALFED adopted the fish as one of its ecosystem restoration indicators. The delta smelt does not have the iconic charisma of the California condor, the docile disposition of the backyard-dwelling desert tortoise, or even the canine cuteness of the San Joaquin kit fox. But as a vulnerable and endemic resident of the delta's open-water habitats, it came to symbolize both the pelagic organism decline and what many observers believed was the delta's slow-motion ecological collapse.[47]

No one knew what was causing the pelagic organism decline, but several theories soon emerged. Entrainment and water quality remained serious concerns. The decline had occurred during a period of relatively high streamflows, which should have ameliorated both of these problems, but other factors could have hindered growth even during favorable years. Shifting patterns of predation, for example striped bass consuming delta smelt, might have had something to do with the decline of prey species, but some of the predators seemed to be in trouble too. Alterations in the distribution and abundance of aquatic microorganisms could have limited the populations of delta smelt and other planktivorous species, but the relationships between fish populations and food availability remained uncertain. Changes in pelagic habitats obviously had some effect, but scientists knew little about the ecological functioning of these spaces or the actual changes that had occurred. Perhaps the most troublesome observation was that the fish species involved in the pelagic organism decline had very different life histories, including survival and reproductive strategies. This suggested a systemic collapse instead of a simpler causal relationship. As one EPA scientist put it, something was "really, really wrong. It is not just the sensitive fish. The cockroaches are dying off!"[48]

By the time the pelagic organism decline brought increased scrutiny to CALFED, other problems had emerged in the organization. Its open, stakeholder-driven decision-making process conflicted with the stepwise procedural requirements of the California and federal environmental policy acts. Its flat organizational structure obscured accountability, and it had never acquired clear decision-making authority over its constituent agencies. The CALFED model seemed to privilege process over product, transparency over substance, consensus over effectiveness. Even its most innovative programs seemed designed not to offend anyone, and as a result they lacked the scope and ambition necessary to achieve their goals. The Environmental Water

Account, for example, helped prevent water delivery reductions but probably never achieved the scale to make a significant difference for fish such as the delta smelt.[49]

In 2005 the "Little Hoover" Commission, California's version of the federal Government Accountability Office, published a review of CALFED's progress. It highlighted CALFED's accomplishments and described the program as a "glass half full." The report argued, however, that despite having spent three billion dollars, CALFED had failed to make acceptable progress on all four of its primary objectives: achieving a reliable water supply, improving water quality, restoring ecosystems, and stabilizing levees. The agency had "demonstrated the propensity for rudderless bureaucracies to get caught in inescapable eddies." According to the commission, fixing the delta required more than just consensus—it required leadership. "CALFED was forged from a crisis," the report concluded, "and to a crisis CALFED has returned."[50]

The release of the Little Hoover Commission's report coincided with a series of harrowing developments. A state appellate court required CALFED to revisit its Environmental Impact Report and Statement because it had not evaluated slashing water deliveries as a management option. The State Water Resources Control Board sent a cease-and-desist order to the directors of the CVP and the SWP demanding that they ensure salinity standards. Another state appellate court gave even more urgency to the levee situation, by ruling that the state would be liable for the failure of any levee even partly financed or maintained with state funds. The National Oceanic and Atmospheric Administration (NOAA) listed yet another species, the southern green sturgeon, as threatened under the ESA. And despite increased precipitation and stream flows, 2005 and 2006 saw the continued decline of the delta's pelagic fish. The collapse persisted through the dry year of 2007, when it seemed that the smelt might disappear entirely.[51]

In retrospect, CALFED's demise began in late 2004 and early 2005, when NOAA and the FWS issued their biological opinions regarding the long-term effects of the CVP and the SWP on listed species in the delta watershed. A biological opinion is an administrative assessment of whether the proposed activities of a federal agency would constitute a taking under the ESA. The Bureau of Reclamation had issued an updated draft operating plan for the CVP as part of the CALFED process, which triggered the ESA review. Both NOAA and the FWS concluded that the bureau's plan did not pose a threat to the persistence of any listed species, and as in the past, they issued "no jeopardy" decisions. The very agencies that were later accused of choosing fish over people had, in fact, decided that the bureau and its partners should be allowed to proceed with business as usual.[52]

Within months, two lawsuits challenged the biological opinions as arbitrary and capricious. The first, filed by the Natural Resources Defense Council (NRDC), targeted the FWS's smelt decision, while the second, filed by the Pacific Coast Federation of Fishermen's Associations, attacked NOAA's salmon and steelhead opinion. Both cases went to the federal district court in the San Joaquin Valley city of Fresno, to be decided by Judge Oliver Wanger. In December of 2007, he issued his first key decision in the cases. Finding an unacceptable risk to the delta smelt, he halted the CVP's and the SWP's pumps for ten days with an interim remedial order and directed the FWS to rewrite its biological opinion. The following year Wanger reached a similar conclusion regarding the NOAA salmon and steelhead biological opinion, and he issued additional temporary pump closures in 2009 and 2010.[53]

Wanger was no tree hugger. A Republican appointee of former president George H. W. Bush, he presided over cases in one of California's most conservative regions. His 2007 order was, at best, ambivalent. In his written decision, he addressed some of the thorniest issues related to the ESA: the complexity of ecological change, the problem of conflicting scientific evidence, the difficulty of assessing risk, the standards for and appropriate scope of injunctive relief, and the tradition of judicial deference to agency expertise. Wanger was cognizant of the economic damage that might result from his order, but he argued that the act's "plain language" and "legislative history" constrained his options. "The Court cannot balance hardships nor does it have any discretion, except to apply the mandate of Congress prescribed by the ESA," he wrote. "It is Congress that struck the balance in favor of affording endangered species the highest of priorities. It is up to the political branches of government, not the court, to solve the dilemma and dislocation created by the required application of the law." Wanger's decision constituted the largest court-ordered water diversion in California history.[54]

Reactions varied from glee to outrage. Fishery groups hailed the moves as important steps toward the revival of commercial and recreational stocks. Environmental organizations such as the NRDC rejoiced as well, but they also had a broader agenda. They saw Wanger's decisions as further proof that they could use the ESA to force changes in water management that would provide numerous benefits, including habitat conservation, the recovery of listed species, reducing long-distance water deliveries, curtailing reliance on infrastructure, restoring streamflows, and improving water quality. Although these were all worthy goals, the causes of the pelagic organism decline remained uncertain. And this uncertainty presented a potential pitfall for future court cases involving species such as the delta smelt that would require the plaintiffs to demonstrate harm.[55]

Government water agencies and private water contract holders—including urban utilities, irrigation districts, and agribusinesses—responded to Wanger's rulings with outrage. How could a small group of fisheries biologists and environmental lawyers cause draconian closures of pumps that supplied water to twenty-five million people and five million acres of farmland? They decried the notion that the regulation of water deliveries, traditionally the province of government agencies, could devolve to a single appointed judge. They argued that that policies to address the delta's myriad problems could not be reduced to shutting off the pumps for a couple weeks to protect a two-inch-long, noncommercial fish species that few people even knew existed a decade and a half earlier. Such measures might not even help the delta smelt, which had declined for unknown reasons, and could encourage groundwater mining or result in crop failures and farm bankrupties. Organizations from the Metropolitan Water District of Southern California to the Latino Water Coalition called for change, and the conservative Pacific Legal Foundation asked the federal government to take the rare step of convening the "God Squad," a committee of high-level government officials that has the power to exempt listed species from ESA protection.[56]

Many environmentalists agreed that endangered species should not determine the agenda for the future of the Bay-Delta. They understood that its problems were too complicated for that to work, and they sympathized with officials who were being asked to prioritize endangered species management within a water storage and delivery system that engineers had not designed for habitat or biodiversity conservation. Yet environmental groups pressed forward with their lawsuits. With CALFED sidelined and the Arnold Schwarzenegger administration's alternative efforts just getting under way, court cases focused on the ESA were driving much of California's water policy.[57]

THE DELTA DENOUEMENT

By 2009 the situation had descended into chaos, and the press had arrived to witness the debacle. Growers were staging rallies in fallow fields; op-eds plastered the pages of national newspapers; the Fox News anchor Sean Hannity was filming sensationalistic on-location stories; the comedian Paul Rodriguez, the son of migrant farm workers, was serving as a public face for the plight of agricultural laborers; and politicians were bringing fishbowls to their speeches on Capitol Hill. Republican Representative Devin Nunes, who became a central figure in the smelt debate, claimed that "tens of thousands of people had been thrown out of work" in a valley where once "someone with few belongings, little education and even no ability to speak English could prosper by picking grapes, milking cows, or hoeing cotton fields." According to Nunes and others, a "federally mandated drought," brought on by a perverse policy of fish before people, had led to an economic and labor crisis.[58]

In fact, the San Joaquin Valley has seen diverse communities suffer from poverty for more than 150 years. During the nineteenth century, East Asian immigrants, first from China and later from Japan and elsewhere, endured violence, were blocked from pursuing more lucrative jobs, and were forced to live in squalid, isolated settlements. During the 1930s, poor white "Okies" sought refuge in the San Joaquin Valley from the ravages of the dust bowl. Beginning in 1942, the Bracero Program attracted thousands of Mexican workers to participate in the United States' World War II agricultural mobilization. Many remained after the war and built California's modern agricultural economy, but they suffered from harsh working conditions, low wages, and constant harassment. When the Bracero Program ended in the 1960s, the farm labor pool shrank, wages increased, and unemployment dropped—but only temporarily.[59]

Over the past half century, the San Joaquin Valley has become, by most measures, the poorest region in the United States. By 2005, California's Twentieth Congressional District, in the heart of the valley, had the lowest median income in the country. The valley's human development index was also among the lowest in the country, roughly equivalent to that of central Appalachia. People there live on average six years less than people in Connecticut. A Congressional Research Service report released in December of 2005 described a litany of social problems that had contributed to this situation, including the prevalence of temporary and seasonal jobs, a saturated labor market, low wages, poor schools, environmental health hazards, and substandard housing. When the report appeared, the valley contained five of the country's top ten farming counties by annual sales, with Fresno and Tulare ranking as numbers one and two.[60]

High levels of unemployment are not new to the region. The town of Mendota, which attracted attention as the center of the valley's economic crisis from 2007 to 2009, saw its unemployment rate increase from 10 percent in 1960 to 30 percent in 2000. Per capita annual income in the town in 2000, after several years of abundant precipitation in California, was just seven thousand dollars, 70 percent below the national average. Mendota lies within the Westlands Water District, which is one of the arid areas in the western San Joaquin Valley that benefited most, in terms of agricultural development, from the delivery of state-subsidized water after World War II. Since the 1960s, however, increased access to water has correlated not with improvements in welfare or working conditions but rather with higher rates of joblessness and poverty.[61]

This situation briefly improved during the housing boom of the early 2000s. By 2005 the San Joaquin Valley was one of the country's hottest housing markets, as families from Sacramento, the San Francisco Bay Area, and other major cities moved to smaller, more affordable outlying communities. The housing boom offered unprecedented opportunities for some farm workers to make the transition from the fields to the construction industry, which offered better-paying jobs, safer working conditions, the opportunity to learn a skilled trade, and the chance to advance in a profession. After the financial collapse of 2007, however, the San Joaquin Valley earned the ignominious distinction of becoming the country's housing-crisis capital. Home building declined by 80 percent, assessed values dropped by up to 75 percent in some areas, and all six of the valley's metropolitan areas ranked among the top twenty nationwide in the percentage of foreclosures. Laid-off construction workers found themselves once again treading water in the deep end of a flooded agricultural labor pool.[62]

So how did delta smelt–related pumping restrictions affect employment and the economy in the San Joaquin Valley? In 2009 and 2010, two academic economists, both well known for their work on labor and agriculture, set out to answer this question. The first was Richard Howitt, from the University of California, Davis, who led a study that used mathematical modeling to predict a $1.6 to $2.2 billion drop in revenues and sixty to eighty thousand job losses from delta smelt–related pumping restrictions. These were astounding numbers, and Howitt noted that shifts in policies or market conditions could change them. Five months later, his team recalibrated its model and reduced its projections by about half, to between $627 and $710 million in revenue losses and thirty-one to thirty-five thousand job losses. By that time, however, many print and broadcast media outlets had accepted the notion that "as many as 80,000" jobs would be lost due to smelt-related water cuts. Howitt gave several interviews on the subject, including one in which he described the situation as a case of "environmental values versus human suffering . . . fish versus jobs and communities."[63]

The second interpretation came from Jeffrey Michael of the Business Forecasting Center at the University of the Pacific. His statistical study differed from Howitt's modeling approach in that it relied on empirical data from the California Employment Development Department and other organizations. According to Michael, Howitt's mathematical model underestimated the importance of other macroeconomic factors, such as the housing crisis, and failed to distinguish between smelt-related water cuts and cuts that would have come anyway due to a lack of precipitation. More importantly, Howitt had assumed an unusually large multiplier effect. The multiplier effect in this case represented the number of additional jobs that would have resulted from increases in farm revenue. Howitt's model used a multiplier more than double that of similar studies, which caused it to overestimate the number of job losses. As Michael pointed out, the San Joaquin Valley had showed an overall increase—not decrease—in farm employment during 2008 and 2009, for reasons entirely unrelated to the delta smelt. He concluded that the total number of jobs lost due to pumping restrictions did not exceed two thousand and might have been as low as zero.[64]

There is no perfect method for understanding the complex and multifaceted relationships among economics, labor, and environmental regulations. In this case, however, it is clear that Howitt vastly overestimated the amount of revenue and number of jobs lost due to delta smelt–related pumping restrictions, failed to place his study in a broader economic and historical context, and probably made the situation worse with his comments to the media. Michael's study offered a much more plausible explanation of the situation on the ground. But the truth is that we will never know exactly how Judge Wanger's decisions affected farm income and employment in the San Joaquin Valley.[65]

Comprehending the effects of the delta smelt pumping restrictions—which caused so much furor and turned a nondescript two-inch baitfish into yet another icon of the environmental culture war—is impossible without a deep understanding of the delta's history. The roots of the pelagic organism decline and the ecological collapse it came to represent began with the levee wars of the nineteenth century and persisted through decades of political conflict, bureaucratic mismanagement, and interminable consensus building in the twentieth century. Judge Wanger's pumping restrictions constituted only the latest episode in a dysfunctional history that has produced a dysfunctional ecosystem, a dysfunctional political system, and a dysfunctional delivery system for what is by far the state's most important natural resource: water.

Blaming a fish for this predicament may seem ridiculous. Yet that is exactly what has too often happened in debates about the delta smelt. Its story, like those of other endangered species, is not a tale of animal versus people but rather a case of people versus people, with some unsuspecting species stuck in the middle. Framing the debate as one of fish versus people can provide convenient cover for pundits and politicians proposing simple solutions or seeking to shift blame to someone else. But saving the delta smelt is not about choosing between fish and people, and there are no simple, cure-all solutions that will heal the delta. Introducing more-efficient water markets or finally building a peripheral canal, two options often proposed as silver bullets, might help improve the situation if done right, but neither could function properly without the resolution of a range of other problems, and if done wrong they could make things worse. Only a comprehensive strategy that provides a clear vision and addresses all of the delta's complex problems might avert catastrophe. Doing so is in the interest of everyone involved because the delta's collapse would be as much of a disaster for cities and farmers as for the fish that live there.[66]

What about the role of habitat? Habitat conservation remains popular in the delta because it supports the local recreational economy, discourages reckless development in flood zones, and provides opportunities for restoring some ecological services. As early as 1971, an EPA task force circulated an internal report that recommended the federal government acquire the entire delta and convert it into a national park or recreation area. According to the authors, such a move would fulfill the public's demand for "some of the amenities that make life worth living." It would also, conveniently for the EPA, "put the Federal Government in a superior position to regulate land and water use, and control water quality in the Delta."[67] A less ambitious proposal has emerged in recent years: to apply for recognition of the delta as a National Heritage Area.

As of 2012, efforts were under way to develop a Bay-Delta habitat conservation plan. A Bay-Delta HCP could, in theory, prevent future emergency pumping restrictions, create more certainty for water contract holders, and provide a more focused, coherent framework for endangered species management. It might also, quite literally, pave the way for a new "alternative conveyance system," another term for a redesigned and repackaged peripheral canal. As in other regions with multiple listed species, many planning participants in the delta believe that an HCP would provide the stability and flexibility to enable other crucial restoration and infrastructure projects. Yet like the other solutions proposed for the delta, an HCP would be no panacea. HCPs usually achieve their goals by setting aside land in the form of nature reserves, but although "protected areas" can aid in some aspects of local resource management, they cannot save species such as the delta smelt or other pelagic fish that depend on regional ecological processes.[68]

The biggest problem, though, is that none of these proposals address the really big questions facing the delta and its fisheries. How much water do the fish need? What constitutes a functional ecosystem? If the delta is going to change in the coming decades, how can we help those who will lose in this transformation? Who will make these hard decisions, and what sorts of institutional arrangements will best foster the necessary changes? And then there is the most basic and important question of all: what do Californians want from the future delta?

People are answering these questions in several ways. In 2006, in response to the Little Hoover Commission's CALFED report, Governor Schwarzenegger launched the Delta Vision Blue Ribbon Task Force with the goal of establishing a "durable" long-term vision and strategic plan for the delta. Its assessment, published the following year, announced that after decades of deadlock and delay, "the time for action is now. The Delta is in crisis, and each day brings us closer to a major disaster. . . . The Delta cannot be 'fixed' by any single action. Nor can water needs be met by any single action. No matter what policy choices are made, we Californians are compelled to change the ways we behave toward the environment and water." The report concluded that avoiding a nightmare scenario—ecological collapse, catastrophic flooding, species extinctions, and judicial receivership—will require Californians to do "almost everything suggested by the major voices in the water wars" to improve and restore the system.[69]

Delta Vision has replaced CALFED as the overarching framework for delta policy and management, but it is only one of several related efforts. Initiatives are also under way to reduce toxic drainage and eliminate incentives for the cultivation of thirsty, low-value crops such as cotton. Municipal water agencies have developed programs to reduce their reliance on the delta. The San Francisco Estuary Project has been working since 1993 to implement its Bay-Delta Comprehensive Conservation and Management Plan, part of the EPA's National Estuary Program. Before his retirement in 2011, Judge Wanger issued rulings that grew increasingly critical of government agencies and called for a new era of more effective public policy. In 2009 the state legislature attempted to address some of the issues he raised when it approved a package of four water-related bills, including one that authorized an $11.14 billion bond measure to help fund the Delta Vision Task Force's recommendations. Schwarzenegger decided not to place the measure on the 2010 ballot because he feared that weary California voters, faced with a record-breaking state budget deficit, might reject any more borrowing. His successor, Jerry Brown, who had also held the office from 1975 to 1983, has pressed forward with plans for an alternative conveyance system but repeated Schwarzenegger's decision and did not include the water bond on California's 2012 ballot. At the time of this writing, the bond remains in limbo, as does so much else for the California Bay-Delta and its namesake fish.[70]

EPILOGUE

Endangered species advocates engage in a wide variety of activities designed to prevent extinctions and promote recoveries—from enforcing trade regulations to eradicating exotic species to breeding animals in captivity. But in the era of conservation biology, creating and expanding protected areas has become the preferred approach for most wildlife agencies and organizations in the United States. As a result, protected areas have increased in number and proliferated in new environments. Early national parks and wilderness areas encompassed some of the country's most picturesque landscapes, but most were alpine zones of rock and ice. Decades later, the addition of more biologically productive and diverse sites reflected changing environmental values, and a raft of legislation, including the federal Endangered Species Act, provided new motivations and mechanisms for habitat conservation. Today habitat conservation efforts often focus on areas such as farmlands, rangelands, timberlands, and pockets of open space in urban regions that no one would consider pristine or sublime and that prior generations of preservationists never recognized as worthy of protection. With the advent of marine protected areas, nature reserves no longer even require land.[1]

During the late twentieth and early twenty-first centuries, the protected area paradigm went global. Nature reserves have existed for decades in many countries. Between 1985 and 2003, however, the total fraction of land worldwide with some form of publicly protected reserve status grew from 3.5 to 10 percent (about 5.29 to about 15.1 million square kilometers). Marine reserves increased from just a few dozen in the early 1970s to more than five thousand in 2012, covering 5.9 percent of all territorial seas. Much of this expansion occurred in the humid tropics, but protected areas have multiplied in nearly every biome and on every continent except Antarctica, which, at least for now, is essentially one big protected area.[2]

Conservationists cite many reasons for the global expansion of protected areas, including not only habitat conservation for endangered species and biological diversity but also sustainable development, scientific research, cultural preservation, and ecosystem services, such as the sequestration of atmospheric carbon that would otherwise contribute to global climate change. If this list makes protected areas seem like a cure-all, perhaps that is the point. The protected areas paradigm owes much of its success to its supporters' ability to adopt new logics over time while presenting nature reserves as solutions to an extraordinary range of social and ecological problems. The rationales are many, but the message is clear. In the words of the British geographer William Adams, the protected area, in all its diverse manifestations, has served as "the dominant 'big idea' of conservation" for more than a century—and it remains so today.[3]

Protected areas form a pillar of conservation biology, and they serve as a prerequisite for many land and wildlife management goals. Many areas throughout the world could benefit—socially, economically, and ecologically—from having more of them. But although they are necessary, they are also insufficient for the conservation of endangered species and biodiversity, the causes with which they are mostly commonly associated. Protected areas bring with them a host of problems, some of which appear to be increasing, and even under the best of circumstances they cannot solve all of the troubles that confront imperiled biota and ecosystems. Indeed, protected areas now face so many compounding and interrelated problems that the time has come to reconsider their central role in species recovery programs. Before the rethinking, though, let's review some of the problems.

Since the 1930s, the U.S. Fish and Wildlife Service has favored refuge administration, which officials believe is less divisive and more effective than species regulation on nonrefuge lands, as a conservation approach. Around one-third of the land in the United States is publicly owned, and about 90 percent of that is federal property. The FWS manages about ninety million acres, or around 14 percent of all federal lands. About half of California is under some form of public ownership. Some endangered species occur mostly or entirely on these public lands, but even those that do usually inhabit multiple-use management areas with competing priorities and activities. Parks, wilderness areas, and wildlife refuges capture only a small fraction of endangered species' habitat. Because they are clustered mainly in Alaska and the West, public lands do not encompass a representative sample of the country's diverse ecosystems, and many have suffered severe degradation through long histories of mismanagement.[4]

Almost a century ago, ecologists first noted that most nature reserves were too small to hold complete biological communities. Many reserves have grown since then, but size remains a limiting factor for all but the very biggest of national parks and wilderness areas. In the United States, only the immense park and reserve complexes of Alaska capture entire ecosystems, while even the vast protected areas of the Northern Rockies, the Colorado Plateau, and the Mojave Desert fall short. Some reserves function as smaller units than their acreage would suggest because of their bizarre shape or destructive activities on their borders that create harmful edge effects for sensitive species.[5]

This situation suggests an urgent need for more public land dedicated to habitat conservation. Yet no realistic program of land acquisition would ever come anywhere near to achieving the scope necessary to protect the majority of listed species. This is particularly true in states such as California, where endangered species habitat often occurs in coastal and valley areas with high property values. Neither the funding nor the political will exists to create a protected area network on the scale that is probably needed to preserve such species, and such an effort would undoubtedly come with a range of social and economic trade-offs and unintended consequences.[6]

Some believe that privately owned reserves can fill the gap. Between 90 and 95 percent of endangered species use some private land, and between one-third and two-thirds depend entirely on private land. At least twelve hundred nonprofit land trusts around the country cite biodiversity conservation as a goal, and all, to some extent, base their work on the premise that achieving this objective requires land use control, often in the form of privately owned reserves with restricted public access. Organizations such as the Nature Conservancy have made important contributions through their purchases and partnerships, but the durability of their efforts will remain in question as new pressures and priorities arise. Land trusts, no matter how effective or well established, cannot conserve endangered species and biological diversity in perpetuity simply through "buying nature."[7]

Efforts to create new reserves, whether public or private, encounter challenges in design and planning. For decades, conservation biologists have worked to develop rational procedures for the selection and design of new areas for nature reserves and reserve networks that would maximize their effectiveness while limiting their cost. Yet most parks, wilderness areas, and wildlife refuges were not designed to optimize endangered-species or biodiversity conservation, and the establishment of new reserves remains an opportunistic and improvisational process. Shortcuts for reserve selection and design, such as focusing on the needs of wide-ranging "umbrella species"—often large carnivores—and assuming that many other plants and animals will be protected in the process, have little data to support them and have met with increased scrutiny. Planning efforts that focus on ecosystem-level considerations, though long hailed by conservationists, have also come under criticism for failing to safeguard the rare and endangered species that populate those ecosystems.[8]

Creating new reserves can also be a politically contentious process. This book has recounted numerous examples of conflicts involving reserve designations on both public and private lands. In the United States, these conflicts usually involve what I call the politics of place: ongoing cultural conversations about who should have access to and control over lands and natural resources. Outside the United States, in the developing countries of the humid tropics and the global south, where so many protected areas have been established in recent decades, the politics of place also has a geopolitical dimension. Social scientists who work in such regions tend to associate protected areas with neoliberal international development programs that force impoverished and indebted countries to adopt Western economic and environmental policies. According to one such scholar, Karl Zimmerer, these programs have fostered "new geographies of conservation," in which lands once used for the local production of essential natural resources have been fenced off and repurposed as reserves for the protection of global biological diversity, often to the near-term detriment of local communities.[9]

Evaluating the success of protected areas presents another challenge. Many nature reserves have inadequate management plans with poorly defined goals. Even for those with clear objectives, such as saving a particular species, establishing a monitoring system within the reserve capable of detecting ecological changes can be difficult and costly. Conservation biologists agree that flexible, hypothesis-based, adaptive management is essential for documenting and confronting changes on the ground, but it can prove difficult in practice. Adaptive management can be especially challenging for public land management agencies, which often have competing mandates and are bound by state and federal laws to engage in stepwise procedures when making decisions that could have significant environmental impacts. Such laws were designed to promote transparency and accountability, not flexibility and nimble adaptation. Perhaps not surprisingly, most donors prefer to support high-profile reserve acquisitions, not the mundane and complicated but essential tasks of daily monitoring and management.[10]

Biologists now recognize that a variety of factors affect population viability and that setting aside a large area of habitat is not the same thing as ensuring the survival of an endangered species. Changes in species interactions, the introduction of exotic species, the spread of disease, and even the cessation of historic land use practices can all have unforeseen consequences that might diminish a reserve's capacity to sustain imperiled populations. Habitat quantity may appear to increase, at least on a map, at the time of a reserve's creation, but maintaining habitat quality requires constant vigilance. Otherwise the reserves will remain even as the species they were created to protect disappear.[11]

In a small subset of cases, establishing new reserves can have detrimental ecological consequences. Reserves can attract predators that hunt protected prey species. Reserves that eliminate grazing can become overrun with weeds that crowd out preferred plant species and increase the risk of catastrophic fires. Reserves can also divert resources from "unprotected" areas and wildlife populations that may prove crucial to future conservation efforts. The case studies in this book provide examples of each of these management quandaries.

Climate change is perhaps the single most important problem facing nature reserves and the species they seek to save in the coming decades. Consider the gentle, adorable, and possibly doomed American pika. Pikas are hamsterlike relatives of rabbits and hares that live on rocky slopes in the high mountains of the North American West. These temperature-sensitive creatures avoid overheating by scampering between patches of shade while gathering flowers and grasses, which they use to make hay. As alpine dwellers, pikas enjoy an extraordinary level of habitat protection: more than 95 percent of their range is on federal land, and 46 percent falls in designated wilderness areas. Yet vast, inhospitable stretches of desert surround many of their isolated habitats, which will limit their opportunities for dispersal to cooler areas as temperatures rise. With the pika's "protected" habitat shrinking due to climate change, it remains unclear what can be done—other than artificial translocation, increasingly known as assisted migration—to save this lovable lagomorph.[12]

Examples such as the American pika, which in 2012 was not even a listed species yet, raise the question of how well habitat conservation efforts in general are working to further the objectives of the ESA. Remember that the act has two main goals: to prevent extinctions and to promote the recovery of listed species. Since 1967 the federal government has listed about fifteen hundred species, subspecies, or distinct vertebrate populations in the United States as threatened or endangered. As of June 2012, it had delisted only fifty-four, ten of which it presumed extinct, twenty-six of which it considered recovered, and eighteen of which it removed from the list for some other reason, usually a taxonomic reclassification or the discovery of a new population. After forty-five years of conservation and recovery efforts, less than 1 percent of the species listed have gone extinct, but less than 2 percent have recovered.[13]

What these numbers mean depends on whom you ask. The ESA's supporters cite the lack of extinctions as proof that the act is working, while its detractors focus on the small number of recoveries as confirmation of its failure. Wiser observers tend to reject both positions, arguing that the results thus far are mixed and that these statistics do not capture the full complexity of the situation. Recovery criteria are often arbitrary, insufficient monitoring makes it difficult to assess the status of many species, and for others it is simply too early to determine whether efforts are succeeding. Evidence suggests that when species receive adequate resources, their status tends to improve, and that some species, while not fully recovered, have made substantial progress. For many others, however, achieving even moderate recovery goals could be decades away—or may never happen. For these species, protection under the ESA, which Congress conceived as a temporary federal receivership program, is becoming a more permanent administrative arrangement.[14]

There are also legal and political reasons why so few species have recovered. The FWS and the National Oceanic and Atmospheric Administration (NOAA) remain chronically understaffed and underfunded. Environmental groups have enormous incentives to get species listed, but they see few benefits and many drawbacks to delisting, and they often sue to prevent the ESA agencies from delisting protected species. Another reason is the lack of satisfactory mechanisms for transferring legal authority. The states are usually anxious to regain control of listed species. Yet the ESA agencies remain reluctant to release control because with few exceptions, the states have not developed adequate plans to ensure that once a species is delisted and returned to their care it will not decline again and end up back on the federal endangered species list.

One fact stands out in the extinction and recovery data. Of the twenty-six species, subspecies, or distinct vertebrate populations that the FWS says have recovered since 1973, all were originally listed because of factors such as overhunting, predation by or competition with exotic species, and pollution—not habitat loss. These are forms of habitat degradation, of course, but their result has been a decline in habitat quality, not habitat quantity. Their recoveries required the removal of one or at most a few limiting factors (hunting for the American alligator, DDT pollution for the brown pelican, etc.), and once those factors had declined to manageable levels, their populations began to rebound. None of these species' recoveries required protecting more area as nature reserves. Conversely, no species that declined mainly due to habitat loss has yet recovered under ESA protection. A reasonable conclusion, therefore, is that although nature reserves have probably helped prevent many extinctions, they have, to date, fostered few if any recoveries. Meanwhile, some of the species that have had the largest areas set aside on their behalf, leading to the reorganization of land use and natural resource management in entire regions, have continued to decline. The Mojave desert tortoise is one of the best examples of this phenomenon, but several other well-known species, including the northern spotted owl, have followed similar trajectories.[15]

Nature reserves are not primeval wildernesses; they are modern land uses shaped by contemporary politics and affected by modern problems. They have an important role to play in the future of biodiversity protection, endangered species recovery, and conservation more generally. But given their challenges and limitations, and the pressures they will increasingly face in future decades, the time has come to move beyond the protected area paradigm and launch a broader agenda for sustainable landscape management.[16]

The American environmental prophet Aldo Leopold once wrote that the "government can't buy 'everywhere.'" For conservation to succeed, the "private landowner must enter the picture." Leopold worked throughout his life to secure the protection of dozens of wilderness areas and wildlife refuges and encouraged efforts to create privately owned reserves wherever the opportunity arose. Yet he recognized that protected areas were not an end in themselves but part of a much larger vision of conservation that encompassed what he called the entire "land community." This community included not only people but also "soils, waters, plants, and animals," not only protected areas but also private property and working landscapes.[17] The fact that he wrote these words in 1935, at the height of the New Deal federal wildlife refuge expansion program, when it seemed that government land acquisition efforts might, in fact, continue indefinitely, makes his insight only more prescient and relevant today. Leopold would have rejected the contemporary framing of endangered species debates as battles of people versus nature. Instead he believed that it takes entire land communities, working together, to achieve a just, prosperous, and sustainable future.

Nature reserves have an important role to play in this future, but a protected area paradigm that attempts to wall off wildlife and confine its management to a small community of experts risks doing the exact opposite of what Leopold advised. What we need now is a more ambitious vision, one that incorporates the insights, advances, and accomplishments of a century of land and wildlife conservation without being bound to the ideas of the past. Conservationists must understand habitat not only as areas to be set aside but also as attributes to be cultivated, not only as quantities to be collected but also as qualities to be nurtured, not only as places to be acquired but also as processes to be maintained. What we need now is to move beyond the preservation of lands in protected areas to the integration of habitats in shared land communities.

Since the terms *habitat* and *endangered species* each combine aspects of science and law, making these changes will require contributions from both fields. Fortunately, many scientists who study endangered species have already begun this work. Combining insights from the allied subfields of landscape, urban, and restoration ecology, conservation biologists are developing new approaches that illuminate the complexity of wildlife-habitat relationships in landscapes with multiple human uses. They are using new techniques to reduce negative interactions between people and wild animals and to highlight the economic and ecological values of wildlife and endangered species in places where people live and work. And they now recognize that wildlife in cities and suburbs, including populations of endangered species once considered lost in urban jungles, are worth protecting, if for no other reason than to serve as ambassadors for the myriad others that most people never see.

In the legal arena, the threat of ESA regulation will remain an indispensible tool for future conservation efforts, but policy makers also need better incentive-based programs to encourage landowner cooperation. Legislators should eliminate perverse subsidies that encourage habitat destruction. The ESA should allow for more flexible adaptive management by permitting more experimental projects to help ailing populations while producing usable knowledge. Congress needs to provide the FWS and NOAA with more support and direction for recovery programs, in addition to the initial listing and critical habitat designation processes. Finally, the ESA needs better mechanisms for federal cooperation with the state and local governments responsible for most land use planning decisions. Such measures could include FWS input in the conservation elements of county general plans, better procedures for transferring authority over recovered species back to the states, and management agreements for species that will remain conservation-dependent for the foreseeable future. Wildlife habitat should be considered in every aspect of land use law and planning—especially in communities with endangered species.[18]

This book has argued that Americans use endangered species as proxies to fight about so many larger social issues because we have developed a political system, shaped by science and law, that produces and sustains debates about the politics of place in the name of habitat conservation. Yet endangered species have diverse and complex habitat needs that we are only beginning to comprehend. Some endangered species require remote wilderness areas or specific habitat features, but others can thrive in rural areas, suburbs, or even cities. Protected areas can neither supply the diverse habitats necessary for recovering the majority of listed species in the United States nor quell all of the conflicts that arise from contemporary conservation debates.

If we want to protect endangered species and biological diversity, then it is time to rethink the meaning of *habitat*, and the role of protected areas in particular, in a broader vision for conservation. Ultimately, this will require creating not just more protected areas but also more sustainable landscapes. Defining what that means and figuring out how to achieve it is one of the greatest environmental challenges of the twenty-first century.

NOTES

INTRODUCTION

1. Biodiversity Project, *Americans and Biodiversity: New Perspectives in 2002* (Washington, DC: Beldon, Russonello, and Stuart, 2002).

2. See, e.g., Bonnie Christensen, "From Divine Nature to Umbrella Species: The Development of Wildlife Science in the United States," in Harold K. Steen, ed., *Forest and Wildlife Science in America: A History* (Durham, NC: Forest History Society, 1999), 19–65; Sally K. Fairfax, Lauren Gwin, Mary Ann King, Leigh Raymond, and Laura A. Watt, *Buying Nature: The Limits of Land Acquisition as a Conservation Strategy, 1780–2004* (Cambridge, MA: MIT Press, 2005).

3. Dale D. Goble, J. Michael Scott, and Frank W. Davis, eds., *The Endangered Species Act at Thirty*, vol. 1, *Renewing the Conservation Promise* (Washington, DC: Island, 2006).

4. Mark Barrow, *Nature's Ghosts: Confronting Extinction from the Age of Jefferson to the Age of Ecology* (Chicago: University of Chicago Press, 2009); Shannon Petersen, *Acting for Endangered Species: The Statutory Ark* (Lawrence: University Press of Kansas, 2002).

5. Daniel J. Rohlf, "Six Biological Reasons Why the Endangered Species Act Doesn't Work—and What to Do about It," *Conservation Biology* 5, no. 3 (September 1991): 273–282; Sheila Jasanoff, *States of Knowledge: The Co-production of Science and the Social Order* (London: Routledge, 2004); J. B. Ruhl, "Reconstructing the Wall of Virtue: Maxims for the Co-evolution of Environmental Law and Environmental Science," *Environmental Law* 37 (2007): 1063–1082; National Research Council, Committee on

Scientific Issues in the Endangered Species Act, *Science and the Endangered Species Act* (Washington, DC: National Academy Press, 1995).

6. Richard White, *"It's Your Misfortune and None of My Own": A New History of the American West* (Norman: University of Oklahoma Press, 1991); Karl Jacoby, *Crimes against Nature: Squatters, Poachers, Thieves, and the Hidden History of American Conservation* (Berkeley: University of California Press, 2001); Michael J. Bean and Melanie Rowland, *The Evolution of National Wildlife Law*, 3rd ed. (Westport, CT: Praeger, 1997).

7. Craig W. Thomas, *Bureaucratic Landscapes: Interagency Cooperation and the Preservation of Biodiversity* (Cambridge, MA: MIT Press, 2003).

8. Christopher M. Klyza and David J. Sousa, *American Environmental Policy, 1990–2006: Beyond Gridlock* (Cambridge, MA: MIT Press, 2008), 249; Dale D. Goble, Susan M. George, Kathryn Mazaika, J. Michael Scott, and Jason Karl, "Local and National Protection of Endangered Species: An Assessment," *Environmental Science and Policy* 2 (1999): 43–59.

9. Richard West Sellars, *Preserving Nature in the National Parks: A History* (New Haven: Yale University Press, 1999).

10. Victor E. Shelford, ed., *Naturalist's Guide to the Americas* (Baltimore: Williams and Wilkins, 1926).

11. Craig L. Shafer, "Conservation Biology Trailblazers: George Wright, Ben Thompson, and Joseph Dixon," *Conservation Biology* 15, no. 2 (April 2001): 332–334.

12. Robert M. Wilson, *Seeking Refuge: Birds and Landscapes of the Pacific Flyway* (Seattle: University of Washington Press, 2010); Nathan F. Sayre, *Ranching, Endangered Species, and Urbanization in the Southwest: Species of Capital* (Tucson: University of Arizona Press, 2006); James C. Scott, *Seeing like a State: How Certain Schemes to Improve the Human Condition Have Failed* (New Haven: Yale University Press, 1998); William Cronon, "The Trouble with Wilderness; or, Getting Back to the Wrong Nature," in Cronon, ed. *Uncommon Ground: Rethinking the Human Place in Nature* (New York: W. W. Norton, 1995), 69–90.

13. Alfred Runte, *National Parks: The American Experience*, 3rd ed. (Lincoln: University of Nebraska Press, 1997); Sellars, *Preserving Nature in the National Parks;* Wilson, *Seeking Refuge;* Sayre, *Ranching, Endangered Species, and Urbanization in the Southwest;* Cronon, "The Trouble with Wilderness." For examples from the political ecology literature, see Richard Peet and Michael Watts, *Liberation Ecologies: Environment, Development, Social Movements* (London: Routledge, 1996); Nik Heynen, James McCarthy, Scott Prudham, and Paul Robbins, eds., *Neoliberal Environments: False Promises and Unnatural Consequences* (London: Routledge, 2007). For an example of the ecological protection versus social justice framing, see Jacoby, *Crimes against Nature.*

14. Michael L. Morrison, "A Proposed Research Emphasis to Overcome the Limits of Wildlife-Habitat Relationship Studies," *Journal of Wildlife Management* 65, no. 4 (October 2001): 613–623.

15. David Bunn, Andrea Mummert, Marc Hoshovsky, Kirsten Gilardi, and Sandra Shanks, *California Wildlife: Conservation Challenges—California's Wildlife Action Plan*, University of California, Davis, Wildlife Health Center and California Department of Fish and Game, 2007; A. P. Dobson, J. P. Rodriguez, W. M. Roberts, and D. S. Wilcove, "Geographic Distribution of Endangered Species in the United States," *Science* 275 (24 January 1997): 550–553; California Department of Fish and Game, *The Status of Rare, Threatened, and Endangered Plants and Animals of California, 2000–2004* (Sacramento: California Department of Fish and Game, 2005).

CHAPTER 1. THE LAND OF THE BEARS

1. Susan Snyder and Mary Scott, "Walking Tour of the Berkeley Bears," n.d. (Bancroft Library, University of California, Berkeley).

2. Allan Kelly, *Bears I Have Met—and Others* (Philadelphia: Drexel Biddle, 1903), 29.

3. Ibid., 33.

4. Ibid., 37.

5. Ibid., 39–43.

6. Allan Kelly, "Trapping a Grizzly," *Cosmopolitan* 9, no. 3 (July 1890): 342–349.

7. Ibid., 349; *San Francisco Examiner*, 5 November 1889, 3.

8. Kelly, "Trapping a Grizzly," 349.

9. The classic account of grizzlies in California is Tracy I. Storer and Lloyd P. Tevis, *California Grizzly* (Berkeley: University of California Press, 1955).

10. Joseph Grinnell, "California's Grizzly Bears," *Sierra Club Bulletin* 23, no. 2 (April 1938): 70–81.

11. Ibid., 70–71, 75.

12. Paul S. Martin, "Prehistoric Extinctions: In the Shadow of Man," in Charles E. Kay and Randy T. Simmons, eds., *Wilderness and Political Ecology: Aboriginal Influences and the Original State of Nature* (Salt Lake City: University of Utah Press, 2002), 1–27.

13. Storer and Tevis, *California Grizzly*, 77–84.

14. See, e.g., Kat M. Anderson, Michael G. Barbour, and Valerie Whitworth, "A World of Balance and Plenty: Land, Plants, Animals, and Humans in a Pre-European California," *California History* 76, nos. 2–3 (Summer–Fall 1997): 12–47.

15. Miguel Costanso, *The Narrative of the Portola Expedition of 1769–1770* (Berkeley: University of California Press, 1910); Susan Snyder, *Bear in Mind: The California Grizzly* (Berkeley: Heyday Books, 2003), 23–27. La Cañada de los Osos is now called Los Osos Valley. It is one of dozens of places around California with names that allude to bears.

16. Snyder, *Bear in Mind*, 25; Herbert Eugene Bolton, *Historical Memoirs of New California by Francisco Palóu* (Berkeley: University of California Press, 1926), 357.

17. William Preston, "Serpent in the Garden: Environmental Change in Colonial California," in Ramón Gutiérrez and Richard J. Orsi, eds., *Contested Eden: California before the Gold Rush* (Berkeley: University of California Press, 1998), 260–298; Storer and Tevis, *California Grizzly*, 112.

18. Ronald M. Yoshiyama, Frank W. Fisher, and Peter B. Moyle, "Historical Abundance and Decline of Chinook Salmon in the Central Valley Region of California," *North American Journal of Fisheries Management* 18, no. 3 (1998): 487–521; Arthur F. McEvoy, *The Fisherman's Problem: Ecology and Law in the California Fisheries, 1850–1980* (Cambridge: Cambridge University Press, 1990), 23.

19. Steven W. Hackel, *Children of Coyote, Missionaries of Saint Francis: Indian-Spanish Relations in Colonial California, 1769–1850* (Chapel Hill: University of North Carolina Press, 2005); McEvoy, *The Fisherman's Problem*, 41, 51.

20. William Preston, "Post-Columbian Wildlife Irruptions in California: Implications for Cultural and Environmental Change," in Kay and Simmons, eds., *Wilderness and Political Ecology*, 111–140.

21. Preston, "Post-Columbian Wildlife Irruptions," 111–112.

22. Joshua Paddison, *A World Transformed: Firsthand Accounts of California before the Gold Rush* (Berkeley: Heyday Books, 1998), 63, 175; Preston, "Post-Columbian Wildlife Irruptions," 111–140; David Igler, *Industrial Cowboys: Miller and Lux and the Transformation of the Far West, 1850–1920* (Berkeley: University of California Press, 2001), 30–33; Edward Bosqui, *Memoirs* (Oakland: Holmes, 1952), 16; Storer and Tevis, *California Grizzly*, 164.

23. Horace Bell, *Reminiscences of a Ranger; or, Early Times in Southern California* (Santa Barbara: Wallace Hebbard, 1927), 255; F. H. Day, "Sketches of the Early Settlers of California: George C. Yount," *Hesperian* 2, no. 1 (1859), 1; C. F. Carter, "Duhaut-Cilly's Account of California in the Years 1827–28," *California Historical Society Quarterly* 8 (1929), 239.

24. Storer and Tevis, *California Grizzly*, 140–162.

25. *San Francisco Daily Evening Bulletin*, 22 January 1858, 3; Storer and Tevis, *California Grizzly*, 195–196; Grinnell, "California's Grizzly Bears," 80.

26. Storer and Tevis, *California Grizzly*, 222–225.

27. Anonymous, "The Coast Rangers: A Chronicle of Events in California, II— Hunting Adventures," *Harper's New Monthly Magazine* 23 (1861): 593–606; Albert S. Evans, *À la California: Sketches of Life in the Golden State* (San Francisco: A. L. Bancroft, 1873), 64.

28. Anonymous, "A California Bear Story," *Spirit of the Times* 26, no. 5 (15 March 1856): 54; Walter Colton, *Three Years in California* (New York: A. S. Barnes, 1850), 120; Lisa Mighetto, *Muir among the Animals: The Wildlife Writings of John Muir* (San Francisco: Sierra Club, 1986); Joaquin Miller, *True Bear Stories* (Chicago: Rand McNally, 1900), 109.

29. L. T. Burcham, "California Rangelands in Historical Perspective," *Rangelands* 3, no. 3 (June 1981): 95–104; Joseph Grinnell, Joseph S. Dixon, and Jean M. Linsdale, *Fur-Bearing Mammals of California: Their Natural History, Systematic Status, and Relations to Man* (Berkeley: University of California Press, 1937), 1:87; Grinnell, "California's Grizzly Bears," 80–81.

30. Grinnell, Dixon, and Linsdale, *Fur-Bearing Mammals*, 75–78; Grinnell, "California's Grizzly Bears," 71–76; Joseph Dixon, "Does the Grizzly Bear Still Exist in California?," *California Fish and Game* 2, no. 2 (April 1916): 65–69.

31. Grinnell, "California's Grizzly Bears," 91–93.

32. Walter Fry, "The California Grizzly," Sequoia National Park, Historic Series, Nature Guide Service, Bulletin 2 (1924), 4 pp.; Grinnell, Dixon, and Linsdale, *Fur-Bearing Mammals*, 94.

33. Charles Howard Shinn, "Grizzly and Pioneer," *Century* 41, no. 19 (November 1890–April 1891): 130–131.

34. Andrew Isenberg, *The Destruction of the Bison: An Environmental History, 1750–1920* (Cambridge: Cambridge University Press, 2001).

35. Harold C. Bryant, "California's Fur-Bearing Mammals," *California Fish and Game* 1, no. 3 (April 1915): 96–107; Adele Ogden, *The California Sea Otter Trade, 1784–1848* (Berkeley: University of California Press, 1975); McEvoy, *The Fisherman's Problem*, 41–47, 237; Kurkpatrick Dorsey, *The Dawn of Conservation Diplomacy: U.S.-Canadian Wildlife Protection Treaties in the Progressive Era* (Seattle: University of Washington Press, 1998).

36. Dale R. McCullough, *The Tule Elk: Its History, Behavior, and Ecology*, University of California Publications in Zoology, no. 88 (Berkeley: University of California Press, 1969); Thomas Farnham, quoted in John E. Skinner, *An Historical Review of the Fish and Wildlife Resources of the San Francisco Bay Area* (Sacramento: Resources Agency of California, 1962), 157.

37. John Work, quoted in Alice B. Maloney, *Fur Brigade to the Bonaventura: John Work's California Expedition, 1832–33* (San Francisco: California Historical Society, 1945), 31.

38. McCullough, *The Tule Elk*; Barton W. Evermann, "An Attempt to Save California Elk," *California Fish and Game* 1, no. 3 (April 1915): 85–96; C. Hart Merriam, "A California Elk Drive," *Scientific Monthly* 13, no. 5 (November 1921): 465–475.

39. Skinner, *An Historical Review*, 141; Joseph Grinnell, Harold C. Bryant, and Tracy I. Storer, *The Game Birds of California* (Berkeley: University of California Press, 1918).

40. R. H. Schmidt, "Gray Wolves in California: Their Presence and Absence," *California Fish and Game* 11 (1991): 79–85; William Dasmann, *Big Game of California* (Sacramento: California Department of Fish and Game, 1975).

41. International Union for Conservation of Nature and Natural Resources, "The IUCN Red List of Threatened Species (2012.2)," www.iucnredlist.org.

42. Theodore H. Hittell, *History of California* (San Francisco: N. J. Stone, 1897), 564; Hubert H. Bancroft, *History of California*, vol. 7 (San Francisco: History Company, 1890), 81.

43. Gray A. Brechin, *Imperial San Francisco: Urban Power, Earthly Ruin* (Berkeley: University of California Press, 1999). The Bay Area population figure includes San Francisco and its four satellite cities—Oakland, San Jose, Sacramento, and Stockton—as described in Richard White, *"It's Your Misfortune and None of My Own": A New History of the American West* (Norman: University of Oklahoma Press, 1991), 391–392.

44. Socrates Hyacinth [Stephen Powers], "Wayside Views of California," *Overland Monthly* 2 (1869): 230.

45. Michael L. Smith, *Pacific Visions: California Scientists and the Environment, 1850–1915* (New Haven: Yale University Press, 1987); Robert E. Kohler, *All Creatures: Naturalists, Collectors, and Biodiversity, 1850–1950* (Princeton: Princeton University Press, 2006).

46. J. Ewan, "San Francisco as a Mecca for Nineteenth Century Naturalists," in Edward L. Kessel, ed., *A Century of Progress in the Natural Sciences, 1853–1953* (San Francisco: California Academy of Sciences, 1955), 1–63; Kohler, *All Creatures*, 18.

47. Richard Marshall Eakin, "History of Zoology at the University of California, Berkeley," *Bios* 27, no. 2 (May 1956): 67–92.

48. Smith, *Pacific Visions*, 5–9.

49. Ibid.

50. A. Starker Leopold, "The Conservation of Wildlife," in Kessel, *A Century of Progress*, 795–807.

51. Harold C. Bryant, "A Brief History of the California Fish and Game Commission," *California Fish and Game* 7, no. 2 (April 1921): 73–86.

52. McEvoy, *The Fisherman's Problem*, 101–116.

53. Karl Jacoby, *Crimes against Nature: Squatters, Poachers, Thieves, and the Hidden History of American Conservation* (Berkeley: University of California Press, 2001); Louis Warren, *The Hunter's Game: Poachers and Conservationists in Twentieth-Century America* (New Haven: Yale University Press, 1999).

54. Leopold, "The Conservation of Wildlife," 796–798.

55. Grinnell, "California's Grizzly Bears," 72.

56. Snyder, *Bear in Mind*, x.

57. Ibid., xi. The California legislature made the grizzly the official state animal in 1953. The grizzly also serves as the mascot for the University of California, Berkeley (Bears), and the University of California, Los Angeles (Bruins).

58. Steve Primm and Karen Murray, "Grizzly Bear Recovery: Living with Success," in Tim W. Clark, Murray B. Rutherford, and Denise Casey, eds., *Coexisting with Large Carnivores: Lessons from Greater Yellowstone* (Washington, DC: Island, 2005), 99–137; Christopher Servheen, "Grizzly Bear Conservation in Montana," U.S. Fish and Wildlife Service, October 2010.

CHAPTER 2. A NEW MOVEMENT

1. Donna Haraway, "Teddy Bear Patriarchy: Taxidermy in the Garden of Eden, New York City, 1908–1936," *Social Text* 11 (Winter 1984–1985): 20–64; Vernon Shephard to Joseph Grinnell, 11 January 1912, "Shephard, Vernon. 1911" correspondence files, Museum of Vertebrate Zoology, University of California, Berkeley.

2. Joseph Grinnell, Joseph S. Dixon, and Jean M. Linsdale, *Fur-Bearing Mammals of California: Their Natural History, Systematic Status, and Relations to Man* (Berkeley: University of California Press, 1937), 89–90; John E. Skinner, *An Historical Review of the Fish and Wildlife Resources of the San Francisco Bay Area* (Sacramento: Resources Agency of California, 1962).

3. Joseph Grinnell to the President of the University of California, 1 July 1913, "Bryant, Harold C. 1915–1921" correspondence files, Museum of Vertebrate Zoology.

4. Etienne Benson, "From Wild Life to Wildlife and Back," *Environmental History* 16, no. 3 (July 2011): 418–422.

5. For examples of works that portray a gradual progression in science and values and attribute these developments to later periods in American history, see Thomas Dunlap, *Saving America's Wildlife: Ecology and the American Mind, 1850–1990* (Princeton: Princeton University Press, 1991); Bonnie Christensen, "From Divine Nature to Umbrella Species: The Development of Wildlife Science in the United States," in Harold K. Steen, ed., *Forest and Wildlife Science in America: A History* (Durham, NC: Forest History Society, 1999), 19–65. Mark Barrow charts a much earlier origin for ideas about endangered species in *Nature's Ghosts: Confronting Extinction from the Age of Jefferson to the Age of Ecology* (Chicago: University of Chicago Press, 2009).

6. Hilda Wood Grinnell, "Joseph Grinnell: 1877–1939," *Condor* 42, no. 1 (January–February 1940): 3–34. Joseph Grinnell was not related to George Bird Grinnell, another prominent Progressive Era conservationist.

7. Barbara R. Stein, *On Her Own Terms: Annie Montague Alexander and the Rise of Science in the American West* (Berkeley: University of California Press, 2001).

8. James R. Griesemer and Elihu M. Gerson, "Collaboration in the Museum of Vertebrate Zoology," *Journal of the History of Biology* 26, no. 2 (Summer 1993): 185–203.

9. Jonathan Peter Spiro, *Defending the Master Race: Conservation, Eugenics, and the Legacy of Madison Grant* (Lebanon, NH: University Press of New England, 2009).

10. There is a large literature on natural history museums during this period. See, for example, Alan E. Leviton and Michael L. Aldrich, eds., *Museums and Other Institutions of Natural History: Past, Present, and Future* (San Francisco: California Academy of Sciences, 2004).

11. Susan Leigh Star and James R. Griesemer, "Institutional Ecology, 'Translations' and Boundary Objects: Amateurs and Professionals in Berkeley's Museum of Vertebrate Zoology," *Social Studies of Science* 19, no. 3 (August 1989): 387–420.

12. Joseph Grinnell to Annie Alexander, 2 and 20 November 1907, "Alexander, Annie 1907" correspondence files, Museum of Vertebrate Zoology; Grinnell, "The Methods and Uses of a Research Museum," *Popular Science Monthly* 77 (August 1910): 163–169.

13. Griesemer and Gerson, "Collaboration in the Museum of Vertebrate Zoology," 193; for a list of Grinnell's publications, see Hilda Wood Grinnell, "Joseph Grinnell," 19–34; C. Hart Merriam and Leonhard Stejneger, *Results of a Biological Survey of the San Francisco Mountain Region and Desert of the Little Colorado, Arizona,* North American Fauna, no. 3 (Washington, DC: Government Printing Office, 1890).

14. Joseph Grinnell, "The Origin and Distribution of the Chestnut-Backed Chickadee," *Auk* 21 (July 1904): 364–378; Grinnell, "The Colorado River as a Highway of Dispersal and Center of Differentiation of Species," *University of California Publications in Zoology* 5 (March 1910): 97–100; Grinnell, "The Colorado River as a Hindrance to the Dispersal of Species," *University of California Publications in Zoology* 12 (March 1914): 100–107; Alden Miller, "Speciation in the Avian Genus *Junco*," *University of California Publications in Zoology* 44 (1941): 173–434; Ernst Mayr, "Alden Holmes Miller, 1906–1965" (biographical memoir, 1973, National Academy of Sciences).

15. Ernst Mayr, "Ecological Factors in Speciation," *Evolution* 1 (1947): 253–288; Joseph Grinnell, "Geography and Evolution," *Ecology* 5 (July 1924): 225–229; James R. Griesemer, "Modeling in the Museum: On the Role of Remnant Models in the Work of Joseph Grinnell," *Biology and Philosophy* 5, no. 1 (1990): 3–36.

16. Grinnell, "The Methods and Uses of a Research Museum," 163–169; Susan E. Chatlin to Jean M. Linsdale, 22 March 1940, "Linsdale, Jean M. 1940" correspondence files, Museum of Vertebrate Zoology.

17. Joseph Grinnell, "The Museum Conscience," *Museum Work* 4 (September–October 1921): 62–63.

18. Robert E. Kohler, *All Creatures: Naturalists, Collectors, and Biodiversity, 1850–1950* (Princeton: Princeton University Press, 2006), 24, 148; Joseph Grinnell to Annie Alexander, 11 May 1911, Joseph Grinnell Papers, Bancroft Library, University of California, Berkeley; Grinnell, "The English Sparrow Has Arrived in Death Valley: An Experiment in Nature," *American Naturalist* 51 (February 1917): 115–128.

19. Joseph Grinnell to Annie Alexander, 2 November 1907, "Alexander, Annie 1907" correspondence files, Museum of Vertebrate Zoology; Grinnell to Alexander, 13 February 1911, Joseph Grinnell Papers, Bancroft Library.

20. Star and Griesemer, "Institutional Ecology," 396–404; Joseph Dixon, "The Timber Wolf in California," *California Fish and Game* 2, no. 3 (July 1916): 125–129; Grinnell, "The Methods and Uses of a Research Museum," 163–169.

21. Craig Moritz, James L. Patton, Chris J. Conroy, Juan L. Parra, Gary C. White, and Steven R. Beissinger, "Impact of a Century of Climate Change on Small-Mammal

Communities in Yosemite National Park, USA," *Science* 322, no. 261 (10 October 2008): 261–264.

22. C. Hart Merriam to Joseph Grinnell, 17 August 1937, "Merriam, C. Hart, 1931–1942" correspondence files, Museum of Vertebrate Zoology; Richard Marshall Eakin, "History of Zoology at the University of California, Berkeley," *Bios* 27, no. 2 (May 1956): 67–90.

23. Aldo Leopold, *A Sand County Almanac, and Sketches Here and There* (Oxford: Oxford University Press, 1989).

24. Karl Jacoby, *Crimes against Nature: Squatters, Poachers, Thieves, and the Hidden History of American Conservation* (Berkeley: University of California Press, 2001), 1–7.

25. Sally Gregory Kohlstedt, *Teaching Children Science: Hands-On Nature Study in North America, 1890–1930* (Chicago: University of Chicago Press, 2010). Detailed discussions between Grinnell and Bryant about Bryant's educational work appear in the correspondence files of the MVZ in the folders labeled "Bryant, Harold C. 1915–1921" and "Bryant, Harold C. 1922–1927."

26. Harold C. Bryant, "California's Fur-Bearing Mammals," *California Fish and Game* 1, no. 3 (April 1915): 96–107.

27. Matthew D. Evenden, "The Laborers of Nature: Economic Ornithology and the Role of Birds as Agents of Biological Pest Control in North American Agriculture, ca. 1880–1930," *Forest and Conservation History* 39 (1995): 172–183; Harold C. Bryant, "F. E. L. Beal and Economic Ornithology in California," *Condor* 18, no. 6 (November–December 1916): 234–236; F. E. L. Beal, *Birds of California in Relation to the Fruit Industry, Part II*, U.S. Department of Agriculture, Biological Survey Bulletin, no. 34 (Washington, DC: Government Printing Office, 1910), 8.

28. Joseph Grinnell, "Bird Life as a Community Asset," *California Fish and Game* 1, no. 1 (October 1914): 20–22; Grinnell, "Bats as Desirable Citizens," *Pacific Rural Press* 85, no. 11 (15 March 1913): 344–345; Grinnell, "The Burrowing Rodents of California as Agents in Soil Formation," *Journal of Mammalogy* 4, no. 3 (August 1923): 137–149.

29. Grinnell, "Bird Life," 20; Harold C. Bryant, "Why Non-game Birds Should Be Protected," *Western Wild Life Call* 1 (7 February 1913): 8; Bryant, "The Cooper Club Member and Scientific Work," *Condor* 16, no. 3 (May–June 1914), 105.

30. Grinnell, "Bird Life," 20; Bryant, "California's Fur-Bearing Mammals," 106.

31. Joseph Grinnell, "Conserve the Collector," *Science* 41 (February 1915): 248–254.

32. Joseph Grinnell to Harold C. Bryant, 26 October 1923, "Bryant, Harold C. 1922–1927" correspondence files, Museum of Vertebrate Zoology.

33. Ibid.

34. James A. Tober, *Who Owns the Wildlife?: The Political Economy of Conservation in Nineteenth Century America* (Westport, CT: Greenwood, 1981), 41–68; Jennifer Price, *Flight Maps: Adventures with Nature in Modern America* (New York: Basic, 1999), 57–110.

35. See, e.g., Golden Gate, "New Laws to Protect California Game," *Forest and Stream* 80, no. 12 (22 March 1913): 368; Joseph Grinnell to Harold C. Bryant, 2 June 1914, "Bryant, Harold C. 1908–1914" correspondence files, Museum of Vertebrate Zoology.

36. Skinner, *An Historical Review*, 210.

37. Walter P. Taylor, "Conserve the Wild Life the Duty of the Individual," *Western Wild Life Call* 1 (7 February 1913): 4.

38. Michael J. Bean and Melanie Rowland, *The Evolution of National Wildlife Law*, 3rd ed. (Westport, CT: Praeger, 1997).

39. Tober, *Who Owns the Wildlife?*, 58–59, 121–128.

40. Anonymous, "Shall California Violate Interstate Comity?," *Western Wild Life Call* 2 (14 March 1913): 1; William L. Finley, "Oregon Calls on California to Do Her Duty," *Western Wild Life Call* 1 (7 February 1913): 12.

41. California Fish and Game Commission, *Twenty-Second Biennial Report for the Years 1910–1912* (Sacramento: State Printing Office, 1913), 8–9.

42. Ibid.

43. Ernest Schaeffle, "The Need of Co-operation in Fish and Game Preservation," *California Fish and Game* 2, no. 2 (April 1916): 77; Arthur F. McEvoy, *The Fisherman's Problem: Ecology and Law in the California Fisheries, 1850–1980* (Cambridge: Cambridge University Press, 1990), 94.

44. Jacoby, *Crimes against Nature*, 121–146.

45. California Fish and Game Commission, *Twenty-Seventh Biennial Report for the Years 1920–1922* (Sacramento: State Printing Office, 1923), 22; Ernest Schaeffle, "The Administration of Fish and Game Laws," *California Fish and Game* 1, no. 5 (October 1915): 209.

46. [Walter P. Taylor], "Nineteen Reasons for the Passage of a Non-sale of American-Killed Wild Game Law in California," *Western Wild Life Call* 1 (7 February 1913): 3–4.

47. Anonymous, "Thirty One States Now Prohibit the Sale of Wild Ducks," *Western Wild Life Call* 4 (4 September 1914): 8.

48. Joseph Grinnell to Walter P. Taylor, 9 May 1913, "Walter P. Taylor, 1913" correspondence files, Museum of Vertebrate Zoology.

49. Walter P. Taylor, "Report of the Secretary to the Officers, Members of the Executive Committee, Advisory Council, Advisory Committee, Official Representatives and Friends," 6 November 1914, "Walter P. Taylor, 1914–1916" correspondence files, Museum of Vertebrate Zoology; H. S. Swarth, "Editorial Notes and News," *Condor* 16, no. 6 (November–December 1914): 262–263.

50. Kurkpatrick Dorsey, *The Dawn of Conservation Diplomacy: U.S.-Canadian Wildlife Protection Treaties in the Progressive Era* (Seattle: University of Washington Press, 1998), 171.

51. [Taylor], "Nineteen Reasons," 3–4.

52. Golden Gate, "Market Hunters Oppose the Fish and Game Commission," *Forest and Stream* 81, no. 23 (6 December 1913): 714.

53. Walter P. Taylor, "The Referendum, the Initiative, and the Wild Life," *Condor* 16, no. 3 (May–June 1914): 148–149; Harold C. Bryant, "A History of the Non-sale of Game in CA," *California Fish and Game* 1, no. 1 (October 1914): 1–2; Taylor, "The Initiative a Failure," *Western Wild Life Call* 4 (4 September 1914): 6.

54. Anonymous, "Non-sale of Game Wins in Southern California but Loses in the North," *Forest and Stream* 83, no. 25 (19 December 1914): 759; Joseph Grinnell to Harry Swarth, 12 November 1914, "Harry S. Swarth, 1914" correspondence files, Museum of Vertebrate Zoology.

55. Hornaday offered these opinions on a visit to Berkeley in 1915, and Harold C. Bryant recounted them in a letter shortly thereafter: Bryant to Walter P. Taylor, 18 September 1915, "Walter P. Taylor, 1914–1916" correspondence files, Museum of Vertebrate Zoology.

56. McEvoy, *The Fisherman's Problem*, 182; California Fish and Game Commission, "Commission's Work Reorganized," *California Fish and Game* 12, no. 1 (January 1926): 29–30.

CHAPTER 3. THE OFFICIAL LANDSCAPE

1. Joseph Grinnell and Tracy I. Storer, "Animal Life as an Asset of the National Parks," *Science* 44, no. 1133 (15 September 1916): 375–380.

2. Craig L. Shafer, "Conservation Biology Trailblazers: George Wright, Ben Thompson, and Joseph Dixon," *Conservation Biology* 15, no. 2 (April 2001): 332–334.

3. A. Starker Leopold, "The Conservation of Wildlife," in Edward L. Kessel, ed., *A Century of Progress in the Natural Sciences, 1853–1953* (San Francisco: California Academy of Sciences, 1955), 798, 800; Aldo Leopold noted a similar trend more than two decades earlier in his *Game Management* (New York: Charles Scribner and Sons, 1933), 13.

4. Ronald C. Tobey, *Saving the Prairies: The Life Cycle of the Founding School of American Plant Ecology, 1895–1955* (Berkeley: University of California Press, 1981); Victor E. Shelford, ed., *Naturalist's Guide to the Americas* (Baltimore: Williams and Wilkins, 1926), 3.

5. Charles C. Adams, "The New Natural History—Ecology," *American Museum Journal* 17 (1917): 491–494; Adams, "Ecological Conditions in National Forests and in National Parks," *Scientific Monthly* 20, no. 6 (June 1925): 561–593; Robert E. Kohler, *Landscapes and Labscapes: Exploring the Lab-Field Border in Biology* (Chicago: University of Chicago Press, 2002), 23–40.

6. Charles C. Adams, *Guide to the Study of Animal Ecology* (New York: McMillan, 1913), 24–27; Victor E. Shelford, "The Preservation of Natural Biotic Communities," *Ecology* 14, no. 2 (April 1933): 241.

7. Mark Barrow, *Nature's Ghosts: Confronting Extinction from the Age of Jefferson to the Age of Ecology* (Chicago: University of Chicago Press, 2009), 201–213; Shelford, *Naturalist's Guide*, 3; Shelford, *Animal Communities in Temperate America: As Illustrated in the Chicago Region* (Chicago: University of Chicago Press, 1913), 10.

8. Adams, *Animal Ecology*, 24–27.

9. Abby J. Kinchy, "On the Borders of Post-war Ecology: Struggles over the Ecological Society of America's Preservation Committee, 1917–1946," *Science as Culture* 15, no. 1 (March 2006): 23–44; Sara Fairbank Tjossem, "Preservation of Nature and Academic Respectability: Tensions in the Ecological Society of America, 1915–1979" (PhD dissertation, Cornell University, 1994), 40–43.

10. Shelford, *Naturalist's Guide*, 3, 85.

11. Shelford, "Natural Biotic Communities," 240–245.

12. Arthur G. Tansley, "The Use and Abuse of Vegetational Concepts and Terms," *Ecology* 16, no. 3 (July 1935): 284–307; Peder Anker, *Imperial Ecology: Environmental Order in the British Empire, 1895–1945* (Cambridge, MA: Harvard University Press, 2001).

13. Victor E. Shelford, W. C. Allee, and C. Stuart Gager, "Proceedings: Business Meetings of the Ecological Society of America at Cleveland, Ohio, December 31, 1930 and January 1, 1931," *Ecology* 12, no. 2 (April 1931): 433; Tjossem, "Preservation of Nature," 7–8.

14. Victor E. Shelford, "Twenty-Five Year Effort at Saving Nature for Scientific Purposes," *Science* 98, no. 2543 (24 September 1943): 280–281; Barrow, *Nature's Ghosts*, 232.

15. Tjossem, "Preservation of Nature," 33–64.

16. Edward A. Goldman, "The Predatory Animal Problem and the Balance of Nature," *Journal of Mammalogy* 6, no. 1 (February 1925): 33.

17. James A. Tober, *Who Owns the Wildlife?: The Political Economy of Conservation in Nineteenth Century America* (Westport, CT: Greenwood, 1981), 87–88.

18. E. L. Fitzhugh and P. W. Gorenzel, "Biological Status of Mountain Lions in California," *Proceedings of the Twelfth Vertebrate Pest Conference* (Lincoln: University of Nebraska, 1986); Jay C. Bruce, *Cougar Killer* (New York: Comet, 1953); Joseph Grinnell, quoted in Jean M. Linsdale, "Facts Concerning the Use of Thallium in California to Poison Rodents: Its Destructiveness to Game Birds, Song Birds, and Other Valuable Wild Life," *Condor* 33, no. 3 (May–June 1931): 92–106.

19. Alfred Runte, "Joseph Grinnell and Yosemite: Rediscovering the Legacy of a California Conservationist," *California History* 69, no. 2 (Summer 1990): 170–181; Joseph Grinnell, "A Conservationist's Creed as to Wildlife Administration," in *Joseph Grinnell's Philosophy of Nature: Selected Writings of a Western Naturalist* (Freeport, NY: Libraries Press, 1943), 165–166.

20. Lee Dice, "The Scientific Value of Predatory Mammals," *Journal of Mammalogy* 6, no. 1 (February 1925): 25–27; E. Raymond Hall, "An Outbreak of House Mice in

Kern County, California," *University of California Publications in Zoology* 20 (1927): 189–203; Joseph Dixon, "Food Predilections of Predatory and Fur-Bearing Mammals," *Journal of Mammalogy* 6, no. 1 (February 1925): 34–46.

21. Thomas Dunlap, *Saving America's Wildlife: Ecology and the American Mind, 1850–1990* (Princeton: Princeton University Press, 1991), 127.

22. Ibid., 49; Barrow, *Nature's Ghosts*, 222–223; Joseph Grinnell, "Wholesale Poisoning of Wild Animal Life," *Condor* 33, no. 3 (May–June 1931): 131–132.

23. California Fish and Game Commission, "The Predatory Mammal," *California Fish and Game* 11, no. 2 (April 1925): 76–78.

24. Walter Fry, "The California Ring-Tailed Cat," *California Fish and Game* 12, no. 2 (April 1926): 77–78; Fry, "The California Badger," *California Fish and Game* 14, no. 3 (July 1928): 204–208; Fry, "The Wolverine," *California Fish and Game* 9, no. 4 (October 1923): 129–134.

25. Aldo Leopold to Joseph Grinnell, 12 July 1922; H. S. Swarth to Leopold, 19 July 1922; Leopold to Swarth, 21 July 1922, "Leopold, Aldo. 1924–1930" correspondence files, Museum of Vertebrate Zoology, University of California, Berkeley. Thomas Dunlap also describes this exchange in *Saving America's Wildlife*, 89–90. In *Nature's Ghosts*, Mark Barrow argues that Leopold's wolf story was a distillation of his ideas and "should not be taken literally" (230).

26. Dunlap, *Saving America's Wildlife*, 48–61 (Reddington quote, 55); Barrow, *Nature's Ghosts*, 223–225.

27. Dunlap, *Saving America's Wildlife*, 48–61; Shelford, Allee, and Gager, "Proceedings," 430–431.

28. Grinnell and Storer, "Animal Life as an Asset," 378; Richard West Sellars, *Preserving Nature in the National Parks: A History* (New Haven: Yale University Press, 1999), 71–75.

29. Horace M. Albright, "The National Park Service's Policy on Predatory Animals," *Journal of Mammalogy* 12, no. 2 (May 1931): 185–186; William B. Lewis to Joseph Grinnell, 21 July and 11 September 1920, "Lewis, William B. closed" correspondence files, Museum of Vertebrate Zoology; Thomas Dunlap, "Wildlife, Science, and the National Parks, 1920–1940," in James E. Sherow, ed., *A Sense of the American West: An Anthology of Environmental History* (Albuquerque: University of New Mexico Press, 1998), 147–160; Sellars, *Preserving Nature*, 119–123.

30. Mark V. Barrow Jr., "Science, Sentiment, and the Specter of Extinction: Reconsidering Birds of Prey during America's Interwar Years," *Environmental History* 7, no. 1 (January 2002): 69–98.

31. Christian C. Young, *In the Absence of Predators: Conservation and Controversy on the Kaibab Plateau* (Lincoln: University of Nebraska Press, 2002).

32. Dunlap, "Wildlife, Science, and the National Parks," 147.

33. Sellars, *Preserving Nature*, 50, 75–82; Craig L. Shafer, "History of Selection and System Planning for U.S. Natural Area National Parks and Monuments: Beauty and

Biology," *Biodiversity and Conservation* 8, no. 2 (February 1999): 189–204; R. Gerald Wright, *Wildlife Research and Management in the National Parks* (Urbana: University of Illinois Press, 1992).

34. For more on the Forest Service's wildlife work, see Theodore Catton and Lisa Mighetto, *The Fish and Wildlife Job on the National Forests: A Century of Game and Fish Conservation, Habitat Protection, and Ecosystem Management* (U.S. Forest Service, 1998).

35. Runte, "Joseph Grinnell and Yosemite," 171; Harold C. Bryant to Joseph Grinnell, 28 December 1914, "Joseph Grinnell, 1913–1914" correspondence files, Museum of Vertebrate Zoology; Mark Daniels to Grinnell, 13 April 1915, "Daniels, Mark. 1915" correspondence files, Museum of Vertebrate Zoology; Sellars, *Preserving Nature*, 121; Grinnell to Charles G. Thomson, 1 July 1929, "Thomson, Charles G." correspondence files, Museum of Vertebrate Zoology.

36. Lowell Sumner, "Biological Research and Management in the National Park Service: A History," *George Wright Forum* 3, no. 4 (1983): 3–27.

37. Craig L. Shafer, "Conservation Biology Trailblazers," 332–344; George M. Wright, Joseph S. Dixon, and Ben H. Thompson, *Fauna of the National Parks of the United States: A Preliminary Survey of Faunal Relations in National Parks* (Washington, DC: U.S. Government Printing Office, 1933), hereafter cited as *Fauna 1*.

38. George M. Wright, Joseph S. Dixon, and Ben H. Thompson, *Fauna of the National Parks of the United States: Wildlife Management in the National Parks* (Washington, DC: U.S. Government Printing Office, 1935); Shafer, "Conservation Biology Trailblazers," 332–344.

39. Shafer, "Conservation Biology Trailblazers," 332–344; I. R. Franklin, "Evolutionary Change in Small Populations," in Michael E. Soulé and Bruce A. Wilcox, eds., *Conservation Biology: An Evolutionary-Ecological Perspective* (Sunderland, MA: Sinauer Associates, 1980), 135–150.

40. Wright, Dixon, and Thompson, *Fauna 1*, 53; Sellars, *Preserving Nature*, 93–98.

41. Wright, Dixon, and Thompson, *Fauna 1*, 21; James A. Pritchard, "The Meaning of Nature: Wilderness, Wildlife, and Ecological Values in the National Parks," *George Wright Forum* 19, no. 2 (2002): 46–56.

42. Sumner, "Biological Research and Management," 10; Sellars, *Preserving Nature*, 93, 204.

43. S. Charles Kendeigh, "Research Areas in the National Parks, January 1942," *Ecology* 23, no. 2 (April 1942): 236–238; Dietmar Schneider-Hector, "Roger W. Toll: Chief Investigator of Proposed National Parks and Monuments: Setting the Standards for America's National Park System," *Journal of the West* 42, no. 1 (Winter 2003): 82–90.

44. Joseph Grinnell to George M. Wright, 16 April 1935, "Wright, George M. 1933–1935" correspondence files, Museum of Vertebrate Zoology.

45. Sumner, "Biological Research and Management," 15.

46. Sellars, *Preserving Nature*, 146–147, 201–204.

47. John Merrick Anderson, *Wildlife Sanctuaries and the Audubon Society: Places to Hide and Seek* (Austin: University of Texas Press, 2000).

48. Robert Fischman, *The National Wildlife Refuges: Coordinating a Conservation System through Law* (Washington, DC: Island, 2003), 34–40; Christopher M. Klyza and David J. Sousa, *American Environmental Policy, 1990–2006: Beyond Gridlock* (Cambridge, MA: MIT Press, 2008), 99.

49. Sally K. Fairfax, Lauren Gwin, Mary Ann King, Leigh Raymond, and Laura A. Watt, *Buying Nature: The Limits of Land Acquisition as a Conservation Strategy, 1780–2004* (Cambridge, MA: MIT Press, 2005).

50. "Announcement," 26 June 1928, "Leopold, Aldo. 1924–1930" correspondence files, Museum of Vertebrate Zoology; Aldo Leopold, "Report to the Committee on American Wild Life," *Proceedings of the American Game Conference*, vols. 15–17: *The American Game Policy and Its Development, 1928–1930* (Washington, DC: Wildlife Management Institute, 1971); Leopold, "American Wild Life"; Leopold to Joseph Grinnell, 4 June 1930, and Grinnell to Leopold, 31 July 1930, "Leopold, Aldo. 1924–1930" correspondence files, Museum of Vertebrate Zoology.

51. Fairfax et al., *Buying Nature*, 112–113; Timothy W. Luke, "The Pleasures of Use: Federalizing Wilds, Nationalizing Life at the National Wildlife Federation," *Capitalism, Nature, Socialism* 12, no. 2 (2001): 3–38.

52. Luke, "The Pleasures of Use," 11–12; U.S. Department of Agriculture, "President's Committee on Wild Life Submits Final Conservation Plan," box 10, folder 2, Joseph and Hilda Wood Grinnell Papers, 1886–1967, Bancroft Library, University of California, Berkeley.

53. Fairfax et al., *Buying Nature*, 90–94. The Migratory Bird Conservation Act of 1929 is different from the Migratory Bird Treaty Act of 1918, though the two are sometimes confused.

54. Fairfax et al., *Buying Nature*, 115.

55. Luke "The Pleasures of Use," 13; James Moffitt, "Federal Wild-Life Restoration Program," *California Fish and Game* 20, no. 2 (April 1934): 163–166; Fairfax et al., *Buying Nature*, 103–106; Charles G. Curtin, "The Evolution of the U.S. National Wildlife Refuge System and the Doctrine of Compatibility," *Conservation Biology* 7, no. 1 (March 1993): 29–38.

56. Shannon Petersen, *Acting for Endangered Species: The Statutory Ark* (Lawrence: University Press of Kansas, 2002), 14; Johnathan P. West and Glenn Sussman, "Implementation of Environmental Policy: The Chief Executive," in Dennis L. Soden, ed., *The Environmental Presidency* (Albany: SUNY Press, 1999), 79–89.

57. Curt D. Meine, *Aldo Leopold: His Life and Work* (Madison: University of Wisconsin Press, 2010), 363.

58. Barrow, *Nature's Ghosts*, 317–322.

59. Robert M. Wilson, "Directing the Flow: Migratory Waterfowl, Scale, and Mobility in Western North America," *Environmental History* 7, no. 2 (April 2002): 247–266.

60. Robert Darland, "He Brought Order to America's Wildlife Management Efforts," *National Wildlife* 38, no. 4 (2000): 45.

61. Robert Sproul, quoted in anonymous, "Dr. Grinnell, Famous U.C. Scientist, Dies: Ornithologist Succumbs to Heart Attack," *San Francisco Examiner*, 30 May 1939.

62. Ralph J. Raitt, "In Memoriam: A. Starker Leopold," *Auk* 101 (October 1984): 868–871; A. S. Leopold, S. A. Cain, C. M. Cottam, I. N. Gabrielson, and T. L. Kimball, *Wildlife Management in the National Parks*, prepared by the Advisory Board on Wildlife Management appointed by Secretary of the Interior Udall (4 March 1963).

63. Anonymous, "A Summary of Mammal Population Estimates and Relative Population Densities," "Wildlife Management and Endangered Species 1955–1985" box, "Rare and Endangered Species General Information, Lists & Acts 1978–1986 (1 of 3)" folder, Yosemite National Park Archives; Sumner, "Biological Research and Management," 16–18; James W. Feldman, "Public Opinion, the Leopold Report, and the Reform of Federal Predator Control Policy," *Human-Wildlife Conflicts* 1, no. 1 (Spring 2007): 112–124.

64. Leopold et al., *Wildlife Management in the National Parks*, 1–4.

65. Sellars, *Preserving Nature*, 224–228; National Academy of Sciences, "A Report by the Advisory Committee to the National Park Service on Research," William J. Robbins, chairman (National Research Council, 1963).

66. National Park Service, *State of the Parks 1980: A Report to Congress* (Washington, DC: National Park Service, 1980), 35; Rich Baker, quoted in Craig W. Thomas, *Bureaucratic Landscapes: Interagency Cooperation and the Preservation of Biodiversity* (Cambridge, MA: MIT Press, 2003), 81.

CHAPTER 4. THE LAWS OF NATURE

1. Richard Nixon, "The President's 1972 Environmental Program," *Weekly Compilation of Presidential Documents* 8 (8 February 1972): 218–224; Shannon Petersen, *Acting for Endangered Species: The Statutory Ark* (Lawrence: University Press of Kansas, 2002), 29–35.

2. Christopher M. Klyza and David J. Sousa, *American Environmental Policy, 1990–2006: Beyond Gridlock* (Cambridge, MA: MIT Press, 2008), 1, 26, 36–37.

3. Dale D. Goble, J. Michael Scott, and Frank W. Davis, eds., introduction to *The Endangered Species Act at Thirty*, vol. 1, *Renewing the Conservation Promise* (Washington, DC: Island, 2006), 3; Holly Doremus, "Lessons Learned," in ibid., 203; Thomas F. Darin, "Designating Critical Habitat under the Endangered Species Act: Habitat Protection versus Agency Discretion," *Harvard Environmental Law Review* 24, no. 1 (2000): 210; *Tennessee Valley Authority v. Hill et al.*, Supreme Court of the United States, no. 76–1701, decided 15 June 1978, 180.

4. Karl Boyd, *Before Earth Day: The Origins of American Environmental Law, 1945–1970* (Lawrence: University Press of Kansas, 2009).

5. Daniel B. Beard, Frederick C. Lincoln, Victor Calahane, Hartley T. H. Jackson, and Ben H. Thompson, *Fading Trails: The Story of Endangered American Wildlife* (New York: Macmillan, 1942); Peter Matthiessen, *Wildlife in America* (New York: Viking, 1959); Rachel Carson, *Silent Spring* (New York: Houghton Mifflin, 1962); A. S. Leopold, S. A. Cain, C. M. Cottam, I. N. Gabrielson, and T. L. Kimball, *Wildlife Management in the National Parks*, prepared by the Advisory Board on Wildlife Management appointed by Secretary of the Interior Udall, 4 March 1963; Raymond F. Dasmann, *The Destruction of California* (New York: MacMillan, 1965).

6. Sara Fairbank Tjossem, "Preservation of Nature and Academic Respectability: Tensions in the Ecological Society of America, 1915–1979" (PhD dissertation, Cornell University, 1994), 6; James A. Tober, *Wildlife and the Public Interest: Nonprofit Organizations and Federal Wildlife Policy* (New York: Praeger, 1989), 9–58.

7. William D. Palmer, "Endangered Species Protection: A History of Congressional Action," *Boston College Environmental Affairs Law Review* 4 (1975): 258, 267.

8. Michael J. Bean and Melanie Rowland, *The Evolution of National Wildlife Law*, 3rd ed. (Westport, CT: Praeger, 1997); Bradford C. Mank, "Can Congress Regulate Intrastate Endangered Species under the Commerce Clause?," *Brooklyn Law Review* 69 (2004): 937; Palmer, "Endangered Species Protection."

9. Holly Doremus, "New Directions in Environmental Law: The Endangered Species Act: Static Law Meets Dynamic World," *Washington University Journal of Law and Policy* 32 (2010): 175–235.

10. Mike McQueen, "Land and Water Conservation Fund: An Assessment of Its Past, Present, and Future," Arlington, VA: Conservation Fund, 2000; Petersen, *Acting for Endangered Species*, 22; Goble, Scott, and Davis, *Endangered Species Act*, 1:6.

11. Palmer, "Endangered Species Protection," 255–258; Petersen, *Acting for Endangered Species*, 4, 23; National Research Council, Committee on Scientific Issues in the Endangered Species Act, *Science and the Endangered Species Act* (Washington, DC: National Academy Press, 1995), 73.

12. Palmer, "Endangered Species Protection," 262–263; Petersen, *Acting for Endangered Species*, 25.

13. Doremus, "New Directions," 175–180; Senate Committee on Environment and Public Works, 97th Congress, 2nd session, *A Legislative History of the Endangered Species Act of 1973, as Amended in 1976, 1977, 1978, 1979, and 1980* (Washington, DC: Congressional Research Service, 1982).

14. Klyza and Sousa, *American Environmental Policy*, 159.

15. U.S. Department of the Interior, "Memorandum: The Meaning of 'Foreseeable Future' in Section 3(20) of the Endangered Species Act," 16 January 2009; Linda C.

Maranzana, "Defenders of Wildlife v. Norton: A Closer Look at the 'Significant Portion of Its Range' Concept," *Ecology Law Quarterly* 29 (2002), 263–281.

16. Palmer, "Endangered Species Protection," 266; Doremus, "New Directions," 177.

17. Dale D. Goble, Susan M. George, Kathryn Mazaika, J. Michael Scott, and Jason Karl, "Local and National Protection of Endangered Species: An Assessment," *Environmental Science and Policy* 2 (1999): 43–59; U.S. Department of the Interior, "Giant Step Forward for Endangered Species Programs," 30 June 1976, carton 159, folder 22, Sierra Club National Legislative Office Records, Bancroft Library, University of California, Berkeley.

18. Petersen, *Acting for Endangered Species*, x.

19. Palmer, "Endangered Species Protection," 266; Doremus, "New Directions," 177.

20. Palmer, "Endangered Species Protection," 283.

21. Kenneth M. Murchison, *The Snail Darter Case: TVA versus the Endangered Species Act* (Lawrence: University Press of Kansas, 2007); Steven L. Yaffee, *Prohibitive Policy: Implementing the Federal Endangered Species Act* (Cambridge, MA: MIT Press, 1982), 48.

22. Goble, Scott, and Davis, *Endangered Species Act*, 1:9.

23. Lindell L. Marsh and Robert D. Thompson, "San Bruno Mountain Habitat Conservation Plan," in David J. Brower and Daniel S. Carol, eds., *Managing Land-Use Conflicts: Case Studies in Special Area Management* (Durham: Duke University Press, 1987), 114–139; Timothy Beatley, *Habitat Conservation Planning: Endangered Species and Urban Growth* (Austin: University of Texas Press, 1994), 54–68; J. B. Ruhl, "How to Kill an Endangered Species, Legally: The Nuts and Bolts of Endangered Species Act 'HCP' Permits for Real Estate Development," *Environmental Lawyer* 5, no. 2 (1999): 345–405; Wayne King, "Builder Stumbles on Potent Foe—Butterflies," *New York Times*, 6 February 1982, A-1.

24. Timothy Egan, "Strongest U.S. Environment Law May Become Endangered Species," *New York Times*, 26 May 1992, A-1.

25. Timothy Egan, "Look Who's Hugging Trees Now," *New York Times*, 7 July 1996; General Accounting Office, "Endangered Species Program: Information on How Funds Are Allocated and What Activities Are Emphasized," June 2002, 2.

26. Klyza and Sousa, *American Environmental Policy*, 2–11, 41.

27. Government Accountability Office, "Endangered Species Act: Many GAO Recommendations Have Been Implemented, but Some Issues Remain Unresolved," December 2008, 1; Daniel J. Rohlf, "Six Biological Reasons Why the Endangered Species Act Doesn't Work—and What to Do about It," *Conservation Biology* 5, no. 3 (September 1991): 273–282.

28. Charles C. Mann and Mark L. Plummer, *Noah's Choice: The Future of Endangered Species* (New York: Alfred A. Knopf, 1995); Michael J. Bean, "Endangered Species,

Endangered Act?," *Environment* 41, no. 1 (January–February 1999): 12–38; Barton H. Thompson Jr., "People or Prairie Chickens: The Uncertain Search for Optimal Biodiversity," *Stanford Law Review* 51 (May 1999): 1127–1185; Gardner M. Brown Jr. and Jason F. Shogren, "Economics of the Endangered Species Act," *Journal of Economic Perspectives* 12, no. 3 (Summer 1998): 3–20.

29. Daniel Pollak, *Natural Community Conservation Planning (NCCP): The Origins of an Ambitious Experiment to Protect Ecosystems* (Sacramento: California Research Bureau, 2001), 7; Kelly O'Keefe, "A 'New American Land Ethic': Utilizing the Endangered Species Act to Settle Land Use Disputes," *Florida State University Law Review* 21 (Winter 1994): 1032.

30. O'Keefe, "'New American Land Ethic,'" 1032–1039.

31. J. B. Ruhl, "Biodiversity Conservation and the Ever-Expanding Web of Federal Laws Regulating Nonfederal Lands: Time for Something Completely Different?," *University of Colorado Law Review* 66 (Summer 1995): 589.

32. Pollak, *Natural Community Conservation Planning*, 10; Eric Fisher, "Habitat Conservation Planning under the Endangered Species Act: No Surprises and the Quest for Certainty," *University of Colorado Law Review* 67 (Spring 1996): 373–374; Craig W. Thomas, *Bureaucratic Landscapes: Interagency Cooperation and the Preservation of Biodiversity* (Cambridge, MA: MIT Press, 2003), 200.

33. Thomas, *Bureaucratic Landscapes*, 60–69, 89, 148; DeAnne Parker, "Natural Community Conservation Planning: California's Emerging Ecosystem Management Alternative," *University of Baltimore Journal of Environmental Law* 6 (Fall 1997): 122–127; Pollak, *Natural Community Conservation Planning*, 5; Howard Sarasohn and William E. Martin, "Cooperative Agreement between the California Department of Fish and Game and the U.S. Fish and Wildlife Service," 1991.

34. Allan A. Schoenherr, *A Natural History of California* (Berkeley: University of California Press, 1995), 339–340.

35. Pollak, *Natural Community Conservation Planning*, 5–6; Lee Jones, "Cooperation Is Key," *Los Angeles Times*, 28 August 1991, B-10; U.S. Fish and Wildlife Service, "Determination of Threatened Status for the Coastal California Gnatcatcher," *Federal Register* 58 (30 March 1993): 16742–16757.

36. Pollak, *Natural Community Conservation Planning*, 16, 11; Pollak, *The Future of Habitat Conservation?: The NCCP Experience in Southern California* (Sacramento: California Research Bureau, 2001), 24; Parker, "Natural Community Conservation Planning," 108–110, 124–128.

37. Thomas, *Bureaucratic Landscapes*, 194, 214; Pollak, *Natural Community Conservation Planning*, 3, 10, 17.

38. Robert Reinhold, "Tiny Songbird Poses Big Test of U.S. Environmental Policy," *New York Times*, 16 March 1993, A-1; O'Keefe, "'New American Land Ethic,'" 1041; Michael Doyle, "New Tactics May Save Rare Bird," *Sacramento Bee*, 26 March 1993, A-1.

39. California Department of Fish and Game, *The Status of Rare, Threatened, and Endangered Plants and Animals of California, 2000–2004* (Sacramento: California Department of Fish and Game, 2005), 2; U.S. Fish and Wildlife Service, "Habitat Conservation Plan Assurances ('No Surprises') Rule," *Federal Register* 63, no. 35 (23 February 1998): 8871–8873.

40. Michael J. Scott, Dale D. Goble, Leona K. Svancara, and Anna Pidgorna, "By the Numbers," in Goble, Scott, and Davis, *Endangered Species Act*, 1:28; Barton H. Thompson Jr., "Managing the Working Landscape," in ibid., 1:107.

41. Kevin D. Batt, "Above All, Do No Harm: Sweet Home and Section Nine of the Endangered Species Act," *Boston University Law Review* 75 (September 1995): 1177–1231; Matthew W. Cheney, "Babbitt v. Sweet Home Chapter of Communities for a Great Oregon: Habitat Modification Becomes a 'Taking' under the Endangered Species Act of 1973," *Ohio Northern University Law Review* 22 (1995): 537.

42. Darin, "Designating Critical Habitat," 209–210; National Research Council, *Science and the Endangered Species Act*, 73.

43. Batt, "Above All, Do No Harm," 1205–1211, 1227; Christopher F. Tate, "Getting out of 'Harm's' Way: Babbitt v. Sweet Home Chapter of Communities for a Great Oregon," *George Mason Law Review* 5 (Fall 1996): 128; Cheney, "Babbitt v. Sweet Home," 549–550.

44. Kristen M. Fletcher, "Conserving Their Kingdom: Habitat Modification as Harm under the Endangered Species Act," *Journal of Legislation* 21 (1995): 136.

45. *Bruce Babbitt, Secretary of the Interior, et al., Petitioners, v. Sweet Home Chapter of Communities for a Great Oregon et al.*, Supreme Court of the United States, no. 94–859, decided 29 June 1995.

46. Cheney, "Babbitt v. Sweet Home," 544, 547–548, 554; *Sweet Home*, at 714 (Justice Scalia dissenting).

47. Darin, "Designating Critical Habitat," 212.

48. Amy Armstrong, "Critical Habitat Designations under the Endangered Species Act: Giving Meaning to the Requirements for Habitat Protection," *South Carolina Environmental Law Journal* 10 (Summer 2002): 81; General Accounting Office, "Endangered Species: Fish and Wildlife Service Uses Best Available Science to Make Listing Decisions, but Additional Guidance Needed for Critical Habitat Designations," August 2003; National Research Council, *Science and the Endangered Species Act*, 74–75.

49. Armstrong, "Critical Habitat Designations," 53–54, 76–77; Darin, "Designating Critical Habitat," 213–222; Kieran Suckling and Martin Taylor, "Critical Habitat and Recovery," in Goble, Scott, and Davis, *Endangered Species Act*, 1:76.

50. Martin F. J. Taylor, Kieran F. Suckling, and Jeffrey J. Rachlinski, "The Effectiveness of the Endangered Species Act: A Quantitative Analysis," *BioScience* 55, no. 4 (April 2005): 360–362; Amy N. Hagen and Karen E. Hodges, "Resolving Critical Habitat Designation Failures: Reconciling Law, Policy, and Biology," *Conservation Biology* 20, no. 2 (April 2006): 400.

51. General Accounting Office, "Endangered Species Act: Types and Number of Implementing Actions," May 1992; Scott et al., "By the Numbers," 24; Suckling and Taylor, "Critical Habitat and Recovery," 76; U.S. Fish and Wildlife Service, "Critical Living Space for Endangered Species Sought," 11 June 1975, and "Critical Habitat Set Forth for Four Endangered Species," carton 160, folder 2, Sierra Club National Legislative Office Records, Bancroft Library.

52. Hagen and Hodges, "Resolving Critical Habitat Designation Failures," 400; Josh Thompson, "Critical Habitat under the Endangered Species Act: Designation, Re-designation, and Regulatory Duplication," *Alabama Law Review* 58 (2007): 902; Suckling and Taylor, "Critical Habitat and Recovery," 78–80; B. H. Thompson Jr., "Managing the Working Landscape," 113.

53. *Conservation Council for Hawai'i et al., Plaintiffs, v. Bruce Babbitt et al., Defendants,* United States District Court, District of Hawaii, no. 97–00098, decided 9 March 1998.

54. Suckling and Taylor, "Critical Habitat and Recovery," 84; Ray Ring, "Rebels with a Lost Cause," *High Country News* 39, no. 23 (10 December 2007): 10–17.

55. U.S. Fish and Wildlife Service, "Notice of Intent to Clarify the Role of Habitat in Endangered Species Conservation," *Federal Register* 64, no. 113 (14 June 1999): 31871–31874; Thomas, *Bureaucratic Landscapes,* 33; U.S. Department of the Interior, Office of the Solicitor, "Memorandum: The Secretary's Authority to Exclude Areas from a Critical Habitat Designation under Section 4(b)(2) of the Endangered Species Act," 3 October 2008; Jonathan M. Hoekstra, William F. Fagan, and Jeffrey E. Bradley, "A Critical Role for Critical Habitat in the Recovery Planning Process?: Not Yet," *Ecological Applications* 12, no. 3 (2002): 701–707; General Accounting Office, "Critical Habitat Designations," 4, 34–35.

56. For examples of refuge conflicts, see Robert M. Wilson, *Seeking Refuge: Birds and Landscapes of the Pacific Flyway* (Seattle: University of Washington Press, 2010), and Nathan F. Sayre, *Ranching, Endangered Species, and Urbanization in the Southwest: Species of Capital* (Tucson: University of Arizona Press, 2006); Holly Doremus, "Science and Controversy," in Goble, Scott, and Davis, eds., *Endangered Species Act,* 2:99.

57. Robert H. MacArthur and Edward O. Wilson, *The Theory of Island Biogeography* (Princeton: Princeton University Press, 1967); Daniel Simberloff, "Experimental Zoogeography of Islands: A Model for Insular Colonization," *Ecology* 50, no. 2 (March 1969): 296–314.

58. Daniel Simberloff and L. G. Abele, "Island Biogeography Theory and Conservation Practice," *Science* 191, no. 4224 (23 January 1976): 285–286; Simberloff, "Biogeographic Approaches and the New Conservation Biology," in S. T. A. Pickett, R. S. Ostfeld, M. Shachak, and G. E. Likens, eds., *The Ecological Basis of Conservation: Heterogeneity, Ecosystems, and Biodiversity* (New York: Chapman and Hall, 1997), 274–284; William D. Newmark, "A Land-Bridge Island Perspective on Mammalian

Extinctions in Western North American Parks," *Nature* 325 (29 January 1987): 430–432; Michael E. Gilpin and Jared M. Diamond, "Subdivision of Nature Reserves and the Maintenance of Species Diversity," *Nature* 285 (19 June 1980): 567–568.

59. Yrjo Haila, "A Conceptual Genealogy of Fragmentation Research: From Island Biogeography to Landscape Ecology," *Ecological Applications* 12, no. 2 (April 2002): 321–334; Etienne Benson, *Wired Wilderness: Technologies of Tracking and the Making of Modern Wildlife* (Baltimore: Johns Hopkins University Press, 2010).

60. Raymond F. Dasmann, "Towards a System for Classifying Natural Regions of the World and Their Representation by National Parks and Reserves," *Biological Conservation* 4, no. 4 (July 1972): 247–255; Craig L. Shafer, "U.S. National Park Buffer Zones: Historical, Scientific, Social, and Legal Aspects," *Environmental Management* 23, no. 1 (January 1999): 51; Thomas, *Bureaucratic Landscapes*, 202.

61. Reed F. Noss, Michael A. O'Connell, and Dennis D. Murphy, *The Science of Conservation Planning: Habitat Conservation under the Endangered Species Act* (Washington, DC: Island, 1997).

62. Kristin Carden, "Bridging the Divide: The Role of Science in Species Conservation Law," *Harvard Environmental Law Review* 30 (2006): 184–195, 215, 241.

63. J. B. Ruhl, "Reconstructing the Wall of Virtue: Maxims for the Co-evolution of Environmental Law and Environmental Science," *Environmental Law* 37 (2007): 1063–1082.

CHAPTER 5. THE CALIFORNIA CONDOR

1. David Smollar, "California's Last Condor in Wild Captured," *Los Angeles Times*, 20 April 1987, A-1; Jay Mathews, "Last Wild Condor of Species Netted," *Washington Post*, 20 April 1987, A-3; John Nielsen, *Condor: To the Brink and Back—the Life and Times of One Giant Bird* (New York: Harper Collins, 2006), 21–24; James A. Tober, *Wildlife and the Public Interest: Nonprofit Organizations and Federal Wildlife Policy* (New York: Praeger, 1989), 59.

2. Nielsen, *Condor*, 21–24.

3. William Cronon, "The Trouble with Wilderness; or, Getting Back to the Wrong Nature," in Cronon, ed., *Uncommon Ground: Rethinking the Human Place in Nature* (New York: W. W. Norton, 1995), 81–82.

4. Paul S. Martin, "Prehistoric Extinctions: In the Shadow of Man," in Charles E. Kay and Randy T. Simmons, eds., *Wilderness and Political Ecology: Aboriginal Influences and the Original State of Nature* (Salt Lake City: University of Utah Press, 2002), 1–27; Noel Snyder and Helen Snyder, *The California Condor: A Saga of Natural History and Conservation* (San Diego: Natural World Academic Press, 2000), 10–11; Steven D. Emslie, "Age and Diet of Fossil California Condors in Grand Canyon, Arizona," *Science* 237, no. 4816 (14 August 1987): 768–770.

5. Lloyd Kiff, "An Historical Perspective on the Condor," *Outdoor California* 44, no. 5 (September–October 1983): 6; Sanford R. Wilbur, *The California Condor, 1966–76: A Look at Its Past and Future*, North American Fauna, no. 72 (Washington, DC: United States Department of the Interior, Fish and Wildlife Service, 1978), 18.

6. Snyder and Snyder, *California Condor*, 30–45; D.D. Simons, "Interactions between California Condors and Humans in Prehistoric Far Western North America," in Sanford R. Wilbur and Jerome A. Jackson, eds., *Vulture Biology and Management* (Berkeley: University of California Press, 1983), 470–494; Wilbur, "The Condor and the Native Americans," *Outdoor California* 44, no. 5 (September–October 1983): 7–8.

7. Harry Harris, "The Annals of *Gymnogyps* to 1900," *Condor* 43, no. 1 (January–February 1941): 3–9; Andrew Jackson Grayson, quoted in "Harry Harris Papers" folder, Ornithology Collections, Section of Vertebrate Zoology, Natural History Museum of Los Angeles County.

8. Patrick Gass, *Gass's Journal of the Lewis and Clark Expedition* (Chicago: A.C. McClurg, 1904), 178, 203, 207; J.H. Flemming, "The California Condor in Washington: Another Version of an Old Record," *Condor* 26 (September 1924): 111–112; Carl B. Koford, *The California Condor* (New York: Dover, 1953), 9–10; Dick Smith and Robert Easton, *California Condor: Vanishing American* (Charlotte: McNally and Loftin, 1964), 68; Snyder and Snyder, *California Condor*, 45–47; H.W. Henshaw, "Autobiographical Notes," *Condor* 22 (1920): 3–10.

9. Kiff, "Historical Perspective," 34; Alexander S. Taylor, "The Great Condor of California," *Hutchings California Magazine* 36 (June 1859): 540–543.

10. Catharine Millikan, "Capture of a Condor in El Dorado Co. Cal. in 1854," *Condor* 2, no. 1 (January–February 1900): 12–13; Kiff, "Historical Perspective," 6, 34; Wilbur, *California Condor*, 71–88.

11. James G. Cooper, "A Doomed Bird," *Zoe* 1 (1890): 248–249; William T. Hornaday, "The Destruction of Our Birds and Mammals: A Report on the Results of an Inquiry," *2nd Annual Report of the New York Zoological Society* (15 March 1898), 77–126; C.W. Beebe, "The California Condor," *Bulletin of the Zoological Society of New York* 20 (1906): 258–259; Graham Renshaw, "The California Condor," *Ovid* 11 (August 1907): 295–298; H.H. Sheldon, "What Price Condor," *Field and Stream* 44 (September 1939): 61–62; see also William Finley, "Life History of the California Condor Part II," *Condor* 10, no. 1 (January–February 1908): 5–10.

12. Smith and Easton, *California Condor*, 75; Koford, *California Condor*, 2–3.

13. E. Ainsworth, "Hunt Starts for Pair of California Condors," *Los Angeles Times*, 10 February 1953, II-22; Lloyd Kiff, quoted in Scott Armstrong, "Flight of the Condor (and Ferret)," *Christian Science Monitor*, 25 September 1991, 8, col. 2.

14. Carlson, "Last Days of the Condor?," A-1; Pat V. Rich, "The Fossil History of Vultures: A World Perspective," in Wilbur and Jackson, *Vulture Biology and Management*, 3–16; Kiff, "Historical Perspective," 5.

15. David Kelly, "Welfare State for Vultures," *Los Angeles Times,* 24 July 2002, A-1.

16. Lloyd Kiff, "A New Epoch for the California Condor," *Peregrine Fund Newsletter* 34 (Fall–Winter 2003): 3; Nielsen, *Condor,* 35.

17. Charles Bergman, *Wild Echoes: Encounters with the Most Endangered Animals in North America* (New York: McGraw-Hill, 1990), 71; Ian McMillan, "An Objection to Feeding Condors," in David Phillips and Hugh Nash, eds., *The Condor Question: Captive or Forever Free?* (San Francisco: Friends of the Earth, 1981), 103.

18. Timothy Carlson, "Last Days of the Condor?," *New York Times,* 8 February 1986, A-1; David Brower, "The Condor and a Sense of Place," in Phillips and Nash, *The Condor Question,* 275; Nielsen, *Condor,* 16, 124.

19. Jennifer Meyer, "To Save the Condor," *Outdoor California* 44, no. 5 (September–October 1983): 3; Brower, "The Condor and a Sense of Place," 275.

20. Finley, "California Condor Part II," 4, 8; Mark Barrow, *Nature's Ghosts: Confronting Extinction from the Age of Jefferson to the Age of Ecology* (Chicago: University of Chicago Press, 2009), 286.

21. William L. Finley, "Life History of the California Condor. Part I. Finding a Condor's Nest," *Condor* 8, no. 6 (November–December 1906): 134; Finley, "Life History of the California Condor Part III: Home Life of the Condors," *Condor* 10, no. 2 (March–April 1908): 58.

22. Barrow, *Nature's Ghosts,* 285–287, 298; William T. Hornaday, *Our Vanishing Wildlife: Its Extermination and Preservation* (New York: New York Zoological Society, 1913), 23–24.

23. Nielsen, *Condor,* 110–111; Barrow, *Nature's Ghosts,* 285–289.

24. Nielsen, *Condor,* 110–111; Barrow, *Nature's Ghosts,* 285–296.

25. Ray Ford, "Saving the Condor: Robert E. Easton's Fight to Create the Sisquoc Condor Sanctuary," *Noticias—Bulletin of the Santa Barbara Historical Society* 32, no. 4 (1986): 78–80.

26. Koford, *California Condor,* 23.

27. Ibid., 129–135; Finley, "Part I," 142.

28. David B. Mertz, "The Mathematical Demography of the California Condor Population," *American Naturalist* 105, no. 945 (September–October 1971): 442; Koford, *California Condor,* 21–23; V. J. Meretsky, N. F. R. Snyder, S. R. Beissinger, D. A. Clendenen, and J. W. Wiley, "Demography of the California Condor: Implications for Reestablishment," *Conservation Biology* 14, no. 4 (August 2000): 957–967.

29. Carl B. Koford, "California Condors, Forever Free?," *Audubon Imprint— Newsletter of the Santa Monica Bay Audubon Society* 3 (April 1979): 1–7.

30. Kiff, "Historical Perspective," 35; Barrow, *Nature's Ghosts,* 297; Koford, *California Condor,* 135.

31. California Fish and Game Commission, *Twenty-Seventh Biennial Report for the Years 1920–1922* (Sacramento: State Printing Office, 1923), 107.

32. Alden H. Miller, Ian I. McMillan, and Eben McMillan, *The Current Status and Welfare of the California Condor*, National Audubon Society, research report no. 6 (1965), 19; Wilbur, *California Condor*, 27; Lloyd Kiff, "A New Beginning for the Condor," *Western Tanager* 58, no. 4 (December 1991): 4.

33. Barrow, *Nature's Ghosts*, 290, 294; Nielsen, *Condor*, 126; Kiff, "Historical Perspective," 36; Wilbur, *California Condor*, 7.

34. David M. Stoms, F. W. Davis, C. B. Cogan, M. O. Painho, B. W. Duncan, J. Scepan, and M. J. Scott, "Geographic Analysis of California Condor Sighting Data," *Conservation Biology* 7, no. 1 (March 1993): 148–159; Kiff, "Historical Perspective," 36.

35. U.S. Fish and Wildlife Service, "Determination of Critical Habitat for American Crocodile, California Condor, Indiana Bat, and Florida Manatee," *Federal Register* 41, no. 187 (24 September 1976): 41914–41916; California Condor Recovery Team, *California Condor Recovery Plan* (U.S. Fish and Wildlife Service, July 1976).

36. Snyder and Snyder, *California Condor*, 370.

37. Ibid., 92–95, 273–275, 298–305; Lloyd Kiff, David B. Peakall, and Sanford R. Wilbur, "Recent Changes in California Condor Egg Shells," *Condor* 81, no. 2 (May 1979): 166–172; Lloyd Kiff, "How Few Is Enough?: The Case for Captive Breeding," *Western Tanager* 46, no. 2 (October 1979): 2.

38. Anonymous, "National Audubon Endorses Captive Propagation and Release of California Condors Because of Precarious State of This Endangered Species: Science Panel to be Set," *Audubon Leader* 18, no. 3 (11 February 1977): 1.

39. Anne and Paul Ehrlich, foreword, and A. Starker Leopold, "To the Condor Advisory Committee," in Phillips and Nash, *The Condor Question*; Snyder and Snyder, *California Condor*, 304; Mark J. Palmer, "Shedding Light on the Controversy: The Sierra Club," *Outdoor California* 44, no. 5 (September–October 1983): 21; Nielsen, *Condor*, 154.

40. Mark Crawford, "The Last Days of the Wild Condor?," *Science* 229, no. 4716 (30 August 1985): 844–845.

41. Bergman, *Wild Echoes*, 82.

42. Snyder and Snyder, *California Condor*, 95, 298–305; Kiff, "How Few Is Enough?," 2–3; Kiff, "New Beginning," 2; Bergman, *Wild Echoes*, 74.

43. Noel Snyder, S. R. Derrickson, S. R. Beissinger, J. W. Wiley, T. B. Smith, W. D. Toone, and B. Miller, "Limits of Captive Breeding in Endangered Species Recovery," *Conservation Biology* 10, no. 2 (April 1996): 338–348; Smollar, "California's Last Condor in Wild Captured," A-1.

44. Oliver Ryder, A. McLaren, S. Brenner, Y. Zhang, and K. Benirschke, "DNA Banks for Endangered Animal Species," *Science* 288, no. 5464 (14 April 2000): 275–277; C. J. Geyer, O. A. Ryder, L. G. Chemnick, and E. A. Thompson, "Analysis of Relatedness in the California Condors, from DNA Fingerprints," *Molecular Biology and Evolution* 10, no. 3 (May 1993): 571–589; Kiff, "New Beginning," 2.

45. Chris Manganiello describes a similar effort to maintain the wildness of a captive species in "From Howling Wilderness to Howling Safaris: Science, Policy and Red Wolves in the American South," *Journal of the History of Biology* 42, no. 2 (May 2009): 325–359; Meretsky et al., "Demography of the California Condor."

46. Joanna M. Miller, "Condor 'Preschool' Teaches Fear," *Los Angeles Times*, 17 August 1995, A-3; Jeffrey P. Cohn, "Saving the California Condor," *Bioscience* 43 (1993): 866; Frank Graham Jr., "The Day of the Condor," *Audubon* 102 (January–February 2000): 46–53; Stephanie Simon, "Biologists Hope to Save Condors with 'Tough Love,'" *Los Angeles Times*, 5 February 1995, A-1.

47. Larry B. Stammer, "First Captive California Condors Freed in Wild," *Los Angeles Times*, 15 January 1992, A-1; David Kelly, "Condor Is Free to Roam after 15 Years in Protective Custody," *Los Angeles Times*, 2 May 2002, B-8; Kiff, "New Epoch," 2; Kiff, "New Beginning," 1.

48. David Kelly, "Last of Three Wild Condor Chicks Is Found Dead," *Los Angeles Times*, 2 May 2002, B-8.

49. Robert A. Jones, "When Ugly Is Okay," *Los Angeles Times*, 19 June 1991, A-3; Mary F. Pols, "Condor Conundrum," *Los Angeles Times*, 28 April 1996, A-3; Nielsen, *Condor*, 197; anonymous, "Arizona Condor Release Program," *Peregrine Fund Newsletter* 27 (Fall–Winter 1996): 5.

50. Sheldon, "What Price Condor," 61–62; Andrew C. Revkin, "The Condor: Is Money Being Wasted on Doomed Species?," *Los Angeles Times*, 23 September 1985, I-3; Michael J. Ybarra, "Is This Bird Worth $20 Million?," *Los Angeles Times Magazine*, (14 September 1997): 16–17, 31–36; Kelly, "Welfare State for Vultures," A-1; "Coveting Condor Land," editorial, *Los Angeles Times*, 16 March 2002, B-20; Nielsen, *Condor*, 149, 214 (Noel Snyder quote).

51. Nielsen, *Condor*, 216.

52. Snyder and Snyder, *California Condor*, 367; Richard C. Bishop and Roland C. Clement, "Conservation of the California Condor (A Socioeconomic Study of a Survival Problem)," *Bulletin of the International Council for Bird Preservation* 12 (1975): 243.

53. Bergman, *Wild Echoes*, 72–79.

54. Alfred Runte, *National Parks: The American Experience*, 3rd ed. (Lincoln: University of Nebraska Press, 1997).

55. Reed Noss, "Sustainability and Wilderness," *Conservation Biology* 5, no. 1 (March 1991): 120–122; Noss, "What Can Wilderness Do for Biodiversity?," *Wild Earth* 1 (Summer 1991): 51–56; Jim Eaton, "Wilderness: From Aesthetics to Biodiversity," *Wild Earth* 1 (Summer 1991): 1–2.

56. Jane Goodall, interview with Michael Krasny, *Forum*, National Public Radio, KQED, San Francisco, 3 October 2005, about her new book: Goodall, Thane Maynard, and Gail E. Hudson, *Hope for Animals and Their World: How Endangered Species Are Being Rescued from the Brink* (New York: Grand Central, 2009).

57. Transcript of Maria Shriver, Kevin Starr, and Governor Arnold Schwarzenegger at the State Quarter Unveiling, 29 March 2004, Library and Courts Building, Sacramento (available at www.sierraclub.org/john_muir_exhibit/coin/unveiling_transcript.aspx, accessed 9 November 2012).

58. Lisa Gosselin, "On Human Intervention," *Audubon* 102 (January–February 2000): 6.

CHAPTER 6. THE MOJAVE DESERT TORTOISE

1. James E. Moore, quoted in Jon Christensen, "Sin City's Lucky Tortoise," *Nature Conservancy* 42, no. 4 (July–August 1992): 13; Moore made similar comments in an interview with the author, Las Vegas, 9 December 2004.

2. Robert F. Thorne, "A Historical Sketch of the Vegetation of the Mojave and Colorado Deserts of the American Southwest," *Annals of the Missouri Botanical Garden* 73, no. 3 (1986): 642–651; Philip V. Wells and Rainer Berger, "Late Pleistocene History of Coniferous Woodland in the Mohave Desert," *Science* 155, no. 3770 (31 March 1967): 1640–1647.

3. Joan S. Schneider and G. Dicken Everson, "The Desert Tortoise (*Xerobates agassizii*) in the Prehistory of the Southwestern Great Basin and Adjacent Areas," *Journal of California and Great Basin Anthropology* 11, no. 2 (1989): 175–202; Gary Paul Nabhan, *Singing the Turtles to Sea: The Camcáac (Seri) Art and Science of Reptiles* (Berkeley: University of California Press, 2003); Anna Noah, "The Zooarchaeology of Joshua Tree National Monument: Results of Analysis of Animal Remains from 24 Archaeological Sites," in Claude N. Warren and Joan S. Schneider, eds., *Phase II, An Archaeological Inventory of Joshua Tree National Park* (U.S. Department of the Interior, Joshua Tree National Park, 2000).

4. Jeffrey E. Lovich and David Bainbridge, "Anthropogenic Degradation of the Southern California Desert Ecosystem and Prospects for Natural Recovery and Restoration," *Environmental Management* 24, no. 3 (October 1999): 309–326; Richard H. Webb and E. B. Newman, "Recovery of Soil and Vegetation in Ghost-Towns in the Mojave Desert, Southwestern United States," *Environmental Conservation* 9, no. 3 (1982): 245–248.

5. Richard Hereford, Robert H. Webb, and Claire I. Longpre, *Precipitation History of the Mojave Desert Region, 1893–2001*, fact sheet 117–03 (Flagstaff, AZ: United States Geological Survey, 2004); H. L. Bentley, "Cattle Ranges of the Southwest: A History of the Exhaustion of the Pasturage and Suggestions for its Restoration," U.S. Department of Agriculture, Farmers Bulletin, no. 72 (Washington, DC: Government Printing Office, 1898); Eric Charles Nystrom, "From Neglected Space to Protected Place: An Administrative History of Mojave National Preserve," prepared for the United States Department of the Interior (National Park Service, Great Basin Cooperative Ecosystem Studies Unit, March 2003).

6. Mathew L. Brooks, "Alien Annual Grasses and Fire in the Mojave Desert," *Madroño* 46, no. 1 (1999): 13–19; Brooks, "Competition between Alien Annual Grasses and Native Annual Plants in the Mojave Desert," *American Midland Naturalist* 114, no. 1 (July 2000): 92–108.

7. Bruce M. Pavlick, *The California Deserts: An Ecological Rediscovery* (Berkeley: University of California Press, 2008), 19–22; George Wharton James, *The Wonders of the Colorado Desert (Southern California)* (London: T. Fisher Unwin, 1906), 196–199; Loye Miller, "Notes on the Desert Tortoise (Testudo agassizii)," *Transactions of the San Diego Society of Natural History* 7, no. 18 (October 1932): 200–201.

8. Edmund Carroll Jaeger, *Denizens of the Desert: A Book of Southwestern Mammals, Birds, and Reptiles* (Boston and New York: Houghton Mifflin, 1922), 263–264.

9. Raymond Lee Ditmars, "Agassiz's Tortoise," in Ditmars, *The Reptile Book: A Comprehensive, Popularised Work on the Structure and Habits of the Turtles, Tortoises, Crocodilians, Lizards and Snakes Which Inhabit the United States and Northern Mexico* (New York: Doubleday, Page, 1907), 69–70.

10. Mary Austin, *The Land of Little Rain* (Boston: Houghton, Mifflin, 1903); John Charles Van Dyke, *The Desert: Further Studies in Natural Appearances* (New York: Charles Scribner's Sons, 1918).

11. Angus M. Woodbury and Ross Hardy, "Studies of the Desert Tortoise," *Ecological Monographs* 18, no. 2 (April 1948): 196; R. Bruce Bury and Ronald W. Marlow, "The Desert Tortoise: Will It Survive?," *National Parks and Conservation Magazine* 47 (June 1973): 12; U.S. Fish and Wildlife Service, "Emergency Determination of Endangered Status for the Mojave Population of the Desert Tortoise," *Federal Register* 54, no. 149 (4 August 1989): 32326.

12. John Van Denburgh, *The Reptiles of Western North America,* vol. 2, *Snakes and Turtles* (San Francisco: California Academy of Sciences, 1922), 989.

13. For examples of early tortoise studies, see Charles F. Harbinson, "The Adobe Tick on Gopherus agassizii," *Herpetologica* 1, no. 1 (July 1936): 80; Charles M. Bogert, "Note on the Growth Rate of the Desert Tortoise, *Gopherus Agassizi,*" *Copeia* 3 (November 1937): 191–192; Clifford H. Pope, *Turtles of the United States and Canada* (New York: Alfred A. Knopf, 1939), 236–245.

14. Vernon Bailey, "The Desert Tortoise: An Example of Unusual Adaptations," *Nature Magazine* 12, no. 6 (December 1928): 372–374; Miller, "Notes on the Desert Tortoise," 187–208; Thomas R. Van Devender, "Natural History of the Sonoran Tortoise in Arizona: Life in a Rock Pile" and "Cenozoic Environments and the Evolution of the Gopher Tortoises (Genus *Gopherus*)," in Van Devender, ed., *The Sonoran Desert Tortoise: Natural History, Biology, and Conservation* (Tucson: University of Arizona Press, 2002), 3–51; David J. Morafka and Kristin H. Berry, "Is *Gopherus agassizii* a Desert-Adapted Tortoise, or an Exaptive Opportunist? Implications for Tortoise Research," *Chelonian Conservation and Biology* 4, no. 2 (December 2002): 263–287.

15. Woodbury and Hardy, "Studies of the Desert Tortoise," 194–196.

16. R. Bruce Bury and Glen R. Stewart, "California Protects Its Herpetofauna," *HISS News Journal* 1, no. 2 (March 1973): 46; Bury and Marlow, "The Desert Tortoise," 10.

17. Paul Lucas, "State Report—Nevada," *The Desert Tortoise Council: Proceedings of 1976 Symposium* (Las Vegas: Desert Tortoise Council, 1976), 10; Lucas, "State Report—Nevada," *The Desert Tortoise Council: Proceedings of 1977 Symposium* (Las Vegas: Desert Tortoise Council, 1977), 25; George K. Tsukamoto, "Keynote Address: The Status of and Future Outlook for the Desert Tortoise in Nevada," *The Desert Tortoise Council: Proceedings of 1982 Symposium* (Las Vegas: Desert Tortoise Council, 1982), 6.

18. Bureau of Land Management, *The California Desert Conservation Area Plan 1980* (Riverside, CA: U.S. Department of the Interior, 1980), 3–5; William I. Boarman, *Threats to Desert Tortoise Populations: A Critical Review of the Literature,* prepared by the U.S. Geological Survey Western Ecological Research Center for the Bureau of Land Management (2002).

19. David Darlington, *The Mojave: Portrait of the Definitive American Desert* (New York: Henry Holt, 1996), 234–241; E. Davidson and M. Fox, "Effects of Off-Road Motorcycle Activity on Mojave Desert Vegetation and Soil," *Madroño* 22 (1974): 381–412; R. H. Webb and H. G. Wilshire, *Environmental Effects of Off-Road Vehicles: Impacts and Management in Arid Regions* (New York: Springer-Verlag, 1983).

20. Shav Glick, "The Battle for the Great Mojave," *Los Angeles Times,* 17 December 1974.

21. Robert C. Stebbins, "Whose Domain Is the Desert?," *Los Angeles Times,* 16 May 1976, I-5; Bart Everett, "How the Desert Is Fragile . . . and Why," *Los Angeles Times,* 10 April 1977, C-1.

22. William D. Rowley, *U.S. Forest Service Grazing and Rangelands* (College Station: Texas A&M University Press, 1985).

23. Public Land Law Review Commission, *One Third of the Nation's Land* (Washington, DC: Government Printing Office, 1970).

24. James A. St. Amant, "The Desert Tortoise Council—a Review, 1974–1976," *Proceedings of 1976 Symposium,* 1; Kristin H. Berry, interview with the author, Moreno Valley, CA, 7 December 2004.

25. Mary Ann Lewis, "Special Report—California: Tortoise Adoption Program of the California Turtle and Tortoise Club," *Proceedings of 1977 Symposium,* 15–16; James A. St. Amant, "State Report—California," ibid., 21.

26. Gloria Nowak, "The Desert Tortoise," *Desert Magazine* 40, no. 2 (February 1977): 25–26; Elizabeth W. Forgey, "Special Report—California: Desert Tortoise Preserve Committee," *Proceedings of 1977 Symposium,* 17–20.

27. Bureau of Land Management, *The California Desert Conservation Area Plan 1980* (Riverside, CA: U.S. Department of the Interior, 1980); Bureau of Land Management,

California Desert Conservation Area, Thirtieth Anniversary, 1976–2006 (Sacramento, CA: Bureau of Land Management, 2006).

28. Kristin H. Berry, interview with the author; anonymous, "1977 Annual Award—a Profile of Recipient, Dr. Kristin H. Berry," *Proceedings of 1977 Symposium*, 6–7.

29. Kristin H. Berry, ed., *The Status of the Desert Tortoise (*Gopherus agassizii*) in the United States* (Long Beach, CA: Desert Tortoise Council, 1984); Leonhard Stejneger, "Annotated List of the Reptiles and Batrachians Collected by the Death Valley Expedition in 1891, with Descriptions of New Species," *North American Fauna* 7 (May 1893): 161–162; George Wharton James, *Wonders of the Colorado Desert*, 196–199; C. L. Camp, "Notes on the Local Distribution and Habits of the Amphibians and Reptiles of Southeastern California in the Vicinity of the Turtle Mountains," *University of California Publications in Zoology* 12 (1916): 513; Jaeger, *Denizens of the Desert*, 258; R. Bruce Bury and Paul S. Corn, "Have Desert Tortoises Undergone a Long-Term Decline in Abundance?," *Wildlife Society Bulletin* 23, no. 1 (Spring 1995): 41–47.

30. Kristin H. Berry and L. L. Nicholson, "The Distribution and Density of Desert Tortoise Populations in California in the 1970s," in Berry, *Status of the Desert Tortoise*, 26–60; Bury and Corn, "Desert Tortoises," 41.

31. U.S. Fish and Wildlife Service, "Finding on Desert Tortoise Petition," *Federal Register* 50, no. 234 (5 December 1985): 49868–49870; Kristin H. Berry, interview with the author.

32. Frank Rowley, "State Report—Utah," *Proceedings of 1977 Symposium*, 30–31; Rowley, "State Report—Utah," *The Desert Tortoise Council: Proceedings of 1978 Symposium* (Las Vegas: Desert Tortoise Council, 1978), 53–54; U.S. Fish and Wildlife Service, "Listing as Threatened with Critical Habitat for the Beaver Dam Slope Population of the Desert Tortoise in Utah," *Federal Register* 45, no. 163 (20 August 1980): 55654–55666.

33. Elliot R. Jacobson, J. M. Gaskin, M. B. Brown, R. K Harris, C. H. Gardiner, J. L. LaPointe, H. P. Adams, and C. Reggiardo, "Chronic Upper Respiratory Tract Disease of Free-Ranging Desert Tortoises (*Xerobates agassizii*)," *Journal of Wildlife Diseases* 27, no. 2 (1991): 296–316; Kristin H. Berry and Sid Slone, *Final Notes from Meetings on Upper Respiratory Disease Syndrome in Desert Tortoises* (U.S. Department of the Interior, Bureau of Land Management, 12–13 October 1989), 3.

34. Elliot Jacobsen, quoted in Berry and Slone, *Final Notes*, 9; Berry, "The Status of the Desert Tortoise in 1990: Current Population Issues in California," in Kent R. Beaman, Fred Caporaso, Sean McKeown, and Marc D. Graff, eds., *Proceedings of the First International Symposium on Turtles and Tortoises: Conservation and Captive Husbandry* (Orange, CA: Chapman University, California Turtle and Tortoise Club, 1991), 80–82.

35. U.S. Fish and Wildlife Service, "Emergency Determination of Endangered Status for the Mojave Population of the Desert Tortoise," *Federal Register* 54, no. 149

(4 August 1989): 32326–32331; U.S. Fish and Wildlife Service, "Emergency Action Taken to Protect the Desert Tortoise," *Endangered Species Technical Bulletin* 14, nos. 9–10 (September–October 1989): 1–6; U.S. Fish and Wildlife Service, "Determination of Threatened Status for the Mojave Population of the Desert Tortoise," *Federal Register* 55, no. 63 (2 April 1990): 12178–12191.

36. Charles Hillinger, "Arizona, Nevada Wooing Industry," *Los Angeles Times,* 3 January 1962, C-17; Gene Sherman, "Nevada Woos Industry with Tax Incentives," *Los Angeles Times,* 14 May 1961, I-1.

37. James E. Moore, interview with the author.

38. Anonymous, "Endangered Tortoise Slows Building Boom in Las Vegas," *New York Times,* 11 September 1989, A-18.

39. James E. Moore, "Statement of Public Lands Conservation Coordinator of the Nature Conservancy of Nevada on the Clark County, Nevada Desert Tortoise Habitat Conservation Plan, before the Fisheries, Wildlife and Drinking Water Subcommittee of the Senate Environment and Public Works Committee," Washington, DC, 19 October 1999, available at http://epw.senate.gov/107th/moo_1019.htm.

40. James E. Moore described the euthanasia controversy in his interview with the author; Ann Schrieber, quoted in Merrick L. Hoben, "Clark County Habitat Conservation Planning Process," in Christine W. Coughlin, Hoben, Dirk W. Manskopf, and Shannon W. Quesada, "A Systematic Assessment of Collaborative Resources Management Partnerships" (group project master's thesis, University of Michigan School of Natural Resources, 1999), 7.6.

41. Paul Selzer, interview with the author, Palm Springs, CA, 7 December 2004.

42. Recon, "Final Clark County Multiple Species Habitat Conservation Plan and Environmental Impact Statement," prepared for the Clark County, Nevada, Department of Comprehensive Planning and Wildlife Service (2000); Lewis Wallenmeyer, Clark County Desert Conservation Program administrator, interview with the author, Las Vegas, 9 December 2004.

43. Bureau of Land Management, *Southern Nevada Public Land Management Act: 10-Year Report to Congress* (Denver: U.S. Department of the Interior, 2008).

44. U.S. Fish and Wildlife Service, *Desert Tortoise (Mojave Population) Recovery Plan* (Portland, OR: U.S. Department of the Interior, 1994).

45. *Desert Tortoise et al. v. Lujan et al.,* Civ. No. 93–0114 MHP (N.D. Cal., 1993).

46. Marla Cone, "Tortoise Land May Get New Protection," *Los Angeles Times,* 28 August 1993, A-22; Frank Clifford, "6 Million Acres Set Aside for Tortoises," *Chicago Sun Times,* 10 February 1994, 10; U.S. Fish and Wildlife Service, "Determination of Critical Habitat for the Mojave Population of the Desert Tortoise," *Federal Register* 59, no. 26 (8 February 1994): 5820–5866.

47. Deborah S. Brennan, "U.S. Agrees to Close Desert Areas, Beef Up Protection of Rare Species," *Los Angeles Times,* 19 January 2001, A-3; Jane Kay, "Compromise

over Desert Protects 24 State Species," *San Francisco Chronicle*, 19 January 2001, A-2.

48. Memorandum to Howard Chapman, National Park Service western regional director, BLM Desert Plan staff, June 5, 1979, with attached Preliminary Study, cited in Frank Wheat, *California Desert Miracle: The Fight for Desert Parks and Wilderness* (San Diego: Sunbelt, 1999), 53.

49. General Accounting Office, "California Desert: Planned Wildlife Protection and Enhancement Objectives Not Achieved" (June 1989); General Accounting Office, "Shortfalls of BLM's Management of Wildlife Habitat in the California Desert Conservation Area, Statement of James Duffus III . . . before the Subcommittee on Public Lands, National Parks and Forests," 2 October 1989.

50. Wheat, *California Desert Miracle*, 300–301.

51. Larry Dilsaver, unpublished manuscript in the possession of the author.

52. General Accounting Office, "BLM's Hot Desert Grazing Program Merits Reconsideration" (November 1992), 2–3.

53. Bureau of Land Management, "California Desert Conservation Area Plan," 56; Mark Muckenfuss, "Herds, History Fade from the Desert," *Press Enterprise* (Riverside, CA), 3 July 2005; Chris Berdik, "Battle Really Heats Up on a Desert in Turmoil," *San Diego Union Tribune*, 2 September, 2001, A-4; Elisabeth M. Hamin, *Mojave Lands: Interpretive Planning and the National Preserve* (Baltimore: Johns Hopkins University Press, 2003).

54. Timm Kroeger and Paula Manalo, *Economic Benefits Provided by Natural Lands: Case Study of California's Mojave Desert* (Washington, DC: Defenders of Wildlife, 2007); Jennifer Warren, "The Playground Becomes the Battleground," *Los Angeles Times Magazine*, 22 April 1990, 21.

55. General Accounting Office, "Research Strategy and Long-Term Monitoring Needed for the Mojave Desert Tortoise Recovery Program" (December 2002), 24–25.

56. William I. Boarman, Marc Sazaki, and W. Bryan Jennings, "The Effect of Roads, Barrier Fences, and Culverts on Desert Tortoise Populations in California, USA," *Proceedings: Conservation, Restoration, and Management of Tortoises and Turtles—an International Conference*, 11–16 July 1993 (New York: New York Turtle and Tortoise Society, 1997), 54–58; Boarman, "Managing a Subsidized Predator Population: Reducing Common Raven Predation on Desert Tortoises," *Environmental Management* 32, no. 2 (September 2003): 205–217.

57. General Accounting Office, "Mojave Desert Tortoise Recovery Program," 12, 17.

58. Richard C. Tracy, R. Averill-Murray, W. I. Boarman, D. Delehanty, J. Heaton, E. McCoy, D. Morafka, K. Nussear, B. Hagerty, and P. Medica, "Desert Tortoise Recovery Plan Assessment," prepared for the U.S. Fish and Wildlife Service (2004).

59. J. Whitfield Gibbons, David E. Scott, Travis J. Ryan, Kurt A. Buhlmann, Tracey D. Tuberville, Brian S. Metts, Judith L. Greene, Tony Mills, Yale Leiden, Sean

Poppy, and Christopher T. Winne, "The Global Decline of Reptiles, Déjà Vu Amphibians," *BioScience* 50, no. 8 (August 2000): 653–666; Michael W. Klemens, *Turtle Conservation* (Washington, DC: Smithsonian Institution Press, 2000), 4.

CHAPTER 7. THE SAN JOAQUIN KIT FOX

1. C. Hart Merriam, "Description of a New Fox from Southern California," *Proceedings of the Biological Society of Washington* 4 (1888): 5–8; Merriam, "Three New Foxes of the Kit and Desert Fox Groups," *Proceedings of the Biological Society of Washington* 15 (1902): 73–74; Joseph Grinnell, Joseph S. Dixon, and Jean M. Linsdale, *Fur-Bearing Mammals of California: Their Natural History, Systematic Status, and Relations to Man* (Berkeley: University of California Press, 1937), 407.

2. Tadlock Cowan, ed., *California's San Joaquin Valley: A Region in Transition* (Washington, DC: Congressional Research Service, 2005); Sarah Burd-Sharps, Kristen Lewis, and Eduardo Borges Martins, *The Measure of America: American Human Development Report, 2008–2009* (New York: Columbia University Press, 2008); James J. Parsons, "A Geographer Looks at the San Joaquin Valley," *Geographical Review* 76, no. 4 (1986): 371–389.

3. Allan A. Schoenherr, *A Natural History of California* (Berkeley: University of California Press, 1995), 516–520.

4. U.S. Fish and Wildlife Service, *Recovery Plan for Upland Species of the San Joaquin Valley* (Portland, OR: U.S. Fish and Wildlife Service, 1998).

5. Linda Nash, *Inescapable Ecologies: A History of Environment, Disease, and Knowledge* (Berkeley: University of California Press, 2006).

6. David Igler, *Industrial Cowboys: Miller and Lux and the Transformation of the Far West, 1850–1920* (Berkeley: University of California Press, 2001); Peter S. Alagona, "Homes on the Range: Cooperative Conservation and Environmental Change on California's Privately Owned Hardwood Rangelands," *Environmental History* 13, no. 2 (April 2008): 287–311.

7. Kenneth W. Umbach, *San Joaquin Valley: Selected Statistics on Population, Economy, and Environment* (Sacramento: California Research Bureau, 2002); National Agricultural Statistics Service, "2007 Census of Agriculture" (Washington, DC: U.S. Department of Agriculture, 2009).

8. Paul Sabin, *Crude Politics: The California Oil Market, 1900–1940* (Berkeley: University of California Press, 2005).

9. Philip Garone, "The Tragedy at Kesterson Reservoir: A Case Study in Environmental History and a Lesson in Ecological Complexity," *Environs: Environmental Law and Policy Journal* 22, no. 2 (1999): 107–144.

10. David J. Germano, Galen B. Rathbun, Lawrence R. Saslaw, Brian L. Cypher, Ellen A. Cypher, and Larry M. Vredenburgh, "The San Joaquin Desert of California:

Ecologically Misunderstood and Overlooked," *Natural Areas Journal* 31, no. 2 (April 2011): 138–147.

11. U.S. Fish and Wildlife Service, *Recovery Plan for Upland Species*, 1–11.

12. W. E. Frayer, Dennis D. Peters, and H. Ross Pywell, *Wetlands of the Central Valley: Status and Trends, 1939 to Mid-1980s* (Portland, OR: U.S. Fish and Wildlife Service, 1989); Philip Garone, *The Fall and Rise of the Wetlands of California's Great Central Valley* (Berkeley: University of California Press, 2011); Robert M. Wilson, *Seeking Refuge: Birds and Landscapes of the Pacific Flyway* (Seattle: University of Washington Press, 2010).

13. Grinnell, Dixon, and Linsdale, *Fur-Bearing Mammals*, 399–420.

14. Ibid., 420; California Fish and Game Commission, *Twenty-Seventh Biennial Report for the Years 1920–1922* (Sacramento: State Printing Office, 1923), 25.

15. Grinnell, Dixon, and Linsdale, *Fur-Bearing Mammals*, 420; Philip Fradkin, "Poison: Killing Pests versus Saving Wildlife," *Los Angeles Times*, 6 December 1970, D-1; Frank Schitoskey Jr., "Primary and Secondary Hazards of Three Rodenticides to Kit Fox," *Journal of Wildlife Management* 39, no. 2 (April 1975): 416–418.

16. Grinnell, Dixon, and Linsdale, *Fur-Bearing Mammals*, 417; Brian Dennis and Mark R. M. Otten, "Joint Effects of Density Dependence and Rainfall on Abundance of San Joaquin Kit Fox," *Journal of Wildlife Management* 64, no. 2 (April 2000): 388–400.

17. Grinnell, Dixon, and Linsdale, *Fur-Bearing Mammals*, 418; Howard O. Clark, Brian L. Cypher, Gregory D. Warrick, Patrick A. Kelly, Daniel F. Williams, and David E. Grubbs, "Challenges in Conservation of the Endangered San Joaquin Kit Fox," in Nina Fascione, Aimee Delach, and Martin Smith, eds., *People and Predators: From Conflict to Coexistence* (Washington, DC: Island, 2004), 121–126; Clark, Warrick, Cypher, Kelly, Williams, and Grubbs, "Competitive Interactions between Endangered Kit Foxes and Nonnative Red Foxes," *Western North American Naturalist* 65, no. 2 (2005): 153–163; Warrick and Cypher, "Factors Affecting the Spatial Distribution of San Joaquin Kit Foxes, "*Journal of Wildlife Management* 62, no. 2 (April 1998): 707–717; Cypher and Kenneth A. Spencer, "Competitive Interactions between Coyotes and San Joaquin Kit Foxes," *Journal of Mammalogy* 79, no. 1 (February 1998): 204–214.

18. Grinnell, Dixon, and Linsdale, *Fur-Bearing Mammals*, 419–420.

19. Lyndal Laughrin, "Distribution and Abundance of the San Joaquin Kit Fox," *Cal-Neva Wildlife* 6 (1970): 86–93; Stephen Morrell, "Life History of the San Joaquin Kit Fox," *California Fish and Game* 58 (1972): 162–174; Clark et al., "Challenges in Conservation," 118–131; Marni E. Koopman, Jerry H. Scrivner, and Thomas T. Kato, "Patterns of Den Use by San Joaquin Kit Foxes," *Journal of Wildlife Management* 62, no. 1 (January 1998): 373–379.

20. Gregory D. Warrick, Howard O. Clark Jr., Patrick A. Kelly, Daniel F. Williams, and Brian L. Cypher, "Use of Agricultural Lands by San Joaquin Kit Foxes," *Western*

North American Naturalist 67, no. 2 (2007): 270–277; Curtis D. Bjurlin, *Effects of Roads on San Joaquin Kit Foxes: A Review and Synthesis of Existing Data* (Davis: University of California, Davis, Road Ecology Center, 2003).

21. Grinnell, Dixon, and Linsdale, *Fur-Bearing Mammals,* 408. Maps from 1920 and 1950 redrawn in Stephen H. Morrell, "San Joaquin Kit Fox Distribution and Abundance in 1975" (Sacramento: California Department of Fish and Game, 1975), 3–4; U.S. Fish and Wildlife Service, *Recovery Plan for Upland Species,* 125.

22. Grinnell, Dixon, and Linsdale, *Fur-Bearing Mammals,* 403; T. P. O'Farrell, *San Joaquin Kit Fox Recovery Plan* (Portland, OR: U.S. Fish and Wildlife Service, 1983), 4–8; U.S. Fish and Wildlife Service, *Recovery Plan for Upland Species,* 125.

23. Lyndal Laughrin, "Distribution and Abundance of the San Joaquin Kit Fox," *Cal-Nevada Wildlife Transactions* 6 (1970): 86–93; Morrell, "San Joaquin Kit Fox"; O'Farrell, *Recovery Plan.*

24. O'Farrell, *Recovery Plan,* 8–11; U.S. Fish and Wildlife Service, *Recovery Plan for Upland Species.*

25. Michael K. Schwartz, Katherine Ralls, Dan F. Williams, Brian L. Cypher, Kristine L. Pilgrim, and Robert C. Fleischer, "Gene Flow among San Joaquin Kit Fox Populations in a Severely Changed Ecosystem," *Conservation Genetics* 6, no. 1 (January 2005): 25–37.

26. For information about the protected status of the San Joaquin kit fox, see the Web sites for the California Fish and Game Code and the U.S. Fish and Wildlife Service's Endangered Species Program.

27. O'Farrell, *Recovery Plan,* 40.

28. Ibid., 35.

29. U.S. Fish and Wildlife Service, *Recovery Plan for Upland Species,* 13–18; Craig Thomas, *Bureaucratic Landscapes: Interagency Cooperation and the Preservation of Biological Diversity* (Cambridge, MA: MIT Press, 2003), 227–256.

30. U.S. Fish and Wildlife Service, *Recovery Plan for Upland Species,* ix; Grinnell, Dixon, and Linsdale, *Fur-Bearing Mammals,* 407.

31. Richard L. Anderson, Linda K. Spiegel, and Karyn M. Kakiba-Russell, *Southern San Joaquin Valley Ecosystems Protection Program: Natural Lands Inventory and Maps* (Sacramento: California Energy Commission, 1991); Metropolitan Bakersfield Habitat Conservation Plan Steering Committee, *Metropolitan Bakersfield Habitat Conservation Plan* (Bakersfield: City of Bakersfield, 1994), iii–iv.

32. Julie Cart, "Suicide Casts a Shadow on Conservation Battle," *Los Angeles Times,* 20 August 2005.

33. Harrison C. Dunning, "Confronting the Environmental Legacy of Irrigated Agriculture in the American West: The Case of the Central Valley Project," *Environmental Law* 23 (1993): 943–969.

34. Danielle Starkey, "California Farmers Hit at Habitat Laws," *Christian Science Monitor,* 25 August 1994.

35. Kenneth Howe, "Angry Farmers Rally against a Rat," *San Francisco Chronicle*, 30 August 1994.

36. Richard Pombo and Joseph Farah, *This Land Is Our Land: How to End the War on Private Property* (New York: St. Martin's Press, 1996); Bettina Boxall, "Foe of Endangered Species Act on Defensive over Abramoff," *Los Angeles Times*, 14 February 2006.

37. James Morton Turner, "'The Specter of Environmentalism': Wilderness, Environmental Politics, and the Evolution of the New Right," *Journal of American History* 96, no. 1 (June 2009): 123–148; James McCarthy, "First World Political Ecology: Lessons from the Wise Use Movement," *Environment and Planning A* 34, no. 7 (2002): 1281–1302.

38. Brian L. Cypher, Patrick A. Kelly, Daniel F. Williams, Howard O. Clark Jr., Alexander D. Brown, and Scott E. Phillips, *Foxes in Farmland: Recovery of the Endangered San Joaquin Kit Fox on Private Lands in California* (Fresno: California State University, Stanislaus, Endangered Species Recovery Program, 2005), 12; J. Michael Bean, "Second Generation Approaches," in Dale D. Goble, J. Michael Scott, and Frank W. Davis, eds., *The Endangered Species Act at Thirty*, vol. 1, *Renewing the Conservation Promise* (Washington, DC: Island, 2006), 274–285.

39. U.S. Fish and Wildlife Service, "Working Together: Tools for Helping Imperiled Wildlife on Private Lands" (December 2005).

40. Sharon Begley, "Survival by Handout?," *National Wildlife Magazine* 35, no. 1 (December–January 1997): 52–57.

41. Brian L. Cypher and Nancy Frost, "Condition of San Joaquin Kit Foxes in Urban and Exurban Habitats," *Journal of Wildlife Management* 63, no. 3 (July 1999): 930–938.

42. Curtis D. Bjurlin and Brian L. Cypher, "Encounter Frequency with the Urbanized San Joaquin Kit Fox Correlates with Public Beliefs and Attitudes toward the Species," *Endangered Species Update* 22, no. 3 (1 July 2005): 107–115.

43. Heidi Ridgley, "Foxy City," *Defenders Magazine* 82, no. 4 (Fall 2007): 14–19; Robert G. Haight, Brian Cypher, Patrick A. Kelly, Scott Phillips, Katherine Ralls, and Hugh Possingham, "Optimizing Reserve Expansion for Disjunct Populations of San Joaquin Kit Fox," *Biological Conservation* 117 (2004): 61–72.

44. Samantha Bremner-Harrison and Brian L. Cypher, *Feasibility and Strategies for Reintroducting San Joaquin Kit Foxes to Vacant or Restored Habitats* (Fresno: California State University, Stanislaus, Endangered Species Recovery Program, 2007).

45. Ross Gerrard, Peter Stine, Richard Church, and Michael Gilpin, "Habitat Evaluation Using GIS: A Case Study Applied to the San Joaquin Kit Fox," *Landscape and Urban Planning* 52 (2001): 239–255; P. J. White, William H. Berry, Julie J. Eliason, and Michael T. Hanson, "Catastrophic Decrease in an Isolated Population of Kit Foxes," *Southwestern Naturalist* 45, no. 2 (June 2000): 204–211.

CHAPTER 8. THE DELTA SMELT

1. W. J. Kimmerer, "Physical, Biological, and Management Responses to Variable Freshwater Flow into the San Francisco Estuary," *Estuaries* 25, no. 6B (December 2002): 1275–1290; Bay Institute, *From the Sierra to the Sea: The Ecological History of the San Francisco Bay-Delta Watershed* (San Francisco: Bay Institute of San Francisco, 1998), 3.37.

2. *Natural Resources Defense Council et al. v. Kempthorne et al.*, U.S. District Court for the Eastern District of California, no. 1:05-cv-01207, decided 14 December 2007; Ellen Hanak, Jay Lund, Ariel Dinar, Brian Gray, Richard Howitt, Jeffrey Mount, Peter Moyle, and Barton "Buzz" Thompson, *California Water Myths* (Sacramento: Public Policy Institute of California, 2009), 9.

3. David A. Fahrenthold, "Saving Species No Longer a Beauty Contest; Homely Creatures Receiving More Help," *Washington Post*, 29 June 2009, A-1; anonymous, "Of Farms, Folks and Fish; California's Water Wars," *Economist*, 24 October 2009; anonymous, "California's Man-Made Drought," *Wall Street Journal*, 2 September 2009; Harold Johnson, "Little Fish Takes Big Bite," *Orange County Register*, 13 November 2009.

4. Little Hoover Commission, "Still Imperiled, Still Important: The Little Hoover Commission's Review of the CALFED Bay-Delta Program" (Sacramento, 17 November 2005), 9; Mark Newton, "The Bay-Delta: A Key to Solving California's Water Problem," *California Update*, September 1996, 1.

5. National Research Council, *A Scientific Assessment of Alternatives for Reducing Water Management Effects on Threatened and Endangered Fishes in California's Bay-Delta* (Washington, DC: National Academies Press, 2010), 8; Norris Hundley, *The Great Thirst: Californians and Water—a History* (Berkeley: University of California Press, 1992), xv.

6. Bay Institute, *Sierra to the Sea*, 2.2–2.64; Peter B. Moyle, William A. Bennett, Cliff Dahm, John R. Durand, Christopher Enright, William E. Fleenor, Wim Kimmerer, and Jay R. Lund, "Changing Ecosystems: A Brief Ecological History of the Delta," report to the California State Water Resources Control Board, Sacramento, CA (February 2010).

7. Philip Garone, *The Fall and Rise of the Wetlands of California's Great Central Valley* (Berkeley: University of California Press, 2011); Peter B. Moyle and Robert D. Nichols, "Decline of the Native Fish Fauna of the Sierra Nevada Foothills, Central California," *American Midland Naturalist* 92, no. 1 (July 1974): 72–83; Moyle et al., *Changing Ecosystems*, 2.

8. Arthur F. McEvoy, *The Fisherman's Problem: Ecology and Law in the California Fisheries, 1850–1980* (Cambridge: Cambridge University Press, 1990), 23; John E. Skinner, *An Historical Review of the Fish and Wildlife Resources of the San Francisco Bay Area* (Sacramento: Resources Agency of California, 1962); Kenneth Thompson,

"Historic Flooding in the Sacramento Valley," *Pacific Historical Review* 29, no. 4 (November 1960): 349–360; Robert Kelley, *Battling the Inland Sea: Floods, Public Policy, and the Sacramento Valley* (Berkeley: University of California Press, 1989, digital version).

9. Kelley, *Battling the Inland Sea*, 2.8, 8.8; Hundley, *The Great Thirst*, 81–86.

10. Hundley, *The Great Thirst*, 81–86.

11. Andrew Isenberg, *Mining California: An Ecological History* (New York: Hill and Wang, 2005); *Edwards Woodruff v. North Bloomfield Gravel Mining Company*, U.S. Circuit Court for the Northern District of California, Civil Case 2900, decided 7 January 1884.

12. William H. Hall, *Irrigation Development* (Sacramento: Superintendent of State Printing, 1886); Kelley, *Battling the Inland Sea*, 9.8–10.12, 12.11–12.12 (E. D. Adams quotes); L. Allan James and Michael B. Singer, "Development of the Lower Sacramento Valley Flood-Control System: Historical Perspective," *Natural Hazards Review* 9 (August 2008): 125–135.

13. Martin D. Mitchell, "The Sacramento–San Joaquin Delta, California: Initial Transformation into a Water Supply and Conveyance Node, 1900–1955," *Journal of the West* 35, no. 1 (1996): 44–53.

14. Hundley, *The Great Thirst*, 251.

15. Ibid., 271.

16. Ibid., 280–286.

17. Mitchell, "Sacramento–San Joaquin Delta," 44–53; W. Turrentine Jackson and Alan M. Patterson, *The Sacramento–San Joaquin Delta: The Evolution and Implementation of Water Policy: An Historical Perspective* (Berkeley: University of California Water Resources Center, 1977), 3–14.

18. Jackson and Patterson, *Sacramento–San Joaquin Delta*, 53, 69, 81.

19. Ibid., 99–105, 151.

20. Hundley, *The Great Thirst*, 309–330; Jackson and Patterson, *Sacramento–San Joaquin Delta*, 108–114, 152–164.

21. Jackson and Patterson, *Sacramento–San Joaquin Delta*, 98, 117, 131, 153, 175; Donald Worster, *Rivers of Empire: Water, Aridity, and the Growth of the American West* (New York: Pantheon, 1985), 330; *United States v. State Water Resources Control Board*, 182 Cal. App. 3d 82 (1986).

22. Hanak et al., *California Water Myths*.

23. CALFED Science Program, *The State of Bay-Delta Science, 2008: Summary for Policymakers and the Public* (November 2007), 12.

24. Bay Institute, *Sierra to the Sea*, 3.1–4.15; Moyle et al., *Changing Ecosystems*, 2–5; W. E. Frayer, Dennis D. Peters, and H. Ross Pywell, *Wetlands of the California Central Valley: Status and Trends, 1939 to Mid-1980s* (Portland, OR: U.S. Fish and Wildlife Service, June 1989), 5.

25. Jackson and Patterson, *Sacramento–San Joaquin Delta*, 3, 12; Moyle et al., *Changing Ecosystems*, 4.

26. Bay Institute, *Sierra to the Sea*, 3.15–3.30; State of California, *Delta Smelt Action Plan* (Sacramento: State of California Resources Agency, 2005).

27. Blue Ribbon Task Force, *Delta Vision Strategic Plan* (Sacramento: State of California Resources Agency, 2008), 56; Jay Lund, Ellen Hanak, William Fleenor, Richard Howitt, Jeffrey Mount, and Peter Moyle, *Envisioning Futures for the Sacramento–San Joaquin Delta* (Sacramento: Public Policy Institute of California, 2007), 94; Bay Institute, *Sierra to the Sea*, 3.8, 4.19; Moyle et al., *Changing Ecosystems*, 5.

28. James and Singer, "Flood-Control System," 1; Bay Institute, *Sierra to the Sea*, 2.25; Lund et al., *Envisioning Futures*, 47.

29. California Department of Finance, "Implementation Status of the CALFED Bay-Delta Program, Years 1 through 5" (November 2005), 57; James and Singer, "Flood-Control System," 8.

30. McEvoy, *Fisherman's Problem*, 46, 67, 78; Ronald M. Yoshiyama, Frank W. Fisher, and Peter B. Moyle, "Historical Abundance and Decline of Chinook Salmon in the Central Valley Region of California," *North American Journal of Fisheries Management* 18, no. 3 (1998): 487–521; Bay Institute, *Sierra to the Sea*, 2.7, 2.11, 3.2–3.3.

31. McEvoy, *Fisherman's Problem*, 101–116; Earl Leitritz, *A History of California's Fish Hatcheries 1870–1960*, Fish Bulletin, no. 150 (Sacramento: California Department of Fish and Game, Inland Fisheries Branch, 1970).

32. Pacific Fishery Management Council, *Review of 2009 Ocean Salmon Fisheries* (Portland, OR: Pacific Fishery Management Council, February 2010).

33. McEvoy, *Fisherman's Problem*, 85; Bay Institute, *Sierra to the Sea*, 4.10; National Research Council, *Scientific Assessment*, 60; anonymous, "Of Farms, Folks and Fish"; Moyle et al., *Changing Ecosystems*, 3.

34. Peter B. Moyle, "Fish Introductions in California: History and Impact on Native Fishes," *Biological Conservation* 9, no. 2 (1976): 101–118; Moyle and Jack E. Williams, "Biodiversity in the Temperate Zone: Decline of the Native Fish Fauna of California," *Conservation Biology* 4, no. 3 (1990): 275–284; Holly Doremus, "Water, Population Growth, and Endangered Species in the West," *University of Colorado Law Review* 72 (Spring 2001): 366.

35. Dale A. Swetnam, "Status of the Delta Smelt in the Sacramento–San Joaquin Estuary," *California Fish and Game* 85, no. 1 (1999): 22–27; California Department of Fish and Game, *A Status Review of the Delta Smelt (*Hypomesus transpacificus*) in California* (Sacramento: California Department of Fish and Game, May 1993), 25–29, 49, 52–65.

36. California Department of Fish and Game, *Status Review*, 36–40.

37. Ibid., 7–12, 16–20, 66, 76–78; Jane Gross, "A Dying Fish May Force California to Break Its Water Habits," *New York Times*, 27 October 1991, section 1, part 1.

38. California Department of Fish and Game, *Status Review*, 69; State Water Resources Control Board, "Draft Water Right Decision 1630: Decision Establishing

Terms and Conditions for Interim Protection of Public Trust Uses of the San Francisco Bay/Sacramento–San Joaquin Delta Estuary" (Sacramento: California Environmental Protection Agency, 1992); General Accounting Office, "Endangered Species: Federal Actions to Protect Sacramento River Salmon" (August 1994), 3.

39. U.S. Fish and Wildlife Service, "Recovery Plan for the Sacramento/San Joaquin Delta Native Fishes" (November 1996), 5–6, 31–34, 42, 52; U.S. Fish and Wildlife Service, "Endangered and Threatened Wildlife and Plants; Critical Habitat Determination for the Delta Smelt," *Federal Register* 59, no. 242 (19 December 1994), 65256–65279.

40. General Accounting Office, "Sacramento River Salmon," 4–9, 72–76; Fish and Wildlife Service, *Recovery Plan*, 5; General Accounting Office, "Endangered Species: Limited Effect of Consultation Requirements on Western Water Projects" (March 1987), 3.

41. Anadromous Fish Restoration Program Core Group, *Habitat Restoration Actions to Double Natural Production of Anadromous Fish in the Central Valley of California* (Portland, OR: U.S. Fish and Wildlife Service, 1995), 7, 29–31; Bureau of Reclamation, *Central Valley Project Improvement Act: 10 Years of Progress* (Sacramento: Bureau of Reclamation,2003), 8, 11; Susan Zakin, "Delta Blues," *High Country News,* 30 September 2002.

42. Little Hoover Commission, *Still Imperiled,* 34; Michael Hanemann and Caitlin Dyckman, "The San Francisco Bay-Delta: A Failure of Decision-Making Capacity," *Environmental Science and Policy* 12 (2009): 712–721; Judith Innes, Sarah Connick, Laura Kaplan, and David E. Booher, "Collaborative Governance in the CALFED Program: Adaptive Policy Making for California Water," working paper (Institute of Urban and Regional Development, UC Berkeley, January 2006), 14–17; E. A. Rieke, "The Bay-Delta Accord: A Stride toward Sustainability," *University of Colorado Law Review* 67 (1996): 341–369.

43. Innes et al., "Collaborative Governance," 15–16; Little Hoover Commission, *Still Imperiled,* 48; Sarah Di Vittorio, Noelle Cole, and Tamar Cooper, "Accountability in Emerging Forms of Governance: A Comparison of the California Bay-Delta Process and the European Water Framework Directive" (Berkeley: University of California Water Resources Center, 16 May 2008).

44. California Department of Finance, "CALFED Bay-Delta Program," 13–19; Innes et al., "Collaborative Governance," 20–22, 32.

45. San Francisco Estuary Project and CALFED, *State of the San Francisco Bay-Delta Estuary 2006: Science and Stewardship* (Oakland: San Francisco Estuary Project, October 2005), 10, 20, 59; General Accounting Office, "Federal Land Management: Federal Land Acquisitions in California since January 1994" (August 2000), 5.

46. Bay Institute, *Sierra to the Sea,* 4.20.

47. U.S. House of Representatives, Subcommittee on Water and Power, "Extinction Is Not a Sustainable Water Policy: The Bay-Delta Crisis and the Implications for California Water Management," oversight field hearing, Vallejo, CA, 2 July 2007.

48. Lund et al., *Envisioning Futures*, 48; Rebecca Bowe, "The Water Wars," *San Francisco Bay Guardian* 43, no. 49 (September 2009); Randall Baxter, Rich Breuer, Larry Brown, Mike Chotkowski, Fred Feyrer, Marty Gingras, Bruce Herbold, Anke Mueller-Solger, Matt Nobriga, Ted Sommer, and Kelly Souza, "Pelagic Organism Decline Progress Report: 2007 Synthesis of Results," prepared by the Interagency Ecological Program for the San Francisco Estuary (Sacramento: State of California Resources Agency, 15 January 2008), 1–4; U.S. House of Representatives, Committee on Resources, "Scientific Assessments of Declining Pelagic Fish Populations in the California Bay-Delta," oversight field hearing, Stockton, CA, 27 February 2006.

49. Innes et al., "Collaborative Governance," 22–32; Tanya Heikkila and Andrea K. Gerlak, "The Formation of Large-Scale Collaborative Resource Management Institutions: Clarifying the Roles of Stakeholders, Science, and Institutions," *Policy Studies Journal* 33, no. 4 (November 2005): 583–612; Dave Owen, "Law, Environmental Dynamism, Reliability: The Rise and Fall of CALFED," *Environmental Law* 37 (Fall 2007): 1200–1204; California Department of Finance, "CALFED Bay-Delta Program," 2, 11.

50. California Department of Finance, "CALFED Bay-Delta Program," 64; Little Hoover Commission, *Still Imperiled*, 1, 23, 51, 59; Owen, "Law, Environmental Dynamism, Reliability," 1201–1202; U.S. House of Representatives, Committee on Resources, "Declining Pelagic Fish Populations," 9; Lund et al., *Envisioning Futures*, 126.

51. Lund et al., *Envisioning Futures*, 94; *Paterno et al. v. State of California et al.*, California Court of Appeals, Third District, no. C040553, decided 17 March 2004; National Oceanic and Atmospheric Administration, "Endangered and Threatened Wildlife and Plants: Threatened Status for Southern Distinct Population Segment of North American Green Sturgeon," *Federal Register* 71, no. 67 (7 April 2006): 17757–17766.

52. National Marine Fisheries Service, Southwest Region, "Biological Opinion on the Long-Term Central Valley Project and State Water Project Operations Criteria and Plan" (October 2004); Department of Water Resources, "Long-Term Central Valley Project and State Water Project Operations Criteria and Plan Biological Assessment for Terrestrial Species Protected under the State Endangered Species Act" (March 2004); *Natural Resources Defense Council et al. v. Kempthorne et al.*, 506 F. Supp. 2d 322, decided 25 May 2007.

53. Lund et al., *Envisioning Futures*, 132; Hanak et al., *California Water Myths*, 9; *Natural Resources Defense Council v. Kempthorne;* U.S. District Court for the Eastern District of California, *The Consolidated Salmonid Cases*, 688 F. Supp. 2d 1013, decided 18 May 2010.

54. *Natural Resources Defense Council v. Kempthorne;* anonymous, "California Turns Back the Taps," *Christian Science Monitor*, 18 September 2007, 8; Owen, "Law, Environmental Dynamism, Reliability," 1151.

55. Owen, "Law, Environmental Dynamism, Reliability," 1203–1204.

56. Valerie Richardson, "It's Farmers vs. Fish for California Water; U.S. Urged to Lift Restrictions," *Washington Times*, 20 August 2009, 1; U.S. House of Representatives, Subcommittee on Water and Power, "Extinction Is Not a Sustainable Water Policy," 24.

57. San Francisco Estuary Project and CALFED, *State of the San Francisco Bay-Delta Estuary 2006*, 8; Brown et al., "Managing Water to Protect Fish," 359–360.

58. Sonia Verma, "How Green WAS My Valley," *Globe and Mail*, 25 July 2009, F-1; Media Matters for America, "Hannity Demands Obama 'Turn This Water On Now' in Central California—but Pumps Have Been On for Months," 23 September 2009, Web; Devin Nunes, "It's Fish versus Farmers in the San Joaquin Valley," *Wall Street Journal*, 14 August 2009; Bowe, "Water Wars."

59. Cletus E. Daniel, *Bitter Harvest: A History of California Farmworkers, 1870–1941* (Ithaca, NY: Cornell University Press, 1981); Worster, *Rivers of Empire*, 296; Hundley, *The Great Thirst*, 238.

60. Tadlock Cowan, ed., "California's San Joaquin Valley: A Region in Transition" (Washington, DC: Congressional Research Service, 12 December 2005); Hundley, *The Great Thirst*, 382.

61. Hundley, *The Great Thirst*, 297, 315; Worster, *Rivers of Empire*, 292; Jeffrey Michael, "Unemployment in the San Joaquin Valley in 2009: Fish or Foreclosure?" (University of the Pacific, Business Forecasting Center, 11 August 2009).

62. RealtyTrac, "Third Quarter Foreclosure Activity Up in 65 Percent of U.S. Metro Areas but Down in Hardest-Hit Cities," 28 October 2010, Web; Michael, "Unemployment in the San Joaquin Valley." The six San Joaquin Valley metropolitan areas that made the top-twenty foreclosures list were Modesto, Stockton, Merced, Bakersfield, Sacramento, and Visalia-Porterville. The Bay-Delta area of Vallejo-Fairfield, just outside the San Joaquin Valley, also appeared on the list.

63. Richard Howitt, Josué Medellín Azuara, and Duncan MacEwan, "Measuring the Employment Impact of Water Reductions" (University of California, Davis, Department of Agricultural and Resource Economics and Center for Watershed Sciences, 28 September 2009); Johnson, "Little Fish Takes Big Bite."

64. Michael, "Unemployment in the San Joaquin Valley"; David Sunding, Newsha Ajami, Steve Hatchet, David Mitchell, and David Zilberman, "Economic Impacts of the Wanger Interim Order for Delta Smelt" (Berkeley Economic Consulting Group, 8 December 2008).

65. Michael Hiltzik, "Debate Muddies Water Wars," *Los Angeles Times*, 14 March 2010, B-1; Peter Gleick, "Drought Impacts on Unemployment Are Grossly Overstated," *Alternet*, 27 August 2009, Web.

66. Hanak et al., *California Water Myths*, 13–33, 56; anonymous, "Stuck in the Delta; Water in California," *Economist*, 24 September 2009.

67. Jackson and Patterson, *Sacramento–San Joaquin Delta*, 158.

68. California Resources Agency, "Bay Delta Conservation Plan Environmental Review Process" (25 September 2009); Hanak et al., *California Water Myths*, 41–42; CALFED Science Program, *The State of Bay-Delta Science*, 6.

69. Blue Ribbon Task Force, *Delta Vision Strategic Plan*, 3–4, 43–53, 103; Delta Vision Committee, "Delta Vision Committee Implementation Report" (31 December 2008), 1–2.

70. *Delta Smelt Consolidated Cases*, U.S. District Court, Eastern District of California, no. 1:09-CV-00407, decided 27 May 2010; Hanak et al., *California Water Myths*, 38–42.

EPILOGUE

1. Craig L. Shafer, "History of Selection and System Planning for U.S. Natural Area National Parks and Monuments: Beauty and Biology," *Biodiversity and Conservation* 8, no. 2 (February 1999): 189–204; Alfred Runte, *National Parks: The American Experience*, 3rd ed. (Lincoln: University of Nebraska Press, 1997); National Research Council, *Setting Priorities for Land Conservation* (Washington, DC: National Academy Press, 1993).

2. Karl S. Zimmerer, "Geographical Perspectives on Globalization and Environmental Issues: The Inner-Connections of Conservation, Agriculture, and Livelihoods," in Zimmerer, ed., *Globalization and New Geographies of Conservation* (Chicago: University of Chicago Press, 2006), 23–29; for statistics on marine protected areas, see the NOAA Web site at www.mpa.gov.

3. Tim Forsyth, *Critical Political Ecology: The Politics of Environmental Science* (London: Routledge, 2003); William M. Adams, *Against Extinction: The Story of Conservation* (London: Earthscan, 2004), 4.

4. Ross W. Gorte, Carol H. Vincent, Laura A. Hanson, and Marc R. Rosenblum, "Federal Land Ownership: Overview and Data" (Congressional Research Service, 8 February 2012); General Accounting Office, "National Wildlife Refuge System: Contributions Being Made to Endangered Species Recovery" (November 1994); Robert P. Davison, Alessandra Falcucci, Luigi Maiorano, and J. Michael Scott, "The National Wildlife Refuge System," in Dale D. Goble, Scott, and Frank W. Davis, eds., *The Endangered Species Act at Thirty*, vol. 1, *Renewing the Conservation Promise* (Washington, DC: Island, 2006), 90–100.

5. Craig L. Shafer, "Conservation Biology Trailblazers: George Wright, Ben Thompson, and Joseph Dixon," *Conservation Biology* 15, no. 2 (April 2001): 332–334; Michael E. Soulé and John Terborgh, *Continental Conservation: Scientific Foundations of Regional Reserve Networks* (Washington, DC: Island, 1999).

6. Mark L. Shaffer, J. Michael Scott, and Frank Casey, "Noah's Options: Initial Cost Estimates of a National System of Habitat Conservation Areas in the United States," *BioScience* 52, no. 5 (2002): 439–443.

7. Amara Brook, Michaela Zint, and Raymond de Young, "Landowners' Responses to an Endangered Species Act Listing and Implications for Encouraging Conservation," *Conservation Biology* 17, no. 6 (December 2003): 1638–1649; Jodi Hilty and Adina M. Merenlender, "Studying Biodiversity on Private Lands," *Conservation Biology* 17, no. 1 (February 2003): 132–137; Sally K. Fairfax, Lauren Gwin, Mary Ann King, Leigh Raymond, and Laura A. Watt, *Buying Nature: The Limits of Land Acquisition as a Conservation Strategy, 1780–2004* (Cambridge, MA: MIT Press, 2005).

8. J. Michael Scott, Frank W. Davis, R. Gavin McGhie, R. Gerald Wright, Craig Groves, and John Estes, "Nature Reserves: Do They Capture the Full Range of America's Biological Diversity?," *Ecological Applications* 11, no. 4 (August 2001): 999–1007; John R. Prendergast, Rachel M. Quinn, and John H. Lawton, "The Gaps between Theory and Practice in Selecting Nature Reserves," *Conservation Biology* 13, no. 3 (June 1999): 484–492; Daniel Simberloff, "Flagships, Umbrellas, and Keystones: Is Single-Species Management Passé in the Landscape Era?," *Biological Conservation* 83, no. 3 (1998): 247–257; Sandy J. Andelman and William F. Fagan, "Umbrellas and Flagships: Efficient Conservation Surrogates or Expensive Mistakes?," *Proceedings of the National Academy of Sciences* 97, no. 11 (23 May 2000): 5954–5959.

9. See, e.g., Nik Heynen, James McCarthy, Scott Prudham, and Paul Robbins, eds., *Neoliberal Environments: False Promises and Unnatural Consequences* (London: Routledge, 2007); Zimmerer, *Globalization and New Geographies.*

10. J. B. Ruhl, "Regulation by Adaptive Management—Is It Possible?," *Minnesota Journal of Law, Science and Technology* 7 (December 2005): 21–57; Holly Doremus, "New Directions in Environmental Law: The Endangered Species Act: Static Law Meets Dynamic World," *Washington University Journal of Law and Policy* 32 (2010): 175–235.

11. Miguel B. Araújo, Paul H. Williams, and Robert J. Fuller, "Dynamics of Extinction and the Selection of Nature Reserves," *Proceedings of the Royal Society of London B* 269 (2002): 1971–1980; Yrjö Haila, "A Conceptual Genealogy of Fragmentation Research: From Island Biogeography to Landscape Ecology," *Ecological Applications* 12, no. 2 (April 2002): 321–334.

12. U.S. Fish and Wildlife Service, "12-Month Finding on a Petition to List the American Pika as Threatened or Endangered," *Federal Register* 75, no. 26 (9 February 2010): 6438–6471.

13. Delisting figures collected from the FWS endangered species Web site on 28 June 2012; J. Michael Scott, Dale D. Goble, John A. Wiens, David S. Wilcove, Michael Bean, and Timothy Male, "Recovery of Imperiled Species under the Endangered Species Act: The Need for a New Approach," *Frontiers in Ecology and the Environment* 3, no. 7 (2005): 383–389.

14. Government Accountability Office, "Many Factors Affect the Length of Time to Recover Select Species" (September 2006); Holly Doremus and Joel E. Pagel, "Why

Listing May Be Forever: Perspectives on Delisting under the U.S. Endangered Species Act," *Conservation Biology* 15, no. 5 (October 2001): 1258–1268.

15. Government Accountability Office, "Many Factors Affect the Length of Time to Recover Select Species" (September 2006); Holly Doremus and Joel E. Pagel, "Why Listing May Be Forever: Perspectives on Delisting under the U.S. Endangered Species Act," *Conservation Biology* 15, no. 5 (October 2001): 1258–1268.

16. Michael L. Rosenzweig, "Beyond Set-Asides," in Goble, Scott, and Davis, *The Endangered Species Act at Thirty*, 1:259–273.

17. Aldo Leopold, unpublished manuscript, ca. 1935, quoted in Curt Meine, *Correction Lines: Essays on Land, Leopold, and Conservation* (Washington, DC: Island, 2004), 55.

18. Barton H. Thompson Jr., "Managing the Working Landscape," in Goble, Scott, and Davis, *The Endangered Species Act at Thirty*, 1:101–126; Timothy D. Hadlock and Jo Ann Beckwith, "Recommendations to Improve Recovery of Endangered Species in the United States," *Human Dimensions of Wildlife* 7 (2002): 37–53; A. Dan Tarlock, "Local Government Protection of Biodiversity: What Is Its Niche?," *University of Chicago Law Review* 60 (Spring 1993): 555–613; Goble, Susan M. George, Kathryn Mazaika, Scott, and Jason Karl, "Local and National Protection of Endangered Species: An Assessment," *Environmental Science and Policy* 2 (1999): 43–59.

SELECTED BIBLIOGRAPHY

Adams, Charles C. "Ecological Conditions in National Forests and in National Parks." *Scientific Monthly* 20, no. 6 (June 1925): 561–593.

———. *Guide to the Study of Animal Ecology.* New York: Macmillan, 1913.

Adams, William M. *Against Extinction: The Story of Conservation.* London: Earthscan, 2004.

Andelman, Sandy J., and William F. Fagan. "Umbrellas and Flagships: Efficient Conservation Surrogates or Expensive Mistakes?" *Proceedings of the National Academy of Sciences* 97, no. 11 (23 May 2000): 5954–5959.

Anderson, John Merrick. *Wildlife Sanctuaries and the Audubon Society: Places to Hide and Seek.* Austin: University of Texas Press, 2000.

Anderson, Kat M., Michael G. Barbour, and Valerie Whitworth. "A World of Balance and Plenty: Land, Plants, Animals, and Humans in a Pre-European California." *California History* 76, nos. 2–3 (Summer–Fall 1997): 12–47.

Anderson, Richard L., Linda K. Spiegel, and Karyn M. Kakiba-Russell. *Southern San Joaquin Valley Ecosystems Protection Program: Natural Lands Inventory and Maps.* Sacramento: California Energy Commission, 1991.

Anker, Peder. *Imperial Ecology: Environmental Order in the British Empire, 1895–1945.* Cambridge, MA: Harvard University Press, 2001.

Araújo, Miguel B., Paul H. Williams, and Robert J. Fuller. "Dynamics of Extinction and the Selection of Nature Reserves." *Proceedings of the Royal Society of London B* 269 (2002): 1971–1980.

Austin, Mary. *The Land of Little Rain*. Boston: Houghton Mifflin, 1903.

Bancroft, Hubert H. *History of California*. Vol. 7. San Francisco: History Company, 1890.

Barrow, Mark. *Nature's Ghosts: Confronting Extinction from the Age of Jefferson to the Age of Ecology*. Chicago: University of Chicago Press, 2009.

Batt, Kevin D. "Above All, Do No Harm: Sweet Home and Section Nine of the Endangered Species Act." *Boston University Law Review* 75 (September 1995): 1177–1231.

Bay Institute. *From the Sierra to the Sea: The Ecological History of the San Francisco Bay-Delta Watershed*. San Francisco: Bay Institute of San Francisco, 1998.

Beal, F. E. L. *Birds of California in Relation to the Fruit Industry, Part II*. U.S. Department of Agriculture, Biological Survey Bulletin, no. 34. Washington, DC: Government Printing Office, 1910.

Bean, Michael J., and Melanie Rowland. *The Evolution of National Wildlife Law*. 3rd ed. Westport, CT: Praeger, 1997.

Beard, Daniel B., Frederick C. Lincoln, Victor Calahane, Hartley T. H. Jackson, and Ben H. Thompson. *Fading Trails: The Story of Endangered American Wildlife*. New York: Macmillan, 1942.

Beatley, Timothy. *Habitat Conservation Planning: Endangered Species and Urban Growth*. Austin: University of Texas Press, 1994.

Bell, Horace. *Reminiscences of a Ranger; or, Early Times in Southern California*. Santa Barbara: Wallace Hebbard, 1927.

Benson, Etienne. *Wired Wilderness: Technologies of Tracking and the Making of Modern Wildlife*. Baltimore: Johns Hopkins University Press, 2010.

Bentley, H. L. "Cattle Ranges of the Southwest: A History of the Exhaustion of the Pasturage and Suggestions for Its Restoration." U.S. Department of Agriculture, Farmers Bulletin, no. 72 (Washington, DC: Government Printing Office, 1898).

Bergman, Charles. *Wild Echoes: Encounters with the Most Endangered Animals in North America*. New York: McGraw-Hill, 1990.

Berry, Kristin H., ed. *The Status of the Desert Tortoise (*Gopherus agassizii*) in the United States*. Long Beach, CA: Desert Tortoise Council, 1984.

Biodiversity Project. *Americans and Biodiversity: New Perspectives in 2002*. Washington, DC: Beldon, Russonello, and Stuart, 2002.

Bjurlin, Curtis D., and Brian L. Cypher. "Encounter Frequency with the Urbanized San Joaquin Kit Fox Correlates with Public Beliefs and Attitudes toward the Species." *Endangered Species Update* 22, no. 3 (1 July 2005): 107–115.

Boarman, William I. "Managing a Subsidized Predator Population: Reducing Common Raven Predation on Desert Tortoises." *Environmental Management* 32, no. 2 (September 2003): 205–217.

————. *Threats to Desert Tortoise Populations: A Critical Review of the Literature.* Prepared by the U.S. Geological Survey Western Ecological Research Center for the Bureau of Land Management, 2002.

Bolton, Herbert Eugene. *Historical Memoirs of New California by Francisco Palóu.* Berkeley: University of California Press, 1926.

Bosqui, Edward. *Memoirs.* Oakland: Holmes, 1952.

Boyd, Karl. *Before Earth Day: The Origins of American Environmental Law, 1945–1970.* Lawrence: University Press of Kansas, 2009.

Brechin, Gray A. *Imperial San Francisco: Urban Power, Earthly Ruin.* Berkeley: University of California Press, 1999.

Brook, Amara, Michaela Zint, and Raymond de Young. "Landowners' Responses to an Endangered Species Act Listing and Implications for Encouraging Conservation." *Conservation Biology* 17, no. 6 (December 2003): 1638–1649.

Brower, David J., and Daniel S. Carol, eds. *Managing Land-Use Conflicts: Case Studies in Special Area Management.* Durham: Duke University Press, 1987.

Brown, Gardner M., Jr., and Jason F. Shogren. "Economics of the Endangered Species Act." *Journal of Economic Perspectives* 12, no. 3 (Summer 1998): 3–20.

Bruce, Jay C. *Cougar Killer.* New York: Comet, 1953.

Bryant, Harold C. "A Brief History of the California Fish and Game Commission." *California Fish and Game* 7, no. 2 (April 1921): 73–86.

Bunn, David, Andrea Mummert, Marc Hoshovsky, Kirsten Gilardi, and Sandra Shanks. *California Wildlife: Conservation Challenges—California's Wildlife Action Plan.* University of California, Davis, Wildlife Health Center and California Department of Fish and Game, 2007.

Burcham, L. T. "California Rangelands in Historical Perspective." *Rangelands* 3, no. 3 (June 1981): 95–104.

Burd-Sharps, Sarah, Kristen Lewis, and Eduardo Borges Martins. *The Measure of America: American Human Development Report, 2008–2009.* New York: Columbia University Press, 2008.

Bureau of Land Management. *The California Desert Conservation Area Plan 1980.* Riverside, CA: U.S. Department of the Interior, 1980.

————. *Southern Nevada Public Land Management Act: 10-Year Report to Congress.* Denver: U.S. Department of the Interior, 2008.

Bureau of Reclamation. *Central Valley Project Improvement Act: 10 Years of Progress.* Sacramento: Bureau of Reclamation, 2003.

Bury, R. Bruce, and Paul S. Corn. "Have Desert Tortoises Undergone a Long-Term Decline in Abundance?" *Wildlife Society Bulletin* 23, no. 1 (Spring 1995): 41–47.

California Condor Recovery Team. *California Condor Recovery Plan*. U.S. Fish and Wildlife Service, July 1976.

California Department of Fish and Game. *The Status of Rare, Threatened, and Endangered Plants and Animals of California, 2000–2004*. Sacramento: California Department of Fish and Game, 2005.

California Fish and Game Commission. *Twenty-Second Biennial Report for the Years 1910–1912*. Sacramento: State Printing Office, 1913.

———. *Twenty-Seventh Biennial Report for the Years 1920–1922*. Sacramento: State Printing Office, 1923.

Carden, Kristin. "Bridging the Divide: The Role of Science in Species Conservation Law." *Harvard Environmental Law Review* 30 (2006): 165–259.

Carson, Rachel. *Silent Spring*. New York: Houghton Mifflin, 1962.

Catton, Theodore, and Lisa Mighetto. *The Fish and Wildlife Job on the National Forests: A Century of Game and Fish Conservation, Habitat Protection, and Ecosystem Management*. U.S. Forest Service, 1998.

Clark, Tim W., Murray B. Rutherford, and Denise Casey, eds. *Coexisting with Large Carnivores: Lessons from Greater Yellowstone*. Washington, DC: Island, 2005.

Colton, Walter. *Three Years in California*. New York: A. S. Barnes, 1850.

Costanso, Miguel. *The Narrative of the Portola Expedition of 1769–1770*. Berkeley: University of California Press, 1910.

Cowan, Tadlock, ed. "California's San Joaquin Valley: A Region in Transition." Washington, DC: Congressional Research Service, 12 December 2005.

Crawford, Mark. "The Last Days of the Wild Condor?" *Science* 229, no. 4716 (30 August 1985): 844–845.

Cronon, William, ed. *Uncommon Ground: Rethinking the Human Place in Nature*. New York: W. W. Norton, 1995.

Curtin, Charles G. "The Evolution of the U.S. National Wildlife Refuge System and the Doctrine of Compatibility." *Conservation Biology* 7, no. 1 (March 1993): 29–38.

Cypher, Brian L., and Nancy Frost. "Condition of San Joaquin Kit Foxes in Urban and Exurban Habitats." *Journal of Wildlife Management* 63, no. 3 (July 1999): 930–938.

Cypher, Brian L., Patrick A. Kelly, Daniel F. Williams, Howard O. Clark Jr., Alexander D. Brown, and Scott E. Phillips. *Foxes in Farmland: Recovery of the Endangered San Joaquin Kit Fox on Private Lands in California*. Fresno: California State University, Stanislaus, Endangered Species Recovery Program, 2005.

Daniel, Cletus E. *Bitter Harvest: A History of California Farmworkers, 1870–1941*. Ithaca, NY: Cornell University Press, 1981.

Darin, Thomas F. "Designating Critical Habitat under the Endangered Species Act: Habitat Protection versus Agency Discretion." *Harvard Environmental Law Review* 24, no. 1 (2000): 209–235.

Darlington, David. *The Mojave: Portrait of the Definitive American Desert.* New York: Henry Holt, 1996.

Dasmann, Raymond F. *The Destruction of California.* New York: Macmillan, 1965.

————. "Towards a System for Classifying Natural Regions of the World and Their Representation by National Parks and Reserves." *Biological Conservation* 4, no. 4 (July 1972): 247–255.

Dasmann, William. *Big Game of California.* Sacramento: California Department of Fish and Game, 1975.

Dice, Lee. "The Scientific Value of Predatory Mammals." *Journal of Mammalogy* 6, no. 1 (February 1925): 25–27.

Ditmars, Raymond Lee. *The Reptile Book: A Comprehensive, Popularised Work on the Structure and Habits of the Turtles, Tortoises, Crocodilians, Lizards and Snakes Which Inhabit the United States and Northern Mexico.* New York: Doubleday, Page, 1907.

Dixon, Joseph. "Does the Grizzly Bear Still Exist in California?" *California Fish and Game* 2, no. 2 (April 1916): 65–69.

————. "Food Predilections of Predatory and Fur-Bearing Mammals." *Journal of Mammalogy* 6, no. 1 (February 1925): 34–46.

Dobson, A. P., J. P. Rodriguez, W. M. Roberts, and D. S. Wilcove. "Geographic Distribution of Endangered Species in the United States." *Science* 275 (24 January 1997): 550–553.

Doremus, Holly. "New Directions in Environmental Law: The Endangered Species Act: Static Law Meets Dynamic World." *Washington University Journal of Law and Policy* 32 (2010): 175–235.

————. "Water, Population Growth, and Endangered Species in the West." *University of Colorado Law Review* 72 (Spring 2001): 361–414.

Doremus, Holly, and Joel E. Pagel. "Why Listing May Be Forever: Perspectives on Delisting under the U.S. Endangered Species Act." *Conservation Biology* 15, no. 5 (October 2001): 1258–1268.

Dorsey, Kurkpatrick. *The Dawn of Conservation Diplomacy: U.S.-Canadian Wildlife Protection Treaties in the Progressive Era.* Seattle: University of Washington Press, 1998.

Dunlap, Thomas. *Saving America's Wildlife: Ecology and the American Mind, 1850–1990.* Princeton: Princeton University Press, 1991.

Eakin, Richard Marshall. "History of Zoology at the University of California, Berkeley." *Bios* 27, no. 2 (May 1956): 67–92.

Eaton, Jim. "Wilderness: From Aesthetics to Biodiversity." *Wild Earth* 1 (Summer 1991): 1–2.

Emslie, Steven D. "Age and Diet of Fossil California Condors in Grand Canyon, Arizona." *Science* 237, no. 4816 (14 August 1987): 768–770.

Evans, Albert S. *À la California: Sketches of Life in the Golden State*. San Francisco: A. L. Bancroft, 1873.

Evenden, Matthew D. "The Laborers of Nature: Economic Ornithology and the Role of Birds as Agents of Biological Pest Control in North American Agriculture, ca. 1880–1930." *Forest and Conservation History* 39 (1995): 172–183.

Evermann, Barton W. "An Attempt to Save California Elk." *California Fish and Game* 1, no. 3 (April 1915): 85–96.

Fairfax, Sally K., Lauren Gwin, Mary Ann King, Leigh Raymond, and Laura A. Watt. *Buying Nature: The Limits of Land Acquisition as a Conservation Strategy, 1780–2004*. Cambridge, MA: MIT Press, 2005.

Fascione, Nina, Aimee Delach, and Martin Smith, eds. *People and Predators: From Conflict to Coexistence*. Washington, DC: Island, 2004.

Fischman, Robert. *The National Wildlife Refuges: Coordinating a Conservation System through Law*. Washington, DC: Island, 2003.

Fitzhugh, E. L., and P. W. Gorenzel. "Biological Status of Mountain Lions in California." *Proceedings of the Twelfth Vertebrate Pest Conference*. Lincoln: University of Nebraska, 1986.

Forsyth, Tim. *Critical Political Ecology: The Politics of Environmental Science*. London: Routledge, 2003.

Frayer, W. E., Dennis D. Peters, and H. Ross Pywell. *Wetlands of the California Central Valley: Status and Trends, 1939 to Mid-1980s*. Portland, OR: U.S. Fish and Wildlife Service, June 1989.

Garone, Philip. *The Fall and Rise of the Wetlands of California's Great Central Valley*. Berkeley: University of California Press, 2011.

Gass, Patrick. *Gass's Journal of the Lewis and Clark Expedition*. Chicago: A. C. McClurg, 1904.

General Accounting Office. "BLM's Hot Desert Grazing Program Merits Reconsideration." November 1992.

———. "California Desert: Planned Wildlife Protection and Enhancement Objectives Not Achieved." June 1989.

———. "Endangered Species: Fish and Wildlife Service Uses Best Available Science to Make Listing Decisions, but Additional Guidance Needed for Critical Habitat Designations." August 2003.

———. "Endangered Species: Limited Effect of Consultation Requirements on Western Water Projects." March 1987.

————. "Endangered Species Act: Types and Number of Implementing Actions." May 1992.

————. "Endangered Species Program: Information on How Funds Are Allocated and What Activities Are Emphasized." June 2002.

————. "Federal Land Management: Federal Land Acquisitions in California since January 1994." August 2000.

————. "National Wildlife Refuge System: Contributions Being Made to Endangered Species Recovery." November 1994.

————. "Research Strategy and Long-Term Monitoring Needed for the Mojave Desert Tortoise Recovery Program." December 2002.

Germano, David J., Galen B. Rathbun, Lawrence R. Saslaw, Brian L. Cypher, Ellen A. Cypher, and Larry M. Vredenburgh. "The San Joaquin Desert of California: Ecologically Misunderstood and Overlooked." *Natural Areas Journal* 31, no. 2 (April 2011): 138–147.

Gibbons, J. Whitfield, David E. Scott, Travis J. Ryan, Kurt A. Buhlmann, Tracey D. Tuberville, Brian S. Metts, Judith L. Greene, Tony Mills, Yale Leiden, Sean Poppy, and Christopher T. Winne. "The Global Decline of Reptiles, Déjà Vu Amphibians." *BioScience* 50, no. 8 (August 2000): 653–666.

Gilpin, Michael E., and Jared M. Diamond. "Subdivision of Nature Reserves and the Maintenance of Species Diversity." *Nature* 285 (19 June 1980): 567–568.

Goble, Dale D., Susan M. George, Kathryn Mazaika, J. Michael Scott, and Jason Karl. "Local and National Protection of Endangered Species: An Assessment." *Environmental Science and Policy* 2 (1999): 43–59.

Goble, Dale D., J. Michael Scott, and Frank W. Davis, eds. *The Endangered Species Act at Thirty.* 2 vols. Washington, DC: Island, 2006.

Goodall, Jane, Thane Maynard, and Gail E. Hudson. *Hope for Animals and Their World: How Endangered Species Are Being Rescued from the Brink.* New York: Grand Central, 2009.

Gorte, Ross W., Carol H. Vincent, Laura A. Hanson, and Marc R. Rosenblum. "Federal Land Ownership: Overview and Data." Congressional Research Service, 8 February 2012.

Government Accountability Office. "Endangered Species Act: Many GAO Recommendations Have Been Implemented, but Some Issues Remain Unresolved." December 2008.

————. "Many Factors Affect the Length of Time to Recover Select Species." September 2006.

Griesemer, James R. "Modeling in the Museum: On the Role of Remnant Models in the Work of Joseph Grinnell." *Biology and Philosophy* 5, no. 1 (1990): 3–36.

Griesemer, James R., and Elihu M. Gerson. "Collaboration in the Museum of Vertebrate Zoology." *Journal of the History of Biology* 26, no. 2 (Summer 1993): 185–203.

Grinnell, Hilda Wood. "Joseph Grinnell: 1877–1939," *Condor* 42, no. 1 (January–February 1940): 3–34.

Grinnell, Joseph. *Joseph Grinnell's Philosophy of Nature: Selected Writings of a Western Naturalist.* Freeport, NY: Libraries Press, 1943.

Grinnell, Joseph, Harold C. Bryant, and Tracy I. Storer. *The Game Birds of California.* Berkeley: University of California Press, 1918.

Grinnell, Joseph, Joseph S. Dixon, and Jean M. Linsdale. *Fur-Bearing Mammals of California: Their Natural History, Systematic Status, and Relations to Man.* Berkeley: University of California Press, 1937.

Grinnell, Joseph, and Tracy I. Storer. "Animal Life as an Asset of the National Parks." *Science* 44, no. 1133 (15 September 1916): 375–380.

Gutiérrez, Ramón, and Richard J. Orsi, eds. *Contested Eden: California before the Gold Rush.* Berkeley: University of California Press, 1998.

Hackel, Steven W. *Children of Coyote, Missionaries of Saint Francis: Indian-Spanish Relations in Colonial California, 1769–1850.* Chapel Hill: University of North Carolina Press, 2005.

Hadlock, Timothy D., and Jo Ann Beckwith. "Recommendations to Improve Recovery of Endangered Species in the United States." *Human Dimensions of Wildlife* 7 (2002): 37–53.

Hagen, Amy N., and Karen E. Hodges. "Resolving Critical Habitat Designation Failures: Reconciling Law, Policy, and Biology." *Conservation Biology* 20, no. 2 (April 2006): 399–407.

Haight, Robert G., Brian Cypher, Patrick A. Kelly, Scott Phillips, Katherine Ralls, and Hugh Possingham. "Optimizing Reserve Expansion for Disjunct Populations of San Joaquin Kit Fox." *Biological Conservation* 117 (2004): 61–72.

Haila, Yrjö. "A Conceptual Genealogy of Fragmentation Research: From Island Biogeography to Landscape Ecology." *Ecological Applications* 12, no. 2 (April 2002): 321–334.

Hanak, Ellen, Jay Lund, Ariel Dinar, Brian Gray, Richard Howitt, Jeffrey Mount, Peter Moyle, and Barton "Buzz" Thompson. *California Water Myths.* Sacramento: Public Policy Institute of California, 2009.

Hanemann, Michael, and Caitlin Dyckman. "The San Francisco Bay-Delta: A Failure of Decision-Making Capacity." *Environmental Science and Policy* 12 (2009): 712–721.

Haraway, Donna. "Teddy Bear Patriarchy: Taxidermy in the Garden of Eden, New York City, 1908–1936." *Social Text* 11 (Winter 1984–1985): 20–64.

Harris, Harry. "The Annals of *Gymnogyps* to 1900." *Condor* 43, no. 1 (January–February 1941): 3–55.

Hereford, Richard, Robert H. Webb, and Claire I. Longpre. *Precipitation History of the Mojave Desert Region, 1893–2001.* Flagstaff, AZ: United States Geological Survey, 2004.

Heynen, Nik, James McCarthy, Scott Prudham, and Paul Robbins, eds. *Neoliberal Environments: False Promises and Unnatural Consequences.* London: Routledge, 2007.

Hilty, Jodi, and Adina M. Merenlender. "Studying Biodiversity on Private Lands." *Conservation Biology* 17, no. 1 (February 2003): 132–137.

Hittell, Theodore H. *History of California.* San Francisco: N. J. Stone, 1897.

Hoekstra, Jonathan M., William F. Fagan, and Jeffrey E. Bradley. "A Critical Role for Critical Habitat in the Recovery Planning Process?: Not Yet." *Ecological Applications* 12, no. 3 (2002): 701–707.

Hornaday, William T. *Our Vanishing Wildlife: Its Extermination and Preservation.* New York: New York Zoological Society, 1913.

Howitt, Richard, Josué Medellín Azuara, and Duncan MacEwan. "Measuring the Employment Impact of Water Reductions." University of California, Davis, Department of Agricultural and Resource Economics and Center for Watershed Sciences, 28 September 2009.

Hundley, Norris. *The Great Thirst: Californians and Water—a History.* Berkeley: University of California Press, 1992.

Igler, David. *Industrial Cowboys: Miller and Lux and the Transformation of the Far West, 1850–1920.* Berkeley: University of California Press, 2001.

Isenberg, Andrew. *The Destruction of the Bison: An Environmental History, 1750–1920.* Cambridge: Cambridge University Press, 2001.

———. *Mining California: An Ecological History.* New York: Hill and Wang, 2005.

Jackson, W. Turrentine, and Alan M. Patterson. *The Sacramento–San Joaquin Delta: The Evolution and Implementation of Water Policy: An Historical Perspective.* Berkeley: University of California Water Resources Center, 1977.

Jacobson, Elliot R., J. M. Gaskin, M. B. Brown, R. K. Harris, C. H. Gardiner, J. L. LaPointe, H. P. Adams, and C. Reggiardo. "Chronic Upper Respiratory Tract Disease of Free-Ranging Desert Tortoises (*Xerobates agassizii*)." *Journal of Wildlife Diseases* 27, no. 2 (1991): 296–316.

Jacoby, Karl. *Crimes against Nature: Squatters, Poachers, Thieves, and the Hidden History of American Conservation.* Berkeley: University of California Press, 2001.

Jaeger, Edmund Carroll. *Denizens of the Desert: A Book of Southwestern Mammals, Birds, and Reptiles.* Boston and New York: Houghton Mifflin, 1922.

James, George Wharton. *The Wonders of the Colorado Desert (Southern California)*. London: T. Fisher Unwin, 1906.

Jasanoff, Sheila. *States of Knowledge: The Co-production of Science and the Social Order*. London: Routledge, 2004.

Kay, Charles E., and Randy T. Simmons, eds. *Wilderness and Political Ecology: Aboriginal Influences and the Original State of Nature*. Salt Lake City: University of Utah Press, 2002.

Kelley, Robert. *Battling the Inland Sea: Floods, Public Policy, and the Sacramento Valley*. Berkeley: University of California Press, 1989.

Kelly, Allan. *Bears I Have Met—and Others*. Philadelphia: Drexel Biddle, 1903.

Kessel, Edward L., ed. *A Century of Progress in the Natural Sciences, 1853–1953*. San Francisco: California Academy of Sciences, 1955.

Kiff, Lloyd. "An Historical Perspective on the Condor." *Outdoor California* 44, no. 5 (September–October 1983): 5–6, 34, 37.

Kinchy, Abby J. "On the Borders of Post-war Ecology: Struggles over the Ecological Society of America's Preservation Committee, 1917–1946." *Science as Culture* 15, no. 1 (March 2006): 23–44.

Klyza, Christopher M., and David J. Sousa. *American Environmental Policy, 1990–2006: Beyond Gridlock*. Cambridge, MA: MIT Press, 2008.

Koford, Carl B. *The California Condor*. New York: Dover, 1953.

———. "California Condors, Forever Free?" *Audubon Imprint—Newsletter of the Santa Monica Bay Audubon Society* 3 (April 1979): 1–7.

Kohler, Robert E. *All Creatures: Naturalists, Collectors, and Biodiversity, 1850–1950*. Princeton: Princeton University Press, 2006.

———. *Landscapes and Labscapes: Exploring the Lab-Field Border in Biology*. Chicago: University of Chicago Press, 2002.

Kohlstedt, Sally Gregory. *Teaching Children Science: Hands-On Nature Study in North America, 1890–1930*. Chicago: University of Chicago Press, 2010.

Leitritz, Earl. *A History of California's Fish Hatcheries—1870–1960*. Fish Bulletin, no. 150. Sacramento: California Department of Fish and Game, Inland Fisheries Branch, 1970.

Leopold, Aldo. *Game Management*. New York: Charles Scribner and Sons, 1933.

———. *A Sand County Almanac, and Sketches Here and There*. Oxford: Oxford University Press, 1989.

Leopold, A. S., S. A. Cain, C. M. Cottam, I. N. Gabrielson, and T. L. Kimball. *Wildlife Management in the National Parks*. Prepared by the Advisory Board on Wildlife Management appointed by Secretary of the Interior Udall. 4 March 1963.

Leviton, Alan E., and Michael L. Aldrich, eds. *Museums and Other Institutions of Natural History: Past, Present, and Future.* San Francisco: California Academy of Sciences, 2004.

Little Hoover Commission. "Still Imperiled, Still Important: The Little Hoover Commission's Review of the CALFED Bay-Delta Program." Sacramento, 17 November 2005.

Lovich, Jeffrey E., and David Bainbridge. "Anthropogenic Degradation of the Southern California Desert Ecosystem and Prospects for Natural Recovery and Restoration." *Environmental Management* 24, no. 3 (October 1999): 309–326.

Luke, Timothy W. "The Pleasures of Use: Federalizing Wilds, Nationalizing Life at the National Wildlife Federation." *Capitalism, Nature, Socialism* 12, no. 2 (2001): 3–38.

Lund, Jay, Ellen Hanak, William Fleenor, Richard Howitt, Jeffrey Mount, and Peter Moyle. *Envisioning Futures for the Sacramento–San Joaquin Delta.* Sacramento: Public Policy Institute of California, 2007.

MacArthur, Robert H., and Edward O. Wilson. *The Theory of Island Biogeography.* Princeton: Princeton University Press, 1967.

Maloney, Alice B. *Fur Brigade to the Bonaventura: John Work's California Expedition, 1832–33.* San Francisco: California Historical Society, 1945.

Manganiello, Chris. "From Howling Wilderness to Howling Safaris: Science, Policy and Red Wolves in the American South." *Journal of the History of Biology* 42, no. 2 (May 2009): 325–359.

Mann, Charles C., and Mark L. Plummer. *Noah's Choice: The Future of Endangered Species.* New York: Alfred A. Knopf, 1995.

Maranzana, Linda C. "Defenders of Wildlife v. Norton: A Closer Look at the 'Significant Portion of Its Range' Concept." *Ecology Law Quarterly* 29 (2002): 263–281.

Matthiessen, Peter. *Wildlife in America.* New York: Viking, 1959.

Mayr, Ernst. "Alden Holmes Miller, 1906–1965." Biographical memoir, 1973. National Academy of Sciences.

———. "Ecological Factors in Speciation." *Evolution* 1 (1947): 253–288.

McCarthy, James. "First World Political Ecology: Lessons from the Wise Use Movement." *Environment and Planning A* 34, no. 7 (2002): 1281–1302.

McCullough, Dale R. *The Tule Elk: Its History, Behavior, and Ecology.* University of California Publications in Zoology, no. 88. Berkeley: University of California Press, 1969.

McEvoy, Arthur F. *The Fisherman's Problem: Ecology and Law in the California Fisheries, 1850–1980.* Cambridge: Cambridge University Press, 1990.

McQueen, Mike. "Land and Water Conservation Fund: An Assessment of Its Past, Present, and Future." Arlington, VA: Conservation Fund, 2000.

Meine, Curt. *Aldo Leopold: His Life and Work*. Madison: University of Wisconsin Press, 2010.

―――. *Correction Lines: Essays on Land, Leopold, and Conservation*. Washington, DC: Island, 2004.

Meretsky, V. J., N. F. R. Snyder, S. R. Beissinger, D. A. Clendenen, and J. W. Wiley. "Demography of the California Condor: Implications for Reestablishment." *Conservation Biology* 14, no. 4 (August 2000): 957–967.

Merriam, C. Hart. "Description of a New Fox from Southern California." *Proceedings of the Biological Society of Washington* 4 (1888): 5–8.

Merriam, C. Hart, and Leonhard Stejneger. *Results of a Biological Survey of the San Francisco Mountain Region and Desert of the Little Colorado, Arizona*. North American Fauna, no. 3. Washington, DC: Government Printing Office, 1890.

Metropolitan Bakersfield Habitat Conservation Plan Steering Committee. *Metropolitan Bakersfield Habitat Conservation Plan*. Bakersfield: City of Bakersfield, 1994.

Michael, Jeffrey. "Unemployment in the San Joaquin Valley in 2009: Fish or Foreclosure?" University of the Pacific, Business Forecasting Center, 11 August 2009.

Mighetto, Lisa. *Muir among the Animals: The Wildlife Writings of John Muir*. San Francisco: Sierra Club, 1986.

Miller, Joaquin. *True Bear Stories*. Chicago: Rand McNally, 1900.

Mitchell, Martin D. "The Sacramento–San Joaquin Delta, California: Initial Transformation into a Water Supply and Conveyance Node, 1900–1955." *Journal of the West* 35, no. 1 (1996): 44–53.

Morafka, David J., and Kristin H. Berry. "Is *Gopherus agassizii* a Desert-Adapted Tortoise, or an Exaptive Opportunist? Implications for Tortoise Research." *Chelonian Conservation and Biology* 4, no. 2 (December 2002): 263–287.

Moritz, Craig, James L. Patton, Chris J. Conroy, Juan L. Parra, Gary C. White, and Steven R. Beissinger. "Impact of a Century of Climate Change on Small-Mammal Communities in Yosemite National Park, USA." *Science* 322, no. 261 (10 October 2008): 261–264.

Morrell, Stephen H. "San Joaquin Kit Fox Distribution and Abundance in 1975." Sacramento: California Department of Fish and Game, 1975.

Morrison, Michael L. "A Proposed Research Emphasis to Overcome the Limits of Wildlife-Habitat Relationship Studies." *Journal of Wildlife Management* 65, no. 4 (October 2001): 613–623.

Moyle, Peter B., William A. Bennett, Cliff Dahm, John R. Durand, Christopher Enright, William E. Fleenor, Wim Kimmerer, and Jay R. Lund. "Changing Ecosystems: A Brief Ecological History of the Delta." Report to the California State Water Resources Control Board, Sacramento, CA. February 2010.

Moyle, Peter B., and Robert D. Nichols. "Decline of the Native Fish Fauna of the Sierra Nevada Foothills, Central California." *American Midland Naturalist* 92, no. 1 (July 1974): 72–83.

Murchison, Kenneth M. *The Snail Darter Case: TVA versus the Endangered Species Act*. Lawrence: University Press of Kansas, 2007.

Nabhan, Gary Paul. *Singing the Turtles to Sea: The Comcáac (Seri) Art and Science of Reptiles*. Berkeley: University of California Press, 2003.

Nash, Linda. *Inescapable Ecologies: A History of Environment, Disease, and Knowledge*. Berkeley: University of California Press, 2006.

National Academy of Sciences. "A Report by the Advisory Committee to the National Park Service on Research." William J. Robbins, chairman. National Research Council, 1963.

National Agricultural Statistics Service. "2007 Census of Agriculture." Washington, DC: U.S. Department of Agriculture, 2009.

National Research Council. *Setting Priorities for Land Conservation*. Washington, DC: National Academy Press, 1993.

National Research Council, Committee on Scientific Issues in the Endangered Species Act. *Science and the Endangered Species Act*. Washington, DC: National Academy Press, 1995.

Newmark, William D. "A Land-Bridge Island Perspective on Mammalian Extinctions in Western North American Parks." *Nature* 325 (29 January 1987): 430–432.

Nielsen, John. *Condor: To the Brink and Back—the Life and Times of One Giant Bird*. New York: Harper Collins, 2006.

NOAA Fisheries. "Biological Opinion on the Long-Term Central Valley Project and State Water Project Operations Criteria and Plan." October 2004.

Noss, Reed F., Michael A. O'Connell, and Dennis D. Murphy. *The Science of Conservation Planning: Habitat Conservation under the Endangered Species Act*. Washington, DC: Island, 1997.

Nystrom, Eric Charles. "From Neglected Space to Protected Place: An Administrative History of Mojave National Preserve." Prepared for the United States Department of the Interior. National Park Service, Great Basin Cooperative Ecosystem Studies Unit, March 2003.

Ogden, Adele. *The California Sea Otter Trade, 1784–1848*. Berkeley: University of California Press, 1975.

Owen, Dave. "Law, Environmental Dynamism, Reliability: The Rise and Fall of CALFED." *Environmental Law* 37 (Fall 2007): 1145–1215.

Paddison, Joshua. *A World Transformed: Firsthand Accounts of California before the Gold Rush*. Berkeley: Heyday Books, 1998.

Palmer, William D. "Endangered Species Protection: A History of Congressional Action." *Boston College Environmental Affairs Law Review* 4 (1975): 255–293.

Parsons, James J. "A Geographer Looks at the San Joaquin Valley." *Geographical Review* 76, no. 4 (1986): 371–389.

Pavlick, Bruce M. *The California Deserts: An Ecological Rediscovery.* Berkeley: University of California Press, 2008.

Peet, Richard, and Michael Watts. *Liberation Ecologies: Environment, Development, Social Movements.* London: Routledge, 1996.

Petersen, Shannon. *Acting for Endangered Species: The Statutory Ark.* Lawrence: University Press of Kansas, 2002.

Phillips, David, and Hugh Nash, eds. *The Condor Question: Captive or Forever Free?* San Francisco: Friends of the Earth, 1981.

Pickett, S. T. A., R. S. Ostfeld, M. Shachak, and G. E. Likens, eds. *The Ecological Basis of Conservation: Heterogeneity, Ecosystems, and Biodiversity.* New York: Chapman and Hall, 1997.

Pollak, Daniel. *The Future of Habitat Conservation?: The NCCP Experience in Southern California.* Sacramento: California Research Bureau, 2001.

———. *Natural Community Conservation Planning (NCCP): The Origins of an Ambitious Experiment to Protect Ecosystems.* Sacramento: California Research Bureau, 2001.

Prendergast, John R., Rachel M. Quinn, and John H. Lawton. "The Gaps between Theory and Practice in Selecting Nature Reserves." *Conservation Biology* 13, no. 3 (June 1999): 484–492.

Price, Jennifer. *Flight Maps: Adventures with Nature in Modern America.* New York: Basic, 1999.

Pritchard, James A. "The Meaning of Nature: Wilderness, Wildlife, and Ecological Values in the National Parks." *George Wright Forum* 19, no. 2 (2002): 46–56.

Public Land Law Review Commission. *One Third of the Nation's Land.* Washington, DC: Government Printing Office, 1970.

Raitt, Ralph J. "In Memoriam: A. Starker Leopold." *Auk* 101 (October 1984): 868–871.

Recon. "Final Clark County Multiple Species Habitat Conservation Plan and Environmental Impact Statement." Prepared for the Clark County, Nevada, Department of Comprehensive Planning and Wildlife Service, 2000.

Rohlf, Daniel J. "Six Biological Reasons Why the Endangered Species Act Doesn't Work—and What to Do about It." *Conservation Biology* 5, no. 3 (September 1991): 273–282.

Rowley, William D. *U.S. Forest Service Grazing and Rangelands.* College Station: Texas A&M University Press, 1985.

Ruhl, J. B. "Biodiversity Conservation and the Ever-Expanding Web of Federal Laws Regulating Nonfederal Lands: Time for Something Completely Different?" *University of Colorado Law Review* 66 (Summer 1995): 555–673.

———. "How to Kill an Endangered Species, Legally: The Nuts and Bolts of Endangered Species Act 'HCP' Permits for Real Estate Development." *Environmental Lawyer* 5, no. 2 (1999): 345–405.

———. "Reconstructing the Wall of Virtue: Maxims for the Co-evolution of Environmental Law and Environmental Science." *Environmental Law* 37 (2007): 1063–1082.

———. "Regulation by Adaptive Management—Is It Possible?" *Minnesota Journal of Law, Science and Technology* 7 (December 2005): 21–57.

Runte, Alfred. "Joseph Grinnell and Yosemite: Rediscovering the Legacy of a California Conservationist." *California History* 69, no. 2 (Summer 1990): 170–181.

———. *National Parks: The American Experience.* 3rd ed. Lincoln: University of Nebraska Press, 1997.

Sabin, Paul. *Crude Politics: The California Oil Market, 1900–1940.* Berkeley: University of California Press, 2005.

Sayre, Nathan F. *Ranching, Endangered Species, and Urbanization in the Southwest: Species of Capital.* Tucson: University of Arizona Press, 2006.

Schmidt, R. H. "Gray Wolves in California: Their Presence and Absence." *California Fish and Game* 11 (1991): 79–85.

Schneider, Joan S., and G. Dicken Everson. "The Desert Tortoise (*Xerobates agassizii*) in the Prehistory of the Southwestern Great Basin and Adjacent Areas." *Journal of California and Great Basin Anthropology* 11, no. 2 (1989): 175–202.

Schneider-Hector, Dietmar. "Roger W. Toll: Chief Investigator of Proposed National Parks and Monuments: Setting the Standards for America's National Park System." *Journal of the West* 42, no. 1 (Winter 2003): 82–90.

Schoenherr, Allan A. *A Natural History of California.* Berkeley: University of California Press, 1995.

Scott, James C. *Seeing like a State: How Certain Schemes to Improve the Human Condition Have Failed.* New Haven: Yale University Press, 1998.

Scott, J. Michael, Frank W. Davis, R. Gavin McGhie, R. Gerald Wright, Craig Groves, and John Estes. "Nature Reserves: Do They Capture the Full Range of America's Biological Diversity?" *Ecological Applications* 11, no. 4 (August 2001): 999–1007.

Scott, J. Michael, Dale D. Goble, John A. Wiens, David S. Wilcove, Michael Bean, and Timothy Male. "Recovery of Imperiled Species under the Endangered Species Act:

The Need for a New Approach." *Frontiers in Ecology and the Environment* 3, no. 7 (2005): 383–389.

Sellars, Richard West. *Preserving Nature in the National Parks: A History.* New Haven: Yale University Press, 1999.

Shafer, Craig L. "Conservation Biology Trailblazers: George Wright, Ben Thompson, and Joseph Dixon." *Conservation Biology* 15, no. 2 (April 2001): 332–334.

———. "History of Selection and System Planning for U.S. Natural Area National Parks and Monuments: Beauty and Biology." *Biodiversity and Conservation* 8, no. 2 (February 1999): 189–204.

———. "U.S. National Park Buffer Zones: Historical, Scientific, Social, and Legal Aspects." *Environmental Management* 23, no. 1 (January 1999): 49–73.

Shaffer, Mark L., J. Michael Scott, and Frank Casey. "Noah's Options: Initial Cost Estimates of a National System of Habitat Conservation Areas in the United States." *BioScience* 52, no. 5 (2002): 439–443.

Shelford, Victor E., *Animal Communities in Temperate America: As Illustrated in the Chicago Region.* Chicago: University of Chicago Press, 1913.

———, ed. *Naturalist's Guide to the Americas.* Baltimore: Williams and Wilkins, 1926.

Sherow, James E., ed. *A Sense of the American West: An Anthology of Environmental History.* Albuquerque: University of New Mexico Press, 1998.

Shinn, Charles Howard. "Grizzly and Pioneer." *Century* 41, no. 19 (November 1890–April 1891): 130–131.

Simberloff, Daniel. "Experimental Zoogeography of Islands: A Model for Insular Colonization." *Ecology* 50, no. 2 (March 1969): 296–314.

———. "Flagships, Umbrellas, and Keystones: Is Single-Species Management Passé in the Landscape Era?" *Biological Conservation* 83, no. 3 (1998): 247–257.

Simberloff, Daniel, and L. G. Abele. "Island Biogeography Theory and Conservation Practice." *Science* 191, no. 4224 (23 January 1976): 285–286.

Skinner, John E. *An Historical Review of the Fish and Wildlife Resources of the San Francisco Bay Area.* Sacramento: Resources Agency of California, 1962.

Smith, Dick, and Robert Easton. *California Condor: Vanishing American.* Charlotte: McNally and Loftin, 1964.

Smith, Michael L. *Pacific Visions: California Scientists and the Environment, 1850–1915.* New Haven: Yale University Press, 1987.

Snyder, Noel, S. R. Derrickson, S. R. Beissinger, J. W. Wiley, T. B. Smith, W. D. Toone, and B. Miller. "Limits of Captive Breeding in Endangered Species Recovery." *Conservation Biology* 10, no. 2 (April 1996): 338–348.

Snyder, Noel, and Helen Snyder. *The California Condor: A Saga of Natural History and Conservation*. San Diego: Natural World Academic Press, 2000.

Snyder, Susan. *Bear in Mind: The California Grizzly*. Berkeley: Heyday Books, 2003.

Soden, Dennis L., ed. *The Environmental Presidency*. Albany: SUNY Press, 1999.

Soulé, Michael E., and John Terborgh. *Continental Conservation: Scientific Foundations of Regional Reserve Networks*. Washington, DC: Island, 1999.

Soulé, Michael E., and Bruce A. Wilcox, eds. *Conservation Biology: An Evolutionary-Ecological Perspective*. Sunderland, MA: Sinauer Associates, 1980.

Spiro, Jonathan Peter. *Defending the Master Race: Conservation, Eugenics, and the Legacy of Madison Grant*. Lebanon, NH: University Press of New England, 2009.

Star, Susan Leigh, and James R. Griesemer. "Institutional Ecology, 'Translations' and Boundary Objects: Amateurs and Professionals in Berkeley's Museum of Vertebrate Zoology." *Social Studies of Science* 19, no. 3 (August 1989): 387–420.

Steen, Harold K., ed. *Forest and Wildlife Science in America: A History*. Durham, NC: Forest History Society, 1999.

Stein, Barbara R. *On Her Own Terms: Annie Montague Alexander and the Rise of Science in the American West*. Berkeley: University of California Press, 2001.

Storer, Tracy I., and Lloyd P. Tevis. *California Grizzly*. Berkeley: University of California Press, 1955.

Sumner, Lowell. "Biological Research and Management in the National Park Service: A History." *George Wright Forum* 3, no. 4 (1983): 3–27.

Tansley, Arthur G. "The Use and Abuse of Vegetational Concepts and Terms." *Ecology* 16, no. 3 (July 1935): 284–307.

Tarlock, A. Dan. "Local Government Protection of Biodiversity: What Is Its Niche?" *University of Chicago Law Review* 60 (Spring 1993): 555–613.

Taylor, Martin F. J., Kieran F. Suckling, and Jeffrey J. Rachlinski. "The Effectiveness of the Endangered Species Act: A Quantitative Analysis." *BioScience* 55, no. 4 (April 2005): 360–362.

Thomas, Craig W. *Bureaucratic Landscapes: Interagency Cooperation and the Preservation of Biodiversity*. Cambridge, MA: MIT Press, 2003.

Thompson, Barton H., Jr. "People or Prairie Chickens: The Uncertain Search for Optimal Biodiversity." *Stanford Law Review* 51 (May 1999): 1127–1185.

Thompson, Kenneth. "Historic Flooding in the Sacramento Valley." *Pacific Historical Review* 29, no. 4 (November 1960): 349–360.

Thorne, Robert F. "A Historical Sketch of the Vegetation of the Mojave and Colorado Deserts of the American Southwest." *Annals of the Missouri Botanical Garden* 73, no. 3 (1986): 642–651.

Tjossem, Sara Fairbank. "Preservation of Nature and Academic Respectability: Tensions in the Ecological Society of America, 1915–1979." PhD dissertation, Cornell University, 1994.

Tober, James A. *Who Owns the Wildlife?: The Political Economy of Conservation in Nineteenth Century America*. Westport, CT: Greenwood, 1981.

———. *Wildlife and the Public Interest: Nonprofit Organizations and Federal Wildlife Policy*. New York: Praeger, 1989.

Tobey, Ronald C. *Saving the Prairies: The Life Cycle of the Founding School of American Plant Ecology, 1895–1955*. Berkeley: University of California Press, 1981.

Tracy, Richard C., R. Averill-Murray, W. I. Boarman, D. Delehanty, J. Heaton, E. McCoy, D. Morafka, K. Nussear, B. Hagerty, and P. Medica. "Desert Tortoise Recovery Plan Assessment." Prepared for the U.S. Fish and Wildlife Service, 2004.

Turner, James Morton. "'The Specter of Environmentalism': Wilderness, Environmental Politics, and the Evolution of the New Right." *Journal of American History* 96, no. 1 (June 2009): 123–148.

U.S. Fish and Wildlife Service. *Desert Tortoise (Mojave Population) Recovery Plan*. Portland, OR: U.S. Department of the Interior, 1994.

———. "Determination of Critical Habitat for American Crocodile, California Condor, Indiana Bat, and Florida Manatee." *Federal Register* 41, no. 187 (24 September 1976): 41914–41916.

———. "Determination of Critical Habitat for the Mojave Population of the Desert Tortoise." *Federal Register* 59, no. 26 (8 February 1994): 5820–5866.

———. "Determination of Threatened Status for the Coastal California Gnatcatcher." *Federal Register* 58 (30 March 1993): 16742–16757.

———. "Determination of Threatened Status for the Mojave Population of the Desert Tortoise." *Federal Register* 55, no. 63 (2 April 1990): 12178–12191.

———. "Emergency Determination of Endangered Status for the Mojave Population of the Desert Tortoise." *Federal Register* 54, no. 149 (4 August 1989): 32326–32331.

———. "Habitat Conservation Plan Assurances ('No Surprises') Rule." *Federal Register* 63, no. 35 (23 February 1998): 8871–8873.

———. *Recovery Plan for Upland Species of the San Joaquin Valley*. Portland, OR: U.S. Fish and Wildlife Service, 1998.

———. "12-Month Finding on a Petition to List the American Pika as Threatened or Endangered." *Federal Register* 75, no. 26 (9 February 2010): 6438–6471.

———. "Working Together: Tools for Helping Imperiled Wildlife on Private Lands." December 2005.

Van Devender, Thomas R., ed. *The Sonoran Desert Tortoise: Natural History, Biology, and Conservation.* Tucson: University of Arizona Press, 2002.

Van Dyke, John Charles. *The Desert: Further Studies in Natural Appearances.* New York: Charles Scribner's Sons, 1918.

Warren, Louis. *The Hunter's Game: Poachers and Conservationists in Twentieth-Century America.* New Haven: Yale University Press, 1999.

Warrick, Gregory D., Howard O. Clark Jr., Patrick A. Kelly, Daniel F. Williams, and Brian L. Cypher. "Use of Agricultural Lands by San Joaquin Kit Foxes." *Western North American Naturalist* 67, no. 2 (2007): 270–277.

Warrick, Gregory D., and Brian L. Cypher. "Factors Affecting the Spatial Distribution of San Joaquin Kit Foxes." *Journal of Wildlife Management* 62, no. 2 (April 1998): 707–717.

Webb, R. H., and H. G. Wilshire. *Environmental Effects of Off-Road Vehicles: Impacts and Management in Arid Regions.* New York: Springer-Verlag, 1983.

Wheat, Frank. *California Desert Miracle: The Fight for Desert Parks and Wilderness.* San Diego: Sunbelt, 1999.

White, Richard. *"It's Your Misfortune and None of My Own": A New History of the American West.* Norman: University of Oklahoma Press, 1991.

Wilbur, Sanford R. *The California Condor, 1966–76: A Look at Its Past and Future.* North American Fauna, no. 72. Washington, DC: United States Department of the Interior, Fish and Wildlife Service, 1978.

Wilbur, Sanford R., and Jerome A. Jackson, eds. *Vulture Biology and Management.* Berkeley: University of California Press, 1983.

Wilson, Robert M. *Seeking Refuge: Birds and Landscapes of the Pacific Flyway.* Seattle: University of Washington Press, 2010.

Woodbury, Angus M., and Ross Hardy. "Studies of the Desert Tortoise." *Ecological Monographs* 18, no. 2 (April 1948): 145–200.

Worster, Donald. *Rivers of Empire: Water, Aridity, and the Growth of the American West.* New York: Pantheon, 1985.

Wright, George M., Joseph S. Dixon, and Ben H. Thompson. *Fauna of the National Parks of the United States: A Preliminary Survey of Faunal Relations in National Parks.* Washington, DC: U.S. Government Printing Office, 1933.

———. *Fauna of the National Parks of the United States: Wildlife Management in the National Parks.* Washington, DC: U.S. Government Printing Office, 1935.

Wright, R. Gerald. *Wildlife Research and Management in the National Parks.* Urbana: University of Illinois Press, 1992.

Yaffee, Steven L. *Prohibitive Policy: Implementing the Federal Endangered Species Act.* Cambridge, MA: MIT Press, 1982.

Yoshiyama, Ronald M., Frank W. Fisher, and Peter B. Moyle. "Historical Abundance and Decline of Chinook Salmon in the Central Valley Region of California." *North American Journal of Fisheries Management* 18, no. 3 (1998): 487–521.

Young, Christian C. *In the Absence of Predators: Conservation and Controversy on the Kaibab Plateau.* Lincoln: University of Nebraska Press, 2002.

Zimmerer, Karl S., ed. *Globalization and New Geographies of Conservation.* Chicago: University of Chicago Press, 2006.

INDEX

active/intensive management, 85, 91,
106, 147–48; for condor recovery, 131,
138, 140, 142–43, 144; for desert
tortoise recovery, 174; for kit fox
recovery, 196
Adams, Charles, 71–73, 79, 84, 146
Adams, E. D., 204
Adams, John Capen "Grizzly," 25, 25 *fig.*,
26, 27
Adams, Victor, 71–75, 72 *fig.*
Adams, William, 226
adaptive management, 228–29, 232
Administrative Procedure Act, 116
aesthetic values, 55, 56, 57
agency cooperation, 60–61; in the
CALFED process, 215; ESA
implementation and, 100, 102–3, 232;
state-federal cooperation, 82, 230, 232
Agnew, Jesse, 27–28
agriculture, 23, 36, 192–93, 203;
beneficial species conservation
arguments, 54; in the Carrizo Plain,
188–89; in the delta, 203; delta water
and, 206, 221–22; farmland retirement

programs, 88, 187, 189; in the Imperial
Valley, 50; predator control and,
76–77; in the San Joaquin Valley, 175,
176–77, 178, 179–80, 183, 187, 204;
San Joaquin Valley conservation
efforts and, 188–89, 189–92; toxic
runoff from, 179, 209. *See also*
ranching
Alaska, 227
Albright, Horace, 80, 85, 87
Alexander, Annie, 45–46, 47–48, 49,
50, 58
Alexander, Samuel, 45
Alta California: Bear Flag Revolt, 29;
condors in, 126; fur trade in, 30–32,
33; gold rush, 126–27, 152–53, 177–78;
grizzlies in, 20–24; San Joaquin Valley
settlement, 177–78; tortoise
consumption in, 153
amateur naturalists, 56, 58
American alligator, 231
American Fisheries Society, 212
American Game Protective
Association, 88

Board of Fish and Game Commissioners.
See California Fish and Game
Commission
bobcat, 23, 31, 77, 181
Bohlen, Curtis, 101
Boone and Crocket Club, 58
Bowen, Delbert, 193
Bracero Program, 220
Britain, ecology in, 74
Brower, David, 130, 131, 146
Brown, Edmund G. "Pat," 206
Brown, Jerry, 207, 224
brown pelican, 231
Bruce, Jay, 77, 80
Brussard, Peter, 168
Bryant, Harold, 53–55, 56, 67, 78
Buena Vista Lake, 32
Building Industry Association of
Southern California, 108–9
Bureau of Biological Survey, 37, 54, 67,
82, 90–92; and predator control
programs, 76, 77–78, 79–80, 91;
renaming of, 86; and wildlife refuges,
89–90, 118. See also U.S. Fish and
Wildlife Service
Bureau of Land Management (BLM),
158; and Carrizo Plain purchase,
188–89; Central Valley Project
reauthorization, 190; and desert
tortoise petition, 163; GAO reviews of
Mojave land management, 170, 171,
173–74; land management authority,
160–61; Mojave conservation plan,
160–61, 169, 170, 171; Mojave Desert
BLM lands, 157, 158–59, 165, 167, 168,
170, 172
Bureau of Reclamation, 130, 136–37, 190,
204. See also Central Valley Project
Burke, Joyce, 169
Burke, Peter, 169
Burnett, Joe, 143
Bush, George H. W., 108, 218
butterflies, 105

Calahane, Victor, 86
CALFED, 214–22, 224; litigation and
breakdown of, 217–22; Little Hoover
Commission report, 217, 224
California: conservation history, 9–10;
early visitors' descriptions, 22; grizzly
as icon of, 13, 28–30, 30 fig., 40–41;
species richness and endangerment
in, 8–9, 9 map; vertebrate extinctions
in, 9
California Academy of Sciences, 32,
35–36, 47, 155; Monarch at, 39 fig., 42
California Acclimatization Society, 211
California Aqueduct, 205 map, 207
California Associated Societies for the
Conservation of Wild Life, 63, 64,
65, 67
California Bay-Delta, 198–224, 202 map,
205 map; Bay-Delta Accord, 214;
CALFED process, 214–17, 219;
current efforts and future prospects,
223–24; early water projects, 34,
202–4; fisheries declines, 209, 210,
215–17; flooding and flood control,
34–35, 201–3, 210, 217; fur trade in, 31;
habitat conservation in, 200–201, 213,
215, 223; Hall hydrology study, 204;
human impacts summarized, 198–99,
208–11; litigation and CALFED's
breakdown, 217–22; multispecies
recovery plan, 213; nonnative species
in, 37, 209–11, 213, 215; peripheral
canal, 202 map, 207, 223; salinity
problems and standards, 206–7, 208,
209, 212, 217; Wagner decisions and
pumping restrictions, 199–200,
218–22; water demand and supply
problems, 208, 213; water quality
problems and mitigation, 208, 209,
213–14, 216; wetlands drainage in,
203. See also Central Valley Project;
delta smelt; water resources and
management

refuges, 176, 187, 189, 214. *See also* California Bay-Delta; San Joaquin Valley

Central Valley Project (CVP), 178, 205 *map*; approval and early history, 204, 206; and CALFED, 217; Central Valley Project Improvement Act, 214; 1993 reauthorization, 190

CESA. *See* California Endangered Species Act

chaparral bear. *See* California grizzly bear

chestnut-backed chickadee, 48

chickcharnie, 33

Chinook salmon, 210, 213

chuckwalla, 155

Chumash tribe, 138

CITES (Convention on the International Trade in Endangered Species of Wild Fauna and Flora), 101

Civilian Conservation Corps, 85, 91

Clark County, Nevada, 164–68, 172; Desert Conservation Plan, 166–67; Multiple Species Habitat Conservation Plan, 167, 188, 195

Clean Air Act, 96

Clean Water Act, 96

climate change, 8, 229–30

Clinton administration, 105–6, 215; Babbitt as interior secretary, 106–7, 109, 171, 214; Bay-Delta Accord, 214; Carrizo Plain monument designation, 188

Coachella Valley, 166, 167

Coachella Valley fringe-toed lizard, 108

coastal sage scrub protection, 108–10

collaborative conservation efforts, 107, 108, 176, 192; California NCCP program, 109–10, 111 *map*; Delta Vision, 224; HCPs as, 107–8; in the San Joaquin Valley, 188–89, 190; shortcomings of consensus processes, 216–17. *See also* agency cooperation;

CALFED; habitat conservation plans

Colorado River, 48, 50

Colorado River Wildlife Council, 159, 161

Colton, Walter, 26

Columbian sharp-tailed grouse, 32

Columbia River, 126

commerce clause, U.S. Constitution, 61, 66, 99

Commissioners of Fisheries (California), 37. *See also* California Fish and Game Commission

Committee on Rare and Endangered Species (FWS), 100

Committee on the Preservation of Natural Conditions (Ecological Society of America), 73

Committee on Wild Life Restoration (Duck Committee), 88–89

competitive exclusion, 48

Condor (journal), 66, 67, 79

conservation advocacy, 81, 98; beneficial species arguments, 54; debates within the Ecological Society of America, 75; economic arguments, 53–55, 56; ethical arguments, 52–57; expansion of federal authority, 4–6, 60–61, 66, 89–90; Grinnell and the Berkeley circle, 43–44, 52–57, 58, 62–68; in nineteenth-century California, 36–38. *See also* conservation organizations; *specific organizations*

conservation biology, 4, 10, 94, 118–21, 124, 145–46; outside North America, 118, 146

conservation controversies and debates, 2–3, 10, 193, 222–23, 232; hands-on vs. hands-off conservation, 85, 131, 135, 139, 140, 144–46, 147–48. *See also* endangered species controversies; *specific issues, locations, and species*

Conservation Council for Hawaii v. Babbitt, 115

federal agencies. *See* government management; *specific agencies*

federal authority, sources and expansions of, 4–6, 60–61, 66, 89–90, 99–100, 160–61

Federal Energy Regulatory Commission, 97

federal lands, 226; Arkansas Act transfers, 203; ESA land acquisition provision, 112; state projects on, 82. *See also* Bureau of Land Management; public lands

federal law, 99; Antiquities Act, 87, 188; Arkansas Act, 203; Bald Eagle Protection Act, 91; California Desert Protection Act, 170–71; Central Valley Project Improvement Act, 214; Federal Land Policy and Management Act, 160–61; golden age of environmental legislation, 96–97, 104; Lacey Act, 60–61; *Martin v. Waddell* and the public trust doctrine, 59; Migratory Bird Conservation Act, 89; Migratory Bird Treaty Act, 66; mining regulations, 159, 171; Southern Nevada Public Land Management Act, 167–68; Taylor Grazing Act, 158; Wilderness Act of 1964, 94, 100, 136, 171; wildlife refuge funding and management, 89–90. *See also* Endangered Species Act

Feinstein, Dianne, 170

Finley, William, 60, 131–32, 134

fire and fire policy, 21, 133

fish and game: state ownership of, 60, 99. *See also* state fish and game codes

Fish and Game Commission. *See* California Fish and Game Commission

Fish and Wildlife Coordination Act, 89–90

fisheries: declines, 209, 210, 211–12, 215–17; delta fisheries improvement

mandates, 214; hatcheries and stocking programs, 210–11; nonnative species introductions, 37, 209, 210–11. *See also* delta smelt

Fisheries Commission, 210–11

fishing, 37, 38, 210, 211

fishing regulation. *See* state fish and game codes

Flint-Cary Act debate, 63–67, 78

flooding and flood control, 34–35, 201–3, 210, 217. *See also* state water projects

Foley, Roger, 103–4

Foreman, Dave, 145

Forest and Stream, 58

Fort Vancouver, 126

foxes, 31. *See also* San Joaquin kit fox

Frémont, John, 29

fringe-toed lizard, 108, 166

Fry, Walter, 78

Fur-Bearing Mammals of California (Grinnell, Dixon, and Linsdale), 175, 180, 181–82, 183

fur seal, 87

fur trade, 30–32, 33, 77, 100–101; kit fox and, 180–81

FWS. *See* U.S. Fish and Wildlife Service

Gabrielson, Ira, 79, 86, 91–92, 136

Galápagos fauna, 47–48

game management, 88, 91, 92

game trade, 32, 33, 59; wild-caught game sale bans, 10, 43–44, 62–68

GAO reviews, of Mojave land management, 170, 171, 173–74

Garcés, Francisco, 153

Gass, Patrick, 126

Geer v. Connecticut, 60, 66

General Accounting Office reviews, of Mojave land management, 170, 171, 173–74

General Land Office, 158

Gilbert, Charles, 45

Gilpin, Michael, 119

Gingrich, Newt, 105

Gleason Mountain, 15–16

"God Squad," 104, 219

Golden Gate Park, Monarch at, 38

Goldman, Edward, 76, 79

gold rush, 126–27, 152–53, 177–78

Gompers, Samuel, 64

Goodall, Jane, 146

gophers, 54

Gopherus agassizii. *See* Mojave desert tortoise

Gosselin, Lisa, 147–48

government management and conservation initiatives, 4, 8; adaptive management challenges, 228–29; agency loyalties, 81; expansions of federal authority, 4–6, 60–61, 66, 89–90; sources of legal authority for, 59–61, 66. *See also* agency cooperation; state fish and game codes; wildlife management; *specific agencies*

Grand Canyon National Park, 53, 143

grazing, 74, 153; on the Carrizo Plain, 188–89; condor foraging and, 130, 136; elimination of, 229; in the Mojave Desert, 153, 157, 167, 169, 171–72; on public lands, 81, 158, 159, 167, 172

great auk, 32

Green Act, 203

green sturgeon, 213, 217

Grinnell, Joseph, 10, 44, 46–52, 46 *fig.*, 58, 146; "Animal Life in the National Parks," 69, 93, 94; birth and background, 45; and condor research, 131, 132; conservationist thinking, 52–53, 58, 86, 135; death of, 92; *Fur-Bearing Mammals of California,* 175, 180, 181–82, 183; and game sale ban campaign, 10, 53–57, 62, 63, 66; grizzly population estimate, 18; later students and successors of, 129–30;

and the MVZ, 46–48, 49–52, 132; national parks wildlife advocacy, 69, 80, 81–86; predator control opposition, 77, 78, 80; research interests and contributions, 48–49, 50

grizzly bear, 18, 40. *See also* California grizzly bear

gulls, 33

Gymnogyps, 129. *See also* California condor

habitat concept, 3, 4, 6, 11

habitat conservation, 2, 3, 5–6, 70, 124; active management and, 106, 147–48, 150; biodiversity focus, 144–45; California's history of, 10; collaborative approaches, 176, 188–89, 192; condor recovery and, 136–38, 140, 142, 143, 144–45; in the delta, 200–201, 213, 215, 223–24; ESA implementation and, 101, 107, 110, 113; in ESA predecessors, 100; ESA provisions, 97–98, 104; in the Leopold Report, 93–94; modern conservation planning, 119–20, 226–31; quantity vs. quality, 229, 232; for the San Joaquin kit fox, 186–87, 194–97; wildlife-wilderness link and, 94. *See also* critical habitat designations; habitat conservation plans; protected natural areas

habitat conservation focus, 70, 81, 106, 137; in early American ecology, 71–76; in modern conservation planning, 119–20, 225–31. *See also* protected areas paradigm

habitat conservation plans (HCPs), 104–5, 107–10, 120, 166–67; California NCCP program, 109–10, 111 *map*; Clark County Multiple Species Habitat Conservation Plan, 167, 188, 195; for the delta, 223–24; desert tortoise, 166; Metropolitan Bakersfield

Habitat Conservation Plan, 110,
195, 197
habitat islands, 118–19
habitat loss, 7, 9, 50, 59; fragmentation,
84; recovery potential and, 230–31.
See also individual species
Hall, E. Raymond, 77
Hall, William, 204
Hannity, Sean, 219
Hardy, Ross, 156, 162
"harm," in the ESA, 103, 112–13
Hawaii, endangered species litigation in,
112, 115
hawks, 76, 78
HCPs. *See* habitat conservation plans
Hearst, William Randolph, 13, 15, 16
heath hen, 33
Heller, Edmund, 79
Henshaw, Henry, 27
herons, 33
Hittell, Theodore, 33
Hornaday, William, 64
house finch, 54
house mouse, 77
Howell, A. Brazier, 79
Howitt, Richard, 221
Hudson's Bay Company, 31
human activities and impacts, 6, 7, 34–35,
51, 74; condor declines and, 126–27,
133, 134, 136–37; in the delta, 198–99,
208–11; FWS unwillingness to
regulate, 118; Las Vegas growth and
the desert tortoise, 164–68; in the
Mojave Desert, 152–53, 156–59;
Mojave mitigation measures, 169;
MVZ research priorities and, 50, 51; in
the San Joaquin Valley, 176–80, 183,
185, 192–93; wildlife population
dynamics and, 85. *See also specific
activities and locations*
hummingbirds, 33
hunting, 9, 56–59; bounty programs,
26–27, 76; of desert tortoises, 152,

153–55; Grinnell's views, 56, 58; of
grizzly bears, 24–25, 27; indigenous
hunting before European settlement,
21–22; of kit foxes, 180–81; in the
national parks, 80, 81; on national
wildlife refuges, 100; for natural
history collections, 56–57, 127, 132;
predator control programs and,
77–78, 79; related wildlife declines,
30–34, 56–57. *See also* fur trade; game
trade
hunting conflicts and debates, 38, 53–59,
64; game sale bans and the Flint-Cary
Act, 10, 43–44, 62–68. *See also*
predators and predator control
hunting regulation, 32, 37, 38, 59–62, 88;
condor hunting ban, 132; debates
about, 57–59; federal law, 60–61;
possession limits, 66. *See also* state fish
and game codes
Hurricane Katrina, 210

immigrants, 38, 62, 220
Imperial Valley, 50, 167
Indians: and the condor, 126, 128, 138;
and the desert tortoise, 152; and the
grizzly, 20; resource use and ecological
impacts, 21–23, 51
insects, 54, 181, 182
Instituto Nacional de Ecología
(Mexico), 143
International Union for the Conservation
of Nature, 92
interstate commerce: federal powers
under the commerce clause, 61, 66, 99;
state law violations and, 60, 100
intrinsic conservation value (in wildlife),
55, 56, 57, 145
invasive speces. *See* nonnative species
irrigation districts, 189, 199, 203
Irvine Company, 110
island biogeography, 118–19
Isolated Facility, 202 *map*

litigation. *See* endangered species litigation; U.S. Supreme Court rulings; *specific cases*

Little Hoover Commission CALFED report, 217, 224

Little Tennessee River, 104

livestock: as condor food source, 126, 136; in early California, 22, 23; feral livestock eradication in Hawaii, 112; grizzly predation, 26–27. *See also* agriculture; grazing; ranching

long-eared kit fox, 180

longfin smelt, 213, 215

Los Angeles Aqueduct, 205 *map*, 208

Los Angeles Times, 141–42, 157

Los Angeles Zoo, 124

Los Osos, 14 *fig.*, 19 *map*, 21

Los Padres National Forest: as condor habitat, 130, 133, 136; condor sanctuary, 128 *map*, 136, 141, 148

Louisiana, endangered species litigation in, 112–13

MacArthur, Robert, 118–19

mallard, 37

maps: California Bay-Delta, 202, 205; California condor range, 128; California critical habitat areas, 117; California grizzly range, 19; California NCCP proposals, 111; California water projects, 205; Mojave desert tortoise range, 151; San Joaquin kit fox range, 184; species richness and endangerment by state, 9

marine habitat conservation, 10, 225–26

Marine Life Protection Act (California), 10

Marine Mammal Protection Act, 96

marine mammals, 30–31, 87. *See also* fur trade

marine wildlife declines, 30–34

market hunting: desert tortoise, 153. *See also* game trade

martens, 31

Martin v. Waddell, 59

Mather, Stephen, 80

Matthiessen, Peter, 98

Mayr, Ernst, 48

McAtee, W. L., 79

McMillan, Eben, 136

McMillan, Ian, 130, 136

megafauna extinctions, 18, 20, 125

Memorandum of Understanding on Biological Diversity, 108

Mendota, 220–21

Merriam, C. Hart, 28, 46, 48, 52, 76, 175

Merriam, Jon, 46

metapopulation theory, 119

Metropolitan Bakersfield Habitat Conservation Plan, 110, 195, 197

Metropolitan Water District, 219

Mexican farm workers, 219–20, 221

Mexican spotted owl, 142

Mexico, condor recovery in, 143

Michael, Jeffrey, 221–22

Midway-Sunset oil field, 178

Migratory Bird Conservation Act, 89

Migratory Bird Treaty Act, 66

Miller, Alden, 48, 129–30, 132, 136

Miller, Henry, 32

Miller, Joaquin, 26

Miller, Loye, 56, 67, 129–30

Millikan, Jesse, 127

Ming-Lin, Taung, 190

mining, 36; California gold rush, 126–27, 152–53, 177–78; federal law, 159, 171; in the Mojave Desert, 152–53, 156–57, 171; off-site pollution impacts, 178, 203; on public lands, 158, 159; Sawyer decision, 203

Mining in the National Parks Act, 171

mink, 31, 76

Mission 66, 86, 93

Missouri v. Holland, 66

pronghorn antelope, 135, 189
property rights. *See* private property
  rights
protected areas paradigm, 6, 7, 118–21,
  151, 200–201, 225–26; challenges
  and shortcomings of, 8, 223, 226–31,
  233; early ecologists and, 71–76;
  future of, 231–33; in modern
  conservation biology, 118–21;
  traditional human uses and, 74; in
  urban and agricultural environments,
  176, 192–96. *See also* habitat
  conservation *entries*; protected
  natural areas
protected natural areas, 3, 6–7, 229; core
  and buffer areas, 74, 84, 120; farmland
  retirement programs, 88, 187, 189;
  marine protected areas, 10, 225–26;
  national parks as, 69, 82–86, 94;
  national wildlife refuges, 87–92;
  optimal design and planning, 119–20;
  outside the U.S., 225–26, 228; on
  private lands, 227; wildlife-wilderness
  link, 94. *See also* habitat conservation
  entries; national parks; wildlife
  refuges
public access: access development in
  the national parks, 85, 86, 93;
  habitat protection and, 142; Mojave
  Desert access increases, 152,
  154, 157
Public Employees for Environmental
  Responsibility, 169
Public Land Law Review Commission,
  158–59
public lands, 226; in California, 226;
  expansions/acquisition of, 75, 88, 90,
  99, 100, 227; federal management
  authority, 160–61; grazing and mining
  on, 158, 159, 172; in Nevada, 165,
  167–68; oil leases on, 178; in the San
  Joaquin Valley, 187; wetlands, 203;
  wise-use movement, 191–92. *See also*

Bureau of Land Management; federal
  lands
public trust doctrine and resources, 59,
  99, 208

quail, 37, 79

Racanelli decision, 208, 214
raccoon, 31, 78
Radanovich, George, 200
rails, 32
ranching: on the Carrizo Plain, 188–89;
  grizzlies and, 26–27; predator control
  and, 76–77; rangeland rehabilitation
  programs, 153; in the San Joaquin
  Valley, 177–78, 183, 185. *See also*
  grazing; livestock
rattlesnakes, 77
ravens, as desert tortoise predators, 173
Reagan administration, 108, 114, 116,
  171, 207
*Recovery Plan for Upland Species of the
  San Joaquin Valley*, 179, 183, 184 *map*,
  187, 196
recovery plans, 185–86; delta fishes, 213;
  Mojave desert tortoise, 168, 169, 174;
  San Joaquin Valley, 179, 183, 184 *map*,
  187. *See also individual species*
recreational uses, 91; Mojave Desert,
  157–58, 159, 172; Wilderness Act and,
  100. *See also* fishing; hunting
red-breasted sapsucker, 54
Red Cloud, 45
red-cockaded woodpecker, 112–13
red fox, 181–82
Redington, Paul, 79
Red Rock Lakes National Wildlife
  Refuge, 91
Renshaw, Graham, 127
Resourceful California, 109
ring-tailed cat, 78
river otter, 31, 32
roadrunner, 79

state wildlife management, 5–6, 10, 34, 37; cooperation challenges, 60–61; desert tortoise protections, 156–57; of ESA-listed species, 102, 230, 232; federal funding for state efforts, 100; predator control programs, 76–77; revenue sources, 89, 156; state-federal cooperation, 82, 230, 232. *See also* California Department of Fish and Game; California Fish and Game Commission; state fish and game codes

state wildlife refuges, 187

*The Status of the Desert Tortoise (*Gopherus agassizii*) in the United States* (Berry et. al.), 161–62

Stebbins, Robert, 157–58

steelhead, 18; NOAA biological opinion, 217–19

Stellar's jay, 54

Stoddard, Herbert, 49

Storer, Tracy, 67, 69, 93, 94

striped bass, 37, 209, 211, 215

strychnine poisoning, 127, 181

sturgeon, 213, 217

Summa Corporation, 165–66

Swarth, Harry, 66, 67, 79

Sweet Home case, 103, 113

SWP. *See* State Water Project

take, defined in the ESA, 101, 103; interpretations of "harm," 103, 112–13

take regulation, 6, 53–54; desert tortoise, 156; fisheries declines and, 211; national wildlife refuges, 100; by state management agencies, 5; under the ESA, 101, 103, 112–13

Tansley, Arthur, 74

Taylor Grazing Act, 158

Taylor, Walter, 62–63, 64, 65, 67, 131

Teapot Dome, 178

Tejon Ranch, 142

Tejon Ranch Conservation and Land Use Agreement, 142

Tellico Dam, 104

Tennessee Valley Authority, 104

Tennessee Valley Authorty v. Hill, 97

terns, 33

The Theory of Island Biogeography (MacArthur and Wilson), 118–19

This Land Is Our Land (Pombo), 191

Thompson, Ben, 86, 90; at the Wildlife Division, 82–85

Thomson, Charles, 82

threadfin shad, 215

threatened species: defined in ESA, 102. *See also* Endangered Species Act; endangered species *entries*

Throop Polytechnic Institute, 45

TNC (Nature Conservancy), 75, 99, 120, 160, 188, 192, 227

translocation, 229

trapping: in the national parks, 80, 81. *See also* hunting *entries*; predators and predator control

trinomial classification, 48

True Bear Stories (Miller), 26

trumpeter swan, 91

tule elk, 32, 189

Udall, Stuart, 93

unemployment, in the San Joaquin Valley, 220–22

U.S. Biological Survey, 32

U.S. Constitution, 60, 61, 66, 99

U.S. Department of Agriculture, 158

U.S. Department of Energy, 157

U.S. Department of the Interior, 158, 171; Babbitt at, 106–7, 109, 171, 214

United States Exploring Expedition, 32

U.S. Fish and Wildlife Service (FWS), early history, 5, 86, 91, 92; Committee on Rare and Endangered Species, 100; ESPA and, 100; *Fading Trails* publication, 98; Kesterson National Wildlife Refuge closure, 179; Wildlife Division and, 86, 91, 92; wildlife